Get a FREE eBook

To register this book, scan the code or go to
www.manning.com/freebook/despoudis

By registering you get

- **FREE eBook copy**
  download in PDF and ePub

- **FREE online access**
  to Manning's liveBook platform

- **FREE audio**
  read and listen online in liveBook

- **FREE AI Assistant**
  it knows the book and what you are reading when it answers

- **FREE in-book testing**
  fun tests to lock in your knowledge

In Manning's liveBook platform you can share discussions and comments with other readers, add your own bookmarks and highlights, insert personal notes anywhere on the page, see color versions of all the book's graphics, download source code and other resources, and more!

To register, scan the code or go to www.manning.com/freebook/despoudis

Build AI-Enhanced Web Apps

Build AI-Enhanced Web Apps

How to get reliable results with React, Next.js, and Vercel

THEO DESPOUDIS

MANNING
SHELTER ISLAND

For online information and ordering of this and other Manning books, please visit www.manning.com. The publisher offers discounts on this book when ordered in quantity.

For more information, please contact

    Special Sales Department
    Manning Publications Co.
    20 Baldwin Road
    PO Box 761
    Shelter Island, NY 11964
    Email: orders@manning.com

© 2026 Manning Publications Co. All rights reserved.

No part of this publication may be reproduced, stored in a retrieval system, or transmitted, in any form or by means electronic, mechanical, photocopying, or otherwise, without prior written permission of the publisher.

Many of the designations used by manufacturers and sellers to distinguish their products are claimed as trademarks. Where those designations appear in the book, and Manning Publications was aware of a trademark claim, the designations have been printed in initial caps or all caps.

∞ Recognizing the importance of preserving what has been written, it is Manning's policy to have the books we publish printed on acid-free paper, and we exert our best efforts to that end. Recognizing also our responsibility to conserve the resources of our planet, Manning books are printed on paper that is at least 15 percent recycled and processed without the use of elemental chlorine.

The author and publisher have made every effort to ensure that the information in this book was correct at press time. The author and publisher do not assume and hereby disclaim any liability to any party for any loss, damage, or disruption caused by errors or omissions, whether such errors or omissions result from negligence, accident, or any other cause, or from any usage of the information herein.

Manning Publications Co. 20 Baldwin Road PO Box 761 Shelter Island, NY 11964	Development editor: Frances Lefkowitz Technical editor: Anirudh Vijay Prabhu Review editor: Kishor Rit Production editor: Keri Hales Copy editor: Kari Lucke Proofreader: Katie Tennant Technical proofreader: Doug Warren Typesetter: Tamara Švelić Sabljić Cover designer: Marija Tudor

ISBN 9781633436084
Printed in the UK by CPI Group Ltd

brief contents

PART 1 BUILDING BASIC GENERATIVE AI WEB APPS 1

- 1 ■ Using generative AI in web apps 3
- 2 ■ Building your first generative AI web application 19
- 3 ■ Connecting AI models with the Vercel AI SDK 54
- 4 ■ Managing conversation and state in your application 88

PART 2 ADVANCED GENERATIVE AI TECHNIQUES AND DEPLOYMENT 127

- 5 ■ Prompt engineering in web applications 129
- 6 ■ Building AI workflows with LangChain.js 166
- 7 ■ Document summarization and RAG with LangChain.js 197
- 8 ■ Testing and debugging techniques 232
- 9 ■ Deployment and security 268

PART 3 HANDS-ON PROJECTS 303

- 10 ■ Building an AI interview assistant: Project walk-through 305
- 11 ■ Building an AI RAG agent: Project walk-through 317

PART 4 ADVANCED INTEGRATIONS AND THE FUTURE OF AI 329

- 12 ■ Integrating web apps with the Model Context Protocol 331
- appendix ■ Running the examples 353

contents

preface xiii
acknowledgments xiv
about this book xvi
about the author xix
about the cover illustration xx

PART 1 BUILDING BASIC GENERATIVE AI WEB APPS 1

1 Using generative AI in web apps 3

- 1.1 What generative AI can do for web applications 4
  Generative AI capabilities 4 ▪ Real-world uses of generative AI 5
- 1.2 How a generative AI web app works 6
  Core components 6 ▪ The flow of user interactions 8
- 1.3 AI tools and the ecosystem 9
- 1.4 Choosing the right model 12
  Model types 12 ▪ Pretrained vs. self-hosted 13
  Performance considerations 13
- 1.5 Generative vs. traditional AI 13
- 1.6 Handling the concerns and implications of generative AI 15
  What are the limitations of generative AI? 15 ▪ Will developers lose jobs because of AI? 16 ▪ Are generative AI outputs reliable? 16

2 Building your first generative AI web application 19

- 2.1 Introducing Astra 20
- 2.2 Project goal and requirements 21
  Goal: Build a simple interactive AI chat interface 21
  Project and technology requirements 22 ▪ *Setting up 23*
  Running the project 24
- 2.3 Under the hood: The generative AI lifecycle 26
- 2.4 Designing for a better user experience 26
- 2.5 Building the major components 28
  Frontend 28 ▪ *Autoscroll 29▪ChatPage 32* ▪ *ChatList 32*
  The backend: Handling API communication 37 ▪ *Tests 41*
  Common challenges and solutions 42
- 2.6 Assessing the app's first iteration 42
- 2.7 Migrating the app to Next.js 43
  Setting up 44 ▪ *Running the project 44*
- 2.8 Routing and configuration on Next.js 45
  File-based routing 45 ▪ *Configuration 46*
  Environment variables in Next.js 47 ▪ *Route groups 47* ▪ *Layout components 48* ▪ *Route API handlers 50* ▪ *Going deeper with Next.js 51*

3 Connecting AI models with the Vercel AI SDK 54

- 3.1 Introducing the Vercel AI SDK 55
  Key features and benefits 55 ▪ *A strategic approach to integration 56* ▪ *Practical integration: The Vercel AI SDK with Astra AI 58*
- 3.2 Handling streaming responses with the Vercel AI SDK 61
  Challenges and how the SDK solves streaming in web applications 62 ▪ *Implementing streaming with the Vercel AI SDK 65* ▪ *Integrating streaming into Astra AI 69*
- 3.3 Working with multiple AI providers 72
  Handling different AI providers and models 72 ▪ *Using the Vercel AI SDK's interoperability 73* ▪ *Astra AI project: Integrating multiple AI providers and models 76*
- 3.4 Enhancing conversational UIs with multimedia content 79
  Introducing OpenAI's vision capabilities 80 ▪ *Astra AI project: Integrating Gemini vision queries 83*

4 Managing conversation and state in your application 88

- 4.1 AI SDK React server components 90

  Overview of RSCs 90 • *Using server actions for AI-powered RSCs 92* • *Updating the UI to use server actions 96 Techniques for generating and streaming UI components 98 Creating streamable UI components from LLM providers with streamUI 99* • *Streaming React components with createStreamableUI 101*

- 4.2 Managing UI state in AI-powered applications 103

  Separating AI and UI state in React/Next.js applications 103 Key components for UI state management 105 Implementing UI state management patterns 108

- 4.3 Structured data generation using the Vercel AI SDK 113

  How structured data generation works 113 • *Techniques for generating structured data from AI responses 114 Tools for implementing type-safe AI-generated content 115 Integrating structured data generation into our web application 117*

- 4.4 Tool and function calling with AI models 121

  Understanding tool calling and function calling in AI models 121 Implementing custom tools and functions with the Vercel AI SDK 123

PART 2 ADVANCED GENERATIVE AI TECHNIQUES AND DEPLOYMENT 127

5 Prompt engineering in web applications 129

- 5.1 Introducing prompt engineering 131

  What exactly are prompts? 132 • *Prompt types 137 Organizing your prompts: Versioning, testing, and optimization 139*

- 5.2 Few-shot learning 146

  Examples of few-shot learning 147 • *General methodology for creating few-shot learning prompts 150*

- 5.3 Chain-of-thought prompting: A deeper dive into reasoning 151

  Example of chain-of-thought prompting 151 • *General methodology for creating chain-of-thought prompts 152*

5.4   Embeddings: Giving AI a sense of meaning   154
      The restaurant menu analogy: A taste of embeddings   154
      Using embeddings in practice: The Vercel AI SDK   158
      Use case: IT support knowledge base   161

5.5   Going deeper into LLM techniques   164
      Tree of thoughts   164 ▪ *Self-refine   164* ▪ *LLM-as-a-judge   164*

6   Building AI workflows with LangChain.js   166

6.1   Introducing LangChain   167
      Chaining calls with LangChain   168 ▪ *Integration with the Vercel AI SDK   173*

6.2   Preparing and storing documents for retrieval using LangChain   178
      Document ingestion using text splitters   180 ▪ *Introducing vector stores   181* ▪ *Document retrieval   182* ▪ *Full example of preparing and storing documents with LangChain   184*

6.3   Using memory components in LangChain to remember conversation history   185

6.4   Utilizing agents in LangChain.js   188
      How LangChain agents work   189 ▪ *Creating an agent using LangChain.js   190* ▪ *Agent integration with the Vercel AI SDK   192* ▪ *Overview of LangChain.js modules   194*

6.5   Going deeper with LangChain.js   194
      LangChain Expression Language   194 ▪ *LangGraph   195*

7   Document summarization and RAG with LangChain.js   197

7.1   Building a document summarization web application with LangChain.js   198
      Summarization app project requirements   198 ▪ *Architecture and workflow   198* ▪ *Building the document summarization web application   202* ▪ *Caveats and limitations of document summarization   205* ▪ *Demonstrating the app   208 Additional considerations for summarizing documents   212*

7.2   Building a RAG web application with LangChain.js   216
      RAG app project requirements   216 ▪ *Key architectural components of RAG   217* ▪ *Technical architecture overview   218* ▪ *RAG system components   219* ▪ *Web app demonstration   223* ▪ *Adding grounding support   225*

8 Testing and debugging techniques   232

- **8.1** Debugging Next.js AI applications   233

  Debugging common Next.js rendering Issues 233 ▪ Debugging client–server problems 237 ▪ Handling state management 238 Performance monitoring 239

- **8.2** Vercel AI SDK troubleshooting   241

  Handling error states in AI-generated content 242 Managing token limits and rate limiting 246

- **8.3** Troubleshooting LangChain.js   250

  Chain execution errors 251 ▪ Troubleshooting model integration problems 254

- **8.4** Testing strategies for AI applications   256

  Unit and integration testing in React and Next.js 256 Mocking LLM responses 258 ▪ Testing Vercel AI SDK responses 260 ▪ Testing LangChain.js 264

9 Deployment and security   268

- **9.1** Building a secure foundation with input validation, rate limits, and middleware   269

  Input validation 270 ▪ Security middleware layer 273

- **9.2** Building a core security and data protection pipeline   275

- **9.3** Setting up authentication and authorization   275

  Simple authentication with Clerk.js and Next.js 277 Practical security control: Rate limiting 280

- **9.4** API key and secrets management   285

  Understanding Next.js environment variables 285 Application-level API keys 286 ▪ User-provided API keys 286

- **9.5** Data protection and compliance   288

  Example: Adding anonymization to our chat messages 288

- **9.6** Deployment considerations for AI web applications   291

  Deployment options 291 ▪ Production deployment checklist 292 Example deployment to Vercel 294 ▪ Alternative deployments: Netlify 299 ▪ Alternative deployments: Hugging Face Spaces 300 ▪ Next steps 300

PART 3 HANDS-ON PROJECTS 303

10 Building an AI interview assistant: Project walk-through 305

10.1 Overview of the application 306
   Key features 306 ▪ Technical implementation 311
   Technology stack overview 311

10.2 Security measures implemented 313

10.3 Challenges during development 313
   State management considerations 313 ▪ Text-to-speech
   integration 314 ▪ Generating feedback 314

10.4 Additional considerations and improvements 315

11 Building an AI RAG agent: Project walk-through 317

11.1 Overview of the application 318
   Key features 318 ▪ Technical implementation 322
   Technology stack overview 322

11.2 Challenges during development 325
   Shared vs. dedicated user data in vector stores 325
   Security considerations around document management and heavy
   workloads 325 ▪ API design and URL structure to minimize
   information exposure 326

11.3 Additional thoughts on AI and the future of web development 327

PART 4 ADVANCED INTEGRATIONS AND THE FUTURE OF AI 329

12 Integrating web apps with the Model Context Protocol 331

12.1 Why the MCP matters for AI integration 332

12.2 MCP architecture 333

12.3 Connecting Next.js and the Vercel AI SDK with the MCP 334
   Architecture overview 335 ▪ Building an end-to-end integration
   with the MCP in Next.js 336 ▪ Benefits of using the MCP for web
   applications with LLMs 340

12.4 Inside an MCP server: Extending web applications 341
   MCP server structure 342 ▪ Additional considerations
   for MCP servers 345

- 12.5 Integrating MCP servers with LangChain.js 345
  - *Architecture overview 346* ▪ *Building an end-to-end integration with LangChain.js 347*

- 12.6 The future of the MCP: Gateways, directories, and MCP-as-a-service 349
  - *MCP gateways 349* ▪ *MCP-as-a-service 350*
  - *MCP directories and registries 351*

- 12.7 Your next steps with MCP servers 352

appendix *Running the examples 353*

index 361

preface

Machine learning, AI, large language models (LLMs), and generative AI are technologies that have fundamentally reshaped our digital landscape, opening up new avenues for innovation. Their primary appeal lies in their ability to facilitate multimodal interactions—combining text, images, and videos—between humans and machines in a remarkably natural way. It's as simple and intuitive as asking a friend or colleague for help. These applications are no longer confined to science fiction; they're gaining new practical uses every day as technological advancements make them increasingly accurate and lifelike.

As a seasoned software engineer deeply involved in building AI-powered products and supporting headless WordPress solutions on Next.js and React, I've had a front-row seat to this transformation. The imminent access to a plethora of open source tools and initiatives, coupled with the sheer accessibility of LLMs and related AI services, sparked an idea: to bridge the gap for web developers eager to harness this technology without needing a deep dive into machine learning theory or Python.

This book was born from a clear vision: AI and its applications are powerful new tools that every developer must be able to use to deliver exceptional value to their users and customers. It's designed primarily as a practical guide, but I've also placed a strong emphasis on explaining the core concepts behind building full-stack generative web applications.

I've specifically chosen JavaScript, Next.js, Vercel, and LangChain.js because they form a powerful, accessible, and incredibly relevant stack for creating generative AI experiences today. My hope is that this book will become your essential companion, making your journey into building AI-driven web applications both enjoyable and profoundly educational.

acknowledgments

Writing a book is a serious undertaking, demanding a significant investment of personal time and effort. Yet, it's a journey we embark on for a greater good, embodying the spirit that "sharing is caring." This endeavor wouldn't be possible without a strong support network, countless late nights, and an unwavering willingness to persevere.

I am immensely grateful to the team at Manning Publications. I thank Andy Waldron, my acquisitions editor, and Brian Sawyer, my former acquisitions editor, for believing in this book's concept from the very beginning and for their invaluable guidance, and Frances Lefkowitz, my development editor, for her insightful feedback and relentless commitment to shaping this manuscript. My thanks also go to Ana Romac and Aira Dučić for their support in marketing efforts. And to the entire production team, including the copy editors, proofreaders, and all those behind the scenes who polished this book into its final form: your meticulous work is truly appreciated.

Thanks also go to my technical editor, Anirudh Prabhu, and technical proofreader, Doug Warren, who painstakingly read through the drafts, providing invaluable feedback that significantly enhanced the accuracy and clarity of this book. Their expertise was critical in refining the content and ensuring its practical relevance.

A special thank you goes to Ivan Martinović and all the other technical reviewers: Aayush Bhutani, Aditi Choudhary, Akshatha Anantharamu, An Nad, Andreas Berggren, Anujkumarsinh Donvir, Anurag Lahon, Arpankumar Patel, Asaad Saad, Ayisha Tabbassum, Bruno Ricardo Santos, Bruno Sonnino, Charlie Gaines, Christopher G. Fry, David Tarvin, Dhruv Kumar Seth, Dinesh Besiahgari, Foster Haines, Gavin Baumanis, Giovanni Costagliola, Giuseppe De Marco, Gustavo Meza De Lama, Guy Batton, Haniel Lopez, Heather Weaver, Ian Lovell, Iman L Hakim, Isabel Rapando, Iyabo Sindiku, James Liu, Jared Duncan, Jeff Martinez, Jereme Allen, John Bortins, Kalyanasundharam

Ramachandran, Karl-Gustav Kallasmaa, Karthikeyarajan Rajendran, Kaushik Dutt, Lei Zhao, Madhu Chavva, Manas Talukdar, Max Sadrieh, Maytham Fahmi, Mian Shah, Mohit Menghnani, Naga Rishyendar Panguluri, Naga Santhosh Reddy Vootukuri, Naveen Achyuta, Nicolas Bievre, Olena Sokol, Onofrei George, Panagiotis Matsinopoulos, Pradeep Kumar Saraswathi, Prasann Pradeep Patil, Prashanth Lakshmi Narayana Chaitanya Josyula, Rashan Smith, Robert Diana, Rod Weis, Ruben Gonzalez-Rubio, Sathya Narayanan Annamalai Geetha, Saurabh Aggarwal, Serhii Onishchenko, Sharmila Devi Chandariah, Simon Verhoeven, Sonu Kapoor, Sophia Willows, Sridhar Rao Muthineni, Swati Tyagi, Thomas Forys, Victor Jones, Vinod Veeramachaneni, and Zeeshan Chawdhary. Your comments helped make this a better book.

about this book

The primary goal of this book is to empower web developers to build dynamic and intelligent websites and applications that use the full potential of large language models and other generative AI capabilities. I aim to equip you with the practical tools and techniques necessary to integrate sophisticated AI features—such as retrieval-augmented generation (RAG), document summarization, and interactive chatbots—directly into your web-based projects, all within the familiar JavaScript ecosystem. You'll also get a tutorial on interacting with the Model Context Protocol to seamlessly extend capabilities beyond what we build ourselves.

Who should read this book

This book is tailored for frontend developers and full-stack web developers who are comfortable with React and Next.js. If you have a basic proficiency in these technologies and are looking to incorporate cutting-edge AI functionalities into your web applications, this book is for you. No prior experience with Python or machine learning is required; we focus entirely on JavaScript and other tools common to web developers. A basic awareness of generative AI concepts and prior experience using tools like ChatGPT or similar interfaces will be beneficial, but the foundational chapters will get you up to speed.

How this book is organized: A road map

This book is divided into 4 parts spanning 12 chapters, designed to progressively build your expertise in full-stack generative AI application development.

- Part 1: Building basic generative AI web apps (chapters 1–4) lays the essential groundwork. I begin by defining what generative AI web applications are, their key components, and recent developments. I then guide you through getting started with React and Next.js for AI applications, followed by a deep dive into the Vercel AI SDK for handling streaming responses, working with multiple AI providers, and managing state with React server components.

- Part 2: Advanced generative AI techniques and deployment (chapters 5–9) moves into more sophisticated methods and crucial deployment considerations. You'll master prompt engineering techniques; learn to use LangChain.js for complex AI workflows and agents; and understand the intricacies of testing, debugging, and securing your generative AI applications for production.
- Part 3: Hands-on projects (chapters 10–11) puts everything into perspective through comprehensive project explorations. I provide full codebases for an AI interview assistant and an AI RAG agent and then dissect their features, architectural decisions, and critical development considerations.
- Part 4: Advanced integrations and the future of AI (chapter 12) moves beyond current best practices to look at what's next. This part is dedicated to the Model Context Protocol, an emerging standard designed to create more seamless, secure, and interoperable connections between your applications and various AI models.

While the book is structured for a linear read to build knowledge sequentially, experienced developers might choose to focus on specific chapters within parts 2 and 3 that align with their immediate interests after completing part 1. The projects in part 3 serve as excellent consolidation exercises and practical references.

About the code

This book contains many examples of source code both in numbered listings and in line with normal text. In both cases, source code is formatted in a `fixed-width font like this` to separate it from ordinary text. Sometimes code is also **in bold** to highlight code that has changed from previous steps in the chapter, such as when a new feature adds to an existing line of code.

In many cases, the original source code has been reformatted; we've added line breaks and reworked indentation to accommodate the available page space in the book. In some cases, even this was not enough, and listings include line-continuation markers (➥). Additionally, comments in the source code have often been removed from the listings when the code is described in the text. Code annotations accompany many of the listings, highlighting important concepts.

You can get executable snippets of code from the liveBook (online) version of this book at https://livebook.manning.com/book/build-ai-enhanced-web-apps. The complete code for the examples in the book is available for download from the Manning website at https://www.manning.com/books/build-ai-enhanced-web-apps, and from GitHub at https://github.com/Generative-AI-Web-Apps/Code.

Full details for running the examples are in the appendix. To run the code examples and projects in this book, you will need

- *Node.js*—Version 18 or higher.
- npm *or Yarn*—For managing project dependencies.
- *Text editor*—Such as VS code.
- *Web browser*—Latest versions of Chrome, Firefox, Safari, or Edge.
- *API keys*—For various AI providers (e.g., OpenAI, Google Gemini), as demonstrated in the examples. Some examples may require paid API access for full functionality.

liveBook discussion forum

Purchase of *Build AI-Enhanced Web Apps* includes free access to liveBook, Manning's online reading platform. Using liveBook's exclusive discussion features, you can attach comments to the book globally or to specific sections or paragraphs. It's a snap to make notes for yourself, ask and answer technical questions, and receive help from the author and other users. To access the forum, go to https://livebook.manning.com/book/build-ai-enhanced-web-apps/discussion.

Manning's commitment to our readers is to provide a venue where a meaningful dialogue between individual readers and between readers and the author can take place. It is not a commitment to any specific amount of participation on the part of the author, whose contribution to the forum remains voluntary (and unpaid). We suggest you try asking the author some challenging questions lest his interest stray! The forum and the archives of previous discussions will be accessible from the publisher's website as long as the book is in print.

about the author

THEO DESPOUDIS is a senior staff software engineer at WP Engine, where he is part of the engineering team building the next generation of AI-powered search products and services for thousands of customers using WordPress. He is also responsible for supporting Headless WordPress solutions on top of Next.js and React. Author of two previous books, and he enjoys sharing his expertise on web development and AI technologies.

about the cover illustration

The figure on the cover of *Build AI-Enhanced Web Apps* is "La Fioraia," or "The Florist." The illustration is taken from an Italian compendium of regional dress costumes first published in Naples in 1853, engraved by Francesco de Bourcard.

In those days, it was easy to identify where people lived and what their trade or station in life was just by their dress. Manning celebrates the inventiveness and initiative of the computer business with book covers based on the rich diversity of regional culture centuries ago, brought back to life by pictures from collections such as this one.

Part 1

Building basic generative AI web apps

Generative AI is changing how we build software, and its integration into web applications is opening up incredible new possibilities. You see it everywhere, from chatbots like ChatGPT to the Gemini web interface. These applications use natural language to interact with powerful models, providing accurate, contextual responses. But what's happening under the hood? This book is your guide to building these cutting-edge experiences, and in this first part, we'll cover the essential groundwork.

We'll start with the basics: what generative AI web apps are, how they function, and the unique advantages they offer. From there, we'll get practical, walking you through the initial setup and configuration to build these applications using React and Next.js. You'll also be introduced to the Vercel AI SDK, a crucial tool that simplifies integrating AI models into your projects. Finally, we'll share strategies for effectively scaling and managing state. By the end of these chapters, you'll have a strong grasp of the fundamentals and be ready to begin your journey into full-stack generative AI development.

Using generative AI in web apps

This chapter covers
- What generative AI web applications are and what they can do
- How generative AI compares to traditional AI
- How generative AI apps work
- Handling the concerns and implications of AI

Generative AI web apps are web applications that integrate advanced AI models—most commonly large language models (LLMs)—to create original text, images, audio, or video. By generating content dynamically rather than relying solely on predefined logic or static data, these apps deliver personalized, adaptive, and highly interactive user experiences. This shift fundamentally changes how we build and engage with digital products, enabling conversational interfaces, intelligent automation, and entirely new categories of applications.

This book teaches you how to harness these capabilities and build scalable, production-ready generative AI web apps. You'll learn how to integrate AI features using popular models and providers such as OpenAI and Google AI while developing your applications with React, Next.js, and the Vercel AI SDK. Toward the end, you'll see how to work with the Model Context Protocol to access external tools and data sources in a secure and standardized way.

I assume that readers have a basic understanding of JavaScript and familiarity with building simple React applications; everything else will be introduced as needed. Our focus is on the concepts and techniques essential for designing, developing, and deploying AI-powered web experiences.

Throughout the book, you'll work through focused, hands-on projects that gradually build your skills and confidence. In the final chapters, you'll apply what you've learned to create two real-world applications: an interview assistant that records voice input and provides AI-generated feedback and a more advanced corporate knowledge management system powered by retrieval-augmented generation (RAG). These projects reinforce key ideas while giving you strong portfolio pieces you can adapt for future work.

The goal of this book is simple: to empower you to build real, working generative AI applications. We'll start with a quick look at how generative AI works, along with its benefits, limitations, and uses.

1.1 What generative AI can do for web applications

Generative AI opens a wide array of opportunities across various domains.

1.1.1 Generative AI capabilities

AI can enhance web apps in many exciting and useful ways:

- *Text generation*—Producing human-like text for content creation, storytelling, and conversational agents. This is perhaps the most prevalent feature, as it all begins with crafting prompts using natural language and conducting follow-up conversations using tools like ChatGPT, Perplexity AI, Anthropic Claude, or Google Gemini.
- *Image generation*—Creating realistic images for artistic purposes, design, and creative projects. DALL-E and Midjourney are well-known image generators.
- *Multimedia generation*—Producing videos, music, and other multimedia content. OpenAI Sora 2 is popular for video generation.
- *Code generation*—Assisting developers in writing code, automating repetitive tasks, and enhancing productivity. GitHub's Copilot and Claude Code are two code generators in wide use.
- *Learning exploration*—Encouraging exploration and experimentation in creative fields, such as art, music, and literature.
- *Problem solving*—Tackling complex problems in various domains, including science, engineering, and medicine, through innovative solutions.
- *Content enhancement*—Improving existing content through editing, enhancement, and refinement. For example, you might generate images in cartoon or art styles like sketch, anime, or filters from a photo.

1.1.2 Real-world uses of generative AI

Let's look at some use cases to see exactly how this technology is so valuable in web development.

USE CASE: DIGITAL MARKETING AGENCY

Say a digital marketing agency wants to explore new creative possibilities for its client's advertising campaigns. The agency wants to create a toolbox that allows it to generate images from text, generate new images from existing images, and create virtual objects based on written prompts. Here's how the agency might use AI to achieve its goals:

- *Image generation*—The agency could integrate generative AI models like DALL-E into its web applications. By using external APIs from AI service providers, users can input text descriptions or prompts and generate corresponding images directly within the application.
- *Image-to-image translation*—The agency could use architectures like CycleGAN or Pix2Pix in its web applications for image-to-image translation. It also has options to use an external provider like stability.ai.
- *Text generation for marketing*—Utilizing state-of-the-art language models like GPT-4 or Llama, the agency intends to empower users to generate compelling marketing copy or product descriptions directly within the web application.

USE CASE: CUSTOMER EXPERIENCE MANAGEMENT

A customer support platform aims to enhance its customer experience management by integrating generative chatbots into its web application. Its AI solution includes

- *Generative chatbots for automated customer support*—The platform could integrate advanced chatbot models such as GPT into its web application to handle customer inquiries and provide real-time assistance.
- *Dynamic response generation for customer feedback*—To address customer feedback, the platform can rely on generative AI models for dynamic response generation using sentiment analysis APIs, such as Google Cloud Natural Language API or IBM Watson Natural Language Understanding, to analyze feedback sentiment. The platform can also use text generation models like GPT-4 via API integration to generate personalized responses based on the sentiment and context of the feedback.

USE CASE: MOCK INTERVIEW APPLICATION WITH GENERATIVE AI AGENTS

A job-training platform aims to enhance its mock interview feature using these tools:

- *AI interviewer agents for simulated interviews*—The platform will incorporate AI agents powered by generative AI models such as GPT-4 into its web application. By using external APIs for chatbot integration and natural language understanding, users can engage in simulated interview experiences in which AI interviewer agents ask questions, evaluate responses, and provide real-time feedback. Additionally, the platform integrates speech-to-text technology to enable users to speak their responses naturally, enhancing the authenticity of the interview experience.

- *Personalized interview scenarios and feedback generation*—To offer personalized mock interview experiences, the platform plans to use generative AI tools like Google Dialogflow for scenario and feedback generation.
- *Adaptive interview difficulty*—Using generative AI insights, the platform aims to provide adaptive interview coaching based on users' performance and feedback.

To explore further about the ecosystem of tools, see the numerous AI tools listed online (https://topai.tools/), where you can search by type or application category.

1.2 How a generative AI web app works

Building scalable generative AI web applications requires orchestrating a multitude of moving parts, including user interaction, data processing, and communication with LLMs. Figure 1.1 provides a broad view of how the key components of a generative AI web application work together to produce content from queries.

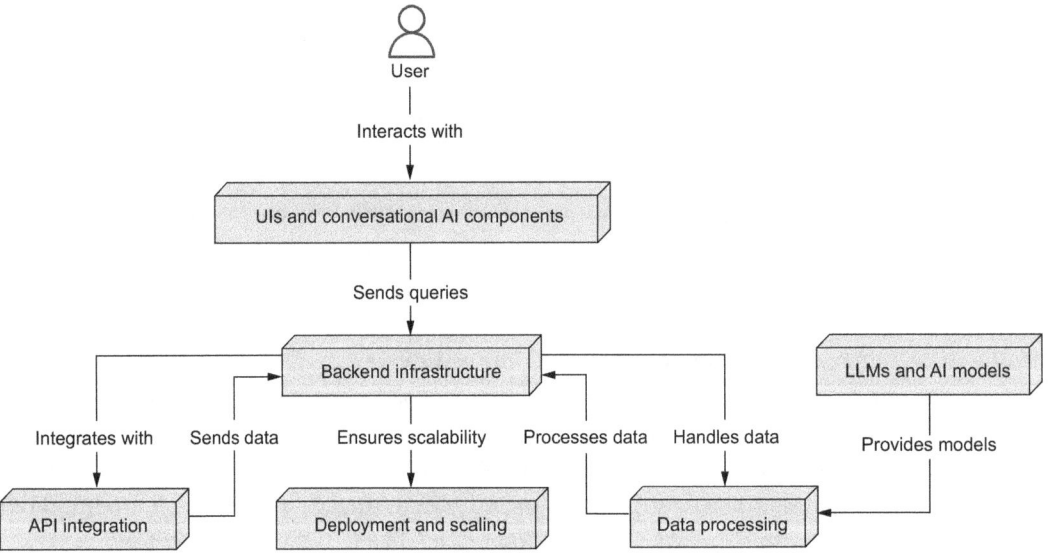

Figure 1.1 The flow of information and interactions between the key components of a generative AI web application

1.2.1 Core components

Let's look at the components in figure 1.1 in more detail.

LLMs AND AI MODELS

At the core of generative AI web apps are the AI models themselves. These models are trained on vast datasets and can generate content such as text, images, video, and even code. LLMs are a crucial class of AI models designed to understand, generate, and process human language. Their "large" designation refers to the immense scale of the data they are trained on (billions of words, sentences, and documents) and the vast number of parameters they contain, allowing them to learn complex patterns in language. Essentially, LLMs work by predicting the most probable next word or sequence of words in a given context, enabling them to produce human-like text, answer questions, summarize information, and more. Tools like ChatGPT rely on these powerful LLMs to perform their "magic" by transforming user prompts into coherent and relevant creative outputs.

UIs AND CONVERSATIONAL COMPONENTS

The user interface (UI) is what users interact with when using the web application with a browser. It includes HTML elements such as buttons, forms, and menus, providing a seamless experience for user queries and receiving AI-generated outputs. Beyond traditional browser-based UIs, generative AI also powers conversational AI components such as chatbots, virtual assistants, and sophisticated AI agents. These agents are programs designed to perform specific tasks autonomously, often by interacting with various other AI APIs and external systems and services, enabling AI functionalities even within nonbrowser applications or operating in the background.

BACKEND INFRASTRUCTURE

Behind the scenes, a robust backend infrastructure handles requests, processes data, and interfaces with AI models—ensuring that generated content is safe, reliable, and accurate, while protecting user privacy and personalization features. Examples of backend infrastructure components for serving LLM agents or interacting with AI models include

- *Caching layers*—Using Redis or Memcached to store frequently accessed data or model responses, the caching layers reduce latency and computational load on the AI models.
- *Containerization and orchestration*—Deploying AI models and associated services involves using Docker containers, managed by orchestration tools like Kubernetes for scalability and ease of management.
- *Serverless functions*—Services like AWS Lambda or Google Cloud Functions can be used to run specific AI-related tasks (like calling APIs) without managing server infrastructure.
- *Model-serving frameworks*—For advanced scenarios, employing specialized tools such as TensorFlow Serving, NVIDIA Triton Inference Server, and Vertex AI can be efficient.

This infrastructure ensures the smooth functioning of the application and efficient communication with external services and APIs.

DATA PROCESSING

A data processing pipeline is responsible for preprocessing raw input data, feeding it into the AI models, and postprocessing the generated output. This pipeline may involve tasks such as data cleaning, normalization, feature extraction, and result formatting.

> **DEFINITION** *Feature extraction* is a data processing technique where the machine learning model identifies meaningful patterns, characteristics, or representations and extracts them from raw data. In AI applications, this could mean detecting key phrases in text or shapes in images. Feature extraction begins with the model learning to automatically extract relevant features from the training data. Then, during inference, the model applies its learned feature-extraction capabilities to new data to understand what it is looking at.

API INTEGRATION

Whether you run an LLM locally or use external APIs, generative AI web apps often integrate with external systems to access additional functionalities or data sources. These APIs could provide services such as natural language processing, image recognition, or sentiment analysis, enhancing the application's capabilities.

DEPLOYMENT AND SCALING

Your web apps need to be deployed and scaled to handle increased spikes and to prevent unwanted service downtime. This task requires careful consideration of infrastructure requirements, resource allocation, and load balancing. Deployment tools and techniques ensure that the application can handle varying levels of traffic and usage.

1.2.2 The flow of user interactions

Now that we've explored the key components of an AI-powered app, let's look at how the user, the app, and the model interact. Figure 1.2 illustrates a typical workflow of actions and information, showing that content creation is a collaborative process between a user and an AI web app.

This user–app interaction can be summed up in four major stages:

1. *User input through the UI interface*—The user submits a query or a prompt, initiating the interaction with the UI. This input can be text prompts, images, selections, or any other format supported by the application.
2. *Backend processing*—The app then routes the query through its internal data processing pipeline, which may include cleaning, feature extraction, and preprocessing, and then selects the most suitable model for the query.
3. *Content generation*—The backend system interacts with both internal and external services or APIs to initialize the generation process in the selected model. This model, which has been pretrained on vast amounts of data (and may be further fine-tuned for specific applications like RAG), then uses its knowledge to generate creative content aligned with the user's input.
4. *Response delivery*—The app then delivers the AI-generated content to the user in the UI. An optional feedback loop allows the user to provide comments and follow-up questions on the results. This feedback can be used to refine the response

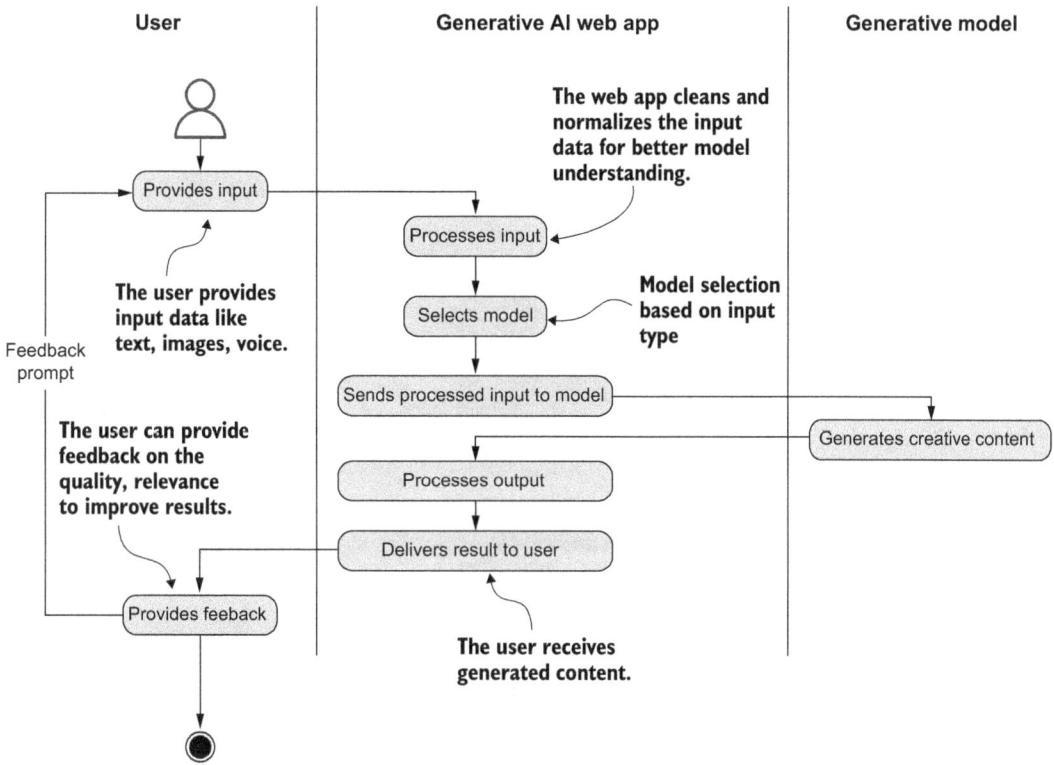

Figure 1.2 How an AI web app works: the user inputs data, and then the app processes it, selects a model, generates content, delivers it, and, optionally, collects feedback.

to this query and to improve the model's performance, thereby enhancing the quality of future responses.

At its core, a web application comprises a service hosted on the public internet. As you can see in figure 1.3, clients, whether web or mobile apps, can access the service to utilize its content and features. The service itself may encompass multiple components that communicate with other services on the public internet to deliver its features. While some services store state in a database system, others may remain stateless.

1.3 AI tools and the ecosystem

To build AI apps, we follow standard software engineering practices, using modern tooling to improve UI/UX, implementing effective testing and deployment strategies, securing APIs against potential threats, and optimizing performance through quality assurance. Let's look at some of these tools and platforms that can streamline the build process.

Many tools, services, and libraries streamline the build process, and this ecosystem continually evolves with new updates and features while striving to improve the accuracy of existing models. Many generative AI tools are available in both commercially

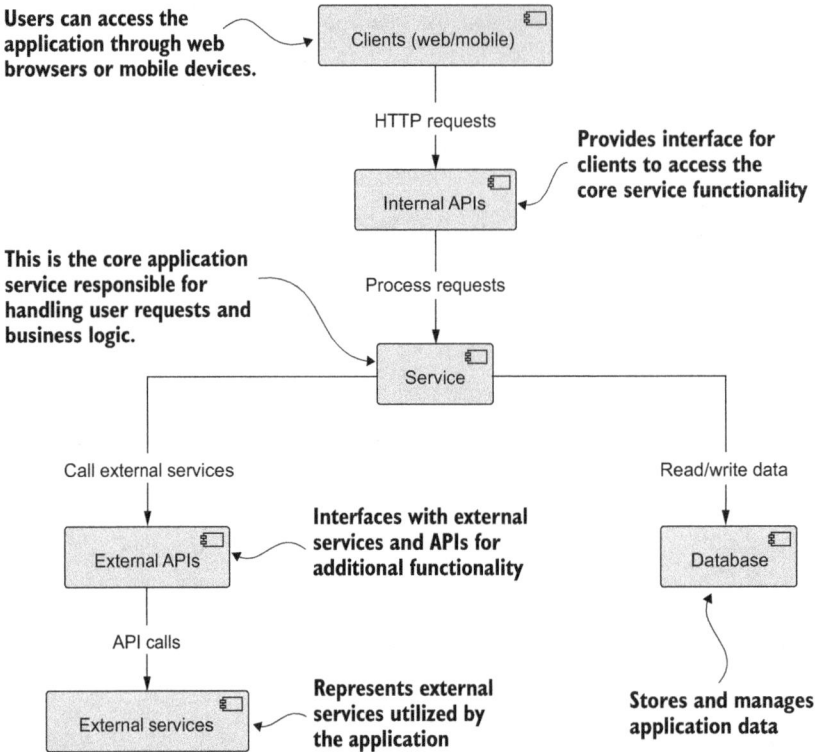

Figure 1.3 Simplified architecture diagram of a web application ecosystem. Clients, such as web browsers and mobile devices, interact with the core application service, which handles user requests and implements business logic. The service interacts with a database to store and manage application data. Additionally, the service communicates with external APIs to access additional functionality and interacts with external services utilized by the application.

licensed and open source versions. Figure 1.4 illustrates the interconnected components of a generative AI web application and the tools we'll use to build the examples in this book.

As we build our apps, we will use JavaScript and React to display our UI interface components, along with Next.js and the Vercel AI SDK to manage the backend and interact with external AI service providers. While the Vercel AI SDK supports various providers, our projects will primarily use Google Gemini models by default, with occasional use of OpenAI models.

React is one of the most popular JavaScript libraries for building user UIs with reusable components. It's easy to learn and has vast support for AI-related components. We will use React to build our UI elements and to present them to the users with accessibility and performance in mind.

Next.js is a framework built on React that simplifies the development of server-rendered and statically generated web applications. It streamlines backend management

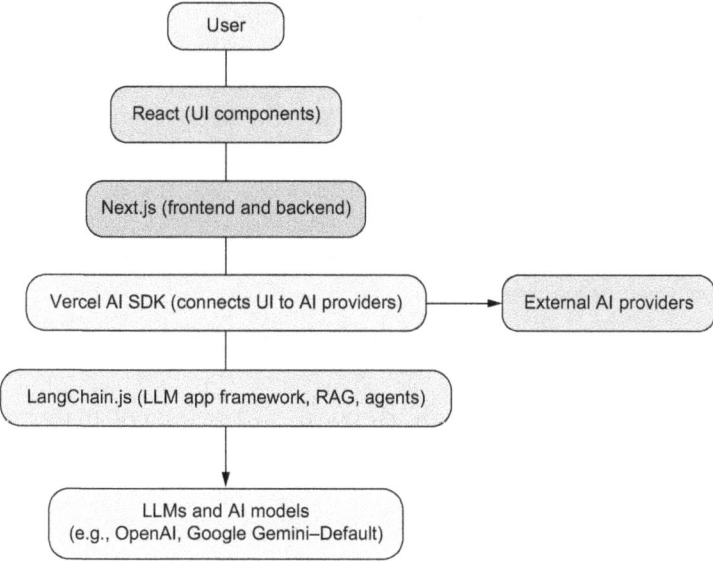

Figure 1.4   Using key technologies to create generative AI web applications

and data fetching, making development faster and more efficient. We will use Next.js to handle all the backend integrations.

The Vercel AI SDK is our cherry on top of the cake. It's an open source library specifically designed to integrate generative AI features into web applications, including specific hooks to handle state, components, and helpers that focus on core logic. We will use Vercel AI SDK tools to interact with external AI service providers and to incorporate AI functionalities seamlessly into our React components.

LangChain.js is a JavaScript framework for building applications with LLMs. It provides a suite of abstractions and building blocks that cover a wide range of application lifecycle scenarios from development to production. We will use LangChain.js to build conversational chatbots using RAG.

Other tools and frameworks for building AI web applications are available. Options include using an LLM API (e.g., the OpenAI.js client) directly or other small toolkits, such as polyfire-js and agentic tools, which offer similar capabilities. However, our choice of Vercel AI SDK has several advantages. First, it provides excellent integration with Next.js and React, allowing for seamless development of our chosen stack. The SDK offers good abstractions for handling multiple AI providers out of the box, saving developers from reinventing the wheel. Its convention-over-configuration approach simplifies setup and usage and offers a good state management solution (via UI and AI state abstractions). While developers could potentially write much of this functionality from scratch, doing so would be tedious.

The same argument applies to using LangChain.js, which offers additional advantages for building sophisticated AI applications. It seamlessly integrates with Next.js and the Vercel AI SDK, provides more specialized tools for building composable conversational chains and agents, and offers practical examples in its documentation. Part of this framework ecosystem also contains tools like LangSmith for building production-grade LLMs and LangGraph for creating agent and multi-agent workflows.

1.4 Choosing the right model

In addition to frontend and backend tooling, we also have to select an LLM model and provider to power our app. For the projects in this book, we'll use several popular models and providers, including

- *OpenAI*—Includes DALL-E 2 for image generation and ChatGPT for language tasks
- *Google AI*—Includes access to its own models, such as Gemini, and integrations with the Vercel AI SDK

There are many considerations when choosing an LLM model and planning how data will flow through the system. Say you're building an app that needs to integrate an LLM model to personalize website content based on user data and preferences. Let's look at the key decisions you'll face. To find the right model for the app, you first need to select the right *type* of model. In this case, you want to select one capable of understanding user preferences and content characteristics. In addition to the model's architecture and approach, the quality and relevance of the model's training data significantly affect its performance. So, you'll want to assess how well the model's training data aligns with your application's specific needs.

1.4.1 Model types

Different types of models excel at different tasks. LLMs are well suited for tasks involving text generation and manipulation, but specific architectures and approaches may be more appropriate for other kinds of tasks:

- *Generative adversarial networks* (GANs) use two competing neural networks to refine image generation so you can create new images based on image inputs. GANs are used to create images on the These Cats Do Not Exist website (https://thesecatsdonotexist.com/) and can also be adapted to generate video.
- *Autoregressive models* predict the next token in a sequence and can generate text one word at a time by predicting the next word in a sentence. This approach can be applied to data other than text and is appropriate for tasks where sequence matters, such as code and music generation, language translation, and time-series prediction. GPT-4 from OpenAI is an autoregressive model.
- *Transformer-based models* analyze relationships within data to excel at tasks like text generation. These models are based on attention mechanisms, allowing them to analyze relationships between different parts of the data. Use transformers when you need global context and large-scale LLM capabilities. Google Bard is an application built on transformer-based LLMs.

- *Variational autoencoders* compress data into a simplified format and then recreate variations of it. This technique is used mostly for anomaly detection or creating slight modifications of existing data—usually images and video, with text less common.
- *Recurrent neural networks* are adept at handling smaller-scale sequential data like text or speech. They can play a role in text-to-speech conversion or music generation but are becoming outdated for these and other large-scale tasks as transformers become more prevalent.

1.4.2 Pretrained vs. self-hosted

You have the choice to use pretrained models offered by cloud providers or third-party services or to create and host your own LLM. While pretrained models offer ease of use, they might lack the level of customization or performance you desire. Building and hosting your own LLMs gives you maximum control over the model's training data, enabling fine-tuning to achieve optimal performance for your specific application. However, this path requires significant computational resources and expertise in machine learning.

For our implementation, we'll use pretrained models via public APIs such as Gemini and OpenAI, which offer a practical way to access state-of-the-art language models without the complexity of hosting and maintaining them ourselves.

1.4.3 Performance considerations

It's important to evaluate a model's latency (inference time) and resource requirements to ensure it delivers a smooth user experience without overloading your infrastructure—or your users' costs. That means defining your user interaction and data flow and finding a model that works well for this flow. In particular, think about

- *UI design*—Determine how users will provide input to the model (e.g., text prompts, selection options) and how the generated output will be presented in the UI.
- *Data preprocessing*—Analyze how user input might need to be transformed or formatted before being fed to the chosen AI model.
- *Output postprocessing*—Consider any postprocessing steps needed on the model's output before integrating it into the final user experience.

1.5 Generative vs. traditional AI

AI is the field of computer science concerned with creating machines that solve problems by mimicking human cognitive abilities. *Machine learning* and *deep learning* are types of AI that enable computers to learn patterns from labeled data and improve their performance without being explicitly programmed. Instead of writing a series of instructions for a computer to identify a picture of a cat, we train a machine learning model to recognize images of cats. Then we can show the computer a picture of a dog, and it will respond: "No, that is not a cat." Figure 1.5 shows the process of training a model to recognize cats.

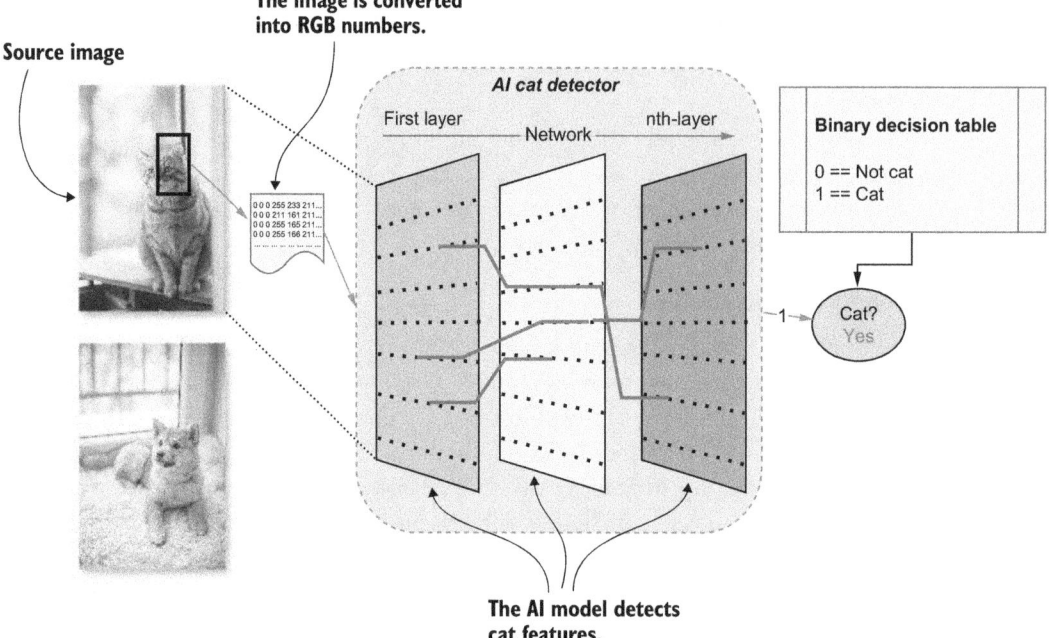

Figure 1.5 AI can be used to detect whether a picture of a cat is, in fact, a cat. It accepts an image as input and responds with *yes* or *no* (or 0 and 1).

Generative AI expands on machine learning's ability to detect patterns. Rather than simply recognizing or classifying data, generative models learn underlying patterns deeply enough to produce entirely new content that resembles the material they were trained on. They can mimic sentence structures, design styles, and musical patterns, generating results that previously required manual human effort.

The development of transformer architectures has propelled generative AI to its current capabilities. The field of AI in computer technology goes back a long time, but two recent developments in the models have revolutionized it: transformers and their core component, self-attention, both introduced in the landmark paper by Vaswani et al., "Attention Is All You Need" (https://arxiv.org/abs/1706.03762).

Transformers are a class of deep learning models that use self-attention mechanisms to process input data in parallel, making them highly effective in capturing long-range dependencies and contextual information within sequences. For example, in a sentence like "The lion, which had been chasing the antelope, finally caught it," transformers can understand that "it" refers to "the antelope" even though several words separate them.

Self-attention enables this understanding by allowing the model to evaluate the relative importance of each word in a sequence. Instead of viewing words in isolation, the model examines the full context to determine which words influence one another. As a result, machines can identify the most meaningful combinations of words to form a sentence.

Transformers revolutionized natural language processing by enhancing both efficiency and accuracy in understanding textual data. They simplify key computation-intensive tasks by reducing the need for large amounts of data. By using an attention mechanism, they help put the meaning of a word in context, considering the words before and after it. Therefore, computers can generate long, semantically sound sentences using only small prompts.

Take, for instance, the task of completing the phrase "green eggs and . . . ." Older natural language processing models often generate responses like "green eggs and unicorns" or "green eggs and spaceships." While grammatically correct, these completions failed to capture the contextual understanding required to produce meaningful and contextually relevant responses based on the original prompt.

The newer class of models has made significant strides in overcoming these limitations. Not only can they form grammatically valid sentences, but they can also provide more contextually relevant answers based on vast amounts of public literature. Today, when prompted with "green eggs and . . .," a model is likely to continue with "ham," referencing the well-known Dr. Seuss book. This demonstrates the model's ability to draw upon extensive knowledge and cultural references to generate responses that are not only syntactically correct but also semantically meaningful and contextually appropriate.

The cool thing about this technology is that it's not confined to text generation tasks; it also finds applications in computer vision for tasks like object detection and image classification, as well as in speech recognition for AI voice assistants. Any media for which feature extraction and semantic understanding are crucial can benefit from the capabilities of transformers.

1.6 Handling the concerns and implications of generative AI

As with any powerful tool, generative AI comes with significant responsibilities and valid concerns. To keep things simple, I will refrain from engaging in abstract philosophical debates about the ethical use of AI and instead provide practical guidelines for the responsible and effective utilization of generative AI in web applications.

1.6.1 What are the limitations of generative AI?

Some of the most crucial challenges and limitations to generative AI include

- *Quality control problems*—These concerns are about ensuring the quality and reliability of generated outputs, especially their accuracy, coherence, and relevance. There is always a chance that the output will be inadequate or unacceptable, which poses a risk of causing more harm than good.
- *Resource intensiveness*—Training our own models for generative AI demands computational resources and infrastructure for training and inference, which can be costly and resource intensive. Not everyone has the budget to run large, expensive GPUs for extended periods of time.

- *Security*—Protecting against potential misuse of generative capabilities for malicious purposes, such as generating fake content, spreading misinformation, or impersonating individuals, is paramount. These trespasses can have a long-lasting and damaging effect on public opinion.
- *Regulatory compliance*—It's imperative to adhere to regulations and guidelines related to data privacy, intellectual property rights, and content authenticity so your tools don't infringe on copyrighted material or create deepfakes. You need to understand and comply with regulations such as the General Data Protection Regulation (GDPR) in Europe and the California Consumer Privacy Act (CCPA) in the United States. These laws dictate how you can collect, store, and process user data, and they are especially relevant when dealing with personally identifiable information (PII). PII is any data that can be used to identify a specific individual, such as names, addresses, phone numbers, and email addresses. You must have a clear strategy for handling PII, including obtaining user consent, securely storing the data, and providing a mechanism for users to request its deletion.

1.6.2 Will developers lose jobs because of AI?

Yes, that is a possibility—but only if we fail to harness this technology to enhance our skills. Imagine you're a skilled furniture maker during the Industrial Revolution, sought after for your craftsmanship. Then, automated machines flood the market, promising to streamline the production of quality furniture at a lower cost. Initially, you might be skeptical of the threat, thinking, "My craft is too intricate to be automated, so I'm safe." But as the machines get better, you may fear that they'll replace you entirely. Notice, however, that two centuries later, there are still carpenters around. Successful furniture makers adapted to technology, learned new skills, and found new opportunities to innovate.

Still, it's undeniable that many jobs were affected by this change and have become obsolete—handloom weavers, blacksmiths, coopers (barrel makers), spinners and carders (textile workers), shoemakers (cobblers), candlemakers, and scribes (copyists). Similarly, in software development, tasks like code generation, documentation, test-case creation, and reviews may become highly automated. Yet, this transformation presents an opportunity for developers to focus on more meaningful and creative aspects of their work. If you aspire to remain relevant and competent in your craft as a developer, my recommendation is to embrace new and innovative technologies like generative AI.

1.6.3 Are generative AI outputs reliable?

As we've seen, generative AI tools are based on natural language, machine learning models that infer their next output based on the set of highest probabilities. This approach introduces two immediate questions:

- How do we trust those probabilities to be consistently accurate?
- How can we address potential language bias in the outputs based on the training data?

VALIDATING AI-GENERATED CONTENT

We let AI generate content for us based on some textual prompt, but how do we know whether the content, based on patterns in the training data, is actually true—or reasonable enough for our use cases? In fact, much of the content generated by AI could be classified as false, inaccurate, or even nonexistent. It's as if the AI is constructing an alternative reality and presenting it as factual information, known as *hallucinating*. Ensuring the accuracy and validity of AI-generated content not only enhances the user experience but also prevents the spread of misinformation that could lead to poor decision making.

In this book, we will take a hands-on approach to validate our generated content. We will explore techniques such as setting clear objectives, carefully framing the context of responses, adjusting certain LLM parameters, conducting cross-validations, and incorporating robust validation processes.

HANDLING BIAS

Bias and discrimination are among the most prevalent problems associated with generative AI technologies, and instances of inaccurate or misleading image generation are of significant concern because they can influence human-made decisions that rely on visual evidence. While there are no easy solutions to tackling bias when using LLMs and generative AI, we can make decisions that will help us in the long run. Restricting the source knowledge base, choosing models trained on diverse datasets, and including bias auditing can help mitigate bias to some extent. *Bias auditing* involves systematically testing a model with diverse inputs to identify and measure any biased behavior.

In this book, we will carefully confine our context and scope of applications to work on factual knowledge bases that do not discriminate against individuals. We will explore practical ways to conduct these audits as we build our applications.

ENHANCING USER EXPERIENCE

Users interacting with your generative AI web apps expect a high-quality experience that keeps them engaged. This means fast and accurate responses, an intuitive interface, a clear presentation of information, and personalization. User experience and satisfaction are pivotal, especially when adding conversational features. Significant progress has been made in LLMs, enabling them to accept a broader range of media inputs and making them more accessible. These models can now generate videos from text (text-to-video) and more. Since natural language can be ambiguous, we aim to provide users with options beyond text to achieve their goals.

This book prioritizes user experience. We'll discuss techniques such as streaming responses, backpropagation, using accessible components from the Vercel AI SDK, and using multiple formats to reduce frustration from repeated trial and error.

Summary

- Generative AI can generate not only text but all sorts of media resources like images, video clips, and audio. This capability greatly enhances their potential use in web applications. Real-world uses of generative AI in web applications range from digital marketing and customer experience management to mock interview applications.
- Generative AI web apps center on powerful models like LLMs to create content from user input. The apps require a whole supporting ecosystem to integrate with the model, including UI and conversational AI components, backend infrastructure, data processing pipelines, API integration, and deployment and scaling mechanisms.
- The apps we build in this book will use JavaScript and React to display the UI interface components, along with Next.js and the Vercel AI SDK to manage the backend and interact with external AI service providers.
- Choosing the right model for an app is a key architectural decision and depends on the task required. Different model types (such as LLMs, GANs, autoregressive, transformers, variational autoencoders, and recurrent neural networks) excel at different kinds of problems. But the model architecture is just one consideration; developers also need to consider the quality and type of data it was trained on.
- Software engineers were using AI long before generative AI came into existence. Common applications include machine learning, search recommendations, chatbots, and computer vision.
- Foundational research like Google's "Attention Is All You Need" laid the groundwork for transformative technologies such as transformers, which simplified natural language processing tasks by using attention mechanisms. Transformers revolutionized language modeling by improving efficiency and accuracy in understanding textual data, thus addressing long-standing challenges faced by traditional AI models.
- Limitations of generative AI include quality control problems, resource intensiveness, security concerns, and regulatory compliance. Concerns include generative AI's potential effects on jobs, the reliability of outputs, handling bias, and enhancing the user experience.

Building your first generative AI web application

This chapter covers

- Setting up a simple generative AI web app with React
- Interfacing with the OpenAI client
- Introducing Next.js and adopting it as our backend service

Let's start our journey by building a simple yet effective conversational app that demonstrates the core principles of large language model (LLM)–powered web applications. By "conversational," I mean that users will interact with our AI app using natural language through text inputs, such as a chat message interface often found on web pages for support or help. Conversational AI can also involve voice input and spoken answers, but our initial focus will be on text-based interactions. Our app will become more versatile as we progress through this book and add more advanced functions. It will eventually be able to accept sound recordings, generate pictures, employ advanced tooling, and even handle queries related to private data. Our goal is to build a flexible app that can select the right model for the task at hand and is highly adaptable, giving us the freedom to customize its behavior.

2.1 Introducing Astra

Our conversational app is an AI persona called Astra. An AI's *persona* defines the unique style, characteristics, and behavioral traits the application exhibits—like Google's Gemini. You can see a screenshot of Astra at work in figure 2.1. In this interaction, a user types a simple query, "Tell me a dad joke." In a matter of seconds, our application, which is powered by an LLM and a few lines of code, processes the request and generates a humorous response.

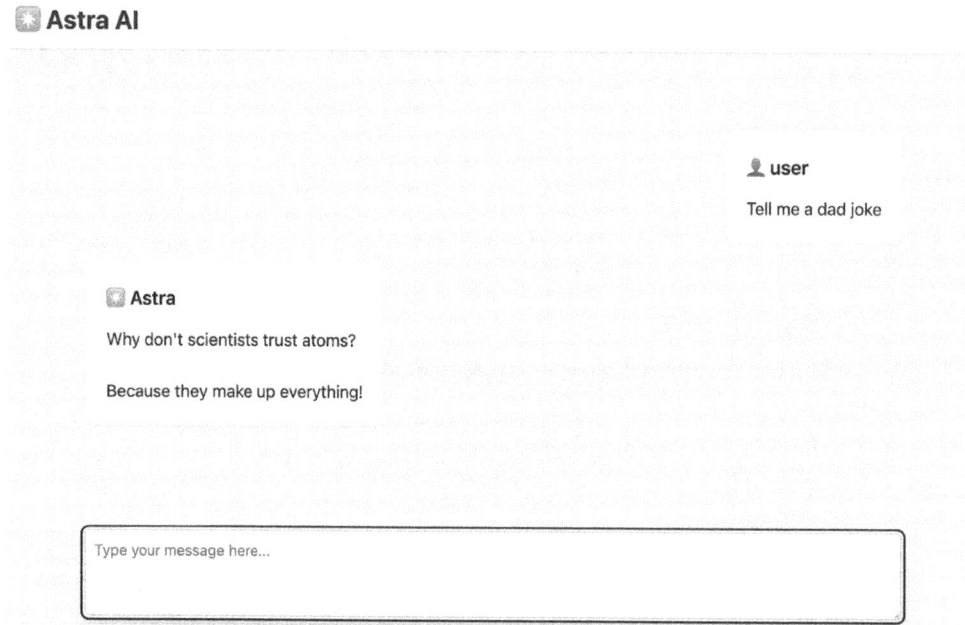

Figure 2.1 A simple conversational UI demonstrating a user query and an LLM-generated response

For our Astra app, we'll use pretrained models via public APIs such as Gemini and OpenAI, which offer a practical way to access state-of-the-art language models without the complexity of hosting and maintaining them ourselves. In fact, we will review two implementations: one built with React and Express.js, and one built with Next.js, with the goal of improving the project in subsequent chapters. By comparing these approaches, you'll gain valuable insights into the strengths and tradeoffs of each framework.

> **NOTE** For step-by-step instructions on how to create and configure API keys for both OpenAI and Google Gemini, including important billing considerations and free tier availability, refer to the appendix.

2.2 Project goal and requirements

When designing software with specific functionality, we typically start with the problem statement and document its requirements.

2.2.1 Goal: Build a simple interactive AI chat interface

Our objective is to create a web application where users can

- Ask questions in natural language
- Receive intelligent responses from an AI agent
- View and scroll through their entire conversation history

Figure 2.2 shows how these interactions relate and the flow started by a user interaction.

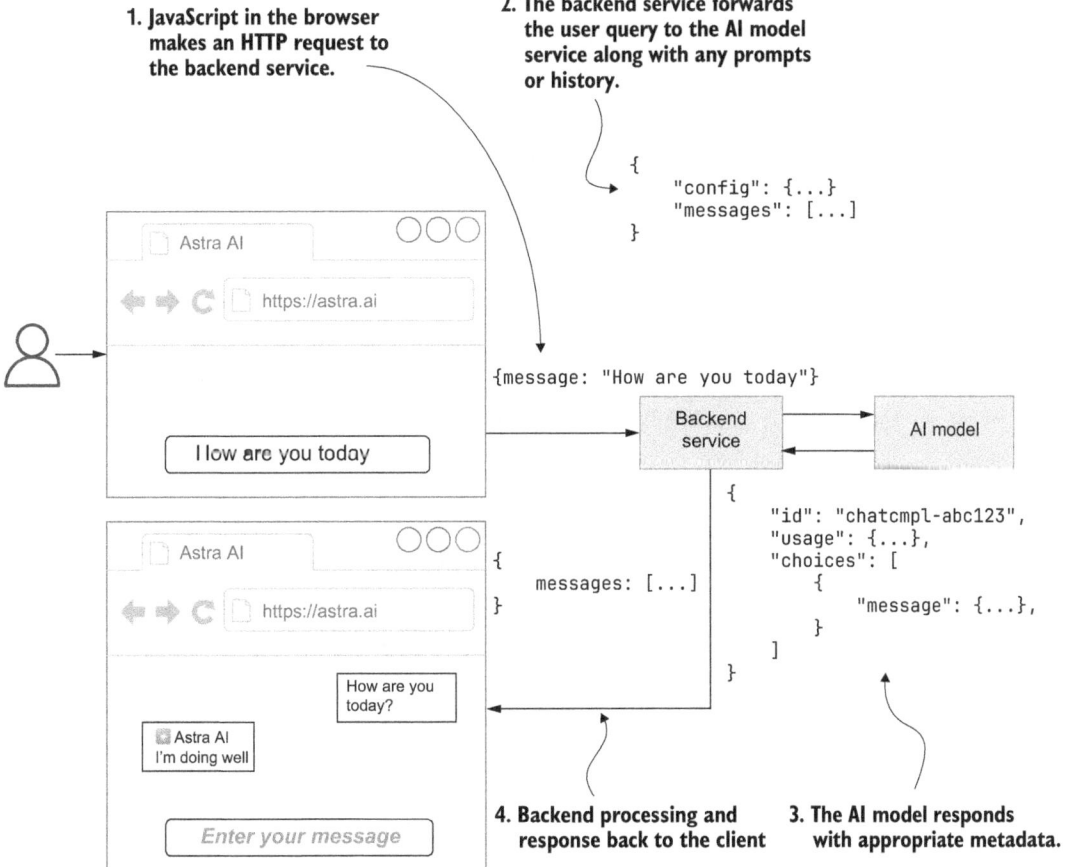

Figure 2.2 The user interaction flow in the chat application. The user types a question and presses Enter. The web UI submits the question to the backend service, which processes it and sends it along with context to the AI model. The AI model responds with a query response, which the backend service verifies and sends back to the web UI to update the conversation messages. This cycle allows for follow-up questions.

In sum, the series of events is as follows:

1. The user is presented with a page that consists of a welcome message and a textbox.
2. The user types a question and presses Enter.
3. The web UI takes the user's question and submits it to the backend service.
4. The backend accepts the query and processes it.
5. The backend submits the query along with some context to the suitable AI model that can understand as well as generate natural language or code.
6. The AI model responds with a query response.
7. The backend service processes the response and verifies its contents.
8. The backend sends the cleaned response back to the web UI.
9. The web UI updates the list of conversation messages.
10. The user can submit follow-up questions.

2.2.2 Project and technology requirements

Given the sequence of events, we can now list our initial requirements for building Astra AI as a simple, user-friendly, and effective chat app. In the first iteration, we want to prioritize a foundational experience. As I introduce concepts throughout this book, we will be enhancing Astra's AI functionality to suit our growing needs:

- *A single page*—The user interface should consist of a single webpage.
- *Welcome message*—A clear and welcoming message should greet the user, introducing Astra AI and its capabilities.
- *Text input box*—A prominent text input box should be readily available for users to type their questions in natural language.
- *Conversation history*—A dedicated area should display the entire conversation history between the user and Astra AI. This allows users to refer to previous interactions and provides context for follow-up questions.
- *Scrolling functionality*—The conversation history area should be scrollable, enabling users to revisit earlier parts of the conversation if needed.
- *Visual design*—A simple interface is preferred for this initial iteration.

To build the Astra AI's initial iteration, we'll use the following technologies. Don't worry if you're unfamiliar with some of the tools mentioned. The example projects are preconfigured to run without any changes on your part. Consequently, you can follow along even if you're new to these tools:

- *Frontend*—React.js
- *Backend*—Node.js
- *CSS framework*—Tailwind.css
- *Build tool*—Vite

- *AI model*—We'll use OpenAI's REST APIs to access pretrained models, so we can integrate natural language processing capabilities into Astra AI without building our own model from scratch.
- *Ephemeral storage*—For this first iteration, we'll avoid storing conversation history.
- *Automated testing*—We will provide unit tests using Vitest.
- *Error handling*—The app will gracefully handle unexpected situations and provide informative messages to the user.
- *Security*—While the initial focus is on functionality, we will utilize basic security measures like input validation and sanitization. No user authentication will be implemented in this iteration.

> **A preconfigured starter project**
>
> To make your journey smoother and let you focus on the core concepts, I've created a starter project that you'll use throughout the book. This project, located in the starter-project folder of the GitHub repository, is a preconfigured, clean, Next.js application.
>
> Think of it as the foundation of your house. I've already handled all the initial setup, like configuring Tailwind CSS, setting up basic routing, and including essential files, so you don't have to. You'll simply copy this project at the beginning of each chapter and build the new features on top of it. You can use the starter project as a base for all the examples in this book, ensuring you have a consistent and ready-to-run environment from the very beginning.
>
> For this first project, we'll start with a clean slate. We won't be using a preconfigured starter project or the Vercel AI SDK just yet, so you can head to the next section.

2.2.3 Setting up

Now let's look at the code that implements the application. To run this example, you'll need Node.js, which you can install by following the instructions on the official Node.js page at https://nodejs.org/en/download/package-manager.

> **NOTE** All examples and projects were developed and tested using Node.js v18 (long-term support [LTS]). I recommend using an LTS version of Node.js for stability, such as v18.x.x or the current LTS. While our code is designed to be compatible with newer versions of Node.js (including v22.x.x or v24.x.x "current" releases), sticking to an LTS version helps ensure a consistent development environment.

While you won't need to write any code in this chapter, feel free to download the complete project and run it yourself to gain practical experience.

> **NOTE** The source code for the examples in this chapter is available at https://github.com/Generative-AI-Web-Apps/Code.

> **Project code: chat-client**
>
> The code for this example project is in the ch02/client-chat folder. The appendix at the end of this book offers instructions on how to set up and create a secret key for OpenAI and other providers.
>
> **Option 1: Using Google (default)**
>
> You can use that example using Google Gemini by running the following command in the source folder from the project root directory:
>
> ```
> $ npm run start -w ch02/client-chat
> ```
>
> You'll also need a Gemini API key to access their REST API:
>
> ```
> // .env
> GEMINI_API_KEY=<SECRET_KEY>
> ```
>
> **Option 2: Using OpenAI**
>
> You can use that example using OpenAI Generative by running the following command in the source folder:
>
> ```
> $ npm run start:openai -w ch02/client-chat
> ```
>
> You'll also need an OpenAI API key to access their REST API:
>
> ```
> // .env
> OPENAI_API_KEY=<SECRET_KEY
> ```

WARNING Make sure that your OpenAI API key is valid to avoid any problems during the installation process. Remember, this secret key should be kept confidential and not shared publicly.

2.2.4 Running the project

If you followed the setup instructions to run the chat-client example project, you should be able to visit http://localhost:5173 and interact with the agent. Figure 2.3 shows a screenshot of the application after some exchange of messages.

A QUICK CHAT WALK-THROUGH

Before we look at the implementation details, let's briefly walk through a simple chat exchange with Astra AI to see the application in action. When you first launch the application, you'll be presented with a welcoming screen, ready for your input. Locate the text box at the bottom of the screen and type your first prompt:

```
Tell me more about yourself
```

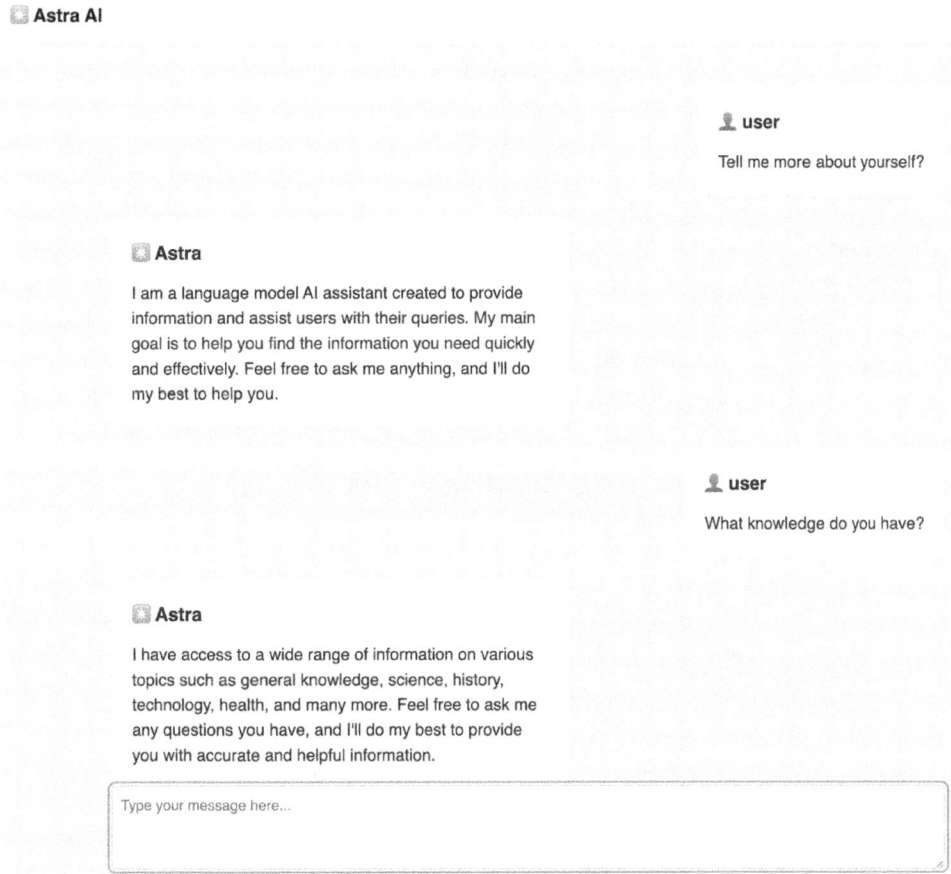

Figure 2.3 A screenshot of Astra AI in action. We can interact with the agent, and it will respond politely.

Upon submitting your query, you'll observe a brief "Please wait" indicator as Astra AI processes your request. Then, Astra AI will provide its response, which will appear in the chat history, and the input text box will be ready for your next question.

For your second interaction, type

```
What knowledge do you have?
```

Astra AI will again process your request and generate another informative response.

PROJECT STRUCTURE OVERVIEW

We take the simplest approach with this example project. Since it's a single feature that we are building, we have all relevant source code with a relevant flat folder hierarchy. For instance, the components folder houses all React components, and the hooks folder stores all custom hooks used in the project. This flat structure is effective for small, focused projects. However, it may not scale well for larger or more complex applications. I'll provide alternative project structures with better scalability when building more intricate features in future chapters.

If you experience problems with the AI not responding to your requests when using OpenAI, it is important to ensure that your OpenAI account has sufficient credits before making API calls; otherwise, you will encounter an `insufficient_quota` error. Additionally, you cannot use the same phone number with different email addresses to obtain additional free credits on OpenAI. If you have already used a free trial, the credits are shared across accounts linked to your phone number. This limitation applies specifically to OpenAI accounts and does not affect the use of other providers such as Google Gemini. Following these guidelines will help you avoid common quota-related errors and ensure smooth API usage with OpenAI.

2.3 Under the hood: The generative AI lifecycle

Let's explore the mechanics that occur when you interact with Astra, our conversational AI agent. Behind the scenes, as you can see in figure 2.4, your message travels from the chat interface to the backend, where it interacts with the AI model and triggers a response. The backend then delivers that response, which updates the chat window and allows you to continue the conversation with Astra. While doing so, the UI displays a loading indicator for the user. Once the new message arrives, the page automatically scrolls to display the last response message.

Some interactive elements are working behind the scenes without user intervention, so we'll want to start with the rules we follow.

2.4 Designing for a better user experience

As we explore the interactivity of our generative AI application, it's important to consider the user experience (UX) when dealing with long responses from LLMs. Here's why:

- *Attention management*—Lengthy, unformatted text blocks can overwhelm users and hinder information processing. To address this, many LLMs allow you to specify both the desired response format through prompts and their delivery method using streaming responses. Requesting content in formats such as Markdown allows for easy rendering with improved readability and structure. This enables features like collapsible sections, code blocks, and bolded text within the application instead of showing a big wall of text.
- *Navigation and control*—Users might struggle to navigate within lengthy responses, so consider adopting automatic scrolling mechanisms or ways to scroll to the top or bottom of the message threads.
- *Engagement and interactivity*—Providing users with ways to interact with the response, like collapsing sections or highlighting keywords, can enhance engagement and understanding.

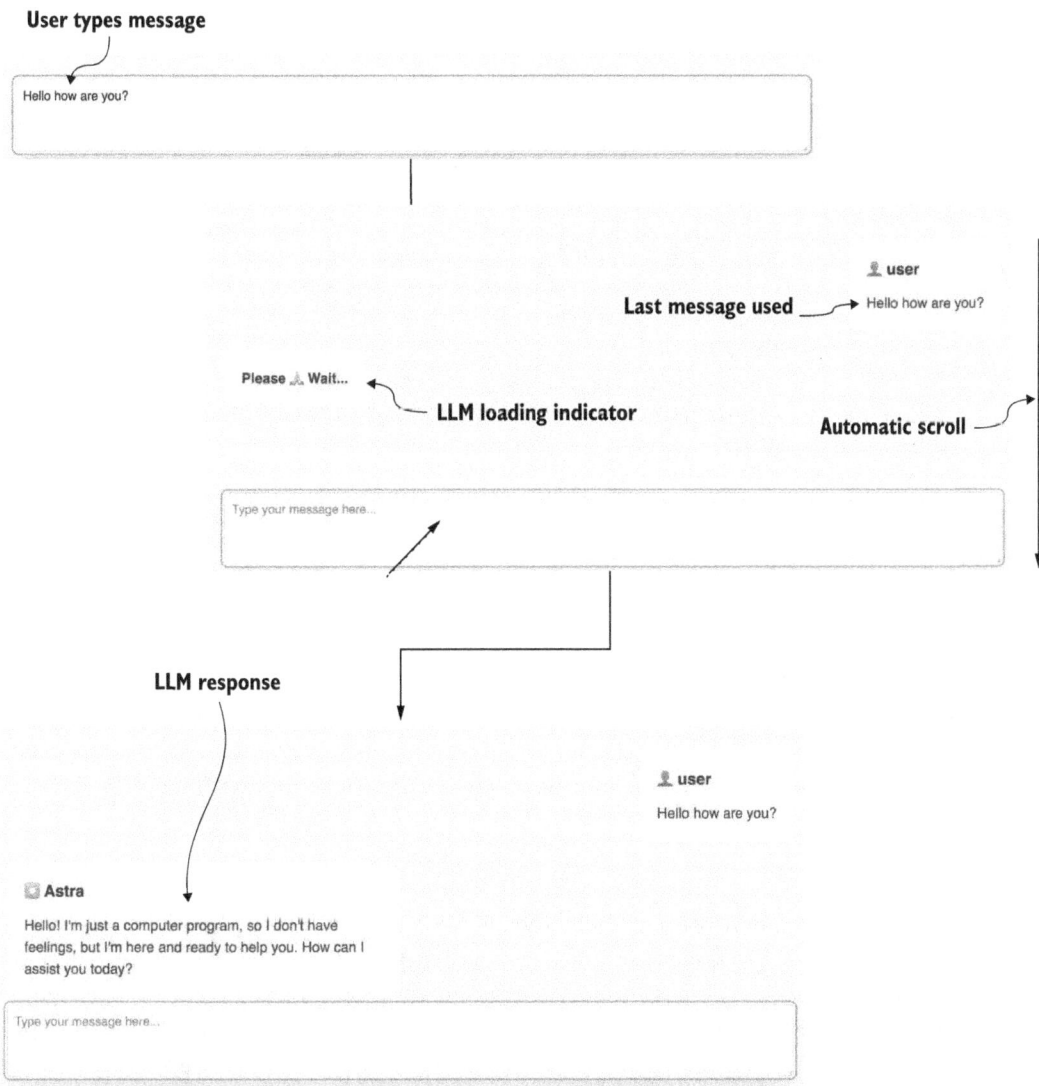

Figure 2.4 A screenshot of Astra's chat interface, showing a conversation history between the user and the AI. Notice the input prompt, a list of past messages, and a loading indicator while the AI (LLM) processes the request. Once a new message is posted, the page is automatically scrolled down.

Throughout the following chapters, we'll explore additional techniques to refine the response content itself through formatting, streaming, and customization, further enhancing the user experience when interacting with the LLM.

Keeping these UX concepts in mind, you'll see that our code example already incorporates automatic scrolling for handling long responses. When a new message arrives in the LLM response, the page will scroll to make it visible so the user doesn't have to scroll manually.

> **React refresher**
>
> Here is a quick refresher intended for readers who need a brief recap of the key React characteristics that we will rely on throughout our development process.
>
> React is primarily a UI library that helps developers write interactive web applications powered by JavaScript. It includes
>
> - *Components*—Reusable, self-contained pieces of UI (e.g., `ChatList`, `TextArea`).
> - *JSX*—A syntax extension for JavaScript that allows writing HTML-like code in React. For example, instead of using `createElement( 'h1, 'Hello');` developers simply use `<h1>Hello</h1>`.
> - *Props*—Read-only data passed from parent to child components.
> - *State*—Mutable data that can change over time, managed within a component.
> - *Hooks*—Functions that let you use state and other React features in functional components.
> - *Virtual DOM*—React's efficient way of updating the UI by comparing virtual representations of the DOM.
> - *Lifecycle methods*—Functions that run at different stages of a component's existence.

2.5 Building the major components

Now that we've outlined the goals and user experience, let's explore the project's structure, focusing on the key architectural components. We'll start with the frontend, where user interactions begin, and then move to the backend, which handles communication with our AI model.

2.5.1 Frontend

The frontend is where the UX comes to life. In this application, we use a component-based architecture to build fluid, responsive chat interactions.

The `<ChatPage/>` component serves as the central building block of the chat interface. Figure 2.2 shows how this component is rendered into the final page. This component is located in the src/pages folder and is responsible for rendering visual elements and managing user interactions. This component handles

- Displaying a list of past conversation messages
- Providing an input field for users to type their questions or prompts
- Submitting user input to the LLM for processing
- Displaying the LLM's generated response
- Incorporating features like automatic scrolling for long responses (as discussed earlier)

NOTE In a React application, the terms *page* and *component* are often used interchangeably, but they typically denote different organizational roles. A page (such as `ChatPage`, often found in a src/pages folder) is a top-level React component specifically associated with a particular route or URL, representing a distinct view or screen in your application. Components (such as ChatList or ChatMessage, typically found in a src/components folder) are smaller, reusable pieces of UI that are nested within pages or other components to build complex user interfaces efficiently.

Figure 2.5 provides the tree hierarchy of this component and its internal components, some of which contain only functionality and not visual presentation (e.g., <AutoScroll/>).

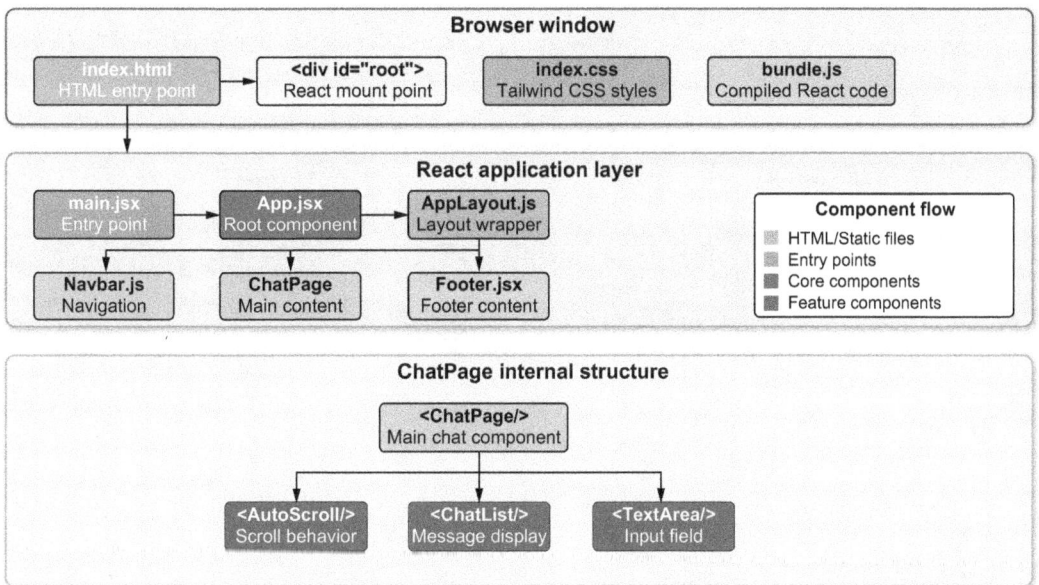

Figure 2.5 The browser loads index.html, which mounts the React application to a root div. The application starts with main.jsx (the entry point), rendering App.jsx. App.jsx uses AppLayout.js for the overall page structure, including Navbar.js, the central ChatPage content, and Footer.jsx. ChatPage further breaks down into three child components: AutoScroll (managing scroll behavior), ChatList (displaying conversation messages), and TextArea (handling user input). Data flows between these components, with ChatList holding the conversation history and TextArea managing the user's message prompt.

Out of the three child components, <AutoScroll/> does not contain any visual representation, so let's look at the process of implementing it.

2.5.2 Autoscroll

One of the most important UX considerations in a chat app is managing the conversation flow. <AutoScroll/> is a React component that automatically scrolls itself into view when it is at the bottom of the viewport and not currently visible.

It receives a `trackVisibility` prop that determines whether the autoscrolling behavior should be enabled. The component uses the `useIsAtBottom` hook to check whether it is at the bottom of the viewport and the `useInView` hook to determine whether it is currently in view. If `trackVisibility` is `true` and the component is at the bottom and not in view, the component smoothly scrolls itself into view using the `scrollIntoView` method.

Figure 2.6 shows how this interaction works. Of course, this is not the only way to implement autoscrolling, but it works quite well in most use cases.

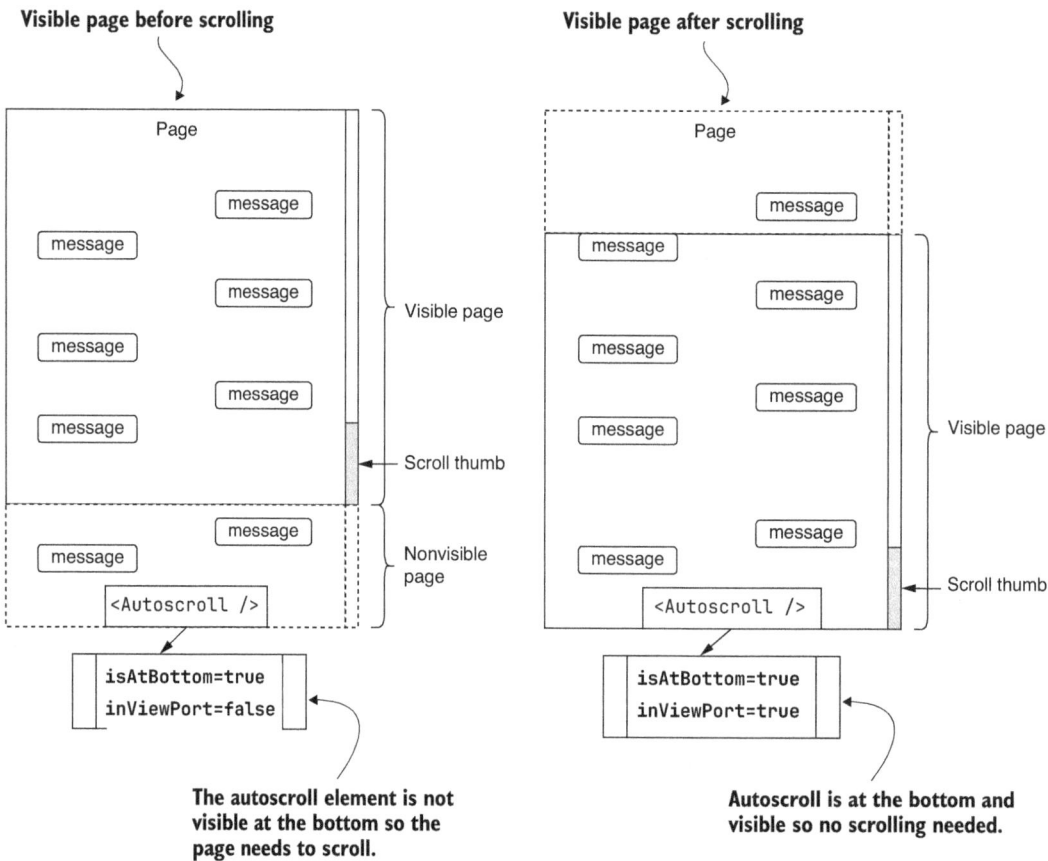

Figure 2.6 The `<Autoscroll/>` component works by triggering a scroll to the bottom of the page. The criteria that trigger the autoscrolling behavior are as follows: the `trackVisibility` prop is set to `true`, the component is at the bottom of the viewport (determined by the `useIsAtBottom` hook), and the component is not currently in view (determined by the `useInView` hook).

You might notice that with the current `AutoScroll` component, if the conversation gets very long, it always forces the view to the bottom when new messages arrive. This can be disruptive if you're trying to read older parts of the chat history. For a more sophisticated user experience, a real-world chat application would enhance the scrolling behavior to

- *Conditional autoscrolling*—Only automatically scrolls to the bottom if the user is already near the bottom of the conversation. If the user scrolls up to review previous messages, autoscrolling should pause to allow uninterrupted reading.
- *Scroll to the Latest button*—When autoscrolling is paused (because the user is viewing older messages and new ones have arrived), a subtle indicator or a Scroll to Latest Message button can appear. Clicking this button manually returns the user to the latest messages.

Listing 2.1 provides a top-level view of the `<ChatPage/>`, `<ChatList/>`, `<AutoScroll/>`, and `<TextArea/>` components. I have omitted some Tailwind CSS classes to improve readability.

> **NOTE** Tailwind CSS is a utility-first framework used in this project for basic styling. While powerful, Tailwind can sometimes result in less readable HTML due to the overuse of CSS classes. For helpful documentation that teaches you how to promote code reusability, see https://tailwindcss.com/docs/reusing-styles. I recommend reviewing it if you plan on working with this framework.

Listing 2.1 The main page component

Form submission logic: useEnterSubmit gives us formRef and onKeyDown to let users submit with Enter.

```
import Textarea from "@/components/ui/textarea";
import ChatList from "@/components/chat/ChatList";

import useEnterSubmit from "@/hooks/use-enter-submit";
import AutoScroll from "@/components/AutoScroll";
import useFocusOnSlashPress from "@/hooks/use-focus-on-slash-press";
import useChatFormSubmit from "@/hooks/use-chat-form-submit";

import { getAssistantResponse } from "@/lib/getAssistantResponse";

const ChatPage = () => {
  // References from custom hooks.
  const { formRef, onKeyDown } = useEnterSubmit();
  const inputRef = useFocusOnSlashPress();

  const { messages, isLoading, handleSubmit, inputValue,
    setInputValue } = useChatFormSubmit(getAssistantResponse);

  const onInputChange = (e) => {
    setInputValue(e.target.value);
  };

  return (
```

Input focus shortcut: useFocusOnSlashPress improves UX by focusing the text box when / is pressed.

Input state updates: keeps inputValue synced with the text area

Chat state and handlers: useChatFormSubmit centralizes state: messages, loading state, submission handler, and input value.

```jsx
      <div>
        {messages.length === 0 && (      ◄── Conditional UI: shows a
          <h1>                               welcome message when empty
            <div>Hello, I'm 🌀 Astra</div>
            <br />
            <span>Ask me anything you want</span>
          </h1>
        )}

        {messages.length > 0 &&                              Conditional UI:
<ChatList messages={messages} isLoading={isLoading} />}  ◄── renders the ChatList

        <form ref={formRef} onSubmit={handleSubmit}>   ◄── Chat form: renders
          <Textarea                                        the text area, wired
            ref={inputRef}                                 to state and handlers
            placeholder="Type your message here..."
            value={inputValue}
            onChange={onInputChange}
            onKeyDown={onKeyDown}
          />
        </form>
        <AutoScroll trackVisibility />   ◄── Autoscroll: keeps the chat window
      </div>                                 pinned to the latest message
  );
};

export default ChatPage;
```

2.5.3 ChatPage

`<ChatPage/>` imports certain components for displaying past conversations located inside the components folder (`<ChatList/>`) and user input (`<Textarea/>`) and includes automatic scrolling support (via `<AutoScroll/>`). Additionally, it uses custom hooks (located in the hooks folder), which are reusable functions that encapsulate state and logic for specific tasks.

2.5.4 ChatList

The `<ChatList/>` component is responsible for a core UI concept: rendering dynamic lists. It takes an array of message objects as a prop and maps over them to display each conversation bubble. This pattern, in which a parent component manages a list of child components, is fundamental to building scalable UIs.

Nested within the `<ChatList/>` component is the `<ChatMessage/>` component. This smaller component renders each message in the conversation history. It takes a single message object as a prop and formats it appropriately, often distinguishing between user messages and AI messages (e.g., by applying different styling or showing an avatar) and a role prop that indicates whether the message came from the "user" or "assistant," and text contains the actual message content.

The `<ChatList/>` component also consumes the application's loading state. The component displays a loading indicator while awaiting the AI response. This message informs the user that the application is currently busy while waiting for the backend to generate the response to the user.

Figure 2.7 provides an outline of the `ChatList` component and its child components. Dividing a page into semantic elements and developing them individually helps you understand how each component fits within the overall design.

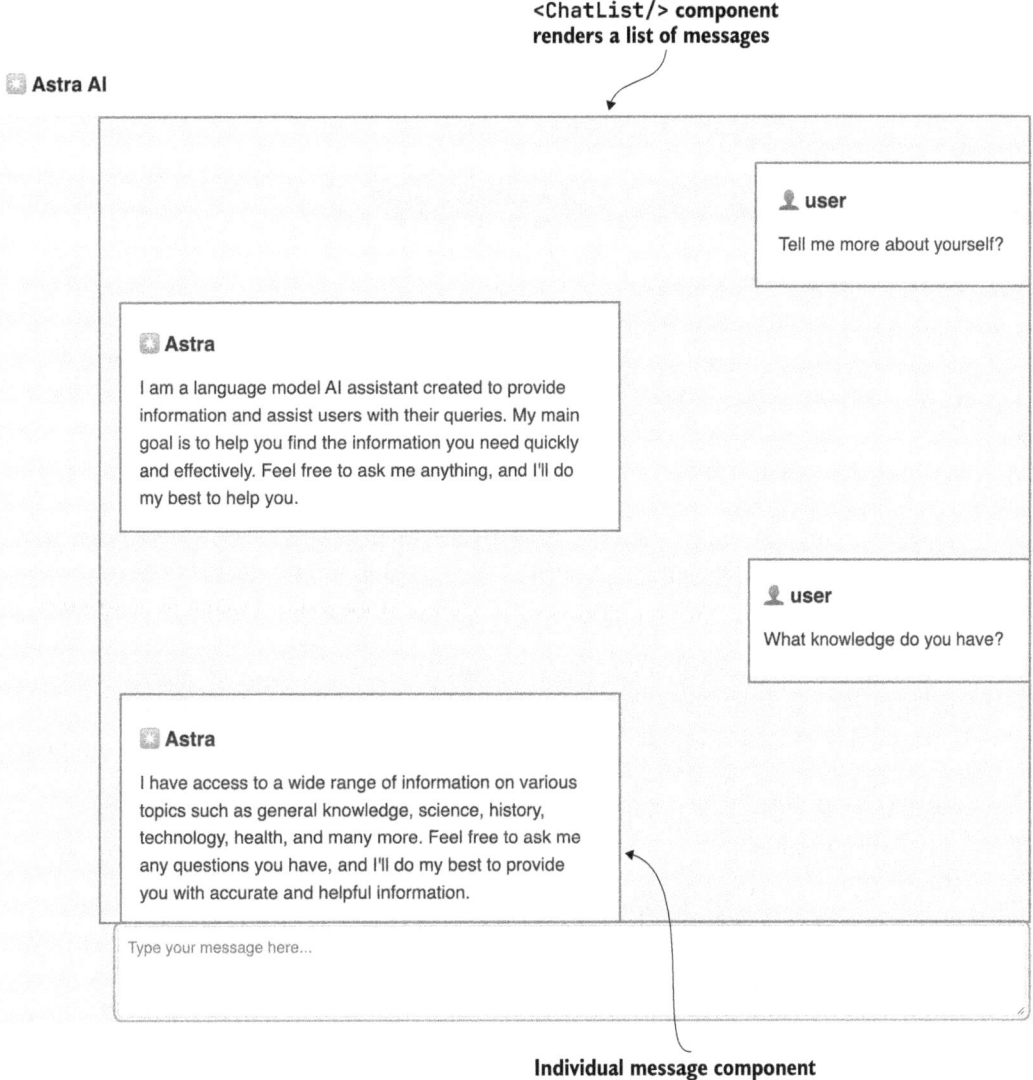

Figure 2.7 The `<ChatList/>` component is highlighted within the Chat page along with the chat message components.

The following listing provides the simplified code view of the `<ChatList/>` component that implements the functionality I just described (ChatList.jsx).

Listing 2.2 Component that lists all conversation messages

```jsx
import ChatMessage from "./ChatMessage";
import ChatBubbleLoading from "./ChatBubbleLoading";

const ChatList = ({ messages, isLoading }) => {
  return (
    <ul>
      {messages.map((message) => (          ◀── Renders each chat message
        <li key={message?.id}>                   dynamically using ChatMessage
          <ChatMessage
            role={message.role}
            text={message.content}
          />
        </li>
      ))}
      {isLoading ? (         ◀── Shows a loading bubble
        <li>                       while the assistant responds
          <ChatBubbleLoading />
        </li>
      ) : null}
    </ul>
  );
};

export default ChatList;
```

`<ChatList/>` maps over the `messages` array to display each message with `<ChatMessage/>`, ensuring new messages appear in real time with the correct role. When `isLoading` is true, `<ChatBubbleLoading />` provides feedback that the assistant is processing a response.

Now that we've seen how the UI is rendered, let's focus on the engine powering chat interaction: the `useChatFormSubmit` hook. This custom hook is a prime example of isolating and reusing complex logic. Instead of cluttering our `<ChatPage/>` component with state management and API calls, we've encapsulated all of that functionality here. This follows the principle of separation of concerns, which is crucial for building maintainable applications.

> **NOTE** Custom React hooks are reusable functions that elevate React components. They can access and manipulate states (`useState`, `useReducer`) and perform side effects (data fetching, subscriptions) using lifecycle methods (`useEffect`). This enables cleaner component logic and improved state management. Hooks promote code reusability, improve readability by separating complex logic, and enhance testability by isolating functionality.

To provide this functionality, we follow some practical steps for creating a custom hook in React:

1. *Define the hook function.* We create a function with a descriptive name that reflects the hook's purpose.
2. *Identify state management needs.* We capture what state the hook needs to manage internally and what it needs to expose externally. It makes sense to keep most of the state internal and only return values that other components need to use.
3. *Create helper functions, if needed.* Sometimes hooks can become complex. We can improve this by defining functions that can encapsulate specific tasks related to state updates or data manipulation. We also consider accepting helper functions as arguments, allowing us to use different implementations on demand.
4. *Implement core functionality.* The core functionality of your hook depends on its purpose. It might involve handling user interactions (like form submissions), managing data fetching (e.g., from APIs), or manipulating UI state (like showing/hiding modals).
5. *Return the hook values.* A key consideration is what values your hook needs to expose. A hook should return an object containing the state variables it manages and any functions it provides for interacting with that state. This allows any component to call the hook to access and manipulate the relevant data and functionalities.

Understanding these core steps is essential before we review the specific implementation details. Let's break down how we used the general guidelines for building custom hooks to create the specific `useChatFormSubmit` hook:

1. *Define the hook function.* Custom hooks begin with use to signal their role and purpose. `useChatFormSubmit` is named to clearly indicate it handles chat form submissions.
2. *Identify state management needs.* Hooks manage dynamic data within components. `useChatFormSubmit` tracks chat messages, the current user input, and the submission's loading status.
3. *Create helper functions (and dependencies).* Hooks often rely on helper functions for complex or external tasks. `useChatFormSubmit` uses a helper, `getAssistantResponse` (passed as an argument), to fetch the LLM response from the backend.
4. *Implement core functionality.* This is the hook's main logic. `useChatFormSubmit` manages the form submission, updates all past messages for the `<ChatList/>` display, and exposes a loading state for user feedback.
5. *Return the hook values.* Hooks provide values (state and functions) for components to use. `useChatFormSubmit` returns an object with
    - *Messages*—Conversation history
    - `isLoading`—Current loading status
    - `handleSubmit`—Function to submit the form
    - `inputValue`—Current input text
    - `setInputValue`—Function to update input text

The following listing provides a closer look at its code that represents this functionality (use-chat-form-submit.js).

Listing 2.3 Function that submits the current message

```js
import { useState } from "react";
import { generateUniqueId } from "@/lib/generateUniqueId";

function useChatFormSubmit(getAssistantResponse) {
  const [messages, setMessages] = useState([]);         // Messages state: holds the conversation history
  const [inputValue, setInputValue] = useState("");     // Input state: current user text
  const [isLoading, setIsLoading] = useState(false);    // Loading state: indicates assistant is processing

  const handleSubmit = async (e) => {
    e.preventDefault();
    const value = inputValue.trim();                    // Trim input: removes leading/trailing spaces
    if (!value) return;                                 // Prevents empty messages

    setIsLoading(true);                                 // Sets loading before fetching response
    setInputValue("");                                  // Clears input after sending
    const userMessage = {
      content: value,
      role: "user",
      id: generateUniqueId(),
    };
    setMessages((currentMessages) =>
[...currentMessages, userMessage]);                     // Adds user message to state
    try {
      const {message} = await getAssistantResponse(value);  // Fetches assistant response
      setMessages((currentMessages) =>
[...currentMessages, responseMessage]);                 // Adds assistant response to state
    } catch (error) {
      console.error(error);                             // Logs errors
    } finally {
      setIsLoading(false);                              // Resets loading after processing
    }
  };

  return { messages, isLoading, handleSubmit, inputValue, setInputValue };
}

export default useChatFormSubmit;
```

This hook manages the chat state, including all messages, the current input, and a loading indicator. handleSubmit processes user input by preventing empty messages, adding the user's message to the state, fetching the assistant's response, and updating the messages again. Errors are logged, and the loading state is reset once processing completes. By encapsulating this logic, the hook keeps the component clean and reusable, making it easy to handle chat interactions consistently across the app.

While this hook manages a single input and interacts with a specific backend endpoint, its design allows for reusability in different parts of our application. That's the power of the custom React hooks in action.

2.5.5 The backend: Handling API communication

The backend is the critical middle layer that connects our frontend to the AI model. Its primary responsibility is to serve as a secure, reliable intermediary between the user interface and the external AI service. This architecture allows us to handle sensitive information such as API keys on the server side, away from the user's browser. Let's explore the key functions of this backend service.

By default, the project uses the Google variant of server.js because of its robust conversation support and developer-friendly API and because it offers a free usage tier that covers the examples in this book. However, users can easily switch to the OpenAI variant, which also offers excellent multimodal capabilities. Please be aware that using OpenAI requires you to provide a credit card and will incur usage-based costs, as it no longer offers a free tier for general API access. You can switch to the OpenAI variant by starting the project with the following npm command:

```
npm run start:openai
```

This command runs the backend using the OpenAI server.openai.js variant, enabling you to use OpenAI tiers and features. This component performs the following key functions:

- *Environment variables*—Before any processing occurs, the backend retrieves essential credentials, like the OpenAI/Google API key, from environment variables. These variables are typically stored in an .env file to enhance security and avoid hardcoding sensitive information in the code itself. Users should create an .env file in the root directory of the project before running the application and add it to their .gitignore as well to prevent accidentally committing sensitive information to version control.
- *Validation*—The backend first receives a POST request from the frontend, likely triggered by user interaction with the chat interface. It parses the request body as JSON to extract the user's input text and performs any necessary validation checks to ensure valid data is processed.
- *Interaction with OpenAI/Google API*—Once the user input is validated, the backend uses the OpenAI/Google client library to interact with the OpenAI/Google API. It sends a request containing the user's input and additional configuration details.
- *Postprocessing*—Upon receiving a response from the OpenAI/Google API, the backend extracts the generated content and constructs a message object.
- *Response transmission*—The backend transmits the constructed message object back to the frontend application as a JSON response. This response will be

received and processed by the frontend to update the chat interface and display the LLM's generated response to the user.

- *Error handling*—The backend incorporates error-handling mechanisms to catch unforeseen problems. In case of errors (e.g., invalid requests, API errors), the backend responds with appropriate status codes to inform the frontend.

A visual representation of the backend layout is depicted in figure 2.8, providing a clear overview of the backend server's functionalities and its interaction with the OpenAI service.

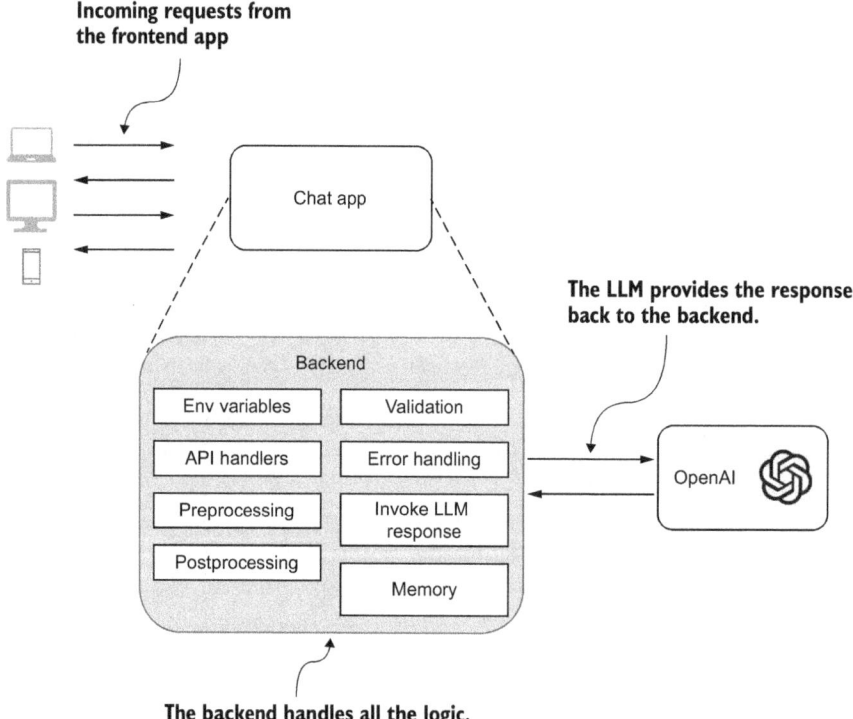

Figure 2.8 The general responsibilities of the backend. The process involves data validation, interaction with the OpenAI API, response processing, and transmission of the generated response back to the frontend application.

Now we will look at the code that powers the OpenAI backend. Listing 2.4 provides a closer look at the code that sets up the server (server.openai.js).

> **NOTE** The code that powers the Google Gemini backend is located in a separate file named server.google.js. This file is almost identical to the OpenAI backend implementation, with the primary difference being the calls made to the respective client libraries for each service.

Listing 2.4 Backend code that uses OpenAI

```
import OpenAI from "openai";
import express from "express";        Loads environment        Retrieves the OPENAI_API_KEY
import cors from "cors";              variables from an        from environment variables for
import "dotenv/config";               .env file                authentication

const apiKey = process.env.OPENAI_API_KEY;
const openai = new OpenAI({ apiKey });            Ensures the API key exists,
if (!apiKey) {                                    throwing an error if not found
  throw new Error("Missing OPENAI_API_KEY environment variable");
}
                                    Parses incoming request     Enables cross-origin
const app = express();              bodies as JSON format       resource sharing to
app.use(express.json());                                        allow requests from
app.use(cors({ origin: "http://localhost:5173" }));             the specified origin
const openaiProvider = new OpenAIHandler(openai);               (likely the chat
                                                                application frontend)
   app.post("/", (req, res) =>
openaiProvider.handleRequest(req, res));          Creates an instance of
                                                  the OpenAIHandler class
app.listen(3000, () => {
  console.log("Started backend server");          Defines a POST route handler that
});                                               delegates the request to the
                                                  handleRequest function within the
       Starts the Express server on port 3000    openaiProvider instance
```

The server.openai.js file sets up an Express server that listens for POST requests from the frontend, handles JSON payloads, and enables cross-origin resource sharing (CORS). The server authenticates with the OpenAI API using the provided API key and delegates incoming requests to the `OpenAIHandler` class. Within `OpenAIHandler`, the `handleRequest` method extracts the user's message from the request, sends it to the OpenAI `chat.completions` endpoint, and formats the assistant's response. Configuration options like `model`, `stop`, and `max_tokens` control which AI model is used, how the response is structured, and its length. Errors are logged and handled gracefully.

While the previous code established the server and API handlers, the heart of server communication lies within the `OpenAIHandler` class. This class, detailed in listing 2.5, is responsible for interacting with the OpenAI service endpoint (Class `OpenAIHandler` in server.js). As you do it, pay particular attention to the configuration values I provide. These values determine the specific OpenAI model used to generate responses (e.g., `gpt-3.5-turbo`) and how the initial system context is configured (e.g., the introductory prompt message).

Listing 2.5 Class that handles OpenAI requests

```
class OpenAIHandler {
  constructor(openai) {           Stores OpenAI client instance; the
    this.openai = openai;         constructor receives an OpenAI client
  }                               instance as an argument and stores it
                                  for future use within the class.
  async handleRequest(req, res) {
```

```
    try {
      const { text } = req.body;
      const { data: completion, response } =
await this.openai.chat.completions.
        .create({
          messages: [
            {
              role: "system",
              content:
                "I'm happy to assist you in any way I can.
How can I be of service today?",
            },
            { role: "user", content: text },
          ],
          model: "gpt-3.5-turbo",
          stop: null,
          max_tokens: 150,
        })
        .withResponse();
      const message = {.
        id: completion.id,
        created: completion.created,
        role: "assistant",
        content: completion.choices[0].message.content,
      };
      res.json({ message });
    } catch (e) {
      console.error(e);
      res.status(500).send("Internal server error");
    }
  }
}
```

- *Generates response using OpenAI; utilizes the stored OpenAI client to generate a response using the chat.completions.create function*
- *Specifies model for response generation; sets the model property to gpt-3.5-turbo to generate the response*
- *Removes stop sequences; sets the stop parameter to null to ensure the generated response is more conversational and avoids stopping at predefined sequences*
- *Limits response length; sets the max_tokens parameter to limit the response length to 150 tokens (can be adjusted based on requirements)*
- *Sends response as JSON; sends the formatted response message as JSON data back to the client*
- *Implements error handling; if an error occurs, it's logged, and a generic Internal Server Error response is sent to the client.*
- *Formats response message; constructs a response message object with relevant properties like ID, creation timestamp, role ("assistant"), and the actual response content extracted from the OpenAI response*

Within the `handleRequest` function, we use the `chat.completions` endpoint of the OpenAI API. This specific endpoint is designed to generate conversational responses tailored to a provided chat history. By using this endpoint, we can analyze the user's input context and craft a relevant, informative response. OpenAI, of course, provides several other endpoints tailored to generating different kinds of requirements.

We are using the specific configuration values that we used for `chat.completions` API for several reasons:

- `stop`—Setting the stop parameter to `null` instructs the OpenAI API to continue generating text until it reaches its internal completion criteria. This enables more elaborate responses that may go beyond a simple one-sentence answer.
- `max_tokens`—This parameter acts as a control mechanism for the response length. Setting it to 150 limits the generated response to a maximum of 150

tokens (words or subwords). This helps maintain conciseness and potentially reduces processing costs associated with longer responses.

NOTE For this book's examples and projects, 150 tokens will generally be sufficient for the initial conversational aspects. However, as you progress to more complex features (such as detailed content generation, summarization of longer texts, or multiturn conversations requiring deeper context), you will likely need to adjust this value upward.

For simplicity, this initial implementation focuses on extracting core information from the OpenAI API response. It constructs a message object containing the response ID, creation time, a designated role (assistant), and the actual content. However, in production environments, additional processing and verification steps would be equally important. These could involve

- *Error handling and retries*—Implementing robust error handling to gracefully handle potential failures during communication with the OpenAI API. This should include mechanisms for retrying failed requests. We will explore comprehensive error-handling strategies in chapter 8.
- *Response validation*—Incorporating logic to verify the validity of the generated responses. This should involve checks for relevance, coherence, or alignment with predefined safety guidelines.

2.5.6 Tests

The tests folder houses a basic testing framework that combines unit tests for individual components. While this doesn't provide exhaustive coverage, establishing a testing infrastructure with tests encompassing various use cases (both normal and unexpected) is essential.

To execute the test suite, navigate to the project's root directory and run the following command:

```
$ npm run test:unit -w ch02/chat-client
```

This command should execute the tests and produce a report detailing the results. The following is the output when running those tests:

```
$ npm run test:unit -w ch02/chat-client
√ tests/unit/ChatPage.test.jsx (3)
  √ ChatPage component (3)
    √ renders initial hello message
    √ updates input value while typing
    √ displays loading state while fetching response

Test Files  1 passed (1)
     Tests  3 passed (3)
  Start at  16:14:32
  Duration  232ms
```

While the `npm run test:unit` command provides a report directly in your terminal (and some local test runners, like Vitest, often used in similar setups, might offer a web-based UI on a localhost port for interactive debugging), there are also excellent online test playgrounds that allow you to explore testing concepts visually.

One such example is the Testing Playground available at https://testing-playground.com/. You can open this URL in your browser to visualize and experiment with testing libraries (such as Testing Library, often used for React components) and interact with the HTML markup.

2.5.7 Common challenges and solutions

As you work through this project, be aware of these common problems and their solutions:

- *API configuration*—If you are having problems with the chat agent not responding, it might be a problem with the provider. First, ensure your .env file is configured with your Google Gemini API key, as Gemini is free for the examples in this book. If you're using OpenAI, note that it requires a credit card and sufficient available credits for API key usage. Double-check your OpenAI account for these details.
- *Handling CORS problems*—Since the backend (Express.js) is served on `localhost:3000` and the frontend (React) is on a different port, you may encounter CORS problems. To fix this problem, make sure that the following line is present in the server.js code:

```
app.use(cors());
```

- *General troubleshooting tips*—If you're experiencing problems, you can also check your browser's console for error messages and verify that both your frontend and backend servers are running.

2.6 Assessing the app's first iteration

Now the chat web application works reasonably well and can be used as a personal AI assistant or LLM agent, but it's rather simple. As you interact with it more, you will notice that it's very bare bones and hasn't got much functionality other than the main feature. Some fundamental characteristics are still missing:

- *Memory and context*—The application lacks the ability to remember or record conversation history. This means it forgets previous interactions upon reloading, leading to a lack of context and repetitive responses. As I mentioned earlier, this is because the message history isn't sent with the request to the backend.
- *UI performance*—The UI experiences loading delays because responses aren't streamed from the backend. They are sent in their entirety after the LLM has finished generating the full response.

- *Security*—The application lacks access restrictions. If deployed, anyone could interact with it, which could lead to unexpected API costs.
- *Improved tooling*—Our current setup uses separate frontend (React) and backend (Express.js) components. A more integrated framework could streamline this process.

We'll address these problems as the chapters progress and especially focus on managing memory and context, streaming, and security considerations. But we can make some enhancements to the base project right away by migrating the backend framework from Express.js to Next.js., a powerful React framework. This shift streamlines the deployment process and has the potential to improve application performance through features like server-side rendering and static site generation. The most compelling benefit lies in the synergy with our existing React codebase. Next.js integrates seamlessly with React, allowing a more cohesive and efficient development environment.

While Next.js is a powerful tool, it's not a one-size-fits-all solution. The best framework choice depends on your specific project requirements and team expertise. However, for complex and dynamic LLM-powered web applications, Next.js offers a compelling set of features that can significantly enhance performance, maintainability, and security.

2.7 Migrating the app to Next.js

To level up our web application and begin to address some of its key limitations, our next step is to migrate to Next.js, a full-stack framework that will simplify our architecture and unlock key features. This isn't about replacing tools; it's about adopting a more cohesive framework to build a more robust application. Migrating to Next.js will allow us to simplify our codebase while maintaining functionality and to use built-in optimizations for performance and deploying for production. It will also unlock built-in server-side rendering and static site generation.

Most of the original project requirements likely remain unchanged for now. The primary difference lies in the build tools used. Previously, we used Vite, a development server and build tool for modern web applications. But with Next.js, you don't necessarily need a separate build tool like Vite. Next.js includes an integrated build system optimized for server-side rendering and static site generation. This simplifies the development process and provides built-in functionalities, such as code splitting and optimization in various environments.

Next.js also includes a command-line interface with several commands for managing your project. Some common commands include

- `next dev`—Starts the development server, allowing you to work on your application with features like hot module replacement
- `next build`—Builds your application for production, optimizing the code and assets for deployment

- `next start`—Starts the production server, serving the built application
- `next export`—Creates a static export of your application, suitable for hosting on platforms like Netlify or Vercel

We will use these commands for building the project while developing the new service.

2.7.1 Setting up

Let's look at the code that uses Next.js instead of React/Express.js. You still need to have Node.js installed on your system before you run the project. Follow the instructions to access the code and run it on your system.

The code for this `chat-client-next` example project can be found in the ch02/chat-client-next folder. You can use this example by running this command in the source folder:

```
$ npm run dev -w ch02/chat-client-next
```

There are two AI provider options. This book's appendix offers instructions on how to set up and create a secret key for AI providers. The first option is Google generative AI, which this application uses by default as its primary LLM. Add your Gemini API key:

```
// .env
GEMINI_API_KEY=<SECRET_KEY>
```

Then, navigate to the / path in your browser to use the Gemini AI version of the application.

The second option is Open AI. Navigate to the /chat-openai path in your browser to use the OpenAI version of the application. First, you need the OpenAI API key (after providing your credit card, initial minimum $5 payment, and pay-as-you-go charges via invoices):

```
// .env
OPENAI_API_KEY=<SECRET_KEY>
```

> **NOTE** For detailed instructions on how to create and configure API keys for both OpenAI and Google Gemini, including important billing considerations and free tier availability, see the appendix.

2.7.2 Running the project

If you followed the instructions for running the chat-client-next example project in the previous section, you should be able to visit `http://localhost:3000` and interact with the agent. It's basically the same application, so I won't post the same screenshot. However, now there are some key differences in the way that the application is structured. We explore some fundamentals on Next.js while we explore the codebase.

2.8 Routing and configuration on Next.js

Compared to our previous Express.js setup, Next.js provides us with a significant advantage with its unique approach to routing using the *app router*. The configuration file is also important, as it helps customize your app's behavior.

2.8.1 File-based routing

Next.js uses a powerful concept called *file-based routing*. This means the very structure of your project folders defines the application's URL routes. Each folder within the src/app directory represents a route segment, and the presence of a page.js file within that folder makes it a publicly accessible page. Figure 2.9 shows an example structure and the corresponding URLs.

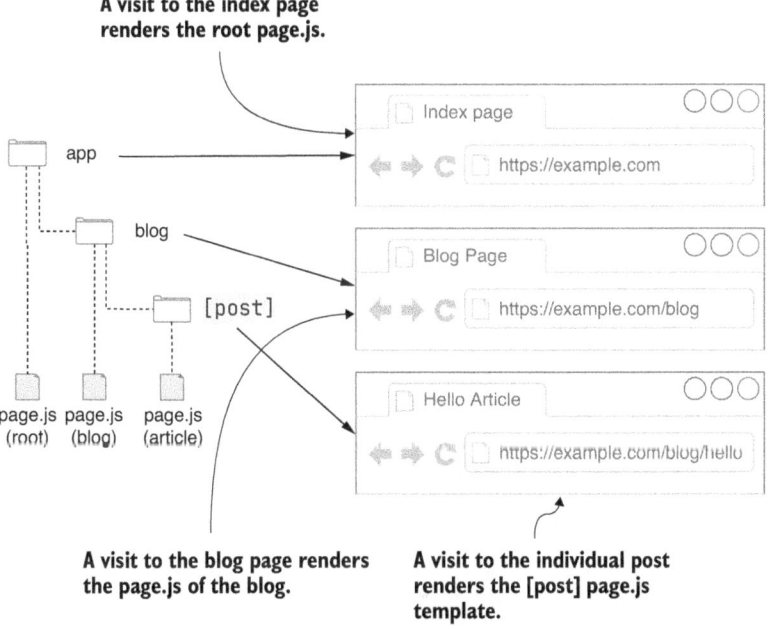

Figure 2.9 File-based routing in Next.js. The root page.js in the app corresponds to the index page (/). The blog page.js in the blog folder corresponds to the blog path (/blog). Finally, the route segment that corresponds to individual articles (wrapped in brackets [ ]) corresponds to the blog post path (/blog/hello).

The app folder acts as a route segment for chat functionality. The presence of a page.js file inside the chat folder creates a publicly accessible page at the URL /. This pattern applies similarly to the blog folder. Here, the page.js file defines a page accessible at /blog. Essentially, the folder structure mirrors the URL segments, and a page.js file within a folder translates to a publicly accessible page at that specific URL.

If you don't want to define a separate route for every single post, you can use a [slug] segment within the route path (e.g., app/blog/[post]/page.js). This [slug] acts as a placeholder for the dynamic part of the URL, which could be anything like "my-first-post" or "welcome-message."

When a user visits a URL with a dynamic segment, Next.js captures that segment value and makes it available to their React component through a params prop. This params prop will be an object containing the extracted data from the dynamic segment (e.g., {slug: "my-first-post"}).

With this in mind, let's review some key directories and files within our Next.js project:

- public—This directory holds static assets like images, favicons, and any files directly accessible by the browser.
- src—This is the heart of our application, containing all the source code for components, pages, layouts, and functionalities:
  - app—This is a key folder that hosts the pages of the application.
  - components—This directory houses reusable UI components like buttons, cards, chat elements, and navigation bars.
  - hooks—This directory stores custom React hooks that encapsulate reusable logic and state management for components.
  - lib—Utility functions and helper code reside in this directory, promoting code organization and reuse.
  - app/(chat)—This looks like a new type of folder wrapped with parentheses. This is called a route group, and I explain how it works and why we use this in section 2.8.6.
  - layout.js—A layout.js file within a folder in the app directory serves as a layout component for that specific route segment. I explain how layout components work and why we use them in section 2.8.4.

NOTE While the projects use the src directory to house the application's source code, it's important to note that Next.js offers flexibility in this regard. Next.js also looks for the app folder at the top level of your project directory if there's no src directory. However, there's one key requirement: the folder must be named app. This flexibility allows developers to customize the project structure to their preferences and existing conventions.

2.8.2 Configuration

As you explore the inner workings of the Next.js project, you also encounter a new file: next.config.mjs. This file acts as the central configuration hub for your Next.js application, allowing you to customize various aspects of its behavior.

You might notice that our next.config.mjs file is currently empty. This doesn't mean it's not important—it simply means that for our current implementation, we don't require any special configuration options offered by Next.js.

NOTE One of the design principles of Next.js is a configuration-free philosophy. It abstracts essential tooling functionalities like bundling, compiling, and optimization without writing a single line of code. That does not mean that all configuration management is bad; it just makes it easier to onboard new developers to the platform.

2.8.3 Environment variables in Next.js

Next.js handles environment variables differently from Express.js. You don't need to use the `dotenv` package as we did before. Instead, use an .env.local or .env file to store your environment variables for your local example. Next.js will then load all variables that are automatically loaded into `process.env`:

```
OPENAI_API_KEY=<OPENAI_SECRET_KEY>
GEMINI_API_KEY= <GEMINI_SECRET_KEY>
```

You'll access these variables in your server-side code (e.g., API routes, `getServerSideProps`) using `process.env.OPENAI_API_KEY`. This keeps your sensitive API keys secure and prevents them from being sent to the user's browser.

However, if you have nonsensitive configuration data that needs to be available in the browser (client-side code), Next.js provides a specific way to "expose" these. To make an environment variable accessible in the browser, you need to prefix its name with `NEXT_PUBLIC_`, for instance:

```
NEXT_PUBLIC_GOOGLE_ANALYTICS_ID=ga_abc
```

It's critical to understand that any variable prefixed with `NEXT_PUBLIC_` will be embedded directly into the client-side JavaScript bundle. This means it will be visible to anyone inspecting the website's source code in their browser. Therefore, you should never use `NEXT_PUBLIC_` for sensitive information like API keys, database credentials, or any other secrets. This feature is strictly for public, nonsensitive configuration values that your frontend code needs to function, such as Google Analytics IDs, public API endpoints, or feature flags.

2.8.4 Route groups

Let's consider what the wrapped parentheses in folder names do in Next.js. The (chat) folder we saw earlier acts as a route group. This means it groups related files for the chat functionality but excludes the folder name itself from the URL path. Inside the route group, we might put more route groups if we include a page.js at some point that Next.js needs to resolve to a page. Why use route groups? There are several advantages:

- *Better code organization*—Grouping related files (layout, page, and potentially API routes) under a namespace keeps your project structure clean and

organized. This makes it easier to locate and maintain code specific to a feature or functionality.
- *Clean URLs*—By using a route group, the folder name (chat) is excluded from the URL path. This results in a cleaner and more user-friendly URL for the application without having to configure anything.
- *Independent layouts*—If you plan to have a distinct layout for the chat section compared to other parts of your application, using a route group allows you to define a separate layout.js file within a group. This ensures that certain pages inherit the specific layout defined within the group.

Interestingly, there's no page.js file directly inside the app folder. So how does Next.js know where to find the index page component? This is because the name you chose for the route (chat) has no effect on the URL path itself. It's purely for organizational purposes within the project structure. In essence, Next.js actively searches for a page.js file within the (chat) folder and uses it as the main component for the chat page, which is also the index page component.

2.8.5 Layout components

In the Next.js project codebase, we renamed the layout component (AppLayout.jsx) to layout.js and moved it inside the (chat) route group. Why is that? This is another file convention that Next.js supports, which allows us to create a hierarchy of layouts. By placing a layout.js file within a folder in the app directory, you define a layout specific to that route segment. These layouts can then be nested within one another.

As an example of how this works, imagine a website with a global header and navigation bar present on all pages. Additionally, you might have a section dedicated to blog posts, with its own specific layout elements, such as sidebars or featured content areas. Here's how nesting layouts can achieve this:

- *Root layout*—A root layout, typically placed at app/layout.js, defines the overall application structure, including the global header and navigation. This layout would wrap all other layouts and pages within your application.
- *Nested layout for blog section*—Within a folder named blog (representing the blog section), you can create a layout.js file. This layout would define elements specific to the blog section, such as sidebars or featured content areas. It would inherit the global elements from the root layout.
- *Individual blog posts*—Each blog post would likely be a separate page (page.js) within the blog route segment (under a folder wrapped in brackets like [post]). These pages would inherit the layouts from both the root and the blog section layout, resulting in a consistent experience with global elements and blog-specific elements.

Figure 2.10 demonstrates visually how you should structure your folders to accommodate different layout trees for each use case.

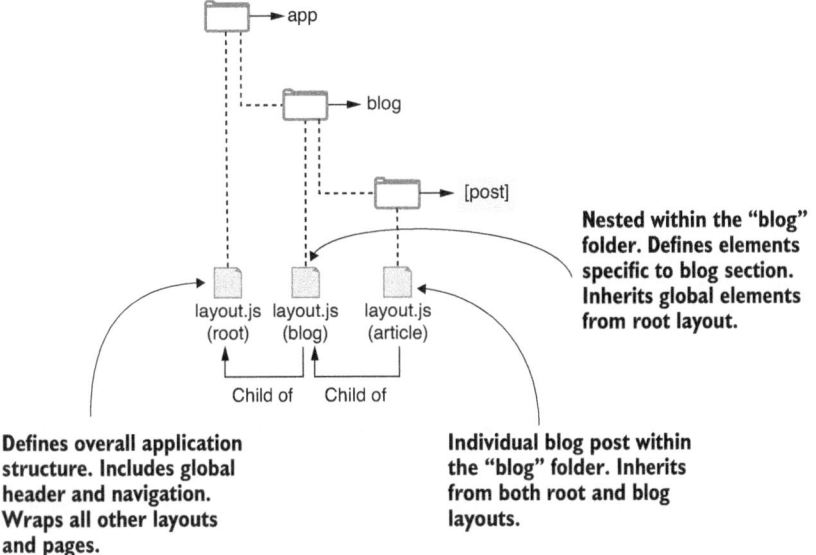

Figure 2.10 This diagram shows nested layouts in Next.js. The root layout wraps all content, while the blog layout adds elements specific to the blog section. Individual blog posts are inherited from both.

Every Next.js application requires a single root layout. This layout, typically defined in a layout.js file at the top level of the app directory, serves as the foundation for your application's UI. It's crucial because it's the only layout component that can include the mandatory <html> and <body> tags. The code in the following listing shows the minimal layout.js used in our application for reference.

Listing 2.6 Root layout component

```
import './index.css';
export const metadata = {        ⬅──  Defines application metadata
  title: 'Astra AI',                   (used for SEO and rendering)
  description: "Hello, I'm 🌟 Astra. Ask me anything you want.",
};

export default function RootLayout({ children }) {   ⬅── Root layout component
  return (
    <html lang="en">
      <body>{children}</body>    ⬅── Renders all the children's components
    </html>                            based on the defined routes
  );
}
```

The children prop in the RootLayout component plays an important role. It acts as a placeholder for all the components that Next.js renders based on your application's file-based routing structure. While you can technically inspect the structure of these child components, there's no need to manipulate them directly within the `RootLayout`. Next.js will handle the rendering of these components based on the defined routes and their corresponding components.

2.8.6 Route API handlers

Finally, we explore how the UI communicates with the backend in Next.js. Since we don't spin up a new server to handle the API processing of the requests and further communication with the Gemini/OpenAI endpoint, we rely on Next.js route handlers.

Next.js route handlers are equivalent to Express.js handlers with some distinct differences:

- *Location*—Next.js route API handlers reside within an api directory of the Next.js project, using route.js or route.ts files—for example, app/api/route.js or app/blog/api/route.js. We can define multiple handlers that can reside in different route paths or segments. This allows for improved code organization due to the separation of concerns within the Next.js structure.
- *Extended handlers*—Next.js route APIs provide built-in access to `NextRequest` and `NextResponse` objects, which are enhanced versions of the Node.js `http.ClientRequest` and `http.ServerResponse` objects, offering convenient functionalities for handling cookies, headers, and revalidation.
- *Convention*—Next.js route API handlers must be specifically named as route.js or route.ts to work.

Code listing 2.7 shows the equivalent API handler that we use to handle all the backend logic (app/(chat)/api/route.js). I've omitted the part that is common between the Express.js and the Next.js implementation for readability; it can be found in the (chat)/api folder in the respective example project.

Listing 2.7 Handling the API backend logic

```
import { GoogleGenerativeAI } from "@google/generative-ai";

export const dynamic = 'force-dynamic';

const openai = new GoogleGenerativeAI (
    process.env.GEMINI_API_KEY || ''
);

export async function POST(req) {
  const { text } = await req.json();
  // Code to request completion data from Google.
  return Response.json({ message });
}
```

- Forces dynamic mode for this route handler to prevent caching
- Initializes the Gemini API client using the API key from environment variables
- Exports the POST request handler function
- Parses the request body as JSON to extract the user's text input
- Returns a JSON response containing the formatted message object
- Calls the Google chat.completions API. This code is the same as the Express.js handler implementation (lines 30-49 in server.js).

Next.js enforces specific conventions for defining route handlers, offering a structured and flexible approach to backend logic. Here are the conventions used in the previous example:

- `export async function POST(req)`—This syntax defines an asynchronous function that handles a specific `POST` HTTP method. It allows us to define different HTTP methods such as `GET`, `PATCH`, and `HEAD`.
- `export const dynamic = 'force-dynamic'`—This line is optional and configures caching behavior for the route handler. By exporting a variable with the specific name "dynamic," Next.js understands how to configure certain caching strategies. By default, dynamic is set to `auto`, enabling caching with the `GET` method and `Response` object. Setting it to `force-dynamic` means that requests are always reevaluated on the server, preventing outdated responses for frequently changing data, such as the OpenAI chat interaction.
- `req.json` and `Response.json`—These helpers are provided by Next.js to parse or respond with JSON as part of the request/response cycle.

Using Next.js's conventional approach for our backend has provided significant benefits for code maintainability and functionality. Arguably, configuring caching behavior for dynamic routes allows us to optimize performance based on the specific needs of each API endpoint. While some of Next.js's conventions are immediately intuitive, others might require more practice to understand.

2.8.7 Going deeper with Next.js

You now have all you need to continue improving your app. For readers who want to go beyond these basic approaches and build highly optimized, scalable apps, this section explores advanced Next.js features, including rendering strategies, data-fetching techniques, and performance optimization.

ADVANCED DATA FETCHING AND RENDERING

Next.js offers a powerful and flexible rendering model. Understanding when and how to use each strategy is key to building a high-performance application:

- *Server-side rendering*—This is a feature where the page's HTML is generated on the server for each request. This is ideal for pages with dynamic, frequently changing data that needs to be up to date for every user. You can implement this by adding the line `export const dynamic = 'force-dynamic'` in the app router, which ensures that the route handler is reevaluated on every request.
- *Static site generation*—This is a prerendering strategy where the HTML is generated at build time. The static HTML files can be served directly from a CDN, making them incredibly fast to load. This is best for pages with static content, such as a blog post or a product page that doesn't change often.
- *Incremental static regeneration*—This is a hybrid approach that allows you to update static pages after you've built your site. You can use revalidation in a fetch request

or `next.revalidatePath()` to specify how often Next.js should check for new data. If a request comes in after the specified time, Next.js will serve the old page while it generates a new one in the background.

PERFORMANCE OPTIMIZATIONS

Next.js offers a few components and configuration parameters that allow fine-grained control of caching and efficiency:

- *Image and font optimization*—The Next.js `<Image />` component automatically optimizes images, serving them in modern formats like WebP or AVIF and resizing them for different devices. Additionally, the `@next/font` module automatically optimizes fonts, removing unused font files and ensuring they are loaded efficiently.
- *Lazy loading*—The `@next/dynamic` module allows you to lazy load components, which means a component and its dependencies are only loaded when they are needed. This is great for large components that are not immediately visible on the page, significantly reducing the initial page load time.
- *Caching with the fetch API*—Next.js extends the native fetch API to provide a powerful caching mechanism. You can control the caching behavior of individual fetch requests using options like `cache: 'no-store'` for dynamic data or `next: { revalidate: 3600 }` to set a revalidation time for static data.

You can explore more detailed features in the official Next.js documentation at https://nextjs.org/docs.

Now we're ready to look at the Vercel AI SDK and see how we can include features like streaming support, backpropagation, and cancellation into our application. These functionalities become particularly relevant when building real-time, interactive conversational interfaces.

Summary

- Building generative AI applications involves several crucial steps. You need to plan a design, the key features it will offer, and how it will be delivered to your users. Then the implementation needs to use all the best practices of UX, security, and testing to ensure it works as intended.
- The planning and design phase focuses on defining the desired features and functionalities of your application. Selecting the right tools to fulfill those needs is crucial for success.
- The simplest conversational chat web app features a way to accept user input (via a message box) and send this to the backend.
- When building user interfaces for generative AI applications, UX becomes paramount, especially when dealing with lengthy LLM responses.
- Security is a top priority for the backend, ensuring the safe handling of user data and application logic. Additionally, performance optimization becomes crucial

as you scale your application and manage complex LLM interactions. Finally, selecting an appropriate LLM that aligns with your application's specific needs is essential.
- While Next.js offers several advantages when building generative AI web applications, overall, it's just a tool that you want to master.
- Next.js uses a file-based routing system, where page routes directly correspond to files and folders within your project structure. This provides a familiar and organized approach to application development.
- Next.js allows you to embed backend logic directly within your application using API routes. These routes benefit from built-in caching mechanisms, optimizing performance and reducing server load for frequently accessed data.

Connecting AI models with the Vercel AI SDK

This chapter covers

- An overview of the Vercel AI SDK for React/Next.js
- Incorporating streaming AI responses into React apps
- Separating AI and UI state in React/Next.js
- Enhancing conversational UIs with multimedia content

While building our minimal AI application, we encountered several challenges. One was *vendor lock-in*. Since our direct API calls created a tight coupling with a single provider, it would be difficult to switch services if we ever needed to. A second challenge concerned streaming responses: delivering AI responses in real time is a critical user experience feature that requires significant, nontrivial architectural changes. Finally, there is the problem of *state management*. As applications grow, managing both UI state and the conversational state (memory) becomes a complex task requiring a robust, scalable solution.

Rather than building custom solutions for each of these problems, a better approach is to use a dedicated framework that provides these capabilities out of the box. Enter the Vercel AI SDK (https://vercel.com/docs/ai), an open source framework developed by Vercel that offers powerful abstractions to streamline the development of AI projects in JavaScript and TypeScript.

In this chapter, we will explore the Vercel AI SDK's key features and see how they provide a more flexible and scalable approach to building AI-powered applications. We will address the three key challenges, starting with provider abstraction and real-time streaming, to build a more robust and professional application. We'll start with the key components of the Vercel AI SDK, and then we'll see how to integrate it into our Astra conversational AI agent app.

3.1 Introducing the Vercel AI SDK

To effectively tackle these challenges, we need a strong and flexible framework that can seamlessly integrate with various large language model (LLM) providers, manage streaming responses, and handle state management efficiently. The Vercel AI SDK is designed to address these needs and more.

3.1.1 Key features and benefits

Table 3.1 outlines some of the key features offered by the Vercel AI SDK. This chapter focuses on the first two features highlighted in the list: *provider abstraction* and s*treaming responses*.

Table 3.1 Key features of the Vercel AI SDK

Feature	Description
Provider abstraction	Provides a unified interface for interacting with different AI providers, allowing seamless switching between providers without modifying the core application logic
Streaming responses	Offers a consistent streaming API that works across different AI providers, enabling real-time display of partial results as they become available
State management	Provides a centralized store for managing conversation history and ensuring synchronization between the UI client and the server code
React server components support	Supports rendering UI elements on the server and streaming them to the client, minimizing the bundle size and improving the UI experience
Generating structured data	Enables the generation of structured data formats that adhere to schemas
Embeddings	Provides utilities for working with embeddings, enabling advanced use cases like semantic search and clustering
React hooks	Offers React hooks (`useChat`, `useCompletion`, `useAssistant`) for simplified integration of chat, completion, and interactive assistant features into React applications

Provider abstraction is the SDK's primary solution to the vendor lock-in problem. Instead of writing code that makes direct API calls to a specific provider (e.g., OpenAI, Google Gemini), the SDK provides a unified interface. This allows you to write one set of code that works with multiple providers. Should you need to switch providers for cost, performance, or availability reasons, the change is a simple configuration update rather than a major architectural refactor.

Streaming responses provides a consistent and unified streaming API that works across different AI providers. This feature directly addresses the challenge of building real-time, dynamic user experiences. With streaming, you can display content as it becomes available from the LLM, dramatically improving perceived performance and user engagement. The SDK handles the complexities of managing the connection and processing the incremental data chunks, freeing you to focus on the UI.

While the SDK offers additional features like state management, React server component support, and the ability to generate structured data, these will be explored in subsequent chapters as we add more complex functionality. For now, understanding these two core features is all you need to get started.

3.1.2 A strategic approach to integration

Introducing a new framework like the Vercel AI SDK into an existing application requires a thoughtful strategy. While our current application is small and the changes will be minimal, it's a perfect opportunity to apply core software development principles that ensure maintainability and scalability for the long run. Let's start by discussing the key guidelines we will follow during our integration process.

SEPARATION OF CONCERNS

Separation of concerns is a crucial principle in software development that promotes modularity, maintainability, and reusability. It involves breaking down a system into distinct components, each with a well-defined responsibility. By ensuring that your application's components are modularized and have clear boundaries, you can easily swap out or modify specific components without affecting the entire codebase.

One effective way to achieve separation of concerns is by distinguishing between intents and actions. An *intent* represents a high-level feature or functionality that your application provides, such as autocomplete, generation, or suggestion. On the other hand, an *action* is the specific implementation or the concrete steps taken to fulfill that intent. Actions often involve calling APIs, interacting with databases, or invoking specific models or algorithms.

For example, let's consider a feature that generates text based on user input. The intent of this feature is to provide text generation capability. The action associated with this intent would be making a request to a specific API or model that can generate the desired text. In this case, we can define an intent called `generateText` and map it to the corresponding action of making a chat completion request to generate the text.

Figure 3.1 illustrates the basic concepts of separating intents from actions. In the diagram, the left part represents the intent `generateText`, while the right part represents the action `chatCompletion`. The arrow between them signifies the connection point that bridges the intent with its corresponding action.

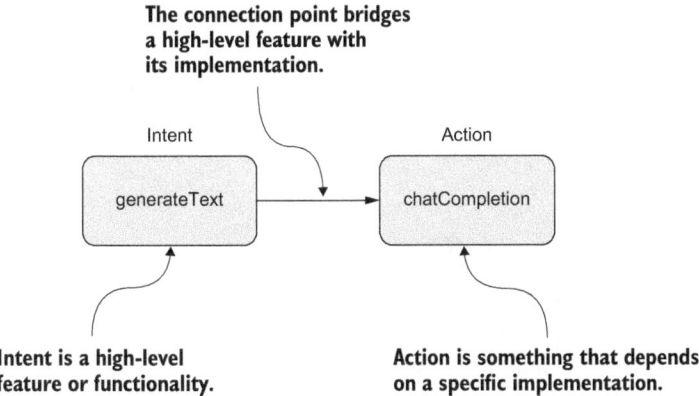

Figure 3.1 Separation of concerns between intents and actions. The intent (left) represents the high-level feature or functionality, such as `generateText`. The action (right) represents the specific implementation or concrete steps to fulfill the intent, such as making a `chatCompletion` request. The arrow signifies the connection point that bridges the intent with its corresponding action, facilitating communication and interaction between the two components.

To implement this separation in your code, you would typically define interfaces or abstractions for intents and actions. The connection point would be responsible for mapping the intents to their respective actions. This can be achieved through various mechanisms such as dependency injection, factory patterns, or configuration files.

ABSTRACTION LAYERS

Introduce abstraction layers between your application logic and external dependencies, such as AI providers or state management solutions. This will allow you to swap out these dependencies with minimal effect on your application's core functionality. We can see that in our existing chat application, we directly call the OpenAI client inside the route handler. This could be problematic if we decide to use a different provider in the future.

INCREMENTAL INTEGRATION

Instead of a complete overhaul, I will introduce the new features one at a time. This reduces the risk of breaking existing functionality and makes the migration process more manageable.

TESTING AND VALIDATION

We will continue to validate our changes with each step to ensure nothing is broken, building a foundation that is both robust and flexible.

DOCUMENTATION AND KNOWLEDGE SHARING

Document your integration process, decisions, and any challenges you encounter. Share this knowledge with your team to ensure a smooth transition and facilitate future maintenance and enhancements.

These guidelines may seem vague and theoretical, but they are critical pieces of thought when developing software, and by following these principles, we can integrate the SDK smoothly. Remember that even if the software is about building AI applications, it still needs to adhere to good practices for maintainability and reliability.

With that consideration, let's attempt to perform *incremental integration* of Vercel AI SDK into Astra AI next.

3.1.3 Practical integration: The Vercel AI SDK with Astra AI

Now that we've established our strategy, let's put it into practice. Our goal is to incrementally replace our existing API calls with the Vercel AI SDK's streamlined utilities. We'll start by addressing our first challenge: text generation.

> **NOTE** The source code for all the examples in this chapter is available at https://github.com/Generative-AI-Web-Apps/Code/tree/main/ch03.

Here's what we're going to build:

- A more efficient text generation system
- A seamless integration that preserves our existing features
- A good foundation for future improvements

Let's start with our first challenge: generating text using a prompt.

GENERATING TEXT USING THE GENERATETEXT UTILITY FUNCTION

The generateText function from the Vercel AI SDK core is designed to generate text in response to a given prompt. This function is particularly useful for noninteractive use cases, such as drafting emails, summarizing web pages, or any scenario where you need to produce written content based on a specific set of instructions. This function can also be used in place of the chat completions API for nonstreaming responses as well, since we only want to request the full response string. The general use of this function is shown in the following listing.

Listing 3.1 generateText example

```
import { generateText } from 'ai';

const { text } = await generateText({
  model,
  messages: [
    {
      role: 'system',
content: "I'm happy to assistyou in any way I can.
         How can I be of service today?",
    },
    { role: 'user', content: text },
  ],
});
```

generateText accepts an object parameter and returns another object with the result of the model API call.

model is the specific instance of the AI model that we use to generate text.

The intent of the `generateText` function is to generate text based on the provided input. It encapsulates the high-level functionality of text generation.

The model parameter in this call is the actual AI model as returned by the Vercel AI SDK provider specification, which allows abstracting the individual providers and the interface with them. For example, one model could be `gpt3.5-turbo` from OpenAI and another one could be `claude-3-opus` from Anthropic. You can easily swap models based on your needs. Section 1.3 goes deeper into this feature if you want to take a quick look at how it works.

What's the benefit of using this approach compared to directly calling the OpenAI endpoint? If you recall from when I talked about the separation of concerns concept earlier, the action associated with the `generateText` function is the specific API call or model invocation that generates the text. In this case, it communicates internally with the AI model specified by the model parameter to generate text. By separating the intent (generating text) from the action (invoking the AI model), the code becomes more modular and flexible.

> **Alternative usage**
>
> You can also use the `generateText` function with a simpler structure, like this:
>
> ```
> const result = await generateText({
>   system: "I'm happy to assist you in any way I can.
>   How can I be of service today?",
>   prompt: text,
>   model: model('gpt-4o'),
>   maxTokens: 512,
> });
> ```
>
> In this alternative usage, we're directly specifying the model and providing a single prompt instead of a series of messages.

Now let's integrate this function into the API route handler.

INCREMENTALlINTEGRATION: UPDATING THE ROUTE HANDLER

As part of our incremental integration strategy, we will first update our existing API route handler to use the Vercel AI SDK. This allows us to test the new functionality without changing any of our frontend code.

> **NOTE** The source code for the following example is available at https://github.com/Generative-AI-Web-Apps/Code/tree/main/ch03/chat-vercel-ai.

Follow these general steps to integrate the Vercel AI SDK and use `generateText`:

1. *Review the installation instructions*—To start using the Vercel AI SDK in our project, we need to install it following the recommended approach for our environment. Since the Vercel AI SDK is a JavaScript library available via Node Package

Manager, we can install it through the command line. The following command adds the library as a dependency to our project:

```
$ npm i ai
```

While this package installs the Vercel AI core features, it does not cover the AI providers feature. For this we need to install the @ai-sdk package, which we will explore later in this chapter.

2 *Update the route handler*—Locate the route handler for the chat completions API and update it to reflect the code in the following listing.

Listing 3.2 Route handler

```
import { createGoogleGenerativeAI } from '@ai-sdk/google';  ◄── Imports the Google AI provider from the @ai-sdk package
import { generateText } from 'ai';  ◄──
import { v4 as uuidv4 } from 'uuid';
                                        Imports the generateText
export const dynamic = 'force-dynamic';  function that calls the provider
                                        and generates a text completion
const model = createGoogleGenerativeAI ({.
  apiKey: process.env.GEMINI_API_KEY || '',   ◄── Creates an instance of the
});                                                Google provider to use for
                                                   interacting with the API
export async function POST(req) {
  const { messages } = await req.json();

  const result = await generateText({   ◄── Calls the generateText function,
    model: model('gemini-2.0-flash'),       providing a Google model instance
    maxTokens: 512,
    messages: [
      {
        role: 'system',
        content: "I'm happy to assist you in any way I can.
How can I be of service today?",
      },
      ...messages,
    ],
  });                         Creates and returns
  const message = {.    ◄──   the response message
    id: uuidv4(),
    role: 'assistant',
    content: result.text, // Extract content from message
  };
  return Response.json({ message });
}
```

To use the drop-in replacement provider for the Google Gemini chat completions API, you need to install an additional dependency:

```
$ npm i @ai-sdk/google
```

The package ai is the core Vercel AI SDK, while @ai-sdk/openai is a separate package specifically designed to integrate with Google's services, and it follows the separation of concerns concept I explained earlier.

3 *Test the functionality*—After each change, you should check the functionality of the code. You can do this either by writing unit and integration tests or more directly by manually testing the site for errors. This will ensure you maintain good progress without losing track of what broke your application.

Now start the development server using the following command from the root folder of the project and visit localhost:3000:

```
$ npm run dev -w ch03/chat-vercel-ai
```

Now we will see that the functionality stays the same and nothing is broken.

That's it! You've successfully integrated the Vercel AI SDK into your app in three simple steps while learning exactly what has changed and why. Now let's start enhancing our existing functionality one feature at a time, beginning with supporting streaming responses. Things are about to get a bit more complex from here on.

3.2 Handling streaming responses with the Vercel AI SDK

While the text generation we've implemented is a great first step, modern AI applications demand a more dynamic experience. The solution is streaming responses, which provides real-time feedback and significantly improves the perceived performance of our application. At its core, streaming is a user experience solution to a technical problem. Large language models (LLMs) are computationally intensive and can be slow to produce a complete response. By delivering the content incrementally as it's generated, we mitigate the perceived wait time and create a more responsive and engaging interaction.

While the previous reasons highlight the benefits of streaming from a user experience perspective, it's important to understand the underlying technical rationale behind its adoption. At its core, the preference for streaming stems from the inherent limitations of LLMs. These models, which power AI applications, are computationally intensive and relatively slow in processing and generating responses. Figure 3.2 depicts the overall throughput of GPT-4 taken from https://artificialanalysis.ai, which is measured in tokens per second; it sits quite low at around 21 tokens per second.

This shows that even the top-tier LLMs really struggle to produce content quickly. Thus, streaming emerges as a solution to mitigate the effect of these limitations on the user experience. By delivering the generated content incrementally, we mitigate the bad user experience of having to wait for a response to be returned to the UI. Overall, it's an acceptable compromise for that kind of problem.

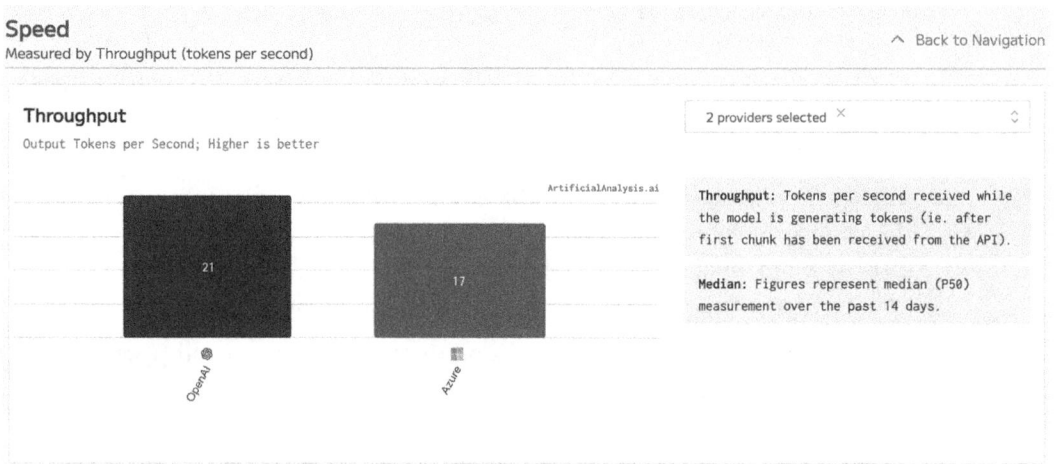

Figure 3.2 Speed comparison of GPT-4 models served from OpenAI versus Azure. The output token throughput is within a mere couple of dozen tokens per second maximum. (Source https://artificialanalysis.ai)

3.2.1 Challenges and how the SDK solves streaming in web applications

While the benefits of streaming are clear, implementing it from scratch presents several technical challenges. The Vercel AI SDK is designed to abstract away these complexities, allowing developers to enable streaming with minimal effort:

- *Asynchronous processing*—Streaming requires handling a continuous flow of data chunks. The SDK's API is built on asynchronous operations, providing a familiar and streamlined way to handle this data flow.
- *Connection management*—The SDK manages the live connection to the server on your behalf, gracefully handling interruptions and reconnections to ensure an uninterrupted experience.
- *Data buffering*—The SDK's built-in hooks and utilities efficiently manage the data as it arrives, taking care of buffering and processing so the UI can be updated smoothly.
- *Error handling*—The SDK provides a centralized and consistent way to handle errors that might occur midstream, allowing you to provide clear feedback to the user without breaking the experience.

How does streaming work, exactly? I will explain this process with some technical details and some diagrams to make it easier to grasp.

HOW STREAMING WORKS

Streaming is a way of transmitting data incrementally rather than all at once. For AI-generated responses, this means content is delivered to the user in real time as the AI model produces it.

The following is a step-by-step explanation of how streaming typically works in a web application:

1. *Client request*—The client (web browser) sends a request to the server, indicating that it wants to receive a streaming response.
2. *Server processing*—The server receives the request and initiates processing the AI-generated response. Instead of waiting for the entire response to be generated, the server starts sending data chunks as soon as they are available.
3. *Chunked transfer encoding*—The server uses a technique called *chunked transfer encoding* to break down the response into smaller chunks. Each chunk is preceded by its size and followed by a newline character. The following is an example of chunked transfer encoding. Suppose the server is sending a response with the following content:

```
Hello, world! This is an example of chunked transfer encoding.
```

Using chunked transfer encoding, the server would break down the response into smaller chunks and send them as follows:

```
1F\r\n
Hello, world! This is an ex
\r\n
1D\r\n
ample of chunked transfer encoding.
\r\n
0\r\n
\r\n
```

When the client receives this chunked response, it reads the size of each chunk, processes the data, and continues reading the next chunk until it encounters the chunk with size 0, indicating the end of the response.

4. *Incremental delivery*—As the server generates and processes the AI response, it sends the data chunks to the client incrementally. The client receives these chunks as they arrive, without waiting for the complete response.
5. *Client-side processing*—The client receives the data chunks and processes them as they arrive. It can update the user interface incrementally, displaying the partially generated content to the user.
6. *Completion*—When the server finishes generating the complete AI response, it sends a final chunk indicating the end of the stream. The client receives this final chunk and concludes the streaming process.

During the streaming process, the client and server maintain an open connection (by setting the connection to "keep-alive" for this header to have this effect), allowing for the continuous flow of data chunks. The client can process and display the received chunks in real time, providing a responsive and interactive user experience.

Figures 3.3 and 3.4 illustrate the difference between a nonstreaming and a streaming response flow. In the nonstreaming version in figure 3.3, the client sends a request to the server, and the server processes the request, generates the complete response, and sends it back to the client in one go. The client then receives the entire response, processes it, and updates the user interface accordingly.

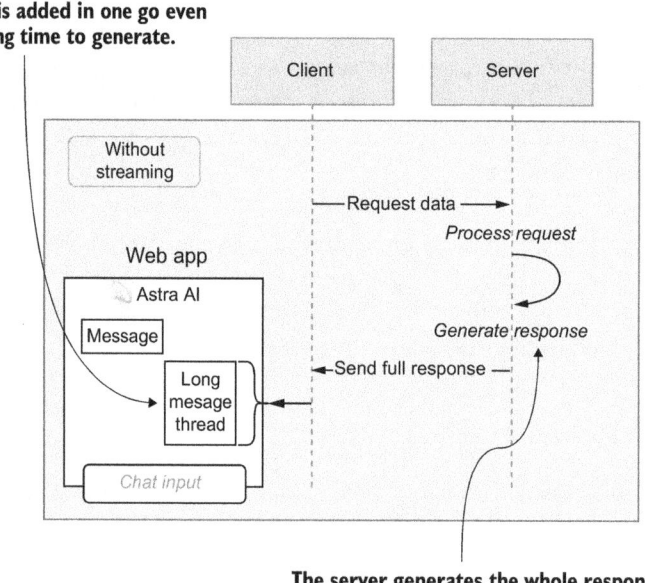

Figure 3.3 Without streaming, the client sends a request and waits for the server to generate and send the full response before displaying it.

Now let's compare the streaming version in figure 3.4. Here, the client sends a request to the server, and the server processes the request and starts generating the response. Now, instead of waiting for the entire response to be ready, the server sends the response in smaller chunks. Each chunk is sent to the client as soon as it is generated. The client receives the chunks one by one, processes them, and updates the user interface incrementally. This process continues until the server sends the final chunk, indicating the completion of the response.

If you think all of that sounds very complicated and difficult to implement, you are right. To handle the challenges associated with streaming, developers need to implement appropriate mechanisms for asynchronous processing, connection management, data buffering, and error handling. Here is where the Vercel AI SDK comes to the rescue, as it simplifies this process by abstracting away many of the low-level details and providing a high-level API for handling streaming responses.

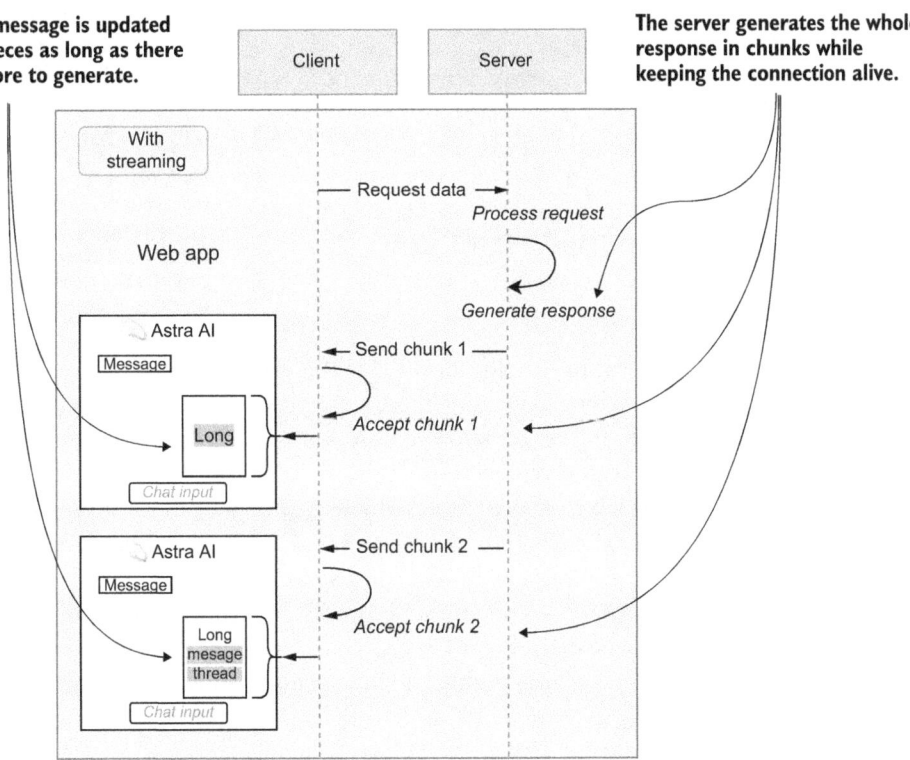

Figure 3.4 With streaming, the client sends a request, and the server sends the response in small chunks that are being streamed back to the client for processing.

3.2.2 Implementing streaming with the Vercel AI SDK

The Vercel AI SDK simplifies streaming with its streamText function and useChat and useCompletion React hooks. These tools handle the complex details of managing the stream and updating the UI, allowing you to focus on building your application.

STREAMING TEXT USING STREAMTEXT

The streamText function is the streaming counterpart to generateText. Instead of returning a full response, it provides an async iterable. You can loop over this iterable, processing each part of the text as it becomes available. The following listing shows an example of how to use streamText.

Listing 3.3 streamText example

```
import { createGoogleGenerativeAI } from '@ai-sdk/google';
import { streamText } from 'ai';

const model = createGoogleGenerativeAI({
  apiKey: process.env.GEMINI_API_KEY || '',
```

Imports the streamText function from the ai package. This function is used to stream text generations from a language model.

```
});
const { textStream } = await streamText({
  model: model('gemini-2.0-flash'),
  prompt: 'Generate 400 words of random content for me please',
});

for await (const textPart of textStream) {
  process.stdout.write(textPart);
}
```

The streamText function is called with an object containing the model (more on this later) and the prompt text.

The code uses a for await...of loop to iterate over the textStream async iterable. This loop allows asynchronous iteration over the text stream, handling each chunk of text as it becomes available.

In this example, we import the `createGoogleGenerativeAI` function from `@ai-sdk/google` to create a Google Gemini model and the `streamText` function from the `ai` package. We then call the `streamText` function with the desired model and prompt, and it returns a `textStream` object.

The `textStream` is an `async iterable`, which means you can use a `for await...of` loop to iterate over the text parts as they are generated. Each `textPart` represents a chunk of the generated text, and you can process or display it in real time.

To understand what an `async iterable` is, look at a simple example that generates a sequence of numbers with a delay between each number. I'll use this example to illustrate the concept of an async iterable and how it can be consumed using a `for await...of` loop.

Listing 3.4 An async iterable example

```
async function* getOneToThree() {
  for (let i = 1; i <= 3; i++) {
    await new Promise(resolve =>
            setTimeout(resolve, 1000));
    yield i;
  }
}
```

An async generator function is declared using the async function syntax.*

The await keyword is used to pause the execution of the async generator function until the promise is returned.

The yield keyword is used to yield the current value of i to the consumer of the async iterable.

In this code, we define an `async generator` function called `getOneToThree`. Inside the function, we use a `for` loop to iterate from 1 to 3. For each iteration, we introduce a delay. After the delay, we use the `yield` keyword to yield the current value of `i`.

When the generator function completes its execution (in this case, after yielding 3), it behaves in a specific way:

1. The generator function automatically returns a promise that resolves to `{ done: true, value: undefined }`.
2. Any subsequent calls to `next()` on the generator object will return this same resolved promise.
3. The `for...of` loop or any other consuming iterator will terminate naturally.

WARNING Be cautious when using infinite generators. Always ensure you have a proper termination condition to avoid infinite loops or memory leaks.

Now let's see how this async iterable can be consumed using a `for await...of` loop in the following listing.

Listing 3.5 Consuming an async iterable

```
(async () => {
  for await (const number of getOneToThree()) {.      ◄──┐  Uses the for await...of
    console.log(number);                                  │  loop to yield the next
  }                                                       │  number in the sequence
})();
```

Table 3.2 shows a step-by-step visualization of how the async iterable is processed. The async iterable allows for asynchronous generation and consumption of values. The `for await...of` loop waits for each value to be yielded by the async iterable before proceeding to the next iteration. This enables the processing of values as they become available, without blocking the execution of other code at the same time. The same process of consuming the stream of values is used when consuming a streaming text response that originates from an AI model.

Table 3.2 What happens on each iteration of the `for await ...of` loop on an async iterable function

Time	Yield	for await...of loop
0	Start	Start
1	Yield 1	console.log(1)
2	Yield 2	console.log(2)
3	Yield 3	console.log(3)
4	End	End

Now let's go back to our example: other than the `textStream` response field, the `streamText` function also provides additional features and callbacks represented in table 3.3.

Table 3.3 Features and result helper functions of the `streamText` utility

Feature	Comment
onFinish callback	You can provide a callback that is triggered when the model finishes generating the response and all tool executions. This callback receives the generated text, tool calls, tool results, finish reason, and usage information.
Result helper functions	The result object returned by `streamText` contains helper functions like `toAIStream()`, `toAIStreamResponse()`, `toTextStreamResponse()`, `pipeTextStreamToResponse()`, and `pipeAIStreamToResponse()` to facilitate integration with AI SDK UI components and streaming responses.

Table 3.3 Features and result helper functions of the `streamText` utility (*continued*)

Feature	Comment
Result promises	The result object also provides promises like `result.text`, `result.toolCalls`, `result.toolResults`, `result.finishReason`, and `result.usage` that resolve when all the required data is available.

While the backend response is streamed to the client, the client (or frontend, in other words) needs to be able to understand how to render the messages in chunks and without sacrificing performance with this flow of updates. This is where some additional helper functions are required in the form of React hooks. I explain them briefly next.

REACT HOOKS FOR A SEAMLESS UI

The Vercel AI SDK provides two powerful React hooks: `useChat` and `useCompletion`, which simplify the creation of conversational user interfaces and text completion capabilities in your application.

Recall that we need to update the UI to handle streaming text responses. While we could potentially modify the existing `useChatFormSubmit` hook to achieve this, the non-trivial implementation details involve managing the streaming response and keeping track of updates.

This hook should eventually handle two crucial things:

- It should handle any fragmented responses, potentially including reassembling the complete message and managing intermediate UI updates.
- Effectively displaying the streaming response requires keeping track of the current state of the message and updating the UI incrementally as new chunks arrive.

The `useChat` and `useCompletion` hooks abstract this functionality without us having to break a sweat.

Here is a quick breakdown of how those hooks work:

- `useChat`—The `useChat` hook allows you to easily create a conversational user interface for your chatbot application. "Conversation" means you can pass a list of messages as a context, and the hook will provide those as context to the AI provider. It also enables the streaming of chat messages from your AI provider, manages the state for chat input, and updates the UI automatically as new messages are received.
- `useCompletion`—The `useCompletion` hook allows you to create text completion–based capabilities for your application. This means that it will only deal with a single prompt and takes a single string as an input compared to the list of messages that `useChat` supports. You simply ask it to complete a sentence, and it will do its best to complete it.

Since we are interested in keeping a conversation with the AI model, we will be using the `useChat` hook. The basic use of this hook is explored in the following code listing.

Listing 3.6 useChat example

```
import { useChat } from 'ai/react';        ◄──  This line imports the useChat
                                                hook from the ai/react library.
export default function Chat() {
  const { messages, input, handleInputChange, handleSubmit} =
    useChat({ api: '/api' });              ◄──
                                                This line calls the useChat hook,
  return (                                      initiating a chat session with the
    <div>                                       LLM. It then uses destructuring to
      <Messages data={messages} />.        ◄──  extract several values from the
      <form onSubmit={handleSubmit}>            object returned by the hook,
        <input                                  including the list of messages and
          value={input}                         the form submission handler.
          placeholder="Ask me something..."
          onChange={handleInputChange}     This is responsible for displaying the
        />                                 conversation history. It receives the
      </form>                              messages array as data.
    </div>
  )
}
```

Compared to the custom useChatFormSubmit hook, there are many similarities, and it's almost a drop-in replacement. The useChat hook accepts an api parameter that will be used to point to the fetch endpoint, which returns to the client. It similarly returns the list of messages and the current value of the prompt. It also provides the form submit handler that we use on a form field. However, behind the scenes, this hook also manages streamed responses in an efficient way without having us do the extra work of implementing them from scratch.

By using the useChat or useCompletion hooks, we can significantly simplify the implementation of streaming-based conversational interfaces and text completion features in our React application. These hooks handle the complexities of managing state, updating the UI, and integrating with the AI provider, allowing you to focus on building engaging user experiences.

3.2.3 Integrating streaming into Astra AI

Let's now bring everything together and enable streaming into our Astra AI project. Based on the previous section, we can identify what we need to modify to enable streaming support.

> **NOTE** The source code for the following example is available at https://github.com/Generative-AI-Web-Apps/Code/tree/main/ch03/chat-streaming.

1. *Replace the* generateText *function with the* streamText *function*—As mentioned, the streamText function from the ai package is suitable for generating streams of text generations from a language model.
2. *Return a streaming text response instance*—Instead of returning the AI stream response object as is, we need to convert it to a StreamingTextResponse that is suitable for

use with the `useChat` and `useCompletion` hooks. This is more like a technical detail, though, since the `streamText` response returns an object of type `StreamTextResult`, which represents a generic way of accessing different stream types and is specific to this package.

The following code listing shows the annotated code that implements these points.

Listing 3.7 API route for chat application

```
import { createGoogleGenerativeAI } from '@ai-sdk/google';
import { streamText } from 'ai';                      ◀─── Imports the necessary utilities
                                                           from the ai package, including
export const dynamic = 'force-dynamic';                    StreamingTextResponse,
                                                           streamText, and StreamData.
const model = createGoogleGenerativeAI ({
  apiKey: process.env.GEMINI_API_KEY || '',
});

export async function POST(req) {
  const { messages } = await req.json();
                                                       Uses the streamText function instead
  const result = await streamText({.          ◀────── of generateText to generate a stream
    model: model('models/gemini-2.0-flash'),           of text from the language model
    maxTokens: 512,
    messages: [
      {
        role: 'system',
        content: "I'm happy to assist you in any way I can.
How can I be of service today?",
      },
      ...messages,
    ],                                                 Creates a new instance of DataStream
  });                                                  to hold the streaming data
  const stream = result.toDataStream();      ◀────
  return new Response(stream, {              ◀────
    status: 200,                                       Converts the AI stream response to
    contentType: 'text/plain; charset=utf-8',          a Response instance, passing the
  });                                                  stream, an empty options object,
    }                                                  and the DataStream instance.
```

This code snippet handles chat message requests by utilizing streaming text generation using the `ai` package to provide a more interactive experience for the user. It manages the streaming data and prepares a formatted response object for the client.

3 Replace the custom `useChatFormSubmit` hook with the `useChat` hook from the `ai` package. This hook, which I explained earlier, understands how to handle streaming chat messages from the AI provider and update the UI whenever there are new messages.

The following listing shows the annotated code that implements these changes inside the chat page.js component. We are listing only the parts that change since the rest of the code for the page remains the same.

Listing 3.8 Main application page

```
'use client';
import React from 'react';
import { Textarea } from '@/components/ui/textarea';
import ChatList from '@/components/chat/ChatList';
import useEnterSubmit from '@/hooks/use-enter-submit';
import useFocusOnSlashPress from '@/hooks/use-focus-on-slash-press';
// import { getAssistantResponse }
// from '@/lib/getAssistantResponse';

import { useChat } from 'ai/react';

const Chat = () => {
  const { formRef, onKeyDown } = useEnterSubmit();
  const inputRef = useFocusOnSlashPress();
  // const { messages, isLoading, handleSubmit, inputValue,
  // setInputValue } = useChatFormSubmit(getAssistantResponse);
  const {
            messages,
            input,
            handleInputChange,
            handleSubmit, isLoading } = useChat({ api: '/api' });
  // ... the rest of the code remains as is
  }
```

- The custom getAssistantResponse function is no longer needed since the useChat hook handles the API communication.
- Imports the useChat hook from the ai/react package to handle the streaming of chat messages
- Removes the custom useChatFormSubmit hook along with its associated state variables and functions
- Uses the useChat hook to manage the chat state, including messages, input, handleInputChange, handleSubmit, and isLoading. Passes the API endpoint /api to the hook.

Now start the development server using the following command from the root of the project, and visit `localhost:3000`:

```
$ npm run dev -w ch03/chat-streaming
```

Streaming improves the user experience by delivering the assistant's response in real time, rather than waiting until the entire answer is generated. This makes conversations feel more natural and interactive. By replacing the custom hook with `useChat` from the `ai` package, we also reduce boilerplate code and gain built-in support for streaming updates.

Now you should see that the generated responses are being streamed sentence by sentence instead of updating all at once. Feel free to ask the AI to generate random long text of 300 to 500 words, for example, and compare the improvement in the user experience.

With streaming implemented, we can now explore some other important features of AI web apps, such as supporting more than one AI provider and being able to swap them on the fly.

3.3 Working with multiple AI providers

So far, we've been working with a single AI model for the AI web application example. However, since the AI landscape is evolving and we have access to multiple AI models, it's useful to be able to adopt and swap providers based on our specific needs. For example, some AI models excel at certain tasks like code generation, but others are good at generating poems. Wouldn't it be great if we could create tools that can employ all models depending on the user's needs?

As you may have guessed, to achieve that, we need to create abstractions, since integrating and managing multiple AI providers and models without effort poses a challenge. We don't want to hardcode every provider API out there, since each provider offers unique capabilities, strengths, and APIs, and that would make the application less flexible and harder to maintain.

In this section, we'll explore how the Vercel AI SDK simplifies working with multiple AI providers and models, enabling developers to focus on building powerful AI applications.

3.3.1 Handling different AI providers and models

Given the explosion of LLMs and AI technologies, every company invested in this space wants to offer its own solution. For example, AI providers, such as OpenAI, Anthropic, Google, and others, have a wide range of language models with varying capabilities and APIs. Each one offers a client or an API that interacts with its models, but there is no requirement to have a common API between them. This creates friction when it comes to integrating multiple clients' various providers into a single application.

For example, consider a scenario where you want to generate text using both OpenAI's GPT-4 and Cohere models. Without a standardized approach, you would need to handle each provider's specific API requirements separately.

Listing 3.9 Calling both OpenAI and Cohere clients

```
import OpenAI from 'openai';
import 'dotenv/config';
const openai = new OpenAI({
  apiKey: process.env.OPENAI_API_KEY,
});
const openaiResponse = await openai.chat.completions.create({
  model: 'gpt-3.5-turbo',
  messages: [{ role: 'user', content: 'What is 7+7 and why?' }],
  max_tokens: 150,
});

import { CohereClient } from "cohere-ai";
const cohere = new CohereClient({
    token: process.env.COHERE_API_KEY,
```

Imports, configures, and uses the OpenAI chat completion functionality

Creates an instance of the Cohere client that interfaces with Cohere AI

max_tokens is a mandatory parameter for the Open AI chat completions API.

```
});

const chat = await cohere.chat({.
  model: "command",
  message: "What is 7+7 and why?",
});
```

> Uses the chat functionality, providing the parameters that it requires. Note that the parameters have different options than the OpenAI client.

Each provider has its own unique way of initializing the client and making API calls, leading to code duplication and increased maintenance. We need a better abstraction for using different clients—not to mention that we may need to create our own client from scratch that interfaces with a custom model in the future as well. Would it be ideal if we had an abstract way to utilize AI model providers with minimal configuration? To address this concern, the Vercel AI SDK offers a nice abstraction over the different AI providers using a language model specification.

3.3.2 Using the Vercel AI SDK's interoperability

The Vercel AI SDK addresses the challenges of working with multiple AI providers by offering a standardized language model specification. This specification acts as an abstraction layer, allowing developers to interact with various models using a unified interface, which is a powerful application of the abstract factory design pattern. This pattern decouples the client code from the specific model implementations, enabling you to switch providers with minimal changes. The following listing shows an example of how you can generate text using different providers and models with the Vercel AI SDK. I have omitted the part that configures the clients for simplicity.

Listing 3.10 Calling the `generateText` function with different models

```
import { generateText } from 'ai';
import { openai } from '@ai-sdk/openai';
import { anthropic } from '@ai-sdk/anthropic';

// OpenAI example
const openaiResponse = await generateText({.
  model: openai('gpt-3.5-turbo'),
  prompt: 'What is 7+7 and why? ',
});

// Anthropic example
const anthropicResponse = await generateText({.
  model: anthropic('claude-v1'),
  prompt: ''What is 7+7 and why?',
});
```

With the Vercel AI SDK, you can easily switch between providers and models by simply changing the model parameter in the `generateText` function. The SDK takes care of the underlying provider-specific details, providing a consistent and intuitive way to interact with different language models.

But how does it work exactly? This is an interesting engineering problem, but it's a great chance to explain in detail the fundamentals so you can apply the same principles in future projects.

LANGUAGE MODEL SPECIFICATION

The code in listing 3.10 implements a well-known design pattern called the abstract factory pattern. This is a creational design pattern that provides an interface for creating families of related or dependent objects without specifying their concrete classes. In the context of the Vercel AI SDK, the abstract factory pattern is used to create instances of language models from different providers.

So what does this have to do with language model specification? This specification is just a place for developers to understand how to add a new provider by implementing the required interface methods for the specification.

Figure 3.5 showcases in broad terms how the abstract factory pattern is applied in the Vercel AI SDK to create instances of language models from different providers while maintaining a consistent interface for generating text.

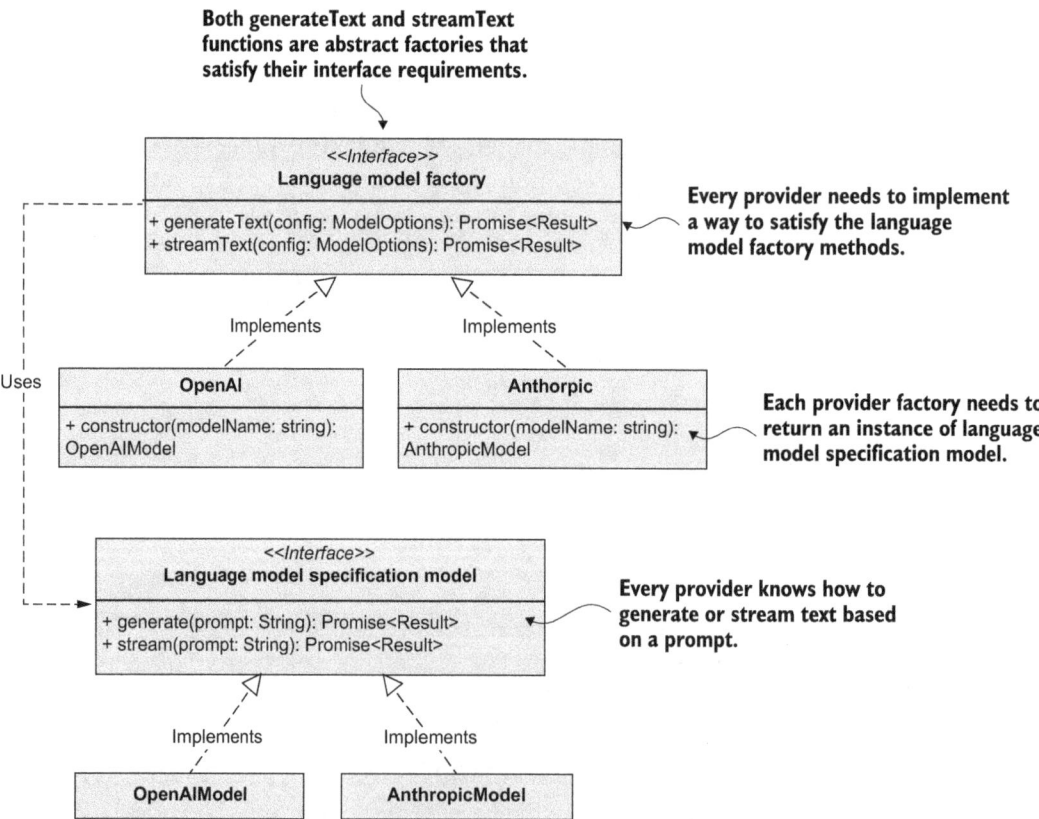

Figure 3.5 Implementation of the abstract factory pattern in the Vercel AI SDK for generating text using different language model providers

> **NOTE** Some functions that follow the specification do not implement the abstract factory pattern in the traditional sense. For example, instead of using classes for the factory, they use regular functions that hold no state. It's important to understand that it's an elegant way of introducing new variants of models without breaking existing client code.

Both `generateText` and `streamText` functions act as abstract factories (listing 3.10). They accept a configuration object that satisfies their interface requirements, which defines the contract for creating instances of language models.

The language model factory interface declares the `generateText` and `streamText` methods. Each provider implementation, such as OpenAI and Anthropic, needs to implement this interface and provide a way to satisfy these methods.

The OpenAI and Anthropic classes are concrete factories that implement the language model factory interface. Their constructors take a model name as a parameter and return an instance of the corresponding language model (`OpenAIModel` or `AnthropicModel`).

The language model specification model interface defines the contract for generating and streaming text based on a prompt. The key point here is that each provider's language model needs to implement the language model specification model interface to define how to generate or stream text based on a prompt, and that pattern decouples the client code from the concrete language model implementations, allowing for easy integration of new providers.

Let's recap:

- *Abstract factories*—The `generateText` and `streamText` functions act as abstract factories, providing a high-level interface for generating or streaming text using language models.
- *Concrete factories*—Provider-specific modules like `@ai-sdk/openai` implement concrete factories that create instances of specific language model implementations.
- *Abstract products*—The language model specification model interface defines the contract for generating and streaming text based on prompts.
- *Concrete products*—Implementations like `OpenAIModel` and `AnthropicModel` are concrete products that implement the language model specification model interface for their respective providers.
- *Decoupling*—The abstract factory pattern decouples the client code from the concrete language model implementations, allowing easy integration of new providers without modifying the existing code.

Now that you have a rough idea of what the language model specification is, we take a brief look at the supported providers.

SUPPORTED PROVIDERS

The Vercel AI SDK supports several popular AI providers out of the box. Table 3.4 lists the provider together with the npm package in which it resides.

Table 3.4 AI providers that implement the language model specification

Provider	Package
OpenAI	@ai-sdk/openai
Anthropic	@ai-sdk/anthropic
Google generative AI	@ai-sdk/google
Google Vertex	@ai-sdk/google-vertex
Mistral	@ai-sdk/mistral

> **NOTE** This list is not definitive, and it may change, as more providers could be added if they implement language model specification. The SDK authors might also include additional providers in the future.

By "supported providers," I mean that you will be able to use the full spectrum of utilities functions from `generateText`, `streamText`, `generateObject`, and `streamObject`.

Additionally, SDK's language model specification is open source, allowing the community to create custom providers for other AI services. Some notable community-contributed providers include

- LLamaCpp (https://github.com/sgomez/ollama-ai-provider)
- Ollama (https://github.com/nnance/llamacpp-ai-provider)

Both providers showcase an example of the flexibility of having a language model specification to extend the support of multiple AI providers under a common abstraction.

3.3.3 Astra AI project: Integrating multiple AI providers and models

Now that we understand the concepts of language model specification, let's put it into practice. We previously imported the `@ai-sdk/google` to create a Google model when we were integrating streaming functionality. We can now expand our feature set by allowing the client to pass on an AI model preference option when sending the request. For this example, we are going to allow switching between two providers: the existing Google `gemini-2.0-flash` model and the OpenAI `GPT-4` model.

> **NOTE** The source code for the following example is available at https://github.com/Generative-AI-Web-Apps/Code/tree/main/ch03/chat-providers.

Here's what we're going to build:

- A backend system that supports multiple AI providers (OpenAI and Google)
- A frontend that can switch between different models based on user preference
- A user interface that allows model selection and comparison

We start with the backend implementation first.

Working with multiple AI providers

BACKEND IMPLEMENTATION: CENTRALIZING PROVIDER LOGIC

First, install the necessary provider packages:

```
$ npm install @ai-sdk/openai @ai-sdk/google
```

Next, we centralize the logic for selecting and initializing a model in a single function, `getSupportedModel`. This function acts as a control center, verifying that the requested provider and model are supported and that the corresponding API key exists before returning the correct model instance. The following listing provides the implementation of the `getSupportedModel` function.

Listing 3.11 Function to get supported models

```
import { createOpenAI } from '@ai-sdk/openai';
import { createGoogleGenerativeAI } from '@ai-sdk/google';

const supportedProviders = {           ◀── Defines the list of supported
  openai: {                                  providers and models
    constructor: createOpenAI,
    models: ['gpt-3.5-turbo', 'gpt-4'],
  },
  gemini: {
    constructor: createGoogleGenerativeAI,
    models: ['models/gemini-2.0-flash'],
  },
};

export function getSupportedModel(provider, model) {
  const providerConfig = supportedProviders[provider];
                                                          ◀── Verifies if the provider
  if (!providerConfig) {                                       is supported
    throw new Error(`Unsupported provider: ${provider}`);
  }

  const { constructor, models } = providerConfig;
                                                          ◀── Verifies if the model
  if (!models.includes(model)) {                               is supported
    throw new Error(`Unsupported model: ${model} for provider: ${provider}`);
  }

  const apiKey =
           process.env[`${provider.toUpperCase()}_API_KEY`];   ◀── Gets the API
  if (!apiKey) {                                                    key from the
    throw new Error(`Missing API key for provider: ${provider}`);   environment
  }

  const providerInstance = constructor({ apiKey });    ◀── Calls the constructor
  return providerInstance(model);                           function that returns an
}                                                           instance of the AI model that
                                                            implements the language
                                                            model specification
```

NOTE Setting up the Google provider requires an API key, which can be obtained by having a valid Google project and generating one in the AI studio page at https://aistudio.google.com/app/apikey.

In this implementation, we define an object called `supportedProviders` that maps provider names to their respective configurations. Each configuration includes the provider constructor function and a list of supported models for that provider.

The `getSupportedModel` function takes two arguments: provider (the provider name) and model (the desired model name). After that, it checks its parameters are correct and the API key is present in the environment. It then calls the provider constructor function with the API key to create an instance of the provider and returns the requested model instance by calling the provider instance with the model's name.

NOTE While the current implementation defines supported providers directly in the code, a more flexible and maintainable approach would be to use external configuration files (like YAML or JSON). Another option is to create a dedicated configuration page where users can enter provider credentials and preferences, which are then stored securely in a database. Both methods make it easier to add or modify AI providers without changing the core application code.

The returned model should be usable within the `streamText` function, and I show how to use this in listing 3.12. For clarity, I show only the half of the code that includes the `getSupportedModel`, as the rest of the code remains the same.

Listing 3.12 Using `getSupportedModel` in the route handler

```
import { StreamingTextResponse, streamText, StreamData } from 'ai';
import { getSupportedModel } from './utils';    ◄── Imports the getSupportedModel function

export const dynamic = 'force-dynamic';

export async function POST(req) {
  const { messages, provider, model } = await req.json();    ◄── Extracts the provider and model preference from the request object
  const result = await streamText({
    model: getSupportedModel(provider, model),    ◄── Gets the supported model instance using the getSupportedModel function
    maxTokens: 512,
    ...
```

By using the `getSupportedModel` function, we can dynamically select the appropriate model instance based on the provider and model values provided in the request body. This approach allows for flexibility and scalability, making it easy to add more providers in the future.

Now the client-side application needs to send the provider and model values in the request body, and the API route handler will automatically select the corresponding model instance. We will see how to update the `useChat` hook to include those parameters next.

FRONTEND IMPLEMENTATION: ENABLING DYNAMIC CONFIGURATION

On the frontend, the useChat hook simplifies this by allowing us to pass additional data to the API using its body parameter. We use React's useState hook to manage the user's selected provider and model and then pass these values directly to the useChat hook.

Listing 3.13 Updating page.js component to allow multiple providers

```
const providers = [.
  { value: 'openai', label: 'OpenAI' },
  { value: 'gemini', label: 'Google AI' },
];

const models = {.
  openai: [
    { value: 'gpt-3.5-turbo', label: 'GPT-3.5-turbo' },
    { value: 'gpt-4', label: 'GPT-4' },
  ],
  gemini: [{ value: 'models/gemini-2.0-flash', label: 'Gemini' }],
};

const Chat = () => {
  const [provider, setProvider] =
          React.useState('openai');
  const [model, setModel] = React.useState('gpt-4');

  const { messages, input, handleInputChange, handleSubmit,
    isLoading } = useChat({
    api: '/api',
    body: { provider, model },
  });
```

- The providers object has a value property (used as the identifier) and a label property (used for display purposes).
- Each model is represented by an object with a value property (used as the identifier) and a label property (used for display purposes).
- We use the useState hook to manage the selected provider and model.
- We pass the selected provider and model values to the body parameter of the useChat hook.

We can verify that this change works by starting the development server and using the <Dropdown/> component to choose the model we currently use. Since the useChat hook manages the list of messages in a unified way, we can literally swap providers on the fly while passing the context to each one of them. Figure 3.6 shows a screenshot of the application after a few interactions with both models.

Feel free to test out different providers and compare their responses. With this functionality in place, you can explore the potential of integrating your own custom-made LLM in the future. This approach allows you to have greater control over the performance and safety of the generated responses.

As we move forward, we will take a look at the world of multimedia content and how it can greatly enhance the user experience in conversational UIs.

3.4 Enhancing conversational UIs with multimedia content

Building a truly engaging conversational UI means moving beyond text. Multimodality, the ability to understand and generate content using multiple modes of input like images, audio, and video, is a crucial next step.

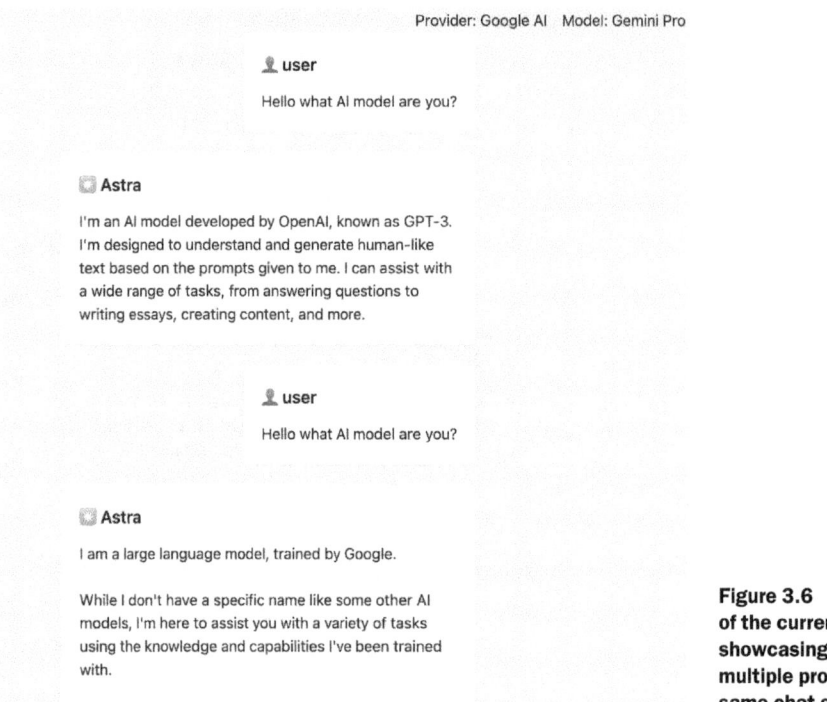

Figure 3.6 Screenshot of the current application showcasing the use of multiple providers in the same chat session

We will focus on integrating image recognition, a feature available in models like OpenAI's GPT-4o and Google's Gemini. The core concept is that the model can process both text and images to generate a more comprehensive and contextually aware response.

3.4.1 Introducing OpenAI's vision capabilities

The latest OpenAI models GPT-4o and GPT-4 are not only capable of understanding and generating text but also possess vision capabilities, allowing them to interpret and generate responses based on images. In this section, I explain how it works, and in the subsequent section, I delve into the implementation details.

HOW IT WORKS

Models with vision capabilities can process and understand images by analyzing the visual content, recognizing objects, and extracting relevant information. This process involves several key steps:

1 *Accepting image input*—The user submits an image along with a text prompt.
2 *Image processing*—The model analyzes the image to identify objects, text, and other significant visual features.
3 *Image comprehension*—The model integrates visual information with the text prompt to generate a comprehensive understanding.

4 *Response generation*—Based on the combined understanding of the image and text, the model generates an appropriate response.

   For example, a user could upload an image of a broken appliance with the prompt, "What is this part, and how do I fix it?" The model would identify the specific part, analyze its condition, and provide a detailed, context-aware answer.

These models can be used for various vision-related tasks, such as image captioning, visual question answering, and even generating new images based on textual prompts and visual references.

> **NOTE** This feature is also called *multimodal AI*. It refers to AI systems that can understand and generate content using multiple modes of input, such as text, images, and sometimes audio.

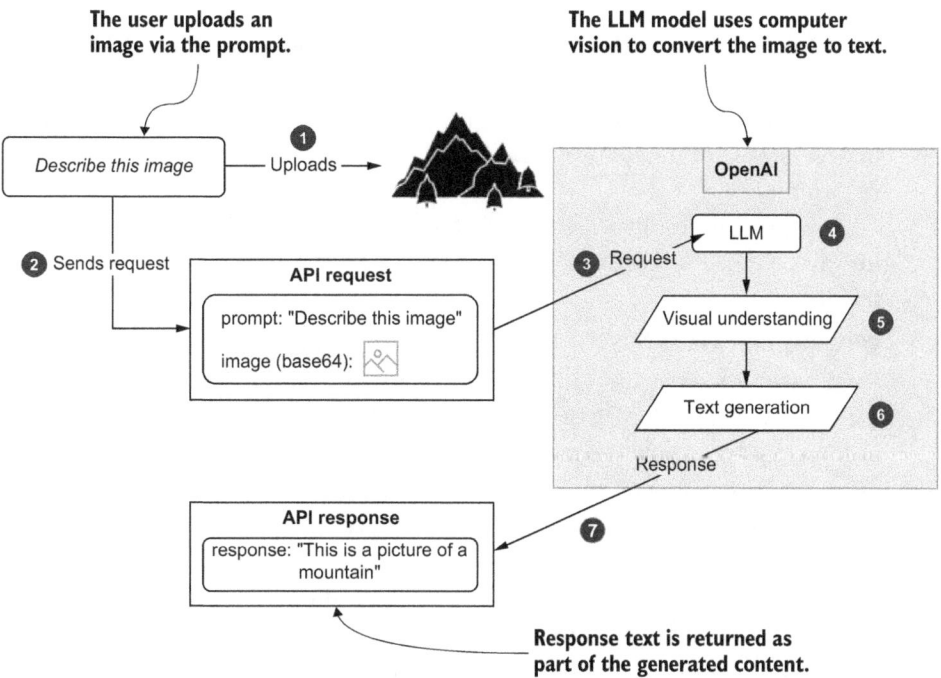

Figure 3.7 The process of sending an image alongside a text prompt to the OpenAI API and how the language model utilizes computer vision techniques to understand the image and generate a relevant text response

Figure 3.7 illustrates the process of integrating visual information into prompts. In this diagram,

1 The client application also provides an interface (file input) for the user to upload an image file.

2 The client application sends an API request to the LLM API, which includes both textual prompts and visual information (e.g., images or image URLs).

3 The API request, with the textual prompts and the binary image data, is sent to the LLM API.

4 The LLM API receives the request and forwards it to the appropriate language model, such as GPT-4o or GPT-4 Turbo or Gemini.

5 The language model processes the visual information (binary image data) through its visual understanding capabilities, analyzing the images and extracting relevant features or semantics.

6 The model then combines the visual understanding with the textual prompts to generate a relevant response or description.

7 The generated response is sent back to the client application through the API response.

What I don't show exactly in this workflow is that the client application is responsible for encoding the image file into a binary format (e.g., using the FileReader API or other techniques) before including it in the API request. The binary image data can be sent as part of the request body or as a separate file upload, depending on the API requirements.

However, as we will see in the following section, the implementation is straightforward. Before we dive into those details, let's clarify some caveats when using this feature.

WHAT ARE THE CAVEATS?

Sending multimedia files along with the prompt is a useful feature, but it has limitations. While some APIs may support sending multiple images as part of a single prompt, it is generally recommended to send one image at a time. Sending multiple images can increase complexity and processing time and may not always yield optimal results. If you need to provide multiple images as context, it's better to break them down into separate prompts or requests.

Another problem is file limitations. Some providers, like OpenAI, allow images up to a certain file size limit (20 MB for OpenAI), while others might accept smaller files. It's advisable to provide high-quality images with lossless compression. If you are hosting your own models, this file size limitation might not be a problem, of course.

Additionally, it's important to consider image content. Models may struggle with images that have low contrast, poor lighting, or excessive noise, which can negatively affect their ability to accurately interpret the content. Ensuring that images are clear and well lit can significantly improve the model's performance and the quality of the generated responses.

Now that we've covered the details of integrating multimedia in prompts, the implementation part is minimal, since we already have all the necessary pieces in place with the Vercel AI SDK. The most technical parts are explained in the next section.

3.4.2 Astra AI project: Integrating Gemini vision queries

In this section, I will guide you through the technical steps to integrate Gemini vision capabilities into your Astra AI project. This involves updating the UI to handle multimedia prompts and using Gemini models for processing images alongside text inputs.

TECHNICAL STEPS TO INTEGRATION

Here's what we're going to build:

- A system that can process multimedia prompts (text + images)
- An updated UI that allows users to upload images alongside text queries
- A backend that uses Gemini vision capabilities to analyze images and provide insightful responses

> **NOTE** The source code for the following example is available at https://github.com/Generative-AI-Web-Apps/Code/tree/main/ch03/chat-multimedia.

Let's start with the backend implementation changes. To handle image data on the backend, you'll need to modify your message-processing logic. Instead of just accepting a text message, the backend should be prepared to receive a message object that includes both text and an image URL. The `processIncomingMessages` function in your route.js file can be updated to check for an `imageUrl` field in the request. If present, it will reformat the last message in the conversation to be an array of "parts." This array includes an object with `type: "text"` for the user's prompt and an object with `type: "image"` containing the image URL. This new, enriched message object is then passed to the `streamText` function.

Listing 3.14 `processIncomingMessages` function in route.js

```
async function processRequestMessages(req) {
  const { messages, data } = await req.json();
  if (!data?.imageUrl) return messages;

  const initialMessages = messages.slice(0, -1);
  const lastMessage = messages[messages.length - 1];

  return [
    ...initialMessages,
    {
      ...lastMessage,
      content: [
        { type: "text", text: lastMessage.content },
        {
          type: "image",
          image: data.imageUrl,
        },
      ],
    },
  ];
};
```

- Parses the incoming request to extract messages and additional data
- If there's no image URL provided in the data, returns the original messages
- Gets the last message
- Modifies the last message so that it includes both its original text content and the additional image content. This ensures that the final message in the conversation contains the multimedia prompt.

The `processRequestMessages` function processes incoming chat messages and adds an image to the last message if an image URL is provided in the request data. We can now use this function to process the request messages before providing them to the `streamText` function. The following listing shows the small snippet of code that provides the updated code.

Listing 3.15 Updating route.js to accept image prompts

```
export async function POST(req) {
  const messages = await processRequestMessages(req);
          const result = await streamText({
              model: model('models/gemini-2.0-flash'),
              maxTokens: 512,
              messages: [
                {
                  role: 'system',
                  content: "I'm happy to assist you
in any way I can. How can I be of service today?",
                },
                ... messages,
              ],
  });
```

Annotations:
- Calls the processRequestMessages to update the prompt messages to include image prompts
- Passes on the messages to the streamText request

That completes the most straightforward part of the implementation. The next section is more challenging, as it involves creating a file uploader and file previewer in JavaScript. To keep things simple, we'll focus on the key concepts and provide essential snippets. The complete code can be reviewed at your convenience in the provided repository.

Updating the frontend to support uploading and previewing images, which will be sent along with the text prompts, involves three main steps:

1. *Creating the file uploader*—We need to create an input field that allows users to select and upload images. This will be accompanied by necessary validations to ensure the uploaded file meets the required criteria (e.g., file type and size).
2. *Previewing the image (optional)*—Once an image is uploaded, it should be displayed to the user for confirmation. This enhances the user experience by allowing them to see the image that will be sent along with the text prompt. However, this step is optional, as it does not hinder the next operation.
3. *Submitting the image with the prompt*—Finally, we need to modify the form submission logic to include the image data along with the text prompt. This will ensure that both text and images are sent to the backend for processing.

   For the code that implements the `FileUploader`, please review the implementation in the code sources accompanying this book. However, for our discussion, I focus solely on the logic for submitting the form with the image data along with the text prompt.

Let's modify the form submission logic in the `<Chat/>` component to include the image data along with the text prompt. You need to update the form `onSubmit` handler to use this new handler from the following listing.

Listing 3.16 Updating the `<Chat />` component that handles file uploads

```
const [imageUrl, setImageUrl] =
         React.useState(null);
const handleUploadFile = async (file, base64) => {
  setImageUrl(base64);
};
const handleOnSubmit = (e) => {
  e.preventDefault();
  const data = { message: e.target.value };
  if (imageUrl) {
    data.imageUrl = imageUrl;
    setImageUrl(null);
  }
  handleSubmit(e, { data });
};
```

- Initializes the state variable imageUrl to null using the useState hook to manage the URL of the uploaded image
- Constructs an object data to hold the form data, including the text message extracted from the event
- Checks if an image URL is available. If imageUrl is not null (i.e., an image has been uploaded), it proceeds to add the image URL to the data object.
- This function handles the form submission, sending the message and the image URL to the appropriate handler.

On the backend, the `processRequestMessages` function extends the chat message format so the last user prompt can carry both text and image data. This allows the Gemini model to receive richer, multimodal input rather than plain text. On the frontend, the `<Chat />` component is updated to include an optional image upload, preview, and submission flow. When a user sends a message with an image, the form handler bundles both into the request body, ensuring they are processed together.

The component that handles all the logic for uploading an image into a string is the `<FileUploader />` component:

```
<FileUploader
    onFileUpload={handleUploadFile}
    maxFileSize = {10 * 1024 * 1024}
/>
```

This component utilizes the DOM API to read the selected file and convert it into a Base64 string. Since this functionality is encapsulated within the component, we won't explore more of its implementation details.

The reasoning behind those changes is to make conversations more powerful and natural: users aren't limited to words; they can upload an image and ask the model to interpret, describe, or analyze it. This capability turns Astra AI into a true multimodal assistant, widening the scope of use cases and making the chat experience more interactive and engaging.

Now let's test these changes. Reload the application and utilize the file upload functionality to upload an image. Then prompt the AI agent to describe what it sees. An example interaction is illustrated in figure 3.8, where the AI agent's response proves to be accurate. This integration enhances the user experience by allowing seamless image uploads and seamless responses from the AI agent.

Figure 3.8 Uploading an image and getting an accurate description from the AI model. This functionality shows how the LLM can generate text descriptions from other media-like images.

Feel free to upload your own images and ask questions about them. To enhance the user experience, consider adding a small preview of the uploaded image alongside the upload area.

> **NOTE** While some LLMs now possess impressive vision capabilities, not all of them do. When choosing a model for your project, it's crucial to verify its capabilities. The Vercel AI SDK provides a helpful compatibility table for various providers and models here: https://mng.bz/Jwea.

We've accomplished a significant amount of work enhancing the functionality of our Astra AI web application. In the next chapter, we'll explore more advanced tools and techniques to further elevate our application's capabilities and user experience.

Summary

- The Vercel AI SDK simplifies AI integration into web applications.
- It also offers features such as provider abstraction, streaming responses, state management, and support for React server components.
- The SDK allows developers to break down complex AI tasks into smaller, more manageable components.
- Guidelines for integrating the SDK include separation of concerns, abstraction layers, incremental integration, testing and validation, and documentation.
- The SDK provides functions like `generateText` and `streamText` for text generation.

- React hooks like useChat and useCompletion are available for creating conversational UI and text completion capabilities.
- Implementing streaming responses with the SDK has challenges like asynchronous processing, connection management, data buffering, and error handling.
- The SDK abstracts away many of these low-level details to simplify handling streaming responses in web applications.
- The SDK uses language model specification to simplify working with different AI providers and models.
- The integration of the SDK enhances functionality and user experience by enabling streaming chat, multiple AI provider support, and integration of OpenAI's vision capabilities.

Managing conversation and state in your application

This chapter covers
- Introducing AI SDK React server components
- Managing UI state in AI-powered applications
- Structured data generation using the Vercel AI SDK
- Tool and function calling with AI models

As we navigate the evolving landscape of AI-powered web applications, we encounter increasingly complex challenges that test the limits of reliability, performance, and scalability. What begins as a straightforward implementation often grows into a sophisticated system with complex interdependencies.

Consider, for example, how to perform state management in AI applications. The seemingly simple task of maintaining conversation history becomes a complex problem between client-side accessibility and server-side security. While storing messages on the client enables quick review, we can't implicitly trust client-provided data. This requires a dual-state approach, demanding meticulous synchronization between client and server to ensure data integrity and security.

For instance, imagine a chat application where the client stores the last 10 messages for quick display. The server, however, maintains the entire conversation history for context and security. When the user sends a new message, the client adds it to its local state and sends it to the server. The server then processes this message, potentially using it with the full history to generate an AI response. The server's response is then sent back to the client, which updates its local state. This process ensures that the client has fast access to recent messages while the server maintains a secure, centralized record of the entire conversation.

But state management is just the tip of the iceberg. As user expectations and business requirements escalate, new challenges emerge. How do we instruct AI models to generate structured data, such as JSON, instead of raw text? Once generated, how can we validate this data to ensure its correctness and usability? Asking those questions early helps reveal the growing complexity of AI-powered web applications and the need for advanced solutions.

React server components (RSCs) and the Vercel AI SDK can provide solutions to some of these concerns by improving the way you build and manage state in AI applications, significantly enhancing performance and user experience. You also need to know how to generate structured, type-safe data directly from AI models, a capability that bridges the gap between raw AI outputs and the structured data your application needs. This approach not only improves reliability but also opens new possibilities for integrating AI-generated content effortlessly into various tools and services.

Finally, *tool* and *function calling* in AI models can greatly expand the capabilities of AI applications. By enabling AI to interact with external resources and perform complex operations, you can create more flexible and stronger web applications that can adapt to real-time data and user needs. Figure 4.1 shows how all of these pieces interconnect.

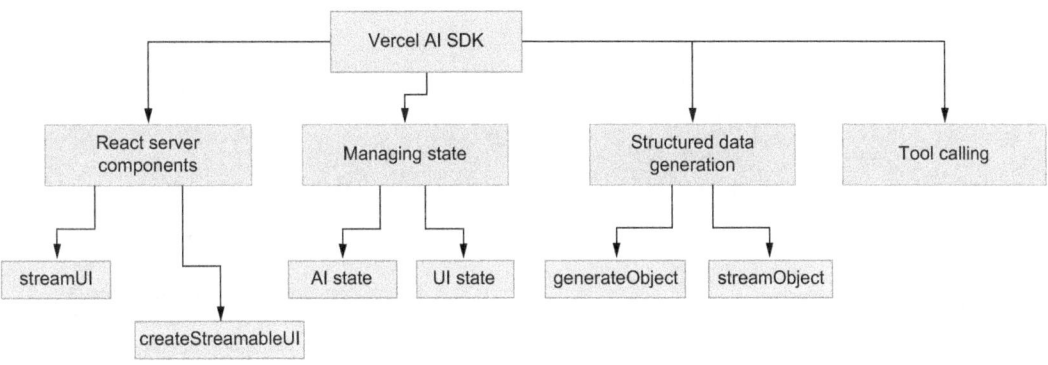

Figure 4.1 The four main topics of this chapter

Now let's update our Astra AI project to incorporate these advanced techniques.

4.1 AI SDK React server components

So far, we've been building conversational UI interfaces with the Next.js app router and have used the Vercel AI SDK to enhance the application features. However, we have not been utilizing the full potential of this framework. For example, we've been developing React components that needed to be shipped to the client and creating dedicated API endpoints to handle text generation and streaming based on user prompts. The generated data needed to be managed securely and sent to the web client to be rendered in the UI.

What if I told you that there is a way to develop React components that work effortlessly on the server side, and we would only need to write code that communicates our intent without manually implementing all the details? This is the essence of RSCs, which are a core feature of Next.js. This section serves as an introduction to this feature, how it works, and how we can use its capabilities to create seamless conversational AI interfaces. By using RSCs, we can focus on the functionality instead of worrying about the nuances of client–server communication, state management, and data fetching.

RSCs offer a new paradigm for building React applications that uses enhanced server-side rendering capabilities. They allow developers to write components that run exclusively on the server, generating HTML that is then sent to the client. This approach offers several advantages, including improved performance, better SEO, and simplified data fetching.

4.1.1 Overview of RSCs

To understand RSCs, we must first grasp how React components are used in a traditional web application. Figure 4.2 shows how the React component tree is typically used.

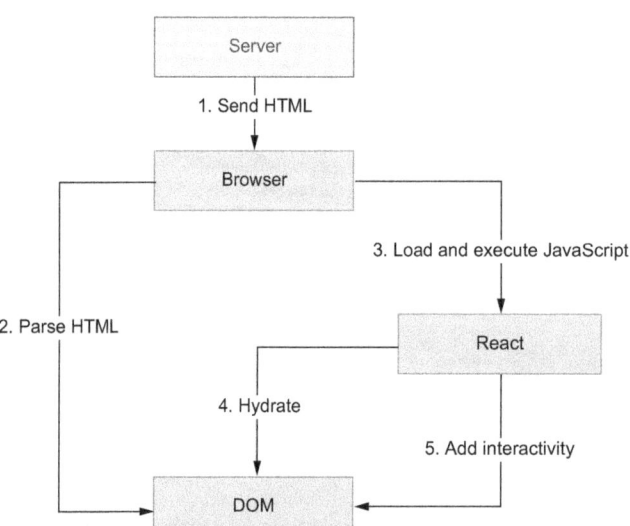

Figure 4.2 Overview of how a traditional React application renders. The React component tree is rendered on the browser. If using server-side rendering, the whole component tree is rendered on the server and then presented to the client. The hydration process then adds interactive elements to the page.

In this traditional approach with server-side rendering, React renders components to a string of HTML and sends that HTML string to the client. Once the HTML DOM is presented, React reruns on the client side, operating over the same rendered HTML and adding interactive elements. This method allows for faster initial page loads compared to solely client-side rendering, but it still requires a hydration step to make the page fully interactive.

RSCs, however, introduce a new way of rendering. They allow specific parts of a React application to be rendered on the server. Figure 4.3 demonstrates how the React component tree is rendered using RSCs.

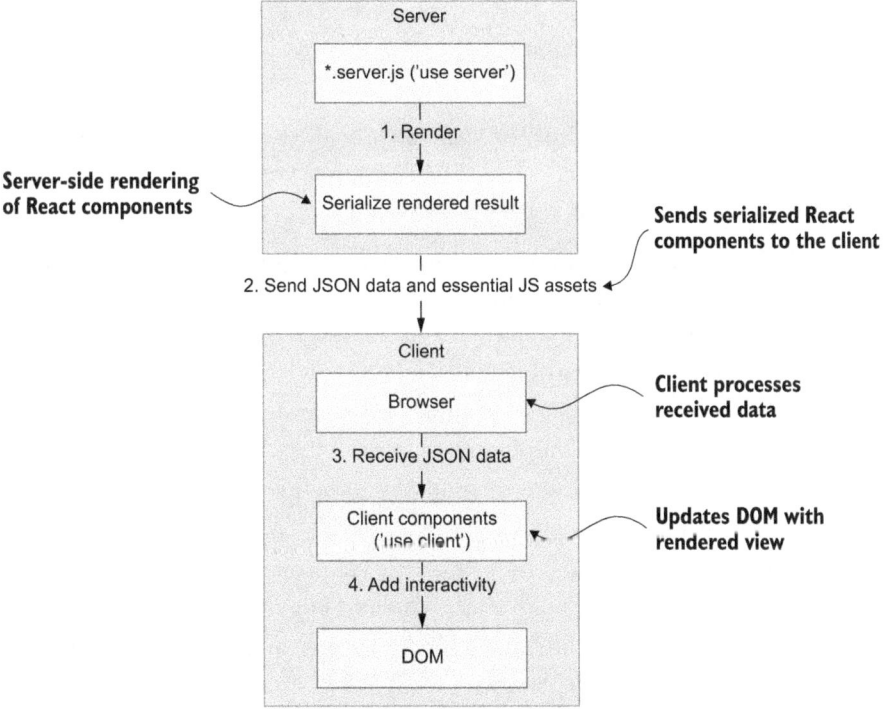

Figure 4.3 RSCs allow specific parts of a React application to be rendered on the server. The components can be streamed to the client incrementally, allowing the client to begin rendering parts of the UI before the entire page is ready.

In this new model, there is no hydration process for server components. Instead, these components are rendered on the server, and their output is sent to the client along with a lightweight JavaScript runtime. Client components are then rendered on the client and integrated into the DOM as HTML tags, adding interactivity where needed.

This approach offers several advantages:

- *Improved performance*—By rendering components on the server, we can reduce the amount of JavaScript sent to the client, leading to faster initial page loads. The client receives the components in a special format that React knows how to render on the fly.
- *Enhanced SEO*—Server-rendered content is more easily indexable by search engines.
- *Better security*—Sensitive operations can be performed on the server, which prevents exposure of API keys and secrets to the client, reducing the attack surface and ensuring that critical logic and data remain protected.
- *Simplified data fetching*—Data can be fetched on the server, eliminating the need for client-side data-fetching logic.

How does this correlate with our AI-powered solution? It turns out that the Vercel AI SDK offers specialized support for RSCs by providing a set of functions that allows us to combine the best of both worlds. By integrating RSCs with AI capabilities, we gain several significant benefits:

- *Real-time AI-generated UI*—RSCs allows us to stream AI-generated content directly from the server to the client, enabling real-time updates without full page reloads. Streaming happens in the background by the framework seamlessly, and we don't have to deal with technical details on how to do it.
- *Reduced client-side bundles*—Complex AI operations can be performed on the server, reducing the computational load on the client device.
- *Enhanced privacy*—Sensitive user data can be processed on the server, with only the results sent to the client.
- *Improved responsiveness*—By offloading AI processing to the server, the client remains responsive even during complex AI operations.
- *Server actions*—RSCs introduce server actions, allowing us to trigger server-side operations without dealing with explicit API endpoints, complex data management, or unnecessary network roundtrips. This feature simplifies our codebase and reduces the potential for errors in client–server communication.

In fact, adopting RSCs with the Vercel AI SDK often results in reducing the overall lines of code rather than increasing them. This reduction mainly comes from eliminating the need for separate API routes for AI operations, removing boilerplate code for client–server communication, and simplifying state management.

In the following sections, we'll dive into practical examples that demonstrate how to refactor existing AI-powered components to use RSCs. You'll see firsthand how this approach can streamline your codebase while enhancing the capabilities and performance of your AI applications.

4.1.2 Using server actions for AI-powered RSCs

Server actions are a Next.js feature that allows you to run server-side code directly from your components. Think of them as server-side functions that you can call directly from your client components (like form elements), eliminating the traditional need for API routes. Let's explore how this magic works.

Here's what we're going to build:

- A server action that showcases how to process user input, interact with the OpenAI API, and return AI-generated responses without the need for explicit API routes
- An updated client code that renders the streamed updates from the server into a UI component that displays the current chat history

NOTE The source code for the examples in this chapter is available at https://github.com/Generative-AI-Web-Apps/Code/tree/main/ch04/chat-rsc.

> **Project code: chat-rsc**
>
> The code for this example project is in the ch04/chat-rsc folder. You can use that example by running this command in the root folder of the project repository:
>
> ```
> $ npm run dev -w ch04/chat-rsc
> ```
>
> You'll also need a Google API key to access their REST API. The appendix at the end of this book offers instructions on how to set up and create a secret key for Google AI and other providers:
>
> ```
> // .env
> GEMINI_API_KEY=<SECRET_KEY>
> ```
>
> For details on setting up and creating API keys, refer to the appendix.

We'll examine the basic implementation of AI-powered RSCs using the Vercel AI SDK. We'll use two main files: a server component file for AI processing and a client component for user interaction.

In this example, we're creating a system that maintains a conversation thread with an AI model. The AI will respond to user inputs based on the conversation history using streaming responses.

Before we dive into the code, let's visualize this communication with our AI model using RSCs. Figure 4.4 shows the flow of data from user input to the final display of the AI's response.

As you can see, user input travels from the client component to the server action, which then interacts with the AI provider. The AI's response is streamed back in chunks, updating the client in real time while maintaining the conversation state in memory. Listing 4.1 shows the code that implements this process.

94 CHAPTER 4 *Managing conversation and state in your application*

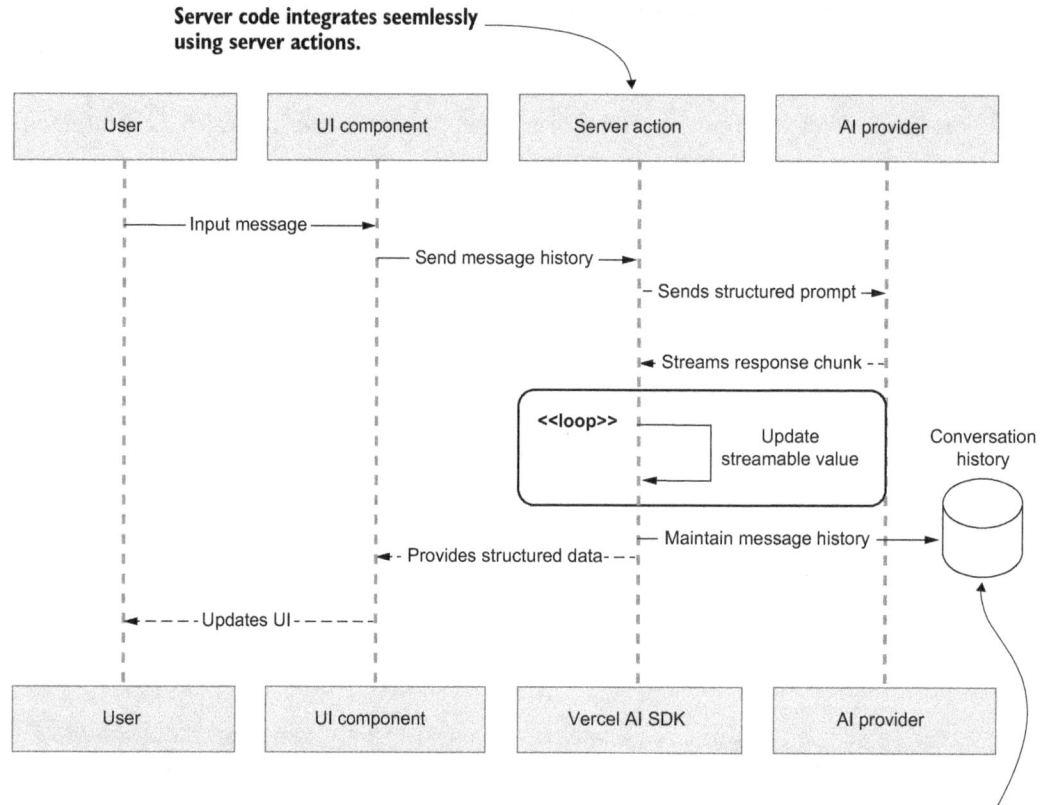

Figure 4.4 React server actions in action. User input travels from the prompt to the AI provider. The response is streamed back in chunks, updating the client in real time while maintaining the conversation state in memory.

Listing 4.1 Server action that creates a streamable conversation

The 'use server' directive indicates that this code should only run on the server, enabling server actions.

Imports necessary functions from the Vercel AI SDK, including createStreamableValue, which is specific to RSCs. This function returns a value that can be used to stream data back to the client.

```
'use server';
import { streamText } from 'ai';
import { createStreamableValue } from 'ai/rsc';

export async function
continueConversation(history, provider, model) {
  'use server';
  const supportedModel = getSupportedModel(provider, model);
  const stream = createStreamableValue();
  (async () => {
    const { textStream } = await streamText({
```

Creates a streamable value that can be updated incrementally and sent to the client in real time

```
      model: supportedModel,
      system: "I'm happy to assist you in any way I can.
How can I be of service today?",
      messages: history,
    });

    for await (const text of textStream) {     ◄──── Iterates over the text stream
      stream.update(text);                            from the AI model, updating
    }                                                 our streamable value with
                                                      each new piece of text
    stream.done();
  })();

  return {                          ◄──── Returns an object containing the
    messages: history,                     conversation history and the new
    newMessage: stream.value,              message as a streamable value, allowing
  };                                       for real-time updates on the client
}
```

This server action encapsulates the entire process of interacting with the supported AI model, generating a response, and preparing it for streaming to the client. The `createStreamableValue` function is a helper function tool provided by the Vercel AI SDK for RSCs. It creates a special type of value that can be continuously updated on the server and streamed to the client in real time. This is particularly useful when dealing with AI-generated content that is produced incrementally.

The `continueConversation` function takes the conversation history as an input, sends it to the AI model, and then streams the response back. It uses the familiar `streamText` function that we explored in chapter 3. This approach allows for a more responsive user experience, as the AI's response can be displayed to the user as it's being generated, rather than waiting for the entire response to be completed.

One key line that you'll notice in the code is the presence of `'use server'`; at the top of the file. This directive is not there by mistake or mere convention—it serves a key purpose in the RSC architecture.

The `'use server'`; directive is a special instruction to the RSC compiler. When this directive is present, it marks the entire file to be used exclusively on the server. All functions and code within this file will only be executed on the server. This allows you to perform operations that require server resources, access databases, or interact with external APIs without exposing these operations to the client. The client (i.e., the browser) will never see or have access to this code. This is a significant security feature, as it allows you to keep sensitive logic, API keys, and other confidential information safely on the server.

It's worth noting that you can also use the `'use server'` directive on individual functions within a file, allowing for more granular control over which functions are server-only. However, when used at the top of a file, it applies to all exports from that file.

In the context of our AI-powered application, this directive ensures that all the logic for interacting with the OpenAI API, handling sensitive data, and managing the streaming of responses happens exclusively on the server. This not only enhances security but also allows for more efficient processing and improved performance.

96 CHAPTER 4 *Managing conversation and state in your application*

> **NOTE** You can use `'use server'` in any server component file within the app directory. You can also use it on a function level. Add `'use server'` at the beginning of an async function body to mark only that function as a server action. Always utilize `'use server'` in code that must run on the server, since Next.js will ensure it's only included in the server bundle.

With this in place, we can now remove the API route handler that we had defined (chat)/api/route.js since we won't be needing it anymore. Any API calls will be handled by the server actions directly in our components.

That completes the backend part of the implementation. The next section deals with the changes to the UI so that we can call the server actions directly.

4.1.3 Updating the UI to use server actions

Our page.js component, which renders the conversational UI, needs to call the provided continueConversation function, passing the message history. We don't have to completely rewrite the existing code. We only need to define a form handler that will call this function and update the client state.

For example, if a user types "What's the weather like today?" our form handler will

1 Capture this input.
2 Add it to the conversation history.
3 Call the continueConversation function with the updated history.
4 Receive and display the AI's response, which might be something like "I'm sorry, I don't have access to real-time weather data. However, I can suggest checking a reliable weather website or app for the most up-to-date information."

This process is visualized in figure 4.5.

The following listing showcases the important parts of our form handler implementation.

Listing 4.2 Form handler implementation for chat messages

```
'use client';
// import declarations here
export const dynamic = 'force-dynamic';
export const maxDuration = 30;

const Chat = () => {
  // ... (state and ref declarations)
// const { messages, input, handleInputChange, handleSubmit,
isLoading } = useChat({ api: '/api' });

  const handleOnSubmit = async (event) => {
    event.preventDefault();
    const value = input.trim();
    setInput('');
```

These export statements ensure that the page is always dynamically rendered and has a maximum execution time of 30 seconds, which is important for handling streaming responses.

This commented-out line shows how we previously used the useChat hook. We're replacing this with our custom implementation using server actions.

The handleOnSubmit function is our custom form submission handler that will use the server action.

AI SDK React server components

```
    if (!value) return;
    setIsLoading(true);
    setMessages([...conversationMessages,
{ role: 'user', content: input }]);
    const { messages, newMessage } = await continueConversation([...
conversationMessages,
{ role: 'user', content: input }], provider, model);
    let textContent = '';
    for await (const delta of readStreamableValue(newMessage)) {
      textContent = `${textContent}${delta}`;
      setMessages([...messages,
{ role: 'assistant', content: textContent }]);
    }
    setIsLoading(false);
  };

  // ... (rest of the component code)

  return (
    // ... (JSX for the chat interface)
  );
};

export default Chat;
```

Updates the local state immediately with the user's message for a responsive UI

Uses readStreamableValue to asynchronously read the streamed response from the server, updating the UI in real time as new content arrives

Calls the continueConversation server action directly, passing the updated conversation history

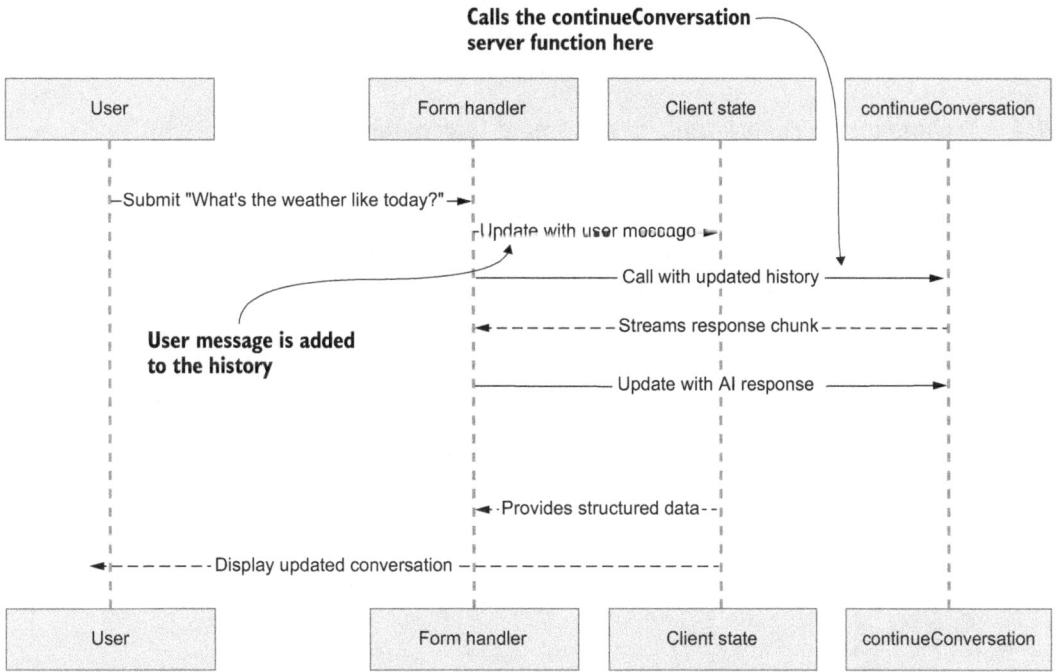

Figure 4.5 UI interaction using server actions. The user submits a message, and the form submission takes place. The call to the continueConversation server action happens on the server and streams the response back to the client.

We're calling the `continueConversation` function directly from our client component, without needing to set up a separate API endpoint.

The `readStreamableValue` function is designed to work in tandem with `createStreamableValue` on the client side. It's specifically used to read and process the streamable value that was created and updated on the server.

When we use the `readStreamableValue`, we can update the UI incrementally as the AI generates its response, providing a more responsive user experience. Finally, we removed the `useChat` since the whole logic is encapsulated in the server actions directly. This means that we don't have to include this code with the final client, reducing the final bundle size.

With these changes implemented, you can now run the web application locally. You'll notice that while the functionality remains the same from a user's perspective, the interactions with the server actions happen seamlessly in the background. The beauty of this approach is that it maintains the lively, interactive feel of a client-side application while enhancing the performance and security benefits of server-side processing.

The final piece of this puzzle is the ability to stream React components directly from within server actions. This approach is highly recommended, as it uses the full power of RSCs and the Vercel AI SDK. To fully utilize this capability, you'll need to understand some additional concepts, particularly around managing AI and UI state. In the next section, we'll peruse a comprehensive walk-through of managing UI state and explore how to use external tools to enhance this process.

4.1.4 Techniques for generating and streaming UI components

Now that we're using server actions for seamless text streaming, we can unlock perhaps the most influential feature: streaming React components directly in response to AI completions. This capability allows us to generate and update complex UI elements based on AI-generated content in real time.

For example, consider an application that can generate and display a weather forecast. As the large language model (LLM)–powered app processes a user's request for weather information, it could stream a series of React components that progressively build a rich, interactive weather display:

1. Initially, it might render a loading component: `<WeatherLoading />`.
2. Then, as it generates the forecast, it could stream city information: `<CityInfo name="New York" />`.
3. Following that, it might add temperature data: `<TemperatureDisplay high={75} low={62} />`.
4. Finally, it could include a weekly forecast: `<WeeklyForecast data={[...]} />`.

The user would see these components appear and update in real time as the AI generates the information, creating a dynamic and engaging experience.

To implement this functionality, we'll introduce two new helper functions: streamUI and createStreamableUI. These functions provide the core functionality for vibrant UI generation based on AI responses.

4.1.5 Creating streamable UI components from LLM providers with streamUI

The streamUI function is an effective tool that allows you to generate and stream UI components based on responses from LLM providers. It orchestrates the process of generating UI components, allowing for active and incremental UI updates. The function takes user input, sends it to the LLM, and based on the response, can either render text directly as a component or call specific tools to generate more complex UI components. The resulting components are then streamed to the client in real time.

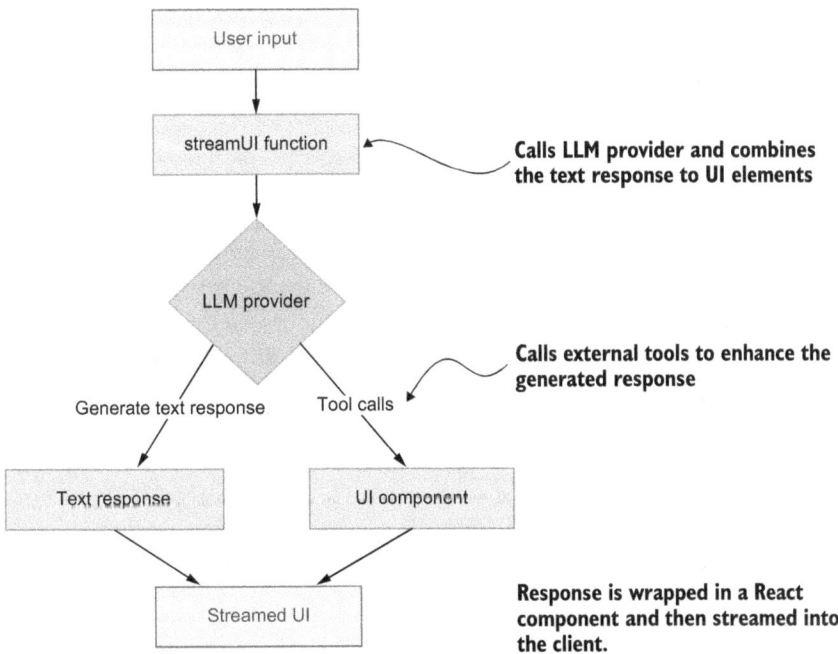

Figure 4.6 Example of how streamUI works. This function orchestrates the process of generating UI components based on LLM responses. It handles both simple text responses and more complex tool calls and then streams the fully rendered components as React nodes into the client.

The streamUI function takes user input and sends it to the LLM provider. Based on the LLM's response, it can either render text directly as a component or call specific tools to generate more complex UI components. This allows components to be streamed to the client in real time.

To understand how it works in practice, see the following listing, where we render a single generated prompt response directly as a <Chat /> message component.

Listing 4.3 Streaming the `<Chat />` component

```
export async function streamComponent(input, history) {
  'use server';
  const result = await streamUI({
    model: openai('gpt-3.5-turbo'),
    messages: [...history, { role: 'user', content: input }],
    text: ({ content, done }) => {
      return <ChatBubble role="assistant" text={content}
  className={`mr-auto border-none`} />;
    },
  });

  return {
    id: generateId(),
    role: 'assistant',
    display: result.value,
  };
}
```

- The streamUI function is called with the OpenAI model and the conversation history, including the new user input.
- The text property is a function that defines how to render the AI's response. It receives the content and a done flag once the response is finished.
- This function returns a ChatBubble component for each piece of content received from the AI, wrapping the AI's response in a React component.
- The result.value contains the streamable UI component, which is assigned to the display property of the returned object.

The `streamComponent` server action sends the conversation history to the supported AI model and then uses the `streamUI` function to process the response. The AI's output is wrapped in a `ChatBubble` component, which can be updated in real time as more content is generated. The function returns an object with the generated response, including a unique ID and the `streamable` UI component.

We can call this action as part of the form submission process and store the results in a variable. This variable will hold the generated React component containing the LLM response, which we can then display to the user. The following listing shows how to do it.

Listing 4.4 Rendering the streamed component into the page

```
'use client';
// imports
export default function Page() {
  const [component, setComponent] = useState();
  const handleInputChange = (event) => {
    setInput(event.target.value);
  };
  const [input, setInput] = useState('');
  return (
    <div>
      <form
        onSubmit={async e => {
          e.preventDefault();
          const value = input.trim();
          setInput('');
          if (!value) return;
```

- Initializes a state variable component to store the streamable UI component returned from the server action

```
            setComponent(await streamComponent(value, []));
        }}
    >
        <TextArea value={input} onChange={handleInputChange} />
    </form>
    <div>{component}</div>.          ◄──────  When the form is submitted, we call
    </div>                                     the streamComponent() server action.
  );
}
                                    The component state is rendered directly
                                    as components, allowing for dynamic
                                    updates as the streamable UI changes.
```

This `PageComponent` demonstrates how to integrate a streamable UI component generated by a server action into a React client component. It maintains two state variables: a component for the streamable UI and input for the user's text input. When the form is submitted, it calls the `streamComponent()` server action. This action generates a streamable UI component based on the input.

The result of the server action is set as the new value of the component state, and it is rendered in the DOM, allowing it to update as new content is streamed from the server. This approach enables real-time updates to the UI based on AI-generated content. The streamable UI component can update incrementally as new content is generated, without requiring full page reloads or explicit polling mechanisms.

Now what about when you want to stream real-time updates to a component from a server action while the content is being updated in real time? In such a case, we use the `createStreamableUI` function, which I will explain next.

4.1.6 Streaming React components with createStreamableUI

When building applications that require real-time updates to components based on server-side actions, the Vercel AI SDK provides the `createStreamableUI` function. This is particularly useful when content needs to be updated as it is processed.

The `createStreamableUI` function complements `streamUI` by providing a way to create and update UI components incrementally. This means you can update the UI components as new updates are received from the AI model, allowing for real-time updates based on ongoing AI processing. This improves perceived performance by showing partial results quickly and enhances the user experience.

For example, in the chatbot interface we are building, the AI generates responses incrementally. Each time a new response chunk is received, the server streams the updates as `streamable` React components that provide immediate feedback to the user without introducing any delays. Figure 4.7 shows how it works.

Compared to the `streamUI` function, the `createStreamableUI` does not really call the LLM provider with the prompt. It instead returns a value object that can be used in place of a React component. This object exposes several methods that the client can use to provide incremental updates:

- `update`—Replaces the existing content with the new content provided
- `done`—Signals that the streaming is complete

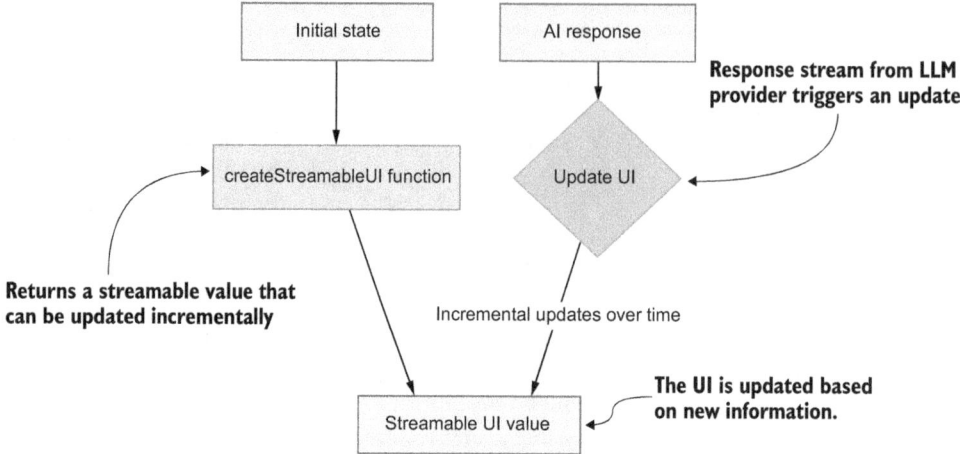

Figure 4.7 createStreamableUI enables the creation of UI components that can be updated incrementally. This capability enables real-time modifications to the user interface as new information is received from the LLM provider.

- append—Adds new content to the existing streamable UI
- error—Handles any errors that occur during the streaming process or displays an error component

The createStreamableUI function in the Vercel AI SDK provides users with immediate updates as processes complete, allowing incremental updates to the UI.

In this example, we create a streamable UI, update it with initial content, append new content as steps are completed, and finally mark it as done. If an error occurs, we use the error method to handle it. This demonstrates how createStreamableUI can be used to walk a user through a two-step process, informing them when each step is complete.

Listing 4.5 Adding incremental UI updates to the stream

```
import { createStreamableUI } from '@vercel/ai-sdk';
export async function continueConversation(history) {
  const ui = createStreamableUI();
  ui.update(<p>Starting process...</p>);
  try {
    await new Promise(resolve => setTimeout(resolve, 1000));
    ui.append(<p>Step 1 complete</p>);

    await new Promise(resolve => setTimeout(resolve, 1000));
    ui.append(<p>Step 2 complete</p>);
```

This initializes a new streamable UI that we can update incrementally.

We use the update method to set the initial content of our UI.

The append method adds new content without replacing the existing content.

```
    ui.update(<p>Process complete!</p>);
    ui.done();
} catch (error) {
    ui.error(error);
}
    return ui;
}
```

- `ui.update(<p>Process complete!</p>);` — Here we use update again to replace all existing content with a final message.
- `ui.done();` — The done method is called to indicate that no more updates will be made.
- `ui.error(error);` — If an error occurs, we use the error method to update the UI accordingly.

How does this approach align with building AI web applications? Both helpers allow us to combine the best of both worlds: server-side component access and seamless client-side updates. This ensures sensitive secrets remain secure on the server while reducing the client-side bundle size.

A significant challenge we face now is managing state, particularly sharing message history between the server and client without introducing complex state management solutions. Based on our experience, proper state management is crucial for maintaining a consistent and responsive user experience.

4.2 Managing UI state in AI-powered applications

As our applications grow, simple state management with React's `useState` hook becomes inadequate. We need to handle not only the messages displayed in the UI but also metadata, AI context, and server-side state, all while ensuring smooth performance and real-time updates.

React's `Context` API, with its `useContext` hook, offers a partial solution for propagating variables, but it falls short when we step into the realm of RSCs. In fact, all React hooks do not work in that space. Moreover, we often need server actions to update conversation messages automatically, ensuring the UI reflects changes without manual state updates.

This leads to a dual-state management approach, which separates AI state and UI state. This is a recommended strategy for building robust, responsive AI-powered applications. UI state handles what the user sees and interacts with, while AI state manages the core data and context that our AI models work with behind the scenes.

4.2.1 Separating AI and UI state in React/Next.js applications

When building AI-powered applications with React or Next.js, it's essential to distinguish between two types of state: AI state and UI state. AI state encompasses all the data and context that the AI model needs to function effectively, and UI state deals with the data and state that directly affect what the user sees and interacts with. This separation allows for more efficient handling of data, improved performance, and better synchronization between the server and client.

Figure 4.8 shows the AI and UI state flow in UI applications. First, the user input is received by a client component. The AI context provider manages both UI and AI states. AI state is sent to a server action, which interacts with the LLM/AI model, and the generated content updates both AI and UI states. Then the AI state is serialized and

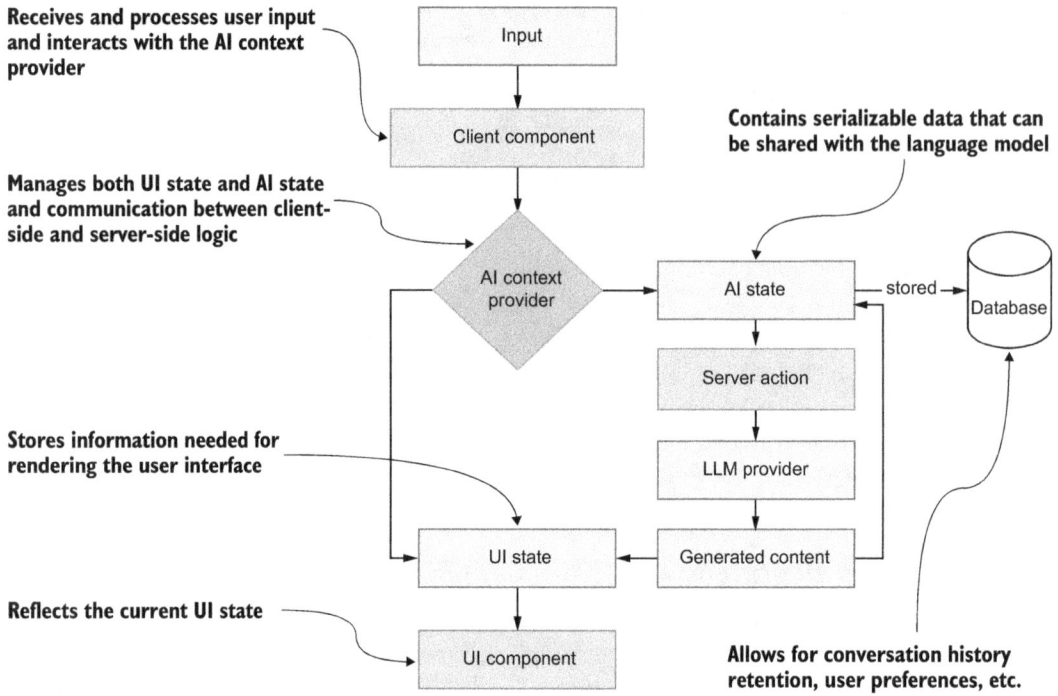

Figure 4.8 AI and UI state representation. Once the user submits a prompt, it goes through a pipeline of events and actions for the final output to be consistent.

can be stored in a database. UI state is used to render the interface, which then accepts new user input.

AI STATE

AI state represents the serializable data that can be shared with the language model and used on the server. It typically includes the following pieces of data:

- Conversation history: messages between user and assistant
- Metadata: for example, timestamps, conversation IDs
- JSON representations of generated components

These kinds of data would almost not be needed in the UI, so there is no need to share them with every conversation thread to the client. They need to be kept in a separate context.

UI STATE

UI state, on the other hand, is a client-side state that encompasses the actual rendered elements and React components. It typically includes components rendered with state parameters:

- *React elements and components*—For instance, <Button isDisabled={true}> or <Input value="hello" />

- *UI state variables*—State stored as variables or as an object: {isLoading: true}
- *Client-side interactivity*—For example, a dropdown menu that shows or hides options based on user selection or a button that updates a counter when clicked

Importantly, UI state is confined to the client and cannot be directly transferred back to the server. Its primary role is to reflect changes in the AI state, ensuring that the user interface accurately represents the current application state.

HOW TO SET UP THE UI AND AI STATE

The Vercel AI SDK provides a set of helpers to facilitate the setup and management of both UI and AI states. These helpers are designed to work seamlessly with React's state management best practices while implementing the principles outlined in our state flow diagram.

4.2.2 Key components for UI state management

Let's explore the essential functions and hooks provided by the Vercel AI SDK that make this possible. There are five key functions you should know: createAI, getMutableAIState, useActions, useUIState, and useAIState.

CREATEAI

createAI is a function that creates an AI context provider. It's the foundation of our state management system, allowing us to define

- *Initial AI and UI states*—For example, the initial AI state might include userProfile: { name: '', email: '' } or currentTask: null.
- *Actions that can be performed* (typically server actions)—These actions are operations that interact with the server, such as fetchUserData, which retrieves user information.
- *Types for both AI and UI states*—Types define the shape and structure of the states. For instance, AIState might include types like UserProfile or Task, while UIState could define types like SidebarState or ThemeSettings.

This function sets up the structure for managing and synchronizing states across your application. You create this function, and then it returns to a React context component, which you can place on the root layout page. Then you will gain access to the server actions and useState hooks to manage both UI and AI state.

Say you are building a web application where users can manage their profiles and settings. At the start, the application needs to load the user's profile and settings from the server and set up the initial UI state.

When the app starts, createAI initializes with an initial AI state. It sets userProfile to have an empty name and email, set to default values (light theme and notifications enabled). It defines server actions like fetchUserData and updateUserSettings. The AIProvider wraps the root layout of the app, making the AI and UI state accessible throughout the application. This setup ensures that any component within AppLayout can access and manage these states and perform actions like fetching data or updating settings. The following listing shows the example reflected as code.

Listing 4.6 Example creating an AI provider

```
const AI = createAI({
  actions: {                                    ◄── Defines your server actions
    fetchUserData: async (userId) => {
      const response = await fetch(`/api/users/${userId}`);
      const data = await response.json();
      return data;
    },
    updateUserSettings: async (settings) => {
      await fetch('/api/settings', {
        method: 'POST',
        headers: { 'Content-Type': 'application/json' },
        body: JSON.stringify(settings),
      });
    }
  },
  initialAIState: {
    userProfile: { name: '', email: '' },
    settings: { theme: 'light', notifications: true },
  },                                            ◄── Defines an initial AI state
  initialUIState: {
    isSidebarOpen: false,
  },                  ◄── Defines an initial UI state
});
...
const AppLayout = ({ children }) => {
  return (
    <AI>.         ◄── Wraps the AI component to the root layout
      {children}      of the app so that the context is available
    </AI>             throughout the children components
  )
}
```

The `createAI` function returns a React context provider component with the defined actions: initial AI and UI states. You will need to place this component on your app layout page so that the hooks discussed after the following sidebar can access the state and actions.

> **Saving and restoring AI state with createAI**
>
> The `createAI` function offers a few useful callbacks for managing AI state persistence. Use the `onSetAIState` callback to save AI state changes to a database—for example:
>
> ```
> onSetAIState: async ({ state, done }) => {
>   if (done) {
>     await saveToDatabase(state);
>   }
> }
> ```

Similarly, you can restore the state of the messages by having a function that loads the contents from the database and passing it into the `initialAIState`:

```
const savedState = await loadFromDatabase();
const AI = createAI({
    initialAIState: savedState,
});
```

GETMUTABLEAISTATE

`getMutableAIState` is a crucial function for managing AI state within server actions. When called, it returns an object that represents the current AI state. You can use this state object to retrieve the latest information about the AI's context, such as conversation history or any other relevant data. Additionally, you can do the following:

- *Update the AI state*—You can add new messages, update existing information, or make any other necessary changes to the AI state.
- *Mark the AI state as "done" (fully updated)*—This is particularly useful in streaming scenarios, signaling that all updates for the current interaction have been completed.

While `getMutableAIState` manages the AI state on the server, it works in conjunction with client-side state management to keep the UI in sync.

USEACTIONS

`useActions` is a hook that provides access to the actions defined in your `createAI` call. It allows client components to trigger server actions and update the AI state.

USEUISTATE

`useUIState` is a hook that provides access to the UI state within client components. It returns the current UI state and a function to update it, similar to React's `useState`.

USEAISTATE

`useAIState` is a hook that provides read-only access to the AI state within client components. This allows you to use the AI state for rendering or logic without directly modifying it.

All these functions and hooks work hand in hand to create a seamless state management system for UI applications. They allow you to

- Separate concerns between AI and UI states.
- Manage complex state updates on both client and server.
- Ensure consistency between what the model sees and what the user interacts with.
- Create reactive UIs that respond to AI-generated content in real time.

4.2.3 Implementing UI state management patterns

We will now refactor our existing Astra AI project to use these powerful new tools. The key architectural upgrades are replacing `streamText` with `streamUI` and introducing `createAI`. These changes will transform our basic chat application into a more robust and flexible system capable of handling complex, dynamic responses and managing state more effectively.

> **NOTE** The source code for the examples in this chapter is available at https://github.com/Generative-AI-Web-Apps/Code/tree/main/ch04/chat-rsc-stream-ui.

Project code: chat-rsc-stream-ui

The code for this example project is in the ch04/chat-rsc-stream-ui folder. You can use that example by running this command in the source folder:

```
$ npm run dev -w ch04/chat-rsc-stream-ui
```

You'll also need a Google API key to access their REST API. The appendix offers instructions on how to set up and create a secret key for Google AI and other providers:

```
// .env
GOOGLE_API_KEY=<SECRET_KEY>
```

For details on setting up and creating API keys, refer to the appendix.

To address these needs, we can use two key architectural upgrades that will improve our state management and response-handling capabilities:

- *Replacing* `streamText` *with* `streamUI`—This helper allows us to stream responses not just as text, but as fully fledged React components.
- *Introducing* `createAI`—This is a comprehensive solution that unifies UI and AI states, providing a single source of truth for our entire application.

These upgrades are focused on improving the underlying architecture of our state management system, and they do not affect the visual representation of the application. By implementing these three key upgrades, we'll transform our basic AI chat application into a more robust, flexible system. Figure 4.9 visually showcases the application architecture before and after the upgrades and changes from `streamText` to `streamUI` and the introduction of `createAI`.

Before the upgrade, the Astra AI project used the `streamText` helper function for managing AI responses. This function streamed text-based responses from the AI model, which were then handled by the React components on the client side. State management was primarily done using React's `useState`.

Managing UI state in AI-powered applications 109

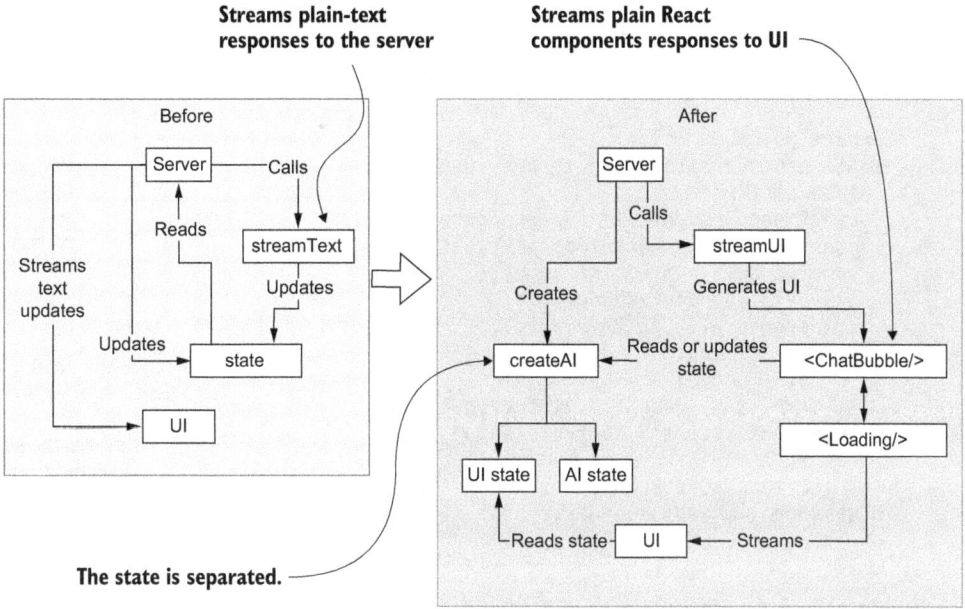

Figure 4.9 The transition from a system with separate management of UI and AI states using streamText for plain-text responses to a unified state management approach using createAI. In the new architecture, streamUI replaces streamText, enabling the streaming of React components and providing a consistent context for both AI and UI states through createAI. This shift enhances the application's ability to manage content and integrates state management more effectively.

After the upgrade, the streamUI function now allows for streaming responses as fully fledged React components instead of plain text. Additionally, the createAI function was introduced to unify AI and UI state management. This function provides a single source of truth for the entire application.

Let's take a close look at the implementation, focusing on the server actions where these changes will have the most effect. We'll walk through the transformation step by step, highlighting the key modifications and their implications for our application's architecture. As we proceed, keep in mind that this new approach will not only solve our current challenges but also open doors to more advanced features.

CHANGES TO SERVER ACTIONS

To refactor our existing server actions to use these tools, we will change the continueConversation action to manage user inputs and conversation history while integrating with createAI for consistent state management.

This action now uses getMutableAIState to manage the conversation history and streamUI to generate a streaming response and updates the AI state accordingly. The createAI function sets up the AI context for the entire application, defining the available actions and initial states.

Listing 4.7 Managing the conversation history with `getMutableAIState`

```
export async function
continueConversation(input, provider, model) {     Gets the mutable AI state to access
  'use server';                                    and update conversation history
  const supportedModel = getSupportedModel(provider, model);
  const history = getMutableAIState();             Uses streamUI
  const result = await streamUI({.                 to generate a
    model: supportedModel,                         streaming
    messages: [...history.get(), { role: 'user', content: input }],   response from
    text: ({ content, done }) => {                                    the AI model
      if (done) {
        history.done([...history.get(),            Combines the existing history
{ role: 'assistant', content: input }]);           with new user input for context
      }
      return <ChatBubble role="assistant" text={content}    Updates the AI state
className={`mr-auto border-none`} />;              when the response
    },                                             is complete
  });

  return {
    id: generateId(),
    role: 'assistant',
    display: result.value,          Returns the streamed UI
  };                                component as the display value
}
export const AI = createAI({.       Creates the AI context with the
  actions: {                        defined action and initial states
    continueConversation,
  },
  initialAIState: [],
  initialUIState: {
    messages: [],
  },
});
```

Notice that we didn't have to pass on the `history` object as a parameter. This `history` object represents the AI state that gets resolved on the server side using the `getMutable-AIState` function. We can call this function anywhere on the server and get the conversation history.

That concludes all the backend updates. The following section deals with the necessary updates needed for the frontend UI.

CHANGES TO THE FRONTEND

To use our new state management system, we need to make some important changes to our frontend components. The AI component, which is created using the `createAI` function, is now set as the parent context provider for the entire application. This allows all child components to access the unified AI and UI state and actions. It wraps the application's layout with the `<AI>` component to provide its context to all descendant components. These modifications will enable us to use the AI context throughout our application, providing access to both actions and state hooks.

Listing 4.8 Adding the AI provider to the layout component

```
import { AI } from './actions';
const AppLayout = ({ children }) => {
  return (
    <AI>            ◄── Sets the AI component to be the parent node,
        <div>           providing its context to the children components
<Header />
        <main>{children}</main>
<Footer />
        </div>
    </AI>
  )
}
```

This setup allows us to use the `useActions`, `useUIState`, and `useAIState` hooks in any child component within our application. Figure 4.10 shows before and after the upgrades and changes from using `useActions`, `useUIState`, and `useAIState` hooks.

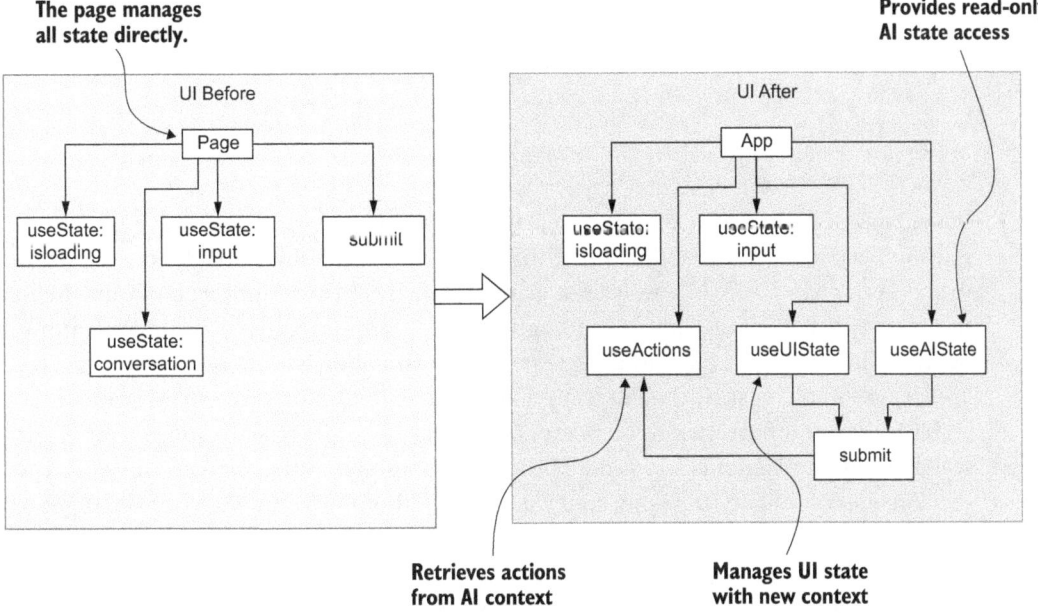

Figure 4.10 The evolution of the chat page component's state management and server actions before and after adopting the new hooks and actions. Before, the component relied on traditional React `useState` hooks to manage input, loading state, and conversation history, with a separate function simulating AI response fetching. The updated implementation integrates the new `useUIState`, `useAIState`, and `useActions` hooks and allows the app to delegate the logic inside those hooks.

Now let's update our chat page component (in page.js) to utilize these new hooks and actions. We'll replace the previous state management with our newly integrated state system.

Listing 4.9 Including new hooks for managing AI and UI state

```
export default function Home() {
  const [provider, setProvider] = useState('openai');      // Uses useUIState to
  const [model, setModel] = useState('gpt-4');             // manage UI-specific state
  const [input, setInput] = useState('');
  const [isLoading, setIsloading] = useState(false);
  const [conversation, setConversation] =                  // Uses useAIState to
useUIState();                                              // access the AI state
  const [aiState] = useAIState();                          // (read-only)
  const { continueConversation } = useActions();           // Retrieves the
                                                           // continueConversation
  const handleSubmit = async (e) => {                      // action from the AI
    e.preventDefault();        // Calls the setUIState to  // context
    setUIState((prev) => ({.   // update the UI state here
      ...prev,
      messages: [...prev.messages, { role: 'user', content: input }],
    }));
    const response =
await continueConversation(input, provider, model);        // Calls the server action
    setUIState((prev) => ({                                // to process user input
      ...prev,                                             // and get AI response
      messages: [...prev.messages, response],
    }));

    setInput('');
  };
};
```

We've replaced the useState for conversation management with useUIState. This hook gives us access to the UI state defined in our AI context. We've also added useAIState to access the AI state. While we're not using it directly in this example, it's available for more complex scenarios where we might need to reference the AI's understanding of the conversation. The continueConversation function is now retrieved using the useActions hook, ensuring we're using the server action defined in our AI context.

With the modifications we've made, our application now uses a more robust and scalable state management system. This upgrade significantly enhances our ability to manage complex state in AI-powered interfaces without introducing visual changes to the user experience.

As an improvement, notice that we keep both the isLoading and value state variables outside of the UI state. See if you can include this inside the UI state instead. What changes do you think you need to make this work? I will leave this to you as a small exercise.

TESTING THE CHANGES

After implementing these modifications, try to rebuild your application and visit the main chat interface. Pay special attention to loading indicators and disabled states during AI responses. You should notice that the application behaves identically to the previous version but with the added benefit of a more centralized and manageable state.

THE TAKEAWAYS

Good state management is key to building responsive, efficient, and user-friendly AI interfaces. Continually refining the state management approach will pay dividends as your application grows in complexity. You will next see some practical use cases of this system, starting with structured data generation.

Structured data generation involves prompting AI models to produce outputs in specific formats, which can greatly enhance feature development. For example, you might instruct an AI model to generate responses in formats such as JSON, Markdown for formatted text, or XML. These formats enable more organized and actionable responses, like creating detailed reports, generating interactive UI elements, or structuring data for further analysis.

4.3 Structured data generation using the Vercel AI SDK

Asking the AI model to generate text for us based on a prompt is a very useful feature, and in most cases, it's sufficient. However, AI models can do better. Why don't we ask the AI model to generate structured, type-safe data directly? After all, we might need to provide their data in another tool as input, so it makes sense to skip the part when we parse the text response and try to manually overcome this limitation.

While generating text is useful, AI models can do more. We can instruct them to generate structured, type-safe data like JSON directly, which is crucial for integrating AI responses into other applications or tools. The Vercel AI SDK provides helpful tools to do this reliably.

In this section, we'll explore how structured object generation works and provide practical examples. We'll then enhance our Astra AI agent to deliver JSON responses, which we can easily display in a React component. This approach opens new possibilities for integrating AI-generated data into various tools and applications.

4.3.1 How structured data generation works

Structured data generation is a process that allows AI models to produce organized, type-safe data instead of raw text. This approach enhances the reliability and usability of AI-generated content in various applications. Let's break down the process by exploring the diagram in figure 4.11.

As shown in the figure, the user initiates an action in a React component, and then the component calls a generation function via the Vercel AI SDK. The allowed schema is predefined by the developer when they call any of the generator functions. Then the SDK sends a structured prompt to the AI model, which in turn returns a raw response. The SDK validates the response using a schema validator, and then the structured data is returned to the client to update the UI.

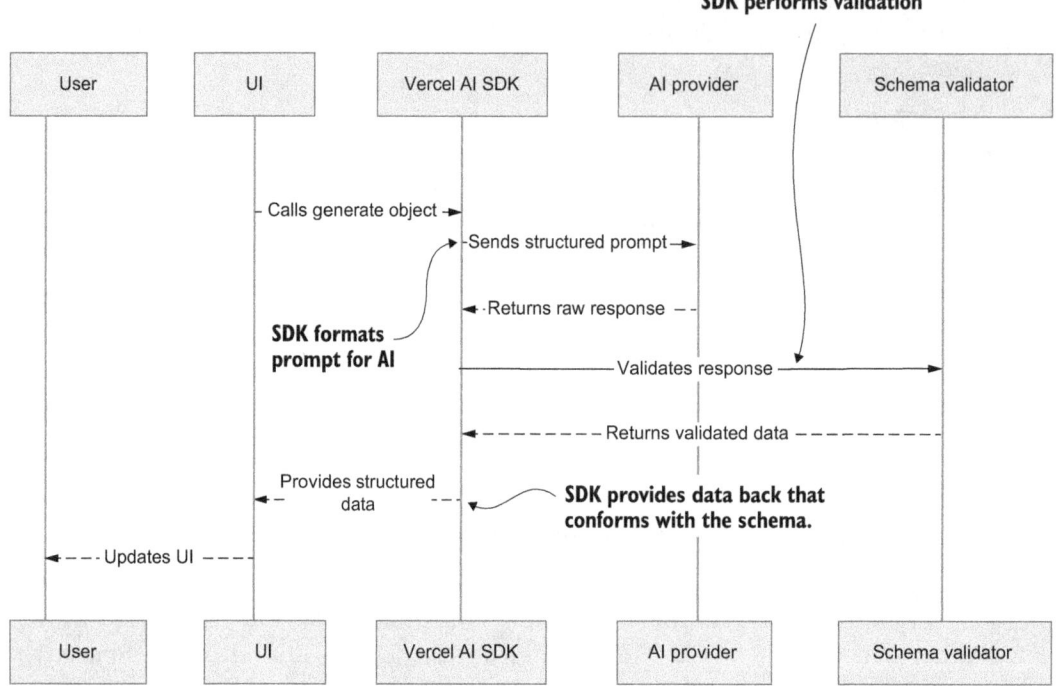

Figure 4.11 This sequence diagram illustrates the process of generating structured data from an AI model using the Vercel AI SDK. The flow begins with a user action and ends with the display of validated, structured data in the user interface. Key components include the React component, Vercel AI SDK, AI model, and schema validator.

This process ensures that the data received from the AI model is not only relevant but also follows a predefined structure, making it easier to integrate into applications. Let's look at the key techniques for generating structured data from AI responses.

4.3.2 Techniques for generating structured data from AI responses

Before we get technical, I explain some techniques we can use to instruct the AI model to respond in a certain format. To effectively generate and handle structured data from AI responses, we can employ several techniques, such as

- *Prompt engineering*—This involves crafting precise, detailed prompts that guide the AI to produce structured outputs like JSON objects with specific fields.
- *Output parsing*—Another way is by using regex patterns or JSON parsing to extract structured data from AI responses. This is trickier but still viable in certain scenarios by allowing flexibility in AI outputs while still obtaining structured data.
- *Function calling*—This is a feature provided by certain AI providers like OpenAI for requesting specific data structures. With this method, we define a function schema that the AI model must adhere to in its response.

- *Zod schema validation*—Zod is a library for schema declaration and validation. By configuring a Zod schema that defines the expected structure and types of the AI response, we ensure type safety and data integrity, catching any inconsistencies in the AI's output. Zod is used in the Vercel AI SDK as the primary schema validator service.
- *Iterative refinement (reprompting)*—If the previous options fail, we can try to use multiple rounds of AI queries to refine and structure the data. This might improve things, but we must be cognizant of the fact that we will be consuming more resources and tokens to achieve a reliable result.
- *Template-based generation*—Here we provide the AI with a template or example of the desired output structure. Then we ask it to fill in the details. This could improve the consistency in the AI's structured outputs.
- *Postprocessing*—As a final step, we can implement a series of data cleaning and structuring steps after receiving the AI response to ensure data quality and consistency.

In practice, a combination of these techniques is often used to achieve reliable results. The choice of techniques depends on the specific requirements of the application, the capabilities of the AI model being used, and the complexity of the desired data structure. As far as we are concerned, we must aim for reliability, consistency, and compliance if we ever want this to work for our end users. Thus, we need to ensure we use all the available tooling.

4.3.3 Tools for implementing type-safe AI-generated content

When working with AI-generated content in a type-safe environment, two key helpers provided by the Vercel AI SDK are particularly useful: generateObject and streamObject. These functions are like the generateText and streamText helpers we explored earlier. They allow developers to integrate structured data generation into their React components while maintaining type safety. Let's analyze them briefly before we see how to integrate them in our web application.

GENERATEOBJECT

The generateObject function is used for one-time generation of structured data from an AI model. It takes a Zod schema and an AI completion function as inputs, sends a prompt to the AI model, and receives a response. The response is then validated against the provided Zod schema. If validation succeeds, it returns the structured, typed object; otherwise, it retries the generation process (up to a specified limit). To use generateObject with schema validation, you'll need to install Zod in your project by running npm install zod. The following listing shows an example.

Listing 4.10 Generating structured responses with Zod

```
import { z } from 'zod';
import { google } from '@ai-sdk/google';
import { generateObject } from 'ai';
```

```
const ProductSchema = z.object({
  name: z.string(),
  description: z.string(),
  price: z.number(),
  category: z.string()
});
```
◀── Defines a Zod schema for a single product, specifying the expected structure and types

```
const ProductListSchema = z.array(ProductSchema);
```
◀── Creates a schema for an array of products using the ProductSchema

```
async function generateProductList(prompt) {
  'use server';
  const {
    object: { products },
  } = await generateObject({
    model: google("models/gemini-2.0-flash"),
    schema: z.object({
      products: ProductListSchema.
    }),
    prompt: `Generate a list of 5 products
related to: ${prompt}. Provide name, description, price,
and category for each product.`,
  });
  return products;
}

generateProductList('A list of cereal types').then(console.table);
```

◀── Uses generateObject to create structured data from the AI response, destructuring the result

◀── Applies the ProductListSchema to ensure the AI generates an array of products

◀── Constructs a detailed prompt for the AI, including the user's input and specific instructions

The generateObject function handles the communication with the AI model and ensures that the response conforms to our defined schema. This provides us with type-safe, structured data that we can directly use in our application without additional parsing or type-checking.

If you run this example code, it will print something similar in the console (figure 4.12). We printed the results using console.table, which renders the data as a table. Since the data is returned in a structured format, we can feed it to other services that expect the same model types.

```
% node example.mjs
```

(index)	name	description	price	category
0	'Honey Nut Cheerios'	'Delicious honey-flavored cereal with a hint of nuttiness'	3.99	'Breakfast Cereal'
1	'Frosted Flakes'	'Crunchy corn flakes coated with a sweet frosting'	2.99	'Breakfast Cereal'
2	'Cinnamon Toast Crunch'	'Toasted squares with a cinnamon and sugar coating'	4.49	'Breakfast Cereal'
3	'Lucky Charms'	'Colorful marshmallow and oat cereal with a touch of magic'	3.79	'Breakfast Cereal'
4	'Raisin Bran'	'Bran flakes with sweet raisins for a nutritious breakfast option'	3.29	'Breakfast Cereal'

Figure 4.12 Structured data generation using the generateObject function. The results of the prompt are printed using console.table to display them in a table format.

STREAMOBJECT

The streamObject function is used for streaming structured data from an AI model and is useful for real-time updates. Similar to generateObject, it takes a Zod schema and a streaming AI function. It streams the AI response and continuously attempts to parse and validate it. As soon as a valid object is parsed, it's returned to the consumer. This process continues, allowing for multiple objects to be streamed over time.

I do not show an example of how this works since it's identical to the previous example with the `streamText`.

4.3.4 Integrating structured data generation into our web application

Now that we understand these helpers, let's see how we can use them in our project to generate JSON responses instead of text responses. We'll modify our Astra AI agent to provide structured data that we can display as a table. Then, when we ask for a specific product category, the AI agent will respond with a product description.

Here's what we're going to build:

- An updated version of our Astra AI chat application that generates structured JSON data instead of plain-text responses, using the `generateObject` helper function
- A modified AI server action that uses a product schema to request and validate JSON output from the AI model
- A user interface that can display this structured product data in a more organized format using a table

NOTE The source code for the examples in this chapter is available at https://github.com/Generative-AI-Web-Apps/Code/tree/main/ch04/chat-rsc-structured-data.

> **Project code: chat-rsc-structured-data**
>
> The code for this example project is in the ch04/chat-rsc-structured-data folder. You can use that example by running this command in the source folder:
>
> ```
> $ npm run dev -w ch04/chat-rsc-structured-data
> ```
>
> You'll also need a Google Gemini API key to access their REST API. The appendix offers instructions on how to set up and create a secret key for Google AI and other providers:
>
> ```
> // .env
> GEMINIGEMINI_API_KEY=<SECRET_KEY>
> ```
>
> For details on setting up and creating API keys, refer to the appendix.

We will reuse the product schema from the generateObject example described in section 1.3.3. As a reminder, `generateObject` is a function that facilitates the creation of structured data from AI responses. It takes a Zod schema and an AI completion function as inputs, sends a prompt to the AI model, and then validates the response against the provided schema. This ensures that we receive type-safe, structured data that conforms to our expected format.

Using this `generateObject` function along with our product schema, we'll modify the AI server action to request a JSON output. This modification will allow us to generate structured product information that can be easily parsed and displayed in our application. The JSON format will enable us to handle complex data structures more efficiently, making it easier to present product details in a user-friendly manner, such as in tables or cards.

CHANGES TO SERVER ACTIONS

To refactor our server actions to use these tools, we only need to export the `generateProductList` instead of the `continueConversation` in the list of actions since we will be changing the response format of the messages.

Listing 4.11 Including the `generateProductList` action

```
export const AI = createAI({
  actions: {
    generateProductList,      ◁── Exports the generateProductList action
  },                              here instead of the continueConversation
  initialAIState: [],
  initialUIState: [],
});
```

With this change, we are now exporting the new server action to generate a structured response. We now simply need to update the UI to render the new message format.

> **NOTE** When working with `createAI`, it's important to include all your server actions within the `createAI` instance, rather than importing them directly in your components. The main reason is that `createAI` creates a context that makes these actions easily accessible throughout your component tree, even in deeply nested client-side components, via the `useActions` hook. Additionally, when used with TypeScript, `createAI` provides type checking for your actions, reducing the likelihood of runtime errors.

CHANGES TO THE FRONTEND

Regarding the changes to the frontend, we need to modify two components:

- `ChatList`—This component now renders not only the list of user prompt history but the list of products from the assistance response result. This means that it needs to render the `ProductListSchema` type in a table format. I do not show exactly how this is implemented, but you can review the code of this component in the provided code sources.
- `page.js`—The main chat page component needs to update the form submit handler to use the new `generateProductList` server action instead of the `continueConversation` action.

We now peruse the relevant changes to the page.js component for the handleOnSubmit function together with some error-handling scenarios. The handleOnSubmit function demonstrates how to integrate the new structured data generation capability into the existing chat interface. It maintains the conversation flow while incorporating the new product list format for AI responses. The error handling ensures a graceful user experience even when problems arise during the AI interaction.

Listing 4.12 Updated page.js component form submit handler

```
const handleOnSubmit = async (event) => {
    event.preventDefault();
    const value = input.trim();
    setInput('');
    if (!value) return;
    setIsloading(true);
    setConversation((currentConversation) => [
      ...currentConversation,
      { id: generateId(), role: 'user', content: value },
    ]);

    try {
        const products = await actions.generateProductList(value);    ◄── Calls the generateProductList server action with the user's input
        const message = { role: 'assistant', products };
        setConversation((currentConversation) => [...currentConversation, message]);    ◄── Adds the AI-generated product list to the conversation state
    } catch (error) {
        console.error('Error generating product list:', error);    ◄── Handles any errors that occur during product list generation
        const errorMessage = { role: 'assistant', products: [{ name: 'Error', description: 'An error occurred while generating the product list.', price: 0, category: 'Error' }] };
        setConversation((currentConversation) => [...currentConversation, errorMessage]);
    } finally {
        setIsloading(false);
    }
};
```

These changes lay the groundwork for a more dynamic and data-rich interaction between the user and our LLM. As we move forward to testing these changes, we'll be able to see how this new structured approach enhances the overall user experience of our application.

TESTING THE CHANGES

Now that we've implemented structured data generation in our Astra AI web application, it's time to put our changes to the test and explore the new capabilities we've unlocked.

Rebuild the application and notice the new changes in the UI. You should observe now that our agent responds with a table format to our queries. Figure 4.13 is a screenshot of some of the interactions I've had with it.

Assistant: Here are some products related to your query:

Name	Description	Price	Category
Error	An error occurred while generating the product list.	$0.00	Error

user

cereal bars

Assistant: Here are some products related to your query:

Name	Description	Price	Category
Chocolate Chip Cereal Bar	Delicious cereal bar with chocolate chips for a sweet treat on the go.	$2.99	Snacks
Fruit and Nut Cereal Bar	Healthy cereal bar packed with dried fruits and nuts for a nutritious snack.	$3.49	Healthy Snacks
Oatmeal Raisin Cereal Bar	Classic oatmeal raisin cereal bar, perfect for breakfast or a quick snack.	$2.79	Breakfast
Peanut Butter Cereal Bar	Creamy peanut butter cereal bar for a protein-packed snack option.	$3.99	Protein Bars
Honey Almond Cereal Bar	Crunchy cereal bar with honey and almonds for a satisfying snack.	$2.69	Nutritious Snacks

Enter product category here...

Figure 4.13 Our Astra AI web application can now respond with structured data. We can ask it to generate product categories, which we render in a table format.

Of course, you can improve this functionality to respond to different kinds of structured responses, each with a different representation.

Feel free to continue experimenting with different types of product categories and query structures. The more you interact with the system, the better you'll understand its capabilities and potential applications in real-world scenarios.

With that, we have explored how to generate structured data using AI models and integrate it into our React components. As we move forward, in the last section of this chapter, we look at an even more advanced capability of AI models: tool and function calling. This feature takes AI interactions to the next level, allowing models to not just generate text or structured data but invoke specific functions or use tools as part of their response process. This allows AI models to perform actions, retrieve real-time information, or execute complex operations as part of their reasoning process.

4.4 Tool and function calling with AI models

AI models are effective tools that excel at generating text and media content based on specific prompts or queries. While these models possess vast knowledge, they may sometimes lack access to real-time, specialized, or rapidly changing information.

What if we could ask the AI model to automate parts of the investigation process to call tools that we provide to aid its results? For example, when asking what the weather is like in a particular region, the AI model would use an API that we provide, call this, and then respond with a structured format.

To address this challenge, developers have introduced tool-calling and function-calling capabilities, which significantly enhance AI models by allowing them to interact with external resources. At their core, *tool calling* and *function calling* in AI models refer to the model's ability to recognize when external information or actions are needed, request the execution of specific functions or tools, and incorporate the results into its response. This process allows the AI to obtain real-time or specialized data, perform actions beyond its training scope, and provide more accurate, relevant responses.

The basic idea of tool and function calling in AI models enables interaction with external functions or tools to perform specific tasks or retrieve information. In this section, we build on the basics we've learned so far in the previous sections about generating structured data and streaming content to instruct the AI model to use tools that we provide. This will unlock new important functionalities that we can include in our Astra AI agent.

4.4.1 Understanding tool calling and function calling in AI models

The process of tool and function calling typically follows a specific flow. First, the AI model identifies the need for external information or action based on the user's query or the context of the conversation. It then generates a structured request for a specific tool or function. The system receives this request and executes the requested tool or function, which might involve calling an API, querying a database, or performing a calculation. The result of this operation is then fed back to the AI model, which incorporates this new information into its final response to the user. Figure 4.4 provides a visual insight into how this process works.

In this process, the user's prompt is sent from their device to your application server, which forwards it to an external AI model service. When the AI model recognizes the need for a tool, it sends a structured request back to your server. This is where the

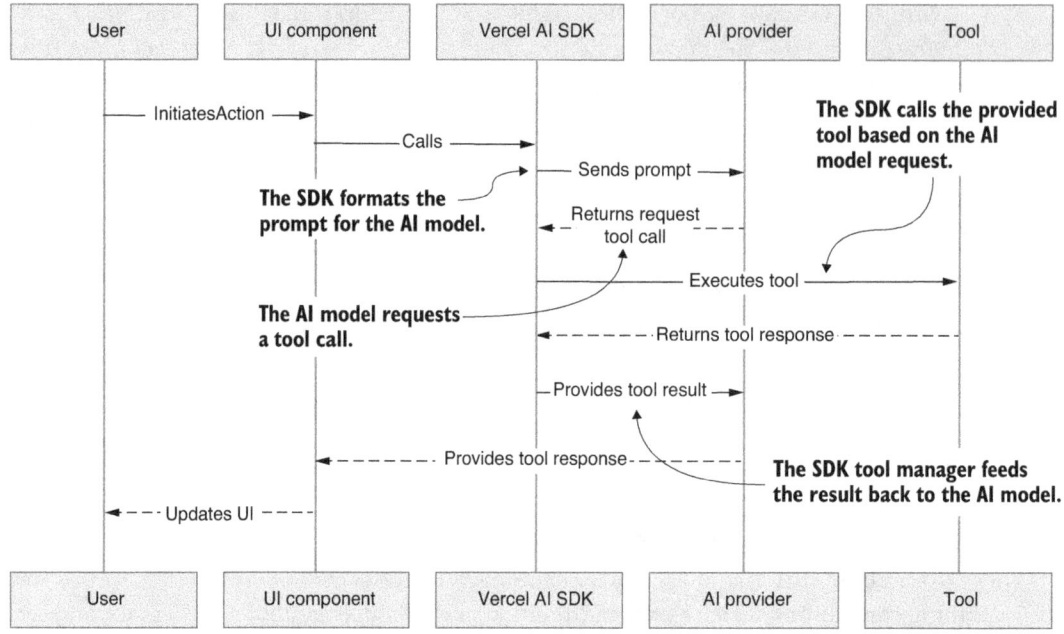

Figure 4.14 The process of tool calling in an AI-powered application using the Vercel AI SDK. This shows how a user action initiates a prompt, which is formatted by the SDK and sent to the AI provider. The AI model may request a tool call, which is then executed by the SDK. The tool's response is fed back to the AI model through the SDK, and finally, the result is used to update the UI for the user.

tool manager, or Vercel AI SDK in our case, comes into play. It interprets the AI's request, executes the appropriate custom tool (which might involve API calls, database queries, or local functions), and collects the result. The SDK then sends this tool result back to the external AI model service. This workflow allows the AI model to use external tools and data while keeping the execution of these tools under our application's control, maintaining a separation between the AI processing and our specific toolset.

Before we continue, I should mention a simpler way to do this. We could also put the response of the external API call directly into the prompt instead of relying on the tool manager. For example, say we make an API call to get the weather data and extract the relevant information from the API response. We can directly inject the response to the prompt and ask the model to provide us with the answer. The following listing shows an example.

Listing 4.13 Getting weather info and displaying it

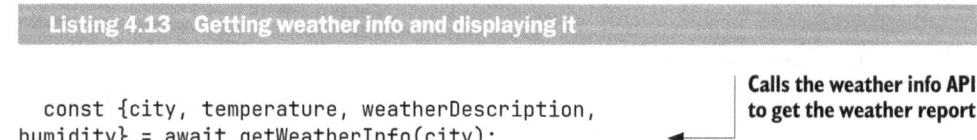

```
  const weatherInfo = `The current temperature in ${city} is
${temperature}°C with ${weatherDescription}. The humidity level is
${humidity}%.`;
  const prompt = `Here is the latest weather update:
${weatherInfo}. How can I help you today?`;
```

Creates the prompt for the AI model by injecting the result of the weather info

Asks the AI model about the weather info

Although a simpler approach, this option is only useful when your application is serving prompts in a specific format. When your application consistently serves prompts in that way, injecting data into these prompts ensures that the format is maintained. It quickly falls apart if you want more flexibility in your responses, though, so you need to be aware of its limitations.

To recap, implementing tools and function calling in AI models offers several significant advantages. It enhances accuracy by providing access to up-to-date information, which is crucial for queries related to current events, real-time data, or rapidly changing fields. It also expands the AI's capabilities, enabling it to perform a wider range of tasks that extend beyond its initial training.

4.4.2 Implementing custom tools and functions with the Vercel AI SDK

The Vercel AI SDK makes it easy to include custom tools and functions. You simply define your custom functions using a Zod schema to specify parameters and then register them with the SDK. Here are the typical steps:

1 *Define your custom tools.* Create functions that represent the tools you want to make available to the AI model. These functions should accept specific parameters and return structured data using the Zod validation library.
2 *Register tools with the SDK.* Use the SDK's tools method to register your custom tools, specifying their names, parameters, and descriptions.
3 *Handle tool response rendering.* Implement logic to render the response of the tool back as React components.

Let's use a simplified example of a weather information tool. I'll explain both the prompt and the tool's parameter.

Here's what we're going to build:

- A weather assistant AI that can provide real-time weather information for specific cities, demonstrating the integration of custom tools with the Vercel AI SDK
- A custom tool that fetches weather data and returns it as a structured React component
- An updated `streamUI` function for rendering of AI responses and tool outputs, including loading states and final weather information displays

In listing 4.13, we first present a proper system message that defines the AI's role as a weather assistant. It instructs the AI to use the `getWeather` function when asked about weather in a specific city. Whether the AI model chooses to call this tool depends on the model's performance and reliability. This call results in a streaming React component based on the fetch state of the weather API.

Listing 4.14 Providing the weather info tool details

```
const supportedModel = getSupportedModel(provider, model);
const result = await streamUI({
  model: supportedModel,
  system: `
    You are a helpful weather assistant.
You can provide weather information for cities.
    If a user asks about the weather in a specific city,
use the 'getWeather' function to fetch the data.
    Always interpret temperatures in Celsius.
  `,
  messages: [
    { role: 'user', content: 'What\'s the weather like in Paris today?' }
  ],
  tools: {
    getWeather: {
      description: 'Get the current weather for a specific city',
      parameters: z.object({
        city: z.string().describe('The name of the city'),
      }),
      generate: async function* ({ city }) {
        yield <LoadingSpinner />

        // Simulating API call
        await sleep(1000)
        const weatherData = await fetchWeatherData(city)

        return <WeatherCard city={city} temperature={weatherData.temperature}
condition={weatherData.condition} />
      }
    }
  }
})
```

The tools object defines custom functions that the AI can call.

getWeather is the name of the tool that the AI will use to fetch weather data.

The description helps the AI understand when and how to use this tool.

parameters uses Zod schema to define and validate the expected input (a city name).

generate is an async generator function that produces the tool's output, including interim loading states.

The `tools` object defines custom functions that the AI can call. In this case, we define a single tool called `getWeather`, which accepts a `description` and `parameters` using the Zod schema. Lastly, the `generate` function is an async generator function that fetches the weather data and returns a `WeatherCard` component with the fetched data.

This tool demonstrates the AI's ability to request and present real-time weather data in a structured format, seamlessly integrating external information into the conversation flow. This also illustrates the versatility of the Vercel AI SDK's interface for AI model interactions. By utilizing this common interface, we can easily swap the `model` parameter to use different AI models while maintaining consistent functionality across the system. This flexibility allows for rapid experimentation and optimization without significant code changes.

To explore this functionality hands-on, I've included the complete example in the source code accompanying this chapter. You can find the project in the ch04/chat-rsc-tool-calls folder. To run the example, follow these steps:

1. Navigate to the root folder of the project repository.
2. Execute the following command:

```
$ npm run dev -w ch04/chat-rsc-tool-calls
```

Open your web browser and visit the local development server address at http://localhost:3000.

Once on the chat page, you can interact with the LLM by asking about the current weather in any city worldwide. The system will render a weather report based on real-time data. Feel free to inquire about the weather in your local city!

You are now equipped with the tools and techniques to utilize the Vercel AI SDK to build interactive generative AI web apps with ease. In the next chapter, we take it to another level by introducing another great tool that integrates well with our framework: *LangChain*.

Summary

- RSCs enable server-side rendering of specific components, improving performance and simplifying data fetching in AI-powered applications.
- The Vercel AI SDK provides helpers like createAI, getMutableAIState, useActions, useUIState, and useAIState for managing AI and UI state in React applications.
- Separating AI state and UI state allows for more efficient handling of data, improved performance, and better synchronization between server and client.
- Structured data generation techniques like prompt engineering, function calling, and Zod schema validation enable AI models to produce organized, type-safe data instead of raw text.
- The generateObject and streamObject functions in the Vercel AI SDK facilitate the creation of type-safe, structured data from AI responses, enhancing reliability and usability.
- Tool-calling and function-calling capabilities allow AI models to interact with external resources, expanding their abilities beyond their initial training data.
- Implementing custom tools with the Vercel AI SDK involves defining functions, registering them with the SDK, and handling their responses as React components.
- The Vercel AI SDK's common interface for AI model interactions enables easy swapping of different AI models while maintaining consistent functionality across the system.

Part 2

Advanced generative AI techniques and deployment

With the basics of building full-stack generative AI web applications with Next.js and the Vercel AI SDK under your belt, it's time to go a step further. In this part, we'll dive deep into advanced techniques and the critical steps needed to take your applications from concept to production. You've already laid the foundation; now, let's make something truly remarkable and get it ready for the real world.

We'll begin with the principles of prompt engineering, showing you how to craft effective prompts to get the exact outputs you need from large language models. Next, you'll be introduced to LangChain.js, a powerful framework that simplifies building complex, context-aware AI applications, with a focus on advanced use cases. Building is only half the battle, so we'll then cover the crucial stages of testing and debugging your applications to ensure they perform as expected. To wrap it up, I'll guide you through the essential steps for securely deploying your applications, making them accessible and reliable for your users.

Prompt engineering in web applications

This chapter covers

- Prompt engineering to optimize AI model outputs in web applications
- Using few-shot learning to enable quick adaptation of AI models to new tasks
- Using chain-of-thought prompting to improve AI reasoning and problem solving
- Using embeddings for semantic search and content recommendations

Our web application aims to provide engaging AI-powered interactions for users. So far, we've focused on the technical foundations, using cutting-edge tools like Next.js, React, and the Vercel AI SDK to seamlessly integrate various AI models. While this has helped improve the overall user experience, we've relied on the same generic prompt message, instructing the AI to be polite and respond to queries. To offer a truly unique solution, we need to go beyond this one-size-fits-all approach. This is called *prompt engineering,* or the art of carefully crafting and refining the prompts and contextual information submitted to the AI model. By fine-tuning the prompts in this chapter, we can enable the AI to perform more efficiently and deliver more accurate, contextual responses that truly meet the needs of our users. We will review important concepts of prompt engineering, experimenting with different prompts and contextual cues to unlock the full potential of the AI models powering our web application.

Effective prompt engineering is essential for optimizing the outputs of AI models in web applications. As generative AI continues to evolve, the ability to effectively communicate with these models through well-crafted prompts becomes crucial for developers and content creators.

Prompt engineering consists of both heuristic and well-defined sets of guidelines to instruct an AI model to fine-tune its output content. By refining the way prompts are constructed, developers can enhance the performance of AI models, leading to improved user experiences in applications.

In this chapter, we explore three prompt engineering strategies, providing insights into how each can be effectively applied to optimize AI model outputs in web applications:

- *Few-shot learning*—This technique allows large language models (LLMs) like GPT and Claude, as well as other AIs, to adapt quickly to new tasks by providing them with a few examples of the desired output. It is particularly beneficial in scenarios where training data is limited or where rapid deployment is necessary, such as customer support chatbots or code generation tools.
- *Chain-of-thought prompting*—This method encourages AI models to engage in a step-by-step reasoning process, thereby helping them deliver more accurate results. By breaking down complex tasks into manageable steps, developers can use AI to tackle a wide range of use cases like code debugging or mathematical problem solving.
- *Embeddings for semantic search and content recommendations*—By representing data in a way that captures its meaning, embeddings allow for more context-aware interactions, leading to more relevant search results and personalized user experiences, like in e-commerce product recommendations or streaming services.

Figure 5.1 provides a quick overview of the concepts that will be explained in this chapter together with some examples.

Of course, the prompt engineering techniques mentioned represent just the initial foundations. As generative AI continues to advance, these techniques will certainly evolve by expanding their scope and potential applications.

In this book, we will take a deep dive into the architectural considerations and practical implementation details of managing prompts. This includes exploring strategies for prompt versioning, testing, and optimization, as well as techniques for integrating prompt engineering into the overall system design.

To follow this chapter effectively, you should be familiar with React, Next.js, and the Vercel AI SDK from previous chapters. A basic understanding of AI model interactions and state management will help you experiment with different prompt

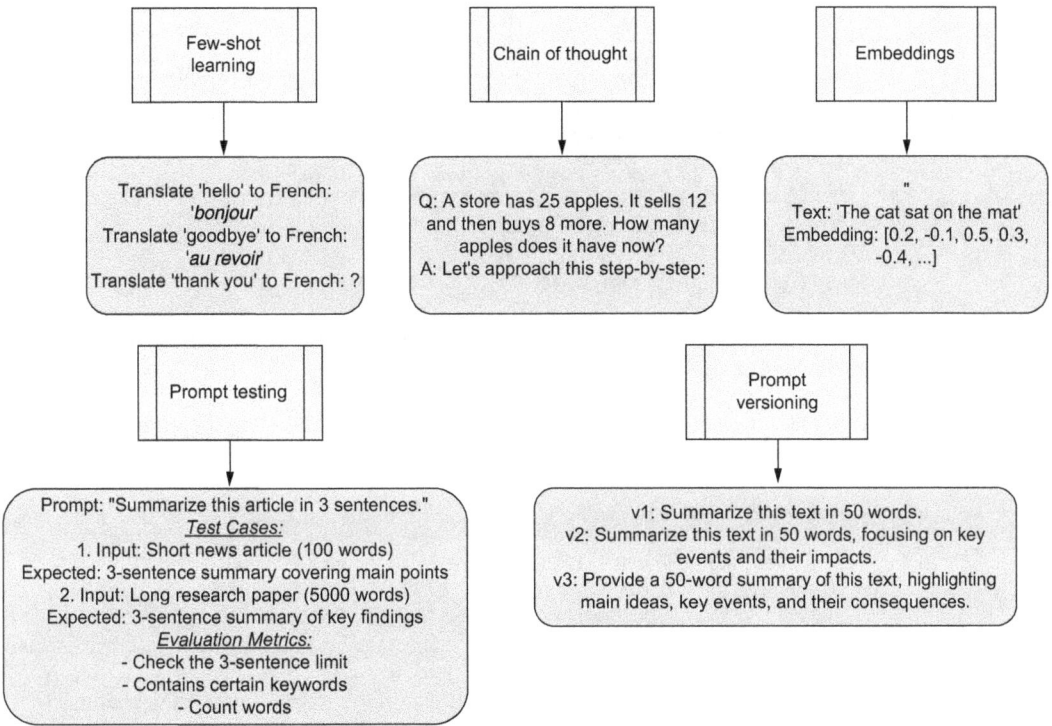

Figure 5.1 What's covered in this chapter

strategies. This chapter assumes you are ready to tackle more advanced AI design techniques, including prompt versioning and testing within a production web application.

5.1 Introducing prompt engineering

"Prompting" and "prompt engineering" are buzzwords that came alive with the explosion of generative AI. The ability to effectively "engineer" prompts has become a sought-after skill, often highlighted in job descriptions related to this field. This book will help you understand how to design and refine prompts to optimize AI model performance.

In this section, we will explore the essence of prompts, the various types available, and the strategies for managing and optimizing them to achieve great performance in AI-driven web applications.

> **Running the chapter examples**
>
> To run the examples provided in this chapter, follow these steps:
>
> 1 Navigate to the chapter directory in your terminal:
>
> ```
> cd ch05
> ```

(continued)

2. Create an .env file in the project root directory and add your Google API key:

   ```
   GEMINI_API_KEY=your_actual_gemini_api_key_here
   ```

3. Execute the desired script using Node.js. For example, to run the embeddings example, use the following command:

   ```
   $ node embeddings.google.js
   ```

   You can run each script individually to explore different functionalities and implementations discussed in this chapter.

   This will print a series of numbers in the console representing the embedding of a text:

   ```
   $ node embeddings.js
   [
     -0.020836005, -0.016921125, -0.004506664,  -0.05085442,  -0.02597347,
      0.029602215,  0.029992402,   0.029107977,  0.010593587, -0.024360698,
     -0.009377503,  0.0066461912, -0.026077522,  0.034726676, -0.016582962,
   ...
   ```

4. If you are using Open AI, there is another file in the same folder named embeddings.openai.js. Create an .env file in the project root directory and add your Google API key:

   ```
   OPENAI_API_KEY =your_actual_openai_api_key_here
   ```

5. Then run the desired script using Node.js. For example, to run the embeddings example, use the following command:

   ```
   $ node embeddings.openai.js
   ```

5.1.1 What exactly are prompts?

At the heart of LLM interaction lies a key concept: *prompts*. These are basically structured communication patterns designed to derive specific responses from AI models. Prompts follow a carefully structured format and are designed to guide the LLM's processing and output generation.

Phrasing a question and submitting it to the AI model involves a key step called *tokenization*. This process is vital, as it transforms our natural language instructions into a format that LLMs can consume efficiently.

Whether it is text, images, or other media, tokenization converts them into sequences of tokens, and vice versa. The process is similar to how computers process high-level programming languages: just as these languages must be compiled into machine code (binary format), our prompts must be tokenized for LLM consumption.

An important practical aspect related to tokens is billing. Many LLM services charge users based on the number of tokens processed, which includes both the tokens in your input prompt and the tokens generated in the model's output. It's important to consider this for both managing and optimizing the cost of interacting with these models.

To better understand the concepts of tokenization, let's visualize the process using a simple prompt as our example. Figure 5.2 illustrates the journey of our prompt through various stages of tokenization and processing, together with an example prompt.

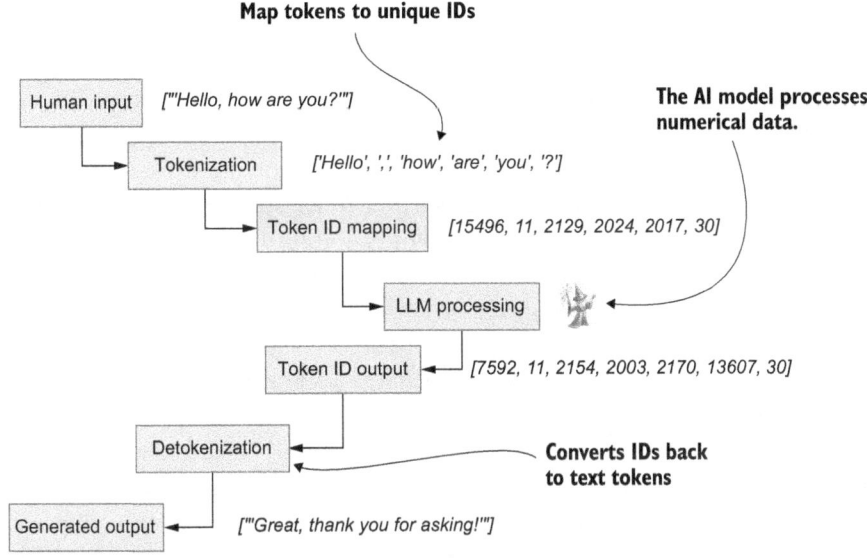

Figure 5.2 The end-to-end process of how human input is transformed, processed by an LLM and converted back into human-readable output

The code on which LLMs operate is a numerical representation in the form of floating-point numbers. They receive numbers as input and produce numbers as output, which are then translated back into human-readable formats like text or images. This numerical intermediary is the key to the LLM's ability to process and generate human-like responses.

The pipeline consists of seven key stages:

1 *Human input*—The raw text provided by the user via an input prompt.
2 *Tokenization*—The process of splitting the input text into tokens and converting them to numerical IDs. These numerical IDs come from a predefined vocabulary or tokenizer model associated with the LLM.
3 *Token IDs*—The numerical representation of the input, ready for LLM processing.
4 *LLM processing*—The core stage where the AI model analyzes the input and generates a response.

5 *Output token IDs*—The LLM's response in numerical format.
6 *Detokenization*—The conversion of numerical IDs back into text tokens.
7 *Human-readable output*—The final stage where tokens are combined into coherent text for the user.

While tokenization is important, we also need to carefully consider the limitations imposed by various LLM providers regarding the size of the prompts and how we control sections within prompts.

In the following section, we take a closer look at two equally important fundamentals in prompt engineering and LLM interaction: max tokens and control tokens.

MAX TOKENS

In your interactions with popular LLMs, you may have encountered the concept of max tokens, which refers to the maximum number of tokens an LLM can process in a single interaction, including both the input (prompt) and the output (generated text). The user input is tokenized into smaller units, such as words or subwords, and each token counts toward the total limit. For example, if an LLM has a maximum context window of 8,192 tokens and your input consists of 200 tokens, only 7,992 tokens remain for the output. Therefore, it's crucial to consider the length of your input to ensure there are enough tokens left for meaningful responses from the model. Balancing input length and output expectations helps optimize interactions with LLMs and enhances overall performance.

For example, GPT-3 models typically have a limit of 4,096 tokens, while GPT-4 can handle up to 8,192 or even 32,768 tokens in some versions. This limit is an important constraint in LLM design and usage; if you exceed this limit, your requests will be rejected. Additionally, enterprise subscription models (e.g., Azure OpenAI) may offer larger context windows or vary by region, allowing for more extensive interactions in specific use cases.

The Gemini models support larger context windows. For example, Gemini 3 Pro and Gemini 3 Flash can handle up to 1,048,576 tokens in input, with an expanded output capacity of 65,536 tokens. This far exceeds the token limits of typical GPT models. Other Gemini variants, such as Gemini 2.5 Flash-Lite and Gemini 2.5 Pro, also support a full 1,048,576-token input limit.

From a billing perspective, most LLM services charge users based on the *total number of tokens processed*—including both input tokens and output tokens. Therefore, longer context windows and larger token limits can lead to higher costs if fully utilized.

But how can we measure how many tokens we use? Quite often, we need a way to count the input tokens to make sure the response doesn't stop midway. While the concept of tokens is universal across LLMs, the specific tokenization algorithms can vary between AI providers. This means that the exact token count for a given piece of text might differ slightly depending on the model and provider you're using.

We can measure our tokens with the help of some open source libraries that calculate the tokens of a prompt together with any system messages we provide as context.

System messages are a specialized type of input that provides instructions, defines the AI's persona, or sets boundaries for its responses within the conversation. For instance, a system message might be "Act as a helpful and encouraging mentor." System messages provide persistent context for the AI's evaluation, whereas the main prompt is the user's direct query for a specific task.

One such library is *tiktoken*, originally developed for OpenAI's models but also useful for other providers with similar tokenization schemes. Let's explore how to use js-tiktoken, the JavaScript port of tiktoken, to calculate tokens for a given prompt in the following listing.

Listing 5.1 Function that counts prompt tokens

```
import { encoding_for_model } from '@dqbd/tiktoken';

function countTokens(text, model = "gpt-3.5-turbo") {
  const enc = encoding_for_model(model);
  const tokens = enc.encode(text);
  enc.free();
  return tokens.length;
}
const prompt =
  "Translate the following English text to French: 'Hello, how are you?'";
const systemMessage
  "You are a helpful assistant that translates English to French.";

const promptTokens = countTokens(prompt);
const systemTokens = countTokens(systemMessage);
const totalTokens = promptTokens + systemTokens;

console.log(`Prompt tokens: ${promptTokens}`);
console.log(`System message tokens: ${systemTokens}`);
console.log(`Total tokens: ${totalTokens}`);
```

- *Imports the encoding_for_model function from the tiktoken library. This function provides the appropriate tokenizer for different GPT models.*
- *Encodes the input text into tokens. This step converts the text into a sequence of token IDs that the model understands.*
- *Counts tokens for the main prompt. This helps ensure the prompt fits within token limits and aids in cost estimation.*
- *Counts tokens for the system message. System messages also contribute to the total token count and should be considered in prompt engineering.*

In a web application like the one we are building, you can use the countTokens function to check if a message exceeds the token limit before sending it to the AI model. By keeping a current tally of available tokens, we can add an indicator next to the input text that shows the user how many tokens they've used as they type. Consider implementing this feature on your own as an extra exercise.

In Google's Gemini, which doesn't provide a standalone tokenizer like OpenAI's tiktoken, you can't count tokens locally yet. Instead, use the Google API itself, which returns token usage info as part of its response. This means you send your prompt to the API and check the token count from the result.

I've included an example in `counting-tokens.google.mjs` that demonstrates this approach. To run it, follow these steps:

1   Install the dependencies:

    ```
    npm install
    ```

2   Set environment variables, and run the script:

    ```
    export GOOGLE_CLOUD_PROJECT="your-project-id"
    export GOOGLE_CLOUD_LOCATION="your-location"
    node counting-tokens.google.mjs
    ```

CONTROL TOKENS

Control tokens (or special tokens) are basically ways to control and guide the behavior, format, or content of the LLM's output from within prompts. In simple terms, we use special marks or keywords to define prompt regions that the LLM needs to apply certain rules and instructions.

There are various types of control tokens depending on the LLM we use. A few example types from the OpenAI GPT-4 model are

- *End-of-text token* (`<|endoftext|>` *or* `(|endoftext|)`)—Marks the end of a sequence of text
- *Beginning-of-sequence token* (`<|startoftext|>` *or* `(|startoftext|)`)—Marks the beginning of a sequence of text
- `<|padding|>`—Used for padding sequences to a fixed length when necessary

The exact tokens can vary depending on the model architecture, the version, and the specific implementation or fine-tuning of the model. For example, the following is the raw user prompt that includes various special tokens commonly associated with OpenAI's GPT-4 in a chat-like environment:

```
<|startoftext|>
<|user|> What is the capital of France?
<|assistant|> The capital of France is Paris.
<|endoftext|>
```

> **NOTE** Control tokens are handled internally by the API. When interacting with the OpenAI API, you don't need to worry about explicitly using special tokens like `<|startoftext|>`, `<|endoftext|>`, or role indicators such as `<|user|>` and `<|assistant|>`. These tokens are managed internally by the model to organize and process the conversation, ensuring seamless interaction. The API abstracts away these details, allowing you to send and receive plain-text messages without needing to manually handle these tokens. While you don't need to manually use control tokens when working with the OpenAI API, it's helpful to understand their purpose—especially when debugging, inspecting raw prompt logs, or fine-tuning models where you may encounter them explicitly.

5.1.2 Prompt types

In the context of the Vercel AI SDK, there are several types of prompts that can be used to interact with AI models. These prompt types—basic text prompts, message prompts, and system prompts—are designed to handle different scenarios and use cases. Additionally, a message prompt can be divided into several types: simple, compound (consisting of additional metadata or attachments), and tool call messages. Figure 5.3 illustrates this hierarchy of prompt types in the context of the Vercel AI SDK.

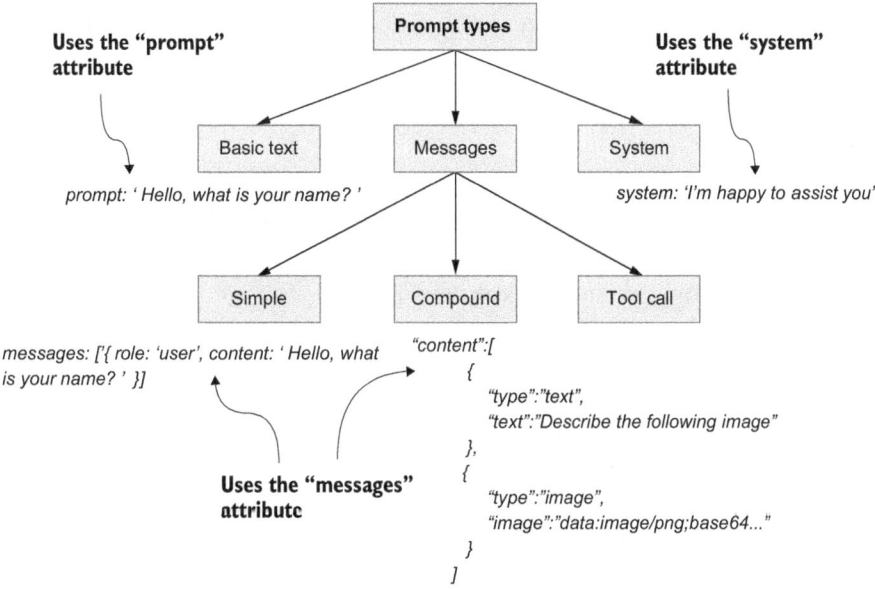

Figure 5.3 The classification of prompt types used in the Vercel AI SDK

BASIC TEXT PROMPTS

Basic text prompts are simple strings that contain instructions or questions for the AI model. They are straightforward and used for single-turn interactions using, for example, the generateText function:

```
generateText({
    prompt: 'Hello, what is your name?',
    model: model("models/gemini-2.0-flash")
});
```

This is essentially the same as using the messages field with a single message inside:

```
generateText({
    messages: [{
        role: 'user',
        content: 'Hello, what is your name?'
    }],
    model: model("models/gemini-2.0-flash")
});
```

The only reason to use this format is when you want a single interaction, since you cannot pass any history of messages like FAQs or one-off queries. Most of the time, you want to use the message prompt type since it is more flexible.

MESSAGES PROMPTS

Messages prompts are more complex and versatile and are typically used in multiturn conversations or when more context is needed. Examples may include language learning agents, retrieval-augmented generation applications, or technical support agents. They can be further categorized into

- *Simple messages*—These are basic messages with a role (e.g., user, assistant) and content.

- *Compound messages*—Compound messages include additional metadata or attachments, such as images or documents. We saw an example in chapter 4 when we were attaching an image to the prompt:

```
system: ({
    "messages":[
        {
            "role":"user ",
            "content":[
                {
                    "type":"text",
                    "text":"Describe the following image"
                },
                {
                    "type":"image",
                    "image":"data:image/png;base64..."
                }
            ]
        }
    ],
    "model": model("models/gemini-2.0-flash")
});
```

- *Tool call messages*—Tool call messages are used to instruct the AI to perform specific functions or API calls. This is basically a compound message using the type `'tool-call'` and passing additional information about the call parameters. Example use cases include automated booking systems, e-commerce, or automation agents:

```
            "content":[
                {
                    "type": "tool-call",
                    "tool": "getWeatherReport",
                    args: { city: 'Dublin' },
                }]
```

SYSTEM PROMPTS

System messages set the context or behavior for the entire conversation. They're typically used at the beginning of a chat session. You need to use the special `system` property that is available. Other reasons to use system messages may also include compliance, messaging, and creating personas:

```
generateText({
    prompt: 'Hello, how are you?',
    model: model("models/gemini-2.0-flash"),
    system: "I'm happy to assist you in any way I can.
How can I be of service today?"
});
```

Generally, when using the Vercel AI SDK, it's important to maintain a consistent approach to prompt types to create complex, interactive AI experiences. The SDK automatically transforms messages into a format wrapped with the appropriate control tokens, allowing developers to focus on crafting effective prompts and managing conversation flow.

5.1.3 Organizing your prompts: Versioning, testing, and optimization

We now explore strategies for prompt versioning, testing, and optimization, providing practical examples to illustrate each approach.

PROMPT MANAGEMENT

Prompt management is important when you want to programmatically handle prompts or store them in a database outside your version control system. This is mainly done for the following reasons:

- *Dynamic updates*—Storing prompts in a database allows you to update them without redeploying your application. This is crucial for fine-tuning prompts based on user feedback or performance metrics.
- *Version control*—A database can easily store multiple versions of the same prompt, allowing you to A/B test different prompt variations or roll back to previous versions if needed.
- *Scalability*—As your application grows, you might need to manage hundreds or thousands of prompts. A database provides better scalability and querying capabilities than storing prompts in code.
- *Access control*—With a database, you can implement role-based access control, allowing different team members (e.g., prompt engineers, data scientists) to modify prompts without touching the application code.

While the Vercel AI SDK doesn't provide a built-in prompt management system, we can design one that integrates well with any existing application structure.

Figure 5.4 depicts an example architecture of a prompt management system for a generative AI web app that generates different PlantUML diagrams from prompts.

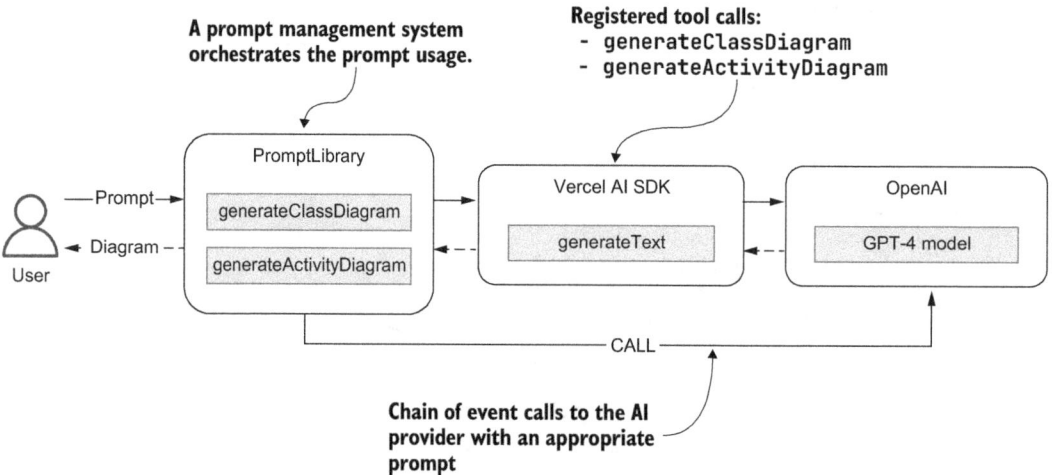

Figure 5.4 Architecture of the PlantUML diagram-generation system using tool calls in the Vercel AI SDK. The system allows users to request diagrams, and the PromptLibrary class handles the generation process by creating prompts, determining the diagram type, and interacting with the Vercel AI SDK to generate the diagram using the AI (OpenAI GPT-4 or other) model and tool calls.

The basic idea is that the system allows users to request diagrams, and the PromptLibrary class handles the generation process. It creates and retrieves prompts, determines the type of diagram requested (class or activity), and calls the appropriate generation method. The generatePlantUML() method then interacts with the Vercel AI SDK's generateText() function, which sends the prompt to the AI model along with tool calls for generating the specific type of diagram. The AI model processes the request and returns the generated text back through the generateText() function, which then returns the generated diagram to the PromptLibrary for display to the user.

While not exactly shown in the figure, we can enroll a database for efficiently handling the prompts used in the diagram-generation process. By storing prompts in a dedicated database, the system can dynamically update prompts based on user feedback or performance metrics without the need for redeploying the application. This flexibility allows for continuous improvement of the prompts.

Additionally, registering the generateClassDiagram function (which uses a prompt specifically designed for generating class diagrams) and the generateActivityDiagram function (which uses a prompt tailored for generating activity diagrams) as tool call functions, we can chain multiple AI calls together. This allows us to combine the results of these individual calls to achieve more complex outcomes.

In the next chapter, we'll explore a library called LangChain, which is designed to simplify the process of chaining AI calls and makes it more powerful. For now, it's important that you understand just the basic concepts and building blocks of prompt management.

PROMPT VERSIONING

In terms of keeping track of prompts as you modify them during the development of the application you are building, you should consider a few things. First, depending on the AI model changes, you will need to keep track of the different versions of prompts to track changes, improvements, and the effects of those changes on the output generated.

Say, for example, you are developing a generative AI web app for content creation for a health blog. You start with a basic prompt:

Version 1: "Write a blog post about the benefits of working out."

As you gather user feedback and analyze the output, you might notice that the posts lack depth. You decide to refine the prompt:

Version 2: "Write a detailed blog post about the benefits of working out, including scientific studies, personal anecdotes, and practical tips."

Those are clearly different versions, so how do you keep track of their effectiveness on the specific AI provider? Here are some practical options:

- *Using a version control system*—Use Git or another version control system to track changes in your prompt files. This would work sufficiently for tracking the difference in wording but not so much when comparing the overall performance of their difference.
- *Using semantic versioning*—A slightly better way is to apply semantic versioning to your prompts, especially for critical ones. This includes crafting a naming scheme that you can use to store the prompts based on their current version or the model that they should apply. Here is an example:

```
// prompts/translation_openai_v1.0.1.ts
export const translationPrompt_openai_v1_0_1 =
"Translate the following text from {source_lang}
to {target_lang}: {text}";
// prompts/translation_openai_v1.1.0.ts
export const translationPrompt_openai_v1_1_0 =
"You are a professional translator. Translate the
following text from {source_lang} to {target_lang},
maintaining the original tone and style: {text}";

// prompts/translation_anthropic_v1.0.0.ts
```

```
export const translationPrompt_anthropic_v1_0_0 =
"As an AI language model, please translate the given
 text from {source_lang} to {target_lang}.
 Ensure that the translation is accurate
 and natural-sounding. Text to translate: {text}";
```

In these examples, we use a simple naming scheme. First, we define the prompt category, which, in this case, is a translation type. Then the filename includes the AI model provider (e.g., OpenAI, Anthropic, Cohere) and the version number. Finally, we use a semantic versioning system, which consists of three components: MAJOR, MINOR, and PATCH, represented in the format MAJOR.MINOR.PATCH:

- *MAJOR version (X)*—This can be used when major updates often involve significant changes to the underlying AI model or the prompt structure that could lead to different interpretations of the prompt.
- *MINOR version (Y)*—This is incremented when minor updates may include enhancements to the prompt that improve its effectiveness without breaking existing functionality.
- *PATCH version (Z)*—This is incremented for patch updates that typically address specific issues identified in the prompt's performance, such as correcting typos, clarifying instructions, or refining output formatting.

In our example, v1.0.1 denotes the first MAJOR version and the first PATCH version of the prompt. This approach allows you to easily track which version of a prompt is optimized for which AI provider, together with any versions that may produce totally different outcomes.

EVALUATING PROMPT EFFECTIVENESS: STRATEGIES FOR TESTING AND EVALUATION

Unit-testing prompts is a challenging aspect of developing AI-powered web applications. The goal is to ensure that changes to prompts don't unexpectedly alter the behavior of the system.

The main issue when dealing with unit-testing prompts is not the way that we write tests but more how we evaluate them in a quick and deterministic manner. Unit tests should test one "unit" or a specific aspect of a system, so there is an issue with how to test something that uses an LLM model to work and that generates a probabilistic result, such as text generation.

This challenge arises from several factors inherent to LLMs:

- *Nondeterministic outputs*—LLMs can produce different outputs for the same input due to their probabilistic nature.
- *Contextual understanding*—LLMs interpret prompts based on their training, which may not always align with human expectations.
- *Variations in output*—LLMs can generate creative and varied responses, making it difficult to define "correct" outputs.

- *Computational cost*—Running full LLM inference for each test can be time consuming and expensive.

To address some of these challenges, we can employ mocking, semantic similarity scoring, and constraint validation.

For writing test cases, we use the Jest framework due to its simplicity and ecosystem. The test cases focus on validating AI-generated text through two approaches: semantic similarity and constraint checking. The first measures how closely the generated response matches an expected output using cosine similarity, ensuring the meaning remains consistent. The second test verifies that the output respects specified constraints, such as word count limits and the inclusion of certain keywords.

MOCKING LLM RESPONSES

Instead of calling the actual LLM for every test, we can mock the responses. The following listing shows an example of mocking the `generateText` function from the `ai` package.

Listing 5.2 Mock testing the prompt

```
import { vi, expect, test } from "vitest";
vi.mock("ai", () => ({
  generateText: vi.fn(),
}));

import { generateText } from "ai";
import { continueConversation } from "./actions";
test('summary generation contains key points', async () => {
  generateText.mockResolvedValue(
"A concise summary of the input text.");

  const result = await continueConversation([
    { role: "user", content: "Long input text..." },
  ]);

  expect(result).toContain("concise summary");
});
```

Annotations:
- vitest mocks the entire ai module, replacing the generateText export with mock functions.
- Imports the actual function we want to test from our application code
- Creates a typed mock function for generateText, allowing TypeScript to provide type checking and autocompletion
- Calls the actual function we're testing, which internally uses the mocked generateText

Running the example code inside the ch05 folder

To run the tests locally, first install the dependencies within the ch05 folder:

`npm install`

Then run all tests once:

`npx vitest run`

Mocking the AI responses allows for faster and more controlled testing by avoiding the overhead of calling the actual LLM. However, it's important to note that this method may not reveal issues related to the real-world behavior of the AI model but rather tests any issues with the logic around it.

SEMANTIC SIMILARITY SCORING

Here the main idea is that instead of exact matching, we use semantic similarity measures to compare outputs to expected results.

Listing 5.3 Testing semantic similarity scoring

```
import { generateText } from "ai";
import stringComparison from 'string-comparison'

function semanticSimilarity(text1, text2) {
  let cos = stringComparison.cosine
  return cos.similarity(text1, text2);
}

test("generated text is semantically similar to expected output", async () => {
  generateText.mockResolvedValue(
    "AI greatly influences modern life in many ways."
  );

  const expected = "AI has a significant impact on modern society.";
  const generated = await generateText(
    "Describe the role of AI in today's world."
  );

  const similarity = semanticSimilarity(expected, generated);
  expect(similarity).toBeGreaterThan(0.7);
});
```

- Imports necessary functions: generateText for AI text generation and string comparison for comparing text similarity
- Defines an expected output to compare against the AI-generated text
- Calculates the semantic similarity between the expected and generated texts
- Asserts that the similarity score is above a threshold (0.7), indicating high semantic similarity

The generated text is then compared to the expected output using the `cosine.simularity` function, which calculates the cosine similarity between them. Finally, the test asserts that the similarity score is above a threshold of 0.7, indicating that the AI-generated text is semantically close to the expected result. Of course, this threshold can be adjusted based on your test criteria.

This approach, although not always bulletproof, allows for more flexible and meaningful testing of AI-generated content, as it evaluates the quality of the output based on semantic understanding rather than exact word matching. This is particularly useful in scenarios where the exact wording may vary but the underlying meaning must remain consistent.

CONSTRAINED VALIDATION

In this kind of testing, we mainly focus on testing that the response from the LLM adheres to any limitations or rules we provided in the prompt. See the following listing, for an example.

Listing 5.4 Testing constraints

```
function validateConstraints(text, minWords, maxWords, requiredWords) {
  const words = text.split(/\s+/);
  return (
    words.length >= minWords &&
    words.length <= maxWords &&
    requiredWords.every((word) =>
      text.toLowerCase().includes(word.toLowerCase())
    )
  );
}
test("generated text meets constraints", async () => {
generateText.mockResolvedValue({
  text: "Regular exercise significantly improves
health and fitness by boosting energy, enhancing mood,
and reducing the risk of many chronic diseases."
});

  const { text } = await generateText({
    model: "fakeModel",
    prompt:
      "Summarize the benefits of exercise in 20-30 words.
Include 'health' and 'fitness'.",
  });

  console.log("Word count:", text.split(/\s+/).length);
  expect(validateConstraints(text, 20, 30, ["health", "fitness"])).
toBe(true);
});
```

- Checks if the generated text meets specific word count requirements and includes required words
- The prompt is used to instruct the AI model on the expected output, including constraints on word count and the necessity of specific keywords.
- Verifies whether the generated text adheres to the defined constraints, ensuring that the test case validates the functionality correctly

In the example, the validateConstraints function is defined to check whether the generated text meets specific conditions: it must contain a certain number of words (minWords and maxWords) and include certain required words (requiredWords). The validateConstraints function splits the text into words and then verifies that the word count falls within the specified range and that all required words are present in the text, regardless of case.

Constrained validation is useful when ensuring that AI outputs follow specific rules (provided in the prompt), making it ideal for scenarios where the generated content must adhere to strict guidelines, such as summaries, reports, or any content requiring specific terminology or structure. However, as you need to preconfigure those rules beforehand, it quickly becomes unwieldy and hard to keep track of unless you create a system that configures the test criteria on the fly.

The preceding list of strategies is not exhaustive, but they can help you catch potential issues early and also ensure that the AI outputs meet specific criteria and deliver consistent, high-quality results.

5.2 Few-shot learning

Having explored the various types of prompts and techniques for testing them, we can now focus on practical prompt engineering techniques that you can implement without the need for fine-tuning or configuring the LLM models you interface with. These methods will allow you to optimize AI outputs efficiently and effectively, enhancing the performance of your generative AI applications.

We start with few-shot learning: this is a simple yet powerful technique in prompt engineering that allows AI models to generalize and adapt to new tasks with just a few examples, rather than requiring extensive training on large datasets.

Imagine trying to teach someone how to cook a specific recipe. Instead of providing them with a full cookbook or a lengthy set of instructions, you simply give them a few examples of how similar dishes are prepared. For instance, if you want them to make a pasta dish, you might show them how to cook spaghetti carbonara and arrabbiata. Depending on the relevance of these examples, they can infer the techniques, ingredients, and general approach needed to create the dish you want.

> **Zero-shot vs. few-shot vs. fine-tuning**
>
> In addition to few-shot learning, there are several other learning techniques used in generative AI, including zero-shot learning and fine-tuning. Each of these methods has its own unique approach and use cases, which can significantly affect the performance of AI models. The following is a brief overview of these techniques and how they differ from few-shot learning:
>
> - *Zero-shot learning* is a technique where the model is tasked with performing a task without seeing specific examples related to that task beforehand. Instead, it relies on its preexisting knowledge and understanding of language to generate responses.
> - *Fine-tuning,* on the other hand, involves taking a pretrained model and further training it on a specific dataset to improve its performance on a particular task or domain. This process adjusts the model's parameters based on the new data. If the operation is successful, it often results in a more accurate model at the cost of being more resource intensive and requiring significant computational power and time.

Before I explain how to implement few-shot learning, let's visualize the general steps involved for crafting prompts using few-shot learning as an example. Based on figure 5.5, we can identify the following steps:

1. *User interaction*—We provide a few examples that demonstrate the desired output format or content.
2. *Provide examples*—We input examples that the model can reference. For instance, we might provide examples of summaries related to AI. This process would be the most crucial, since it will determine the outcome.

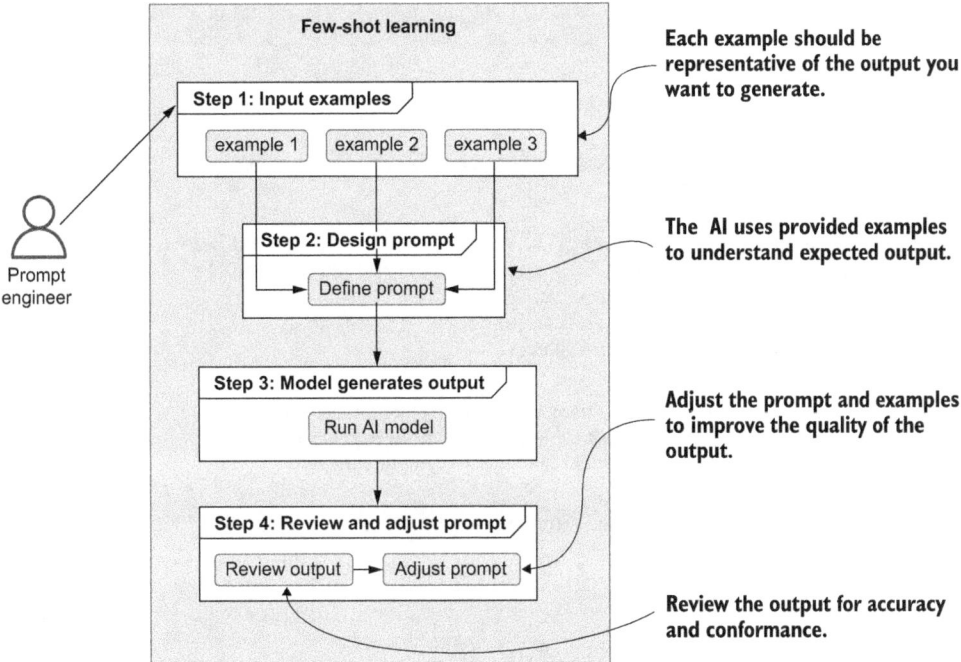

Figure 5.5 The step-by-step procedure for few-shot learning, where users provide a few examples to guide the AI model. The process involves compiling these examples into a prompt, generating output using the AI model, and then reviewing and adjusting the output as needed to achieve the desired results.

3 *Design prompt*—We craft a prompt that incorporates the provided examples, setting clear expectations for the model.
4 *Model generates output*—The LLM processes the prompt and generates an output based on the examples provided.
5 *Review output*—The generated output is then reviewed. In this case, the output might be a summary generated by the AI, such as "AI significantly affects modern society." However, in that case, our aim is to validate how the prompt is reliable and accurate enough to be used for subsequent queries.

The most important step when using this technique is the second one, where we provide examples. These examples should serve as a guide, helping the model to understand what is expected in terms of content, style, and structure. The key advantage of this technique is that it reduces ambiguity in the prompt, allowing the model to produce outputs that are more aligned with the user's intentions.

5.2.1 Examples of few-shot learning

In this example, we will generate a list of programming languages based on a few provided examples. The prompt is a simple and straightforward one with three representative examples.

Listing 5.5 Few-shot learning prompt

```
const prompt = `
  List some popular programming languages along with
a brief description of each:

  1. JavaScript: A versatile language primarily used for web development.
  2. Python: Known for its readability and used in data
science and web development.
  3. Java: A widely-used language for building
enterprise-level applications.

  4.`;
```

- This part of the prompt sets the context for the task, asking the AI to list popular programming languages with descriptions.
- The first three items provide examples of programming languages and their descriptions, guiding the model on the expected format.
- The prompt ends with an incomplete list item (4.), which may prompt the AI to generate additional examples to complete the list.

To execute this example, run the script using Node.js with the following command when within the ch05 folder while making sure you have your Google API key provided in an .env file beforehand:

```
$ node few-shot-learning.google.js
```

This will print some programming language details similar to figure 5.6.

```
% node few-shot-learning.google.js                                          (main)
Generated Programming Languages: Here are some more popular programming languages:

4.  **C#**: A modern, object-oriented language developed by Microsoft, widely used for Window
s desktop applications, web development (ASP.NET), and game development (Unity).
5.  **C++**: A powerful, high-performance language used for systems programming, game develop
ment, embedded systems, and applications requiring direct hardware access.
6.  **PHP**: A server-side scripting language primarily used for web development, powering a
large percentage of websites and web applications.
7.  **Swift**: Apple's modern, powerful, and intuitive programming language for building apps
 across all Apple platforms (iOS, macOS, watchOS, tvOS).
8.  **Go**:
Chatbot Responses: I'm sorry to hear you're having trouble with your Wi-Fi disconnecting. Tha
t can be really frustrating! Let's try to figure out what's going on. To start, could you tel
l me:

1.  **What type of device are you using when you experience the disconnections?** (e.g., lapt
op, phone, tablet)
2.  **Have you tried restarting your modem and router?** This is often the first and easiest
fix.
3.  **Are other devices in your home also experiencing the same Wi-Fi disconnections?** This
will help determine if the problem is with your device or the network itself.
```

Figure 5.6 The output of the few-shot learning responses from the AI model

Note that the wording of the prompt does not specify how many programming languages the AI model should list. In my machine, it generated about 15 examples, but in yours it might be different. By using "some" in the instructions, the model may interpret this as an open-ended request and generate more examples than intended. To avoid this, it would be better to provide a more precise instruction, such as

```
List 5 popular programming languages along with a brief description of each:
```

When your prompts are specific and unambiguous, you minimize the risk of the AI misinterpreting your intent. This clarity allows the model to focus on the key elements you want to emphasize, leading to more consistent and reliable outputs.

Now let's see a more realistic example. Say you want to craft a prompt designed for a customer support chatbot that utilizes few-shot learning to adapt its tone and sentiment based on example interactions for different use cases. The example prompt in the following listing demonstrates how to guide the AI model to generate responses for a customer support web application.

Listing 5.6 Example of few-shot learning for a customer support bot

```
const system = `
  You are a customer support chatbot. Adapt your tone and
sentiment based on the following example interactions
for each supported use case:
  **Use Case 1: Technical Support**
  **User:** My internet connection is really slow.
Can you help me?
  **Chatbot:** I'm sorry to hear that you're experiencing
slow internet speeds. Let's troubleshoot this together.
Can you please provide me with your current
speed test results?

  **Use Case 2: Billing Inquiry**
  **User:** I was charged twice for my subscription this
month. What happened?
  **Chatbot:** I understand how concerning double charges
can be. Let me check your account details and resolve this
issue for you right away.

  **Use Case 3: General Inquiry**
  **User:** What are your customer support hours?
  **Chatbot:** Our customer support team is available 24/7
to assist you with any questions you may have.
  Now, respond to the following user inquiries using the
appropriate tone and sentiment:
`;
```

- The use case title sets the context for the kind of issue the user might present.
- This represents a typical user query within the technical support use case. It's a specific issue that the user is facing, which the chatbot needs to address.
- This is the chatbot's response to the user query in use case 1. The response showcases empathy and willingness to help. This example illustrates the tone and sentiment the chatbot should adopt for technical support interactions.

Each of these calls to the support function represents a different type of user query that the chatbot might handle, utilizing the tone and sentiment based on the provided examples in the prompt.

5.2.2 General methodology for creating few-shot learning prompts

Now that you have a good grasp of the examples, let's look at a general template for creating few-shot learning prompts. We can identify the following key steps for creating a nicely formatted prompt utilizing few-shot learning:

1 *Set the context for the task.* Begin by clearly defining the role of the AI or chatbot. Describe the overall task it needs to accomplish. This adjusts the AI model's outputs with your expectations.
Example: "You are a customer support chatbot. Adapt your tone and sentiment based on the following example interactions for each supported use case."

2 *Identify the example use cases.* List different scenarios or use cases that the AI might encounter. Each use case should represent a different type of interaction the AI needs to handle.
Example: "Use Case 1: Technical Support"

3 *Provide example interactions.* For each use case, provide a clear example of a user query and the appropriate AI response. For example,
User—"My internet connection is really slow. Can you help me?"
Chatbot—"I'm sorry to hear that you're experiencing slow internet speeds. Let's troubleshoot this together. Can you please provide me with your current speed test results?"

4 *Ensure variety across examples.* Use diverse examples that cover different aspects of the use case, such as technical issues, billing inquiries, or general questions.
Example: "Use Case 2: Billing Inquiry," "Use Case 3: General Inquiry"

5 *Conclude with an instruction or directive.* After providing the examples, instruct the AI on how to respond to new queries using the tone and sentiment demonstrated in the examples. For example,
"Now, respond to the following user inquiries using the appropriate tone and sentiment."

The examples serve as a blueprint for the AI to adapt its communication style to different scenarios. Feel free to practice this methodology for the following examples to help your AI model adapt to specific tasks without requiring extensive fine-tuning or retraining.

- *Customer support for e-commerce platform*—In an e-commerce setting, a customer support chatbot must handle various inquiries, from order status checks to product return requests.
- *Educational tutoring support*—In an online tutoring application, an AI model needs to provide step-by-step guidance to students on various subjects like biology or chemistry.

As a quick recap, few-shot learning offers an accessible and efficient way to guide AI models in generating contextually appropriate responses by providing just a handful of examples. The more diverse and relevant examples you provide, the higher-quality results you will receive (depending on the AI model's performance and maturity).

5.3 Chain-of-thought prompting: A deeper dive into reasoning

In the previous section, we explored the concept of few-shot learning and how it can be used to guide LLMs in generating desired outputs by providing relevant examples. Now we look at another complementary technique called chain-of-thought prompting, which encourages LLMs to break down a problem into smaller, manageable steps and provide a step-by-step explanation of their reasoning process. By explicitly asking the model to show its work, chain-of-thought prompting helps to ensure that the final answer is not only correct but also based on easy-to-verify steps.

As an analogy, imagine a student working on a complex math problem. Instead of simply writing down the final answer, the teacher encourages the student to explain their thought process step by step. In that case, the teacher would reward the student who articulates the answer in a clear way, every step of the way.

5.3.1 Example of chain-of-thought prompting

Let's consider a simple example of using chain-of-thought prompting to solve a math problem that calculates percentages:

```
Prompt: Solve the following problem step-by-step:
What is 25 percent of 80?

Answer:
   1. Understand the question:
      We need to find 25% of 80.
   2. Convert the percentage to a decimal number:
      25% = 25/100 = 0.25
   3. Multiply the decimal by 80:
      0.25 × 80 = 20
Therefore, 25% of 80 is 20 percent.
```

In this example, the prompt's instruction to "Solve the following problem step-by-step" explicitly asks the model to show its work; the model responds by breaking down the problem into three steps and demonstrating its reasoning process.

Of course, just asking the model to break down the steps of each calculation does not guarantee that each step will be correct. There might be cases when the model misinterprets the problem, leading to incorrect intermediate steps or conclusions. This can occur for several reasons:

- *Misunderstanding the problem*—The model may not fully grasp the nuances of the question or the specific requirements of the task.
- *Ambiguous prompts*—Natural language can often be ambiguous, and the way a problem is phrased may lead the model to interpret it differently than intended. Wrong punctuation, minced words, and commas can affect the meaning of the

prompt and cause misinterpretation and incorrect calculation. For example, a question like "What is half of the sum of 20 and 30?" could be misinterpreted, resulting in an incorrect calculation if the model fails to recognize that it should first calculate the sum before halving it based on the rules of math.

- *Model limitations*—Despite advancements in AI and natural language processing, models like GPT-4 are not perfect. They are trained on vast datasets and can generate sound responses, but they do not possess true understanding or reasoning capabilities. Therefore, they might hallucinate parts of their answers or just provide false statements. For example, sometimes the AI model fails to count the specific number of characters in a word, leading to inaccuracies.

- *Overfitted examples*—If the model is provided with examples that are overly specific or not representative of the broader problem space, it may "overfit" to those examples. For instance, if the examples only cover problems with single-digit numbers, the model may struggle when presented with larger numbers or more complex expressions. This can result in the model applying the wrong logic or methodology when faced with a slightly different problem.

For all of these reasons, it is essential to validate the correctness of each step in the reasoning process, especially for complex calculations or tasks that require precise answers. This validation is crucial because even though chain-of-thought prompting encourages the model to articulate its reasoning, it does not guarantee that every step will be accurate.

However, chain-of-thought prompting is a very accessible technique since it does not require us to fine-tune the AI model or undergo complex training processes. This accessibility is one of the key advantages of using chain-of-thought prompting in various applications.

5.3.2 General methodology for creating chain-of-thought prompts

Just as with few-shot learning methodologies, developing effective chain-of-thought prompts requires a systematic approach. After all, we are not called "engineers" without a reason! The following methodology focuses on guiding LLMs to explain their reasoning process clearly and logically, aiming for accurate and reliable results. Figure 5.7 is a visualization of the general steps involved for crafting prompts using chain-of-thought reasoning as an example.

Here are the general steps involved:

1 *Define the structure of the prompt.* Begin by establishing a clear format for the prompt that outlines the AI's expected response. By providing a well-structured template, you can ensure that the model understands the required information and the format in which it should be presented. For example, "Calculate the area of a circle: Area = $\pi * R^2$."

In this example, the prompt states the task at hand (calculating the area of a circle) and provides the formula to be used. This structure sets the stage for the model to follow a specific pattern when generating its output.

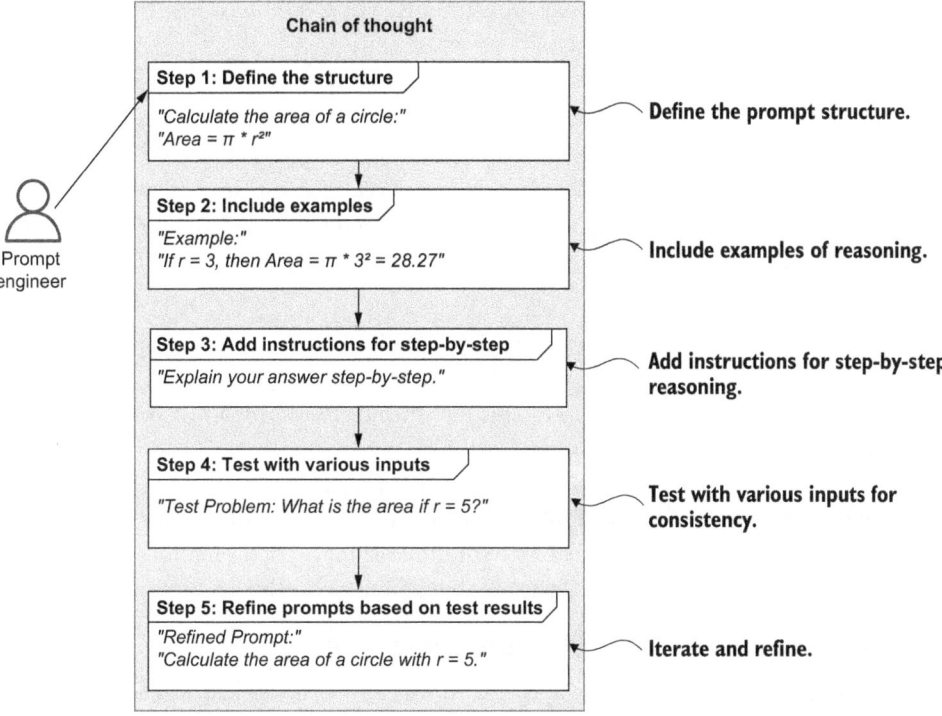

Figure 5.7 The key steps involved in creating chain-of-thought prompts that encourage LLMs to articulate their reasoning process step-by-step

2. *Provide examples.* Here we incorporate few-shot learning techniques, which include relevant examples that demonstrate how to approach similar problems. These examples serve as a guide for the model, helping it understand the expected reasoning process and the level of detail required in the final response. For example, "Example: If r = 3, then Area = $\pi * 3^2$ = 28.27."

This example walks through the calculation of the area of a circle with a radius of 3 using the provided formula.

3. *Ensure step-by-step reasoning.* To ensure that the model provides a clear and logical explanation of its reasoning, it's important to include explicit instructions that prompt it to break down the problem into individual steps. For example, "Explain your answer step-by-step."

By adding this directive, you encourage the model to explain its thought process in a structured manner.

4. *Test for consistency.* Before finalizing the prompt, it's important to verify it with various inputs to test that the model consistently follows the specified format and reasoning process. If you find any inconsistencies or errors in the model's responses,

you can make necessary adjustments. For example, "Test Problem: What is the area if r = 5?"

5 *Iterate and refine.* Let's say that the preceding steps revealed that the results were inconsistent. In that case, you may need to refine the prompt to improve clarity, address any issues identified, and further encourage the desired reasoning process. For example, "Refined Prompt: Calculate the area of a circle with r = 5."

Here we used explicit wording to eliminate any confusion about what shape we are referring to and remove the need for the model to guess the type of the shape from the question.

To recap, chain-of-thought prompting enhances the reasoning capabilities of LLMs by guiding them to present each individual step involved in solving a specific problem. When implemented effectively, this technique can significantly boost the model's performance with less effort.

Now we will explore the concept of embeddings and how they can be effectively utilized within the Vercel AI SDK. Embeddings serve as a powerful tool for representing words, phrases, or images as vectors in a high-dimensional space, enabling applications such as semantic search and retrieval-augmented generation, which I expand on in chapter 7.

5.4 Embeddings: Giving AI a sense of meaning

When a user inputs a prompt, the AI model converts the words into embeddings. Each word or token in the prompt is transformed into a vector that reflects its meaning and context within the sentence. The primary purpose of embeddings is to encapsulate individual measurable properties of the data, allowing AI models to use these features for tasks such as recommendations, classifications, and similarity searches.

Embeddings are thus numerical representations of data that effectively capture relationships and patterns within complex datasets. Processing various types of input, such as plain text, images, or audio, AI models require this data to be transformed into low-dimensional vectors (tuples of floating-point numbers). This transformation simplifies the data while retaining its essential features, resulting in embeddings.

5.4.1 The restaurant menu analogy: A taste of embeddings

Imagine you run a restaurant and a customer asks, "Can you recommend a dish similar to spaghetti carbonara?" The human staff knows that means they like creamy pasta dishes. The staff doesn't have to scan every ingredient of every dish; they can intuitively search for similar concepts.

This is what embeddings do for AI. The "customer order" is the user's query, which is converted into a vector. The "menu items" are also precomputed vectors. The system then performs a similarity search to find the closest menu items in the embedding space. The "attributes" (like "pasta" or "creamy") are the dimensions that define the vectors, capturing the essential qualities of each dish. This process allows for fast, relevant recommendations without the need for complex keyword matching. Figure 5.8 shows the main components of embeddings using a restaurant menu analogy.

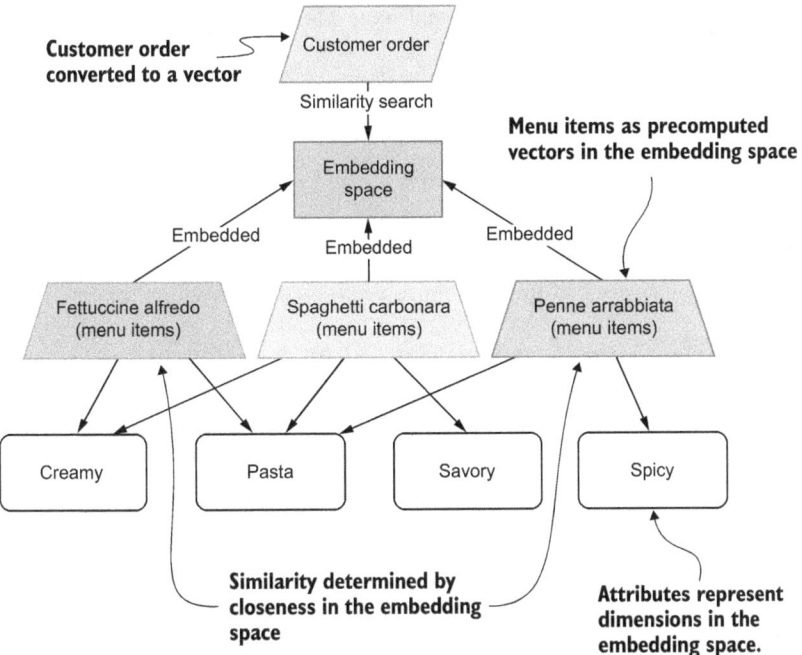

Figure 5.8 The concept of embeddings using a restaurant menu analogy. The "embedding space" represents a multidimensional space where both customer orders (queries) and menu items are mapped as vectors. Each menu item (e.g., spaghetti carbonara) is a precomputed vector, while the customer order is converted to a query vector. Similarity between items is determined by their proximity in this space. Attributes like "pasta" or "creamy" represent dimensions of the embedding space. A similarity search finds the closest match and items similar to the query, mirroring how embedding-based systems in machine learning find relevant results for given inputs.

Here's a breakdown of figure 5.8:

- *Customer order as query vector*—The "customer order" is represented as a query vector in this space. This is analogous to how a user's input or search query would be converted into a vector in an embedding-based system.
- *Menu items as vectors*—Each menu item (spaghetti carbonara, fettuccine alfredo, and penne arrabbiata) is also represented as a vector in the same space. These would be precomputed embeddings of known items in the system.
- *Similarity search*—A similarity search is performed by comparing the customer order vector to the menu item vectors within the embedding space. This represents how embedding-based systems find similar items or relevant responses.
- *Closest match and similar items*—The system can rank results based on their similarity to the query by comparing their distances.
- *Attributes*—Each menu item is connected to various attributes ("pasta," "creamy," "savory," "spicy"). These attributes can be thought of as dimensions or features in the embedding space that contribute to the position of each item's vector.

Now, before we embark on the practical examples, I want to clarify a few facts and answer a few questions about embeddings.

WHAT DO EMBEDDINGS LOOK LIKE?

Let's explore some examples to get a sense of how embeddings are visually represented:

- *Word embeddings*—These are used to represent words as vectors in a low-dimensional space. These embeddings capture relationships between words. When visualized in 2D or 3D space, related words tend to cluster together.

  For example, a word embedding might look something like this:

  ```
  const catEmbedding = [0.23, -0.56, 0.12, 0.87, -0.34, ...]
  ```

  While these numbers appear random to humans, they encode rich semantic information. Figure 5.9 is taken from tensorflow.org (https://projector.tensorflow.org/), demonstrating a more realistic example:

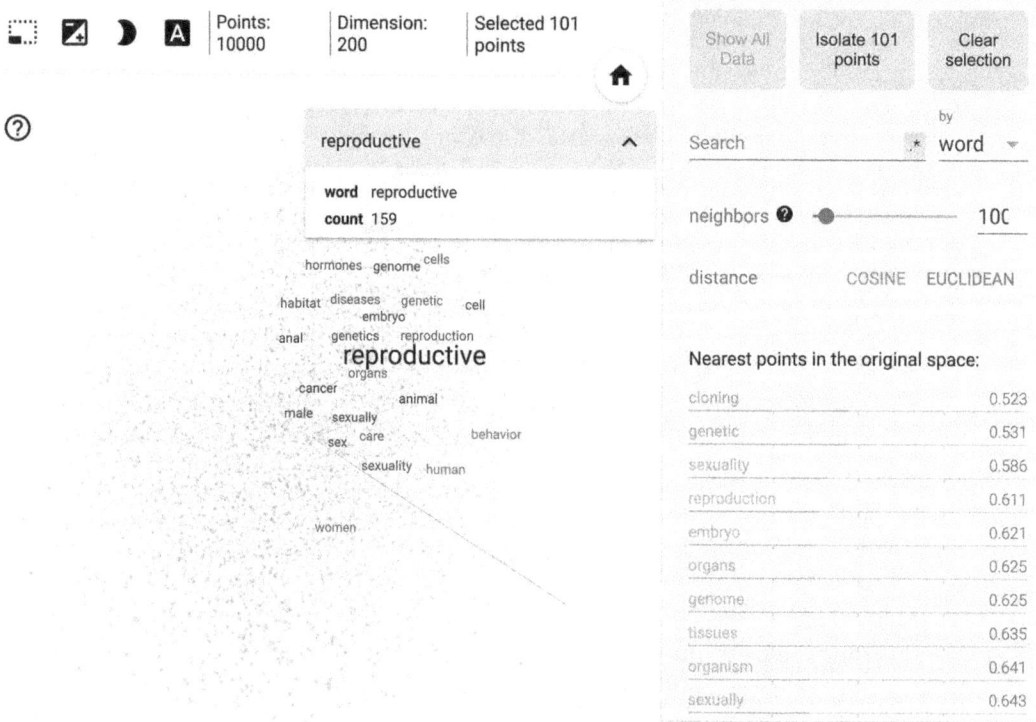

Figure 5.9 A 2D projection of word embeddings in a 200-dimensional space, focusing on the term "reproductive" and its semantic neighbors. The visualization shows 10,000 points, with 101 points selected for detailed view. The right panel lists the 10 nearest neighbors to "reproductive" in the original space, with their cosine distances. This representation demonstrates how word embeddings capture semantic relationships together in the vector space. (https://projector.tensorflow.org/)

- *Image embeddings*—These are like what word embeddings are for words. They are numerical representations of images. When visualized, similar images will be close together in the embedding space. For example, images of dogs would be near each other, while images of cars would be in a different cluster.
- *Graph embeddings*—These are optimized data structures that are used for capturing the relationships between nodes. When visualized, nodes that are well connected in the graph will be close together in the embedding space. For example, in a social network graph, users with many mutual friends would be embedded closer together.

In practical terms, it's important to associate embeddings with lists of floating-point numbers. To the human eye, these numbers may not make any sense, but to machine learning models, they are powerful representations of complex information. This brings us to the following clarification.

EMBEDDINGS ARE NOT LIKE MACHINE LANGUAGE IN COMPUTERS

Don't get confused by thinking that embeddings are a language for AI models. They are fundamentally different in terms of their purpose, functionality, and level of abstraction.

Machine language, also known as machine code, is the lowest-level programming language that is directly understood by a computer's CPU. It consists of binary code (0s and 1s) that represents instructions for the CPU to execute. It is specific to hardware architecture, and it is not human readable.

Embeddings, on the other hand, are numerical representations of data (such as words, sentences, or images) in a continuous vector space; they are also not human readable. They are used in machine learning to capture semantic meaning and relationships between different pieces of data. The AI model does not use them for following instructions in a procedural manner. Instead, they serve as input data for machine learning models, which can then perform tasks such as classification, clustering, or recommendation. This distinction is important when working with different embedding schemes at different levels of abstraction.

EMBEDDINGS ARE TIED TO A PARTICULAR MODEL

In the current state, embeddings are highly specific to the architecture and training of the AI models that generate them. As a result, embeddings produced by one model may not be compatible with those from another model.

Mixing and matching embeddings from different models arbitrarily can lead to inaccurate or misleading results, as the semantic meanings captured by the embeddings may differ significantly. For instance, embeddings generated by OpenAI may not match with those from a different provider, such as a local model or another AI provider. This, of course, can create issues when storing embeddings in systems that cater to multiple AI models, particularly when having to cater for increased storage and versioning requirements.

Therefore, it is important to develop a system that uses embeddings from the same or compatible model for tasks such as similarity comparisons, clustering, or input to downstream models. This ensures that the relationships and patterns captured in the embeddings are relevant.

WHY STORE EMBEDDINGS IN A DATABASE?

You may wonder why we should store embeddings in a database and not generate them on the fly for each user query. There are several reasons, but let's discuss just a few:

- *Efficiency*—Generating embeddings can be computationally intensive and time consuming, especially for large datasets. By storing them beforehand, we avoid the overhead of repeated calculations, allowing for faster response times.
- *Scalability*—For applications with a high volume of queries, storing embeddings enables the system to scale effectively. It can handle multiple user requests simultaneously without overwhelming the AI model or the system's resources.
- *Cost effectiveness*—Many AI models, particularly those hosted in the cloud, incur costs based on usage. For example, using the OpenAI embeddings consumes API credits. By storing embeddings once, we can reduce the number of calls made to the AI model, leading to lower operational costs and a more cost-effective solution.

It's worth noting that embedding models are generally deterministic for a specific version of an AI model. This means that if you generate embeddings using the same input and the same embedding model version, you should receive the same output consistently. This behavior is distinct from the generative models used for text completion, which can often produce probabilistic outputs even for the same prompt designed for general purposes. However, if the embedding model version changes or if there are updates to the underlying algorithms or training data, the embeddings produced may differ even for the same input.

5.4.2 Using embeddings in practice: The Vercel AI SDK

The Vercel AI SDK offers two essential helper functions for obtaining embedding values from input text: `embed` and `embedMany`. These functions simplify the process of generating embeddings of a particular AI model using the familiar concepts used in the `generateText` class of functions. The following is a detailed breakdown of each function, including their usage, parameters, and typical use cases.

The purpose of the `embed` function is to generate embeddings for a single input value. This is particularly useful when you need to obtain the semantic representation of a specific piece of text, such as a sentence or phrase. The following code listing shows how to print the embedding vector values of a sentence.

Listing 5.7 Creating a single embedding

```
import { embed } from "ai";
import { createGoogleGenerativeAI } from "@ai-sdk/google";

const google = createGoogleGenerativeAI({ apiKey });

const { embedding } = await embed({
```

Indicates the import of the embed function, which is essential for generating embeddings from text

```
    model: google.textEmbeddingModel("text-embedding-004"),
    value: "The quick brown fox jumps over the lazy dog",
});

console.log(embedding);
```

Highlights the specification of the embedding model being used from the Google Gemini API

Points out the input text for which the embedding is generated, demonstrating how to provide a specific value for analysis

The `model` parameter specifies the embedding model to use, and the `value` is the input text for which you want to generate an embedding.

The purpose of `embedMany` is to generate embeddings for multiple independent input values in a single call. This is particularly efficient when you have a batch of text data that you want to process simultaneously.

Listing 5.8 Creating multiple embeddings

Indicates the import of the embedMany function, which is essential for generating embeddings from text values

```
import { embedMany } from "ai";
import { createGoogleGenerativeAI } from "@ai-sdk/google";

const google = createGoogleGenerativeAI({ apiKey });

const { embeddings } = await embedMany({
    model: google.textEmbeddingModel("text-embedding-004"),
    values: [
        'The quick brown fox jumps over the lazy dog',
        'A journey of a thousand miles begins with a single step',
        'To be or not to be, that is the question',
    ],
});

console.log(embeddings);
```

Highlights the specification of the embedding model being used from the Google Gemini API

Points out the input values for which the embedding is generated, demonstrating how to provide multiple values for analysis

The values parameter is not a single text but a list of text strings. The model will return the list of embeddings that correspond to each provided input string in the same order.

If you run any of the examples provided, you will get a bunch of floating-point numbers back:

```
$ node ch05/embeddings.google.js
[
     -0.0450604,   -0.014942412,
   -0.037350334,   -0.025503622,
    0.033759177,    0.030023085,
   0.0025531165,   -0.016676709,
   -0.0071603837,  -0.011624326
]
```

What can you really do with those numbers? One of the most effective ways to utilize embeddings is by storing them in a database and employing them for similarity searches. This approach enables us to efficiently retrieve relevant information based on user queries. Let's explore the process in more detail step by step.

STORING AND RETRIEVING WITH EMBEDDINGS

In the general case, we aim to develop a system that generates a list of embedding values based on the body of knowledge we want to serve. Once this knowledge is embedded, when a user submits a query, the system can compile a list of similar queries or relevant recommendations that align with the original query. This functionality can then be integrated into our web application, enabling us to display the results in an intuitive and user-friendly manner. Figure 5.10 showcases the general steps involved in this process.

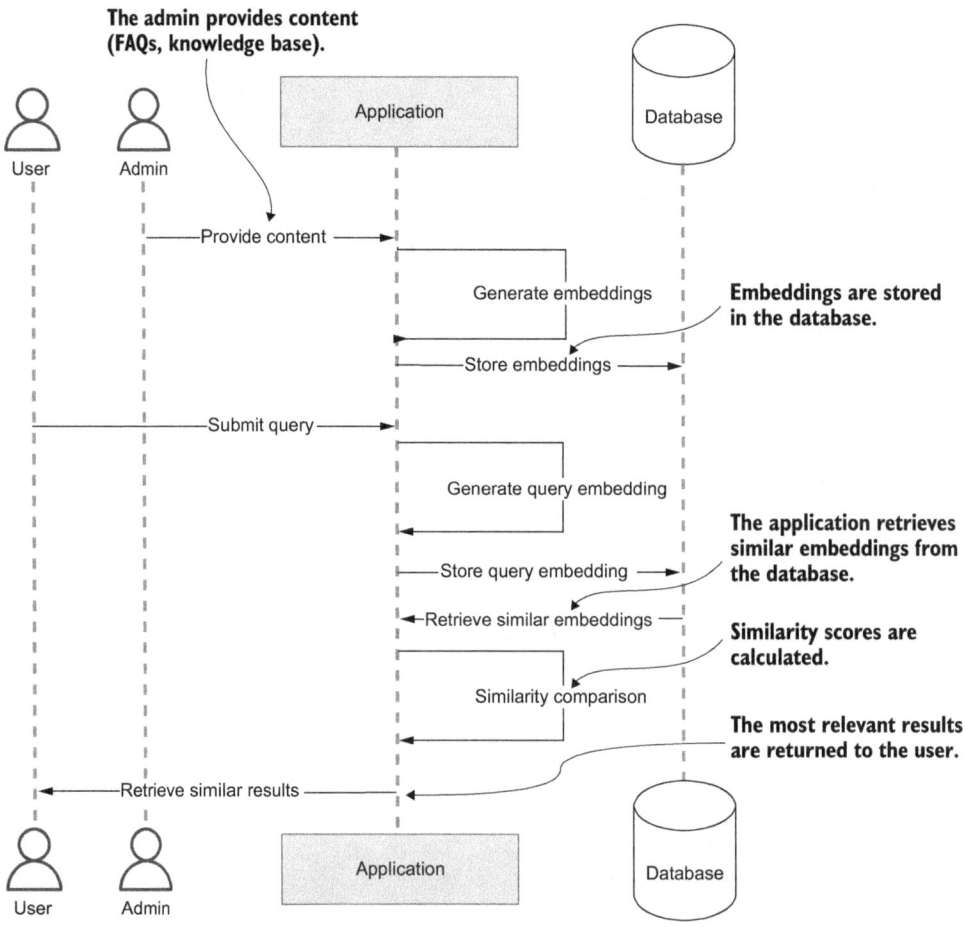

Figure 5.10 The workflow of an information retrieval system that utilizes embeddings to enhance user query responses. An admin provides content, such as common questions and knowledge base articles, to the application, which generates embeddings for this content and stores them in a database. When a user submits a query, the application generates a corresponding query embedding and stores it as well. The system then retrieves similar embeddings from the database and calculates similarity scores to identify the most relevant results. Finally, these results are returned to the user.

The key steps involved in this process are

- *Store embeddings*—The first step is to save the generated embeddings in a database designed for vector storage. This can be a dedicated vector database (e.g., Pinecone, Milvus), which is purpose built for high-performance vector operations, or a general-purpose database that has added vector search capabilities (e.g., PostgreSQL with pgvector, MongoDB, Couchbase, Neo4j). This allows for efficient storage and retrieval of the embeddings.
- *Query processing*—When a user submits a query, we generate an embedding for that query using the same model that was used for the stored embeddings. This ensures that the query embedding is compatible with the stored embeddings, allowing for accurate comparisons.
- *Similarity search*—With the query embedding and the stored embeddings, we can employ various similarity search algorithms to identify the most relevant results. Popular algorithms include *cosine similarity*, which measures the cosine of the angle between two vectors (where a higher cosine value, closer to 1, indicates greater similarity), and *Euclidean distance*, which calculates the straight-line distance between two points (vectors) in a multidimensional space (where a shorter distance indicates greater similarity).
- *Return results*—Based on the similarity scores, we can retrieve and present the most similar items or answers to the user. This could be in the form of a ranked list of relevant information, such as articles, documents, or specific answers to the user's query.

Let's put all of those concepts into practice as we take a look at a very simple use case of an IT support knowledge base utilizing embeddings for the retrieval of similar Q/As or articles.

5.4.3 Use case: IT support knowledge base

Imagine a product designed to assist users with common IT-related questions and issues. By using embeddings and storing them in a database, the system can provide quick and relevant answers to user queries. Here's how it works:

1. *Embedding generation*—Each IT support question and its corresponding answer are converted into embeddings and stored in a database. This step will be performed before the application is deployed.
2. *User query*—When a user asks a question, the system generates an embedding for this query using the same model.
3. *Similarity search*—The system compares the query embedding with stored embeddings to find the closest match.
4. *Response*—The system retrieves and presents the corresponding answer to the user.

The following is a sample code that walks you through each step of the process using JavaScript.

Embedding generation

In this step, we'll convert a list of IT support questions into embeddings and store them in memory.

Listing 5.9 Converting text to embeddings

```
const embeddingDB = {};          ◄── This line defines an object (embeddingDB)
const questions = [                  to serve as an in-memory database, which
  "How do I reset my password?",     stores the question embeddings.
  "What should I do if my computer won't start?",   ◄── Defines an array of sample
];                                                      questions for the IT support
                                                        knowledge base

const answers = [                                              ◄── Defines an array
  "To reset your password, go to the login page and click          of corresponding
'Forgot Password'. Follow the instructions to reset                answers to the
your password.",                                                   questions defined
  "If your computer won't start, check the power cable, try        in the "questions"
restarting it, and if the issue persists, contact support.",       array
];

for (let i = 0; i < questions.length; i++) {
  const { embedding } = await embed({
    model: google.textEmbeddingModel("text-embedding-004"),
    value: questions[i],
  });                                           ◄── This line saves each generated
  embeddingDB[questions[i]] = embedding;            embedding in the embeddingDB
}                                                   object, using the question as the key
                                                    and the embedding as the value.
```

Here, we loop through the questions array, generate embeddings using OpenAI's embedding model, and store each embedding in an in-memory object (`embeddingDB`) with the question as the key. We use an in-memory object instead of a vector database because it's not important at this point, as it will complicate the example.

Next, we allow the application to accept user queries; we use the `embed` function to generate an embedding for the query.

User query

When a user asks a question, the system generates an embedding for that query. We simply use the embed function to get the embeddings of the query.

Listing 5.10 Embedding the user query

```
const userQuery = "I forgot my password";
const { embedding: queryEmbedding } = await embed({
  model: google.textEmbeddingModel("text-embedding-004"),
  value: userQuery,
});
```

Here we create an embedding for the user's query using the same model used for the stored questions. We will use the variable `queryEmbedding` next as an input to perform the most crucial part of the whole process, which is similarity searching.

SIMILARITY SEARCH

We compare the user's query embedding with the stored embeddings to find the most similar question. We use a simple `cosineSimilarity` function here to find out the most relevant question from the corpus.

Listing 5.11 Performing similarity search on the embeddings

```
let maxSimilarity = -1;              // Sets up a variable to keep track of the highest
                                     // cosine similarity found during the loop
let mostRelevantQuestion = "";       // Sets up a variable to store the
                                     // question corresponding to the
                                     // highest similarity found

for (const [question, storedEmbedding] of Object.entries(embeddingDB)) {
  const similarity =
cosineSimilarity(queryEmbedding, storedEmbedding);   // Calculates the cosine
  if (similarity > maxSimilarity) {                  // similarity between
    maxSimilarity = similarity;                      // the current stored
    mostRelevantQuestion = question;                 // embedding and the
  }                                                  // query embedding
}
```

If the current similarity is the highest seen so far, this block updates maxSimilarity and records the corresponding question as the most relevant one.

This `cosineSimilarity` function and the loop will allow you to identify the question in the knowledge base that is most similar to the user's query based on their embeddings. Here we only store the most similar question, but we can also tweak the algorithm to store the top 5 or 10 questions that have close similarity with the original query.

RESPONSE

The last part is simply returning the most relevant question matched to the user. This could also be part of the response as a list of relevant questions, or we can ask the AI model to write a nicely formatted output.

Listing 5.12 Returning the most relevant question

```
const relevantAnswer = answers[questions.indexOf(mostRelevantQuestion)];
console.log(`Most relevant question: ${mostRelevantQuestion}`);
console.log(`Relevant answer: ${relevantAnswer}`);
```

Of course, this process, while effective, can be enhanced in several ways. For instance, implementing the system could benefit from incremental learning, allowing it to update and refine its knowledge base continuously as new questions and answers emerge. Incorporating a feedback loop where users can rate the relevance of the provided answers enables the system to learn from real interactions, improving its accuracy and user satisfaction over time.

5.5 Going deeper into LLM techniques

Here we summarize the key research that is revolutionizing how we interact with and evaluate LLMs. If you're focused on practical application rather than theoretical depth, you can skip this section.

5.5.1 Tree of thoughts

The *tree-of-thoughts* framework is an advanced prompting technique that improves an LLM's reasoning abilities by simulating human problem solving. Unlike the chain-of-thought method, which follows a single linear path, tree of thoughts enables the model to explore multiple reasoning paths in a tree-like structure. This approach is particularly effective for complex tasks that require strategic planning or multistep lookahead, such as solving mathematical problems or creative writing.

For more information, see the following:

- "Tree of Thoughts: Deliberate Problem Solving with Large Language Models" by Yao et al., https://arxiv.org/abs/2305.10601
- Tree of Thoughts (ToT), https://www.promptingguide.ai/techniques/tot

5.5.2 Self-refine

Self-refine is an innovative approach that allows an LLM to iteratively improve its own outputs without the need for additional training data or reinforcement learning. The process works in a feedback loop: an LLM generates an initial output and then provides itself with feedback on how to improve it. Based on this feedback, the model refines its original output. This cycle can be repeated until the output meets a desired quality standard. This technique is highly effective for tasks with complex or hard-to-define goals, such as review rewriting or code optimization.

For more information, see the following:

- "Self-Refine: Iterative Refinement with Self-Feedback" by Madaan et al., https://arxiv.org/abs/2303.17651
- Project page, https://github.com/madaan/self-refine

5.5.3 LLM-as-a-judge

The *LLM-as-a-judge* technique uses the power of LLMs to evaluate the quality of text generated by other LLMs. This is an alternative to traditional human evaluation, which can be costly and time consuming. By providing a "judge" LLM with a set of guidelines, it can assess various aspects of a generated text, such as correctness, tone, or conciseness. While this method offers advantages in efficiency and consistency, potential biases in the judge LLM might occur; careful prompt design is essential to ensure reliability.

For more information, see the following:

- "A Survey on LLM-as-a-Judge" by Huang et al., https://arxiv.org/abs/2411.15594
- "LLM-as-a-Judge: A Complete Guide to Using LLMs for Evaluations," https://www.evidentlyai.com/llm-guide/llm-as-a-judge

So far, we've been working with the simplest example of a generative AI application. To build more sophisticated applications, we now turn to LangChain, a framework that allows you to chain together components such as language models, APIs, and other tools. In the next chapter, we will use LangChain to significantly enhance our app's capabilities and integrate more personalized user interactions.

Summary

- Prompt engineering is a critical technique for optimizing AI model outputs in web applications, enhancing user interactions and experiences.
- Few-shot learning enables AI models to adapt quickly to new tasks by providing a limited number of examples, making it especially beneficial in scenarios with limited training data.
- Chain-of-thought prompting encourages AI models to engage in step-by-step reasoning, improving accuracy by breaking complex tasks into manageable components.
- Embeddings facilitate semantic search and content recommendations, allowing for more context-aware interactions and personalized user experiences.
- Tokenization transforms natural language instructions into a format that AI models can efficiently process, ensuring effective communication between users and models.
- *Max tokens* refers to the maximum number of tokens an AI model can process in a single interaction, encompassing both input and output, which is crucial for ensuring requests are not rejected.
- Control tokens guide the behavior and output of AI models, allowing developers to define specific rules and instructions within prompts.
- Different types of prompts include basic text prompts, message prompts, and system prompts, each designed for distinct use cases and interactions with AI models.
- Effective prompt management involves storing prompts in a database for dynamic updates, version control, scalability, and access control.
- Prompt versioning allows developers to track changes to prompts over time, assessing their effect on AI outputs and user experiences.

Building AI workflows with LangChain.js

This chapter covers

- Using LangChain.js core features to build context-aware AI applications
- `PromptTemplate`, few-shot learning, and other strategies for prompt management
- Chaining calls to improve generative AI responses
- Preparing and storing information for efficient document ingestion and retrieval
- Using memory components in LangChain.js to remember conversation history
- Integrating LangChain.js with the Vercel AI SDK

As we have explored using large language models (LLMs) for generating content, we've primarily focused on single interactions. In these scenarios, we send a prompt along with relevant context history, parse the response, and then display it to the end user. However, what if we want a more flexible approach that accommodates more complex scenarios?

Imagine needing to engage in multiple interactions with LLMs before arriving at a final output. Perhaps we want to utilize various tools and combine their responses into a structured format. This need arises because LLM responses are often not in the desired format or may lack the accuracy required for real-life applications.

In many cases, we find ourselves needing to implement quality control steps that could involve reengaging with the LLMs to refine or validate the information provided. This process of "chaining" calls—where multiple interactions with LLMs and other tools are orchestrated—is essential for creating robust and reliable AI-driven solutions.

Chaining these steps together allows you to build more powerful and versatile AI applications that can handle complex tasks beyond simple prompt–response interactions. Implementing the necessary library code that performs all those tasks is a daunting process, but luckily for us, there is a specialized framework for this purpose called LangChain.

In this chapter, we'll work with the basic features of LangChain, including helpers for prompt management, memory, agents, content ingestion, and retrieval. Then we'll apply this knowledge by integrating LangChain's capabilities into our app and using it alongside the Vercel AI SDK.

6.1 Introducing LangChain

LangChain (https://js.langchain.com/) is a tool/framework dedicated to providing abstractions that make it easier to chain multiple steps together into a cohesive workflow. The core concept in LangChain for this purpose is the chain, or what is more technically a series of linked function call that, together, provide functionality. LangChain deals with the underlying technicalities of managing the API interactions, parsing and transforming content and interacting with various database stores and providers while exposing a composable API for developers to use.

The LangChain ecosystem of tools is huge, and exploring all of its available features would require us to write another book entirely. Instead, we focus on the main concepts that will allow us to combine its features with our existing web application. Our main goal here is to understand how things work together and how to integrate each relevant feature in the most suitable way.

The LangChain project library is provided in two programming languages: one with Python and one in JavaScript, which is called LangChain.js. The LangChain.js project is organized into several modules, each serving a specific purpose in the development of LLM-powered applications. Table 6.1 provides a quick overview of the main modules.

Table 6.1 The main modules available from the LangChain.js library

Module	Description
langchain/prompts	Manages prompt templates and input variables
langchain/agents	Implements autonomous agents that can use tools and make decisions

Table 6.1 The main modules available from the LangChain.js library (*continued*)

Module	Description
`langchain/chains`	Combines multiple components into reusable pipelines
`@langchain/core`	Core package that exposes many common utilities and functions
`@langchain/community`	Community packages
`langchain/vectorstores`	Various vector database store integrations
`langchain/storage`	Provides abstractions for storing data in memory or in databases
`langchain/document_loaders`	Provides helpers for loading documents from various sources
`@langchain/openai`, `@langchain/anthropic`	Provide LLM integration classes with various providers
`langchain/output_parsers`	Exposes classes that transform outputs from LLMs into a more suitable format

These modules work together to provide a comprehensive toolkit for building advanced LLM applications. As we progress, we'll work on how to use these modules effectively in our project.

6.1.1 Chaining calls with LangChain

Let's begin by exploring the concepts of chains and how to manage prompts with LangChain. Chains are a fundamental feature in LangChain that allow you to combine multiple operations into a single, reusable workflow. They are particularly useful for creating complex AI workflows that require multiple steps of processing, such as retrieving information, analyzing it, and generating a response.

Chains are constructed using specific functions that are available through the *runnables* interface. Runnables in LangChain provide a powerful way to create flexible and reusable workflows for processing data. They allow you to chain various operations, enabling complex interactions with LLMs and other tools.

HOW RUNNABLES WORK

A runnable is essentially a unit of work that can be invoked, batched, or streamed. Each runnable can take input, perform some processing, and produce output, which can then be passed to another runnable in a chain. Runnables use the LangChain Expression Language (LCEL), which is basically a declarative way of composing functions that are resistant to code changes and includes baked-in support for retries and fallbacks. Figure 6.1 illustrates a simple chain that consists of four main components, represented by rectangles.

The arrows between the shapes show the flow of data from one component to the next. Each component's output serves as the input for the subsequent component in the chain. The `toUpperCase` and `VowelCount` perform some number processing first before providing these numbers as a prompt to the LLM. The last chain is the `StringOutputParser`, which is a special function that processes the LLM's output and returns a formatted string.

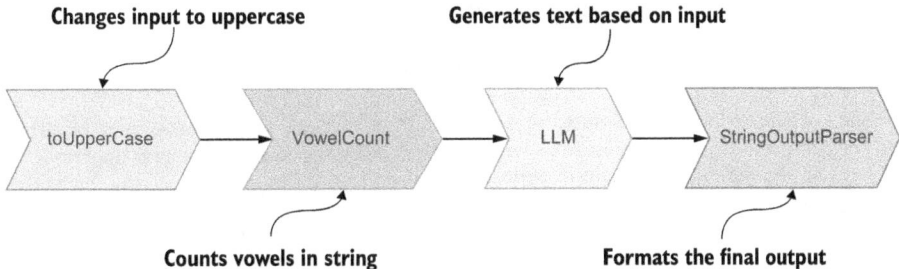

Figure 6.1 A typical LangChain operation chain where it processes data sequentially through a `toUpperCase` function, then a `VowelCount` function, then via the LLM, and finally via the `StringOutputParser` to parse the output.

> **Files: simple-chain.openai.js, simple-chain.google.js**
>
> The code for this example project is in the ch06 folder. To run these examples, first navigate into the ch06 directory from your project root (e.g., if you were in the ch05 folder, you would run `cd ../ch06`):
>
> ```
> $ npm install
> $ node simple-chain.openai.js
> ```
>
> If you are using Google AI, there is a separate file named agents.google.js in the same folder:
>
> ```
> $ npm install
> $ node simple-chain.google.js
> ```
>
> You'll need an OpenAI API key to access their REST API or a Google API key for Google services. The appendix offers instructions on how to set up and create a secret key for OpenAI and other providers:
>
> ```
> // .env
>
> OPENAI_API_KEY=<SECRET_KEY>
> GEMINI_API_KEY=<YOUR_GEMINI_API_KEY>
> ```
>
> For details on setting up and creating API keys, refer to the appendix.

The following listing shows the code for this simple chain.

Listing 6.1 Example using runnable chains

```
import { StringOutputParser } from "@langchain/core/output_parsers";
import { ChatPromptTemplate } from "@langchain/core/prompts";
import { RunnableLambda } from "@langchain/core/runnables";
```

```
import { ChatOpenAI } from "@langchain/openai";
import "dotenv/config";
const apiKey = process.env.OPENAI_API_KEY;

const toUpperCase = (input) => {        ◄──┐ Takes an input object and converts
  return {                                  │ the "text" property to uppercase
    uppercased: input.text.toUpperCase(),
  };
};

const vowelCountFunction = (input) => {  ◄──┐ Counts the number of
  const vowels = input.uppercased.match(/[AEIOU]/gi);  │ vowels in the uppercase text
  return {
    vowelCount: vowels ? vowels.length : 0,
  };                                          ┌ Initializes the ChatOpenAI
};                                            │ model with the API key and
const model = new ChatOpenAI({ openAIApiKey: apiKey,  │ specifies the model to use
model: "gpt-4o" });                         ◄─┘
const prompt = ChatPromptTemplate.fromTemplate("Show the number {vowelCount}
two times.");                               ◄──┐
const chain = RunnableLambda.from(toUpperCase).   │ Creates a prompt
  .pipe(RunnableLambda.from(vowelCountFunction))  │ template that will
  .pipe(prompt)                                   │ be used to format
  .pipe(model)                   ┌ Creates a chain │ the input for the
  .pipe(new StringOutputParser());│ of operations   │ language model

await chain.invoke({text: "hello world"})   ┌ Invokes the chain with the input
.then((output) => {                ◄────────┘ "hello world" and logs the output
    console.log(output);
});
```

We start by defining two functions: `toUpperCase` to convert text to uppercase and `vowelCountFunction` to count vowels in the uppercase text. It's crucial to pay attention to the order of these pipe events, as they determine the flow of data processing. The chain first converts the input to uppercase, then counts the vowels, applies a prompt template with the vowel count, passes it to the `ChatOpenAI` model, and finally parses the output as a string. This sequence ensures that each step builds upon the results of the previous one to produce the final output. The chain is then invoked with the input `"hello world"`, and the result is logged to the console.

With the prompt now set to `"Show the number {vowelCount} two times,"` the language model will generate a more conversational response. For example, when running `simple-chain.openai.js`, you might see output similar to this:

```
% node simple-chain.openai.js
3 3
```

Alternatively, you can achieve the same functionality using `RunnableSequence.from`. This method allows you to create a sequence of runnables that are executed in order, which can be particularly useful for operations that are independent yet need to be processed sequentially. As a quick example, here is the same chain using `RunnableSequence.from`:

```
const sequence = RunnableSequence.from([
  RunnableLambda.from(toUpperCase),
  RunnableLambda.from(vowelCountFunction),
  prompt,
  model,
  new StringOutputParser(),
]);
```

The first approach uses `.pipe()` to chain operations sequentially, while the second uses `RunnableSequence.from()` to define all steps in a single array. The choice between them is mainly a matter of coding style preference.

Now contrast this approach with how the Vercel AI SDK typically interacts with AI models. In Vercel's architecture, API calls are often made directly to the AI model without intermediate processing steps like those seen in runnables. While Vercel allows for straightforward interactions with LLMs, it may lack the flexibility and composability that runnables provide.

Later in this chapter, we will see how to integrate this approach with the Vercel AI SDK to have the best of both worlds. Before we do that, let's explore how to manage prompts effectively using the provided `ChatPromptTemplate`.

MANAGING PROMPT TEMPLATES

In the preceding listing, we saw the use of the wrapper class that creates a prompt template instead of passing a single string directly. This is an example of the *factory method* pattern, which provides a way to encapsulate the creation logic of objects since the pipe methods in the chain require a specific object instance to work.

This encapsulation allows for cleaner code and promotes reusability, as different parts of an application can generate prompts dynamically based on varying input values. For instance, different modules like customer service or marketing could use the same template structure while dynamically inserting different values for tone, length, or content based on their specific needs. The use of placeholders (e.g., with `{vowelCount}`) within the template string allows the framework to perform validation checks.

What's also useful is that the `@langchain/core/prompts` package provides a factory method for constructing few-shot learning prompts in a structured manner. Recall from the last chapter that with few-shot learning, we can enhance the performance of language models by providing them with example inputs and outputs. This technique allows the model to better understand the context and format of the desired responses.

Figure 6.2 shows the various parameters of the function `FewShotPromptTemplate` that is used for creating a prompt in this way, followed by a code listing that demonstrates its implementation.

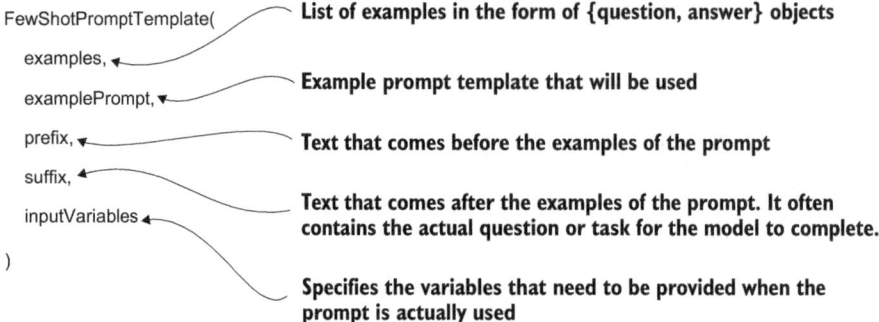

Figure 6.2 The `FewShotPromptTemplate` class takes five key parameters: `examples` (a list of question-answer pairs serving as reference examples), `examplePrompt` (a template for formatting each example), `prefix` (introductory text preceding the examples), `suffix` (concluding text following the examples, typically containing the main task or question), and `inputVariables` (specifying the variables to be provided when the prompt is used).

The following listing shows how to use the `FewShotPromptTemplate` to construct a comprehensive prompt template that uses few-shot learning that can be formulated in interactions with LLMs such as OpenAI.

Listing 6.2 Creating a few-shot prompt template

```
const examplePrompt = PromptTemplate.fromTemplate(
  "Question: {question}\nAnswer: {answer}"
);
const prefix = `You are an intelligent assistant designed
to answer questions accurately and concisely.
Below are some examples of how to approach different
types of questions. Pay attention to whether follow-up
questions are needed and how the final answer is presented.
After reviewing these examples, please answer the user's
question in a similar format.

Remember:
1. Determine if follow-up questions are needed.
2. If yes, ask the follow-up and provide an intermediate answer.
3. Always conclude with a final answer.

Here are some examples:`;

const prompt = new FewShotPromptTemplate({
  examples,
  examplePrompt,
  prefix,
  suffix: "Question: {input}",
  inputVariables: ["input"],
});
```

The examplePrompt defines how each example should be formatted using placeholders for dynamic content.

The prefix provides context and guidelines for how to respond based on previous examples, ensuring consistency in output.

The FewShotPromptTemplate combines all components (examples, formatter, prefix) into a single template that can be formatted with user input.

```
const formatted = await prompt.format({
  input: "What is the capital of Canada?",
});
```
◄— The format method generates a complete prompt by inserting user input into the template.

If you run this example from the command line, you will see the formatted output that can be used as a prompt. Run it from the root folder of the project source code using the following command:

```
$ node few-shot-chain.js
```

This would print the prompt template in the console, which you can review and adjust if needed.

Now that we have a robust method for constructing various structured prompts and a way to compose chains, we can explore how to integrate these functionalities into our web application using the Vercel AI SDK.

6.1.2 Integration with the Vercel AI SDK

Integrating LangChain's features with the Vercel AI SDK allows developers to utilize the best of both worlds when building generative AI web apps. Recall that, in the current state, the Vercel AI SDK is best used for handling interactions with structured data, streaming UI elements, and utilizing various tools.

However, its primary limitations lie in its focus on seamless integration with Next.js server components and the abstractions it provides for efficient UI updates. While these features are beneficial, tasks such as document ingestion and retrieval, prompt management, and chaining calls are left to the developer to implement independently. As an improvement to our existing knowledge, we want to utilize better abstractions that deal with more complex scenarios, such as handling large datasets by indexing documents or consolidating complex retrievals of relevant search queries.

This is where LangChain becomes an invaluable addition. We next explore how to integrate LangChain into our project.

INTEGRATING PROMPT TEMPLATES

Integrating a prompt template exported by the LangChain library into the existing project is a straightforward process. We can take the previously created few-shot prompt template and import it into the actions.jsx file, which handles the server-side logic. By formatting the prompt with user input—representing the user's query—we can seamlessly incorporate it into the `streamUI` history messages. The following listing shows the changes to the actions.jsx file.

Listing 6.3 Integrating prompt template into the conversation handler

```
import { prompt } from '../../lib/fewShotPrompt';   ◄— Imports the few-shot prompt template from the specified module

export async function continueConversation(input, provider, model) {
```

```
  'use server';
  const supportedModel = getSupportedModel(provider, model);
  const history = getMutableAIState();
  const formattedPrompt = await prompt.format({         ◄─── Formats the user input
    input                                                    using the imported prompt
  });                                                        template before sending it
  const result = await streamUI({                            to the AI model
    model: supportedModel,
    messages: [...history.get(), { role: 'user',         ─── Incorporates the formatted
content: formattedPrompt }],                            ◄─── prompt into the message history
    text: ({ content, done }) => {                           for streaming responses
      if (done) {
        history.done([...history.get(), { role: 'assistant', content }]);
      }
      return <ChatBubble role="assistant"
text={content} className={`mr-auto border-none`} />;
    },
  });

  return {
    id: generateId(),
    role: 'assistant',
    display: result.value,
  };
}
```

The code now imports the exported prompt template from listing 6.2. Within the continueConversation function, user input is formatted using prompt.format(), generating a structured prompt that includes relevant examples. This formatted prompt is then included in the streamUI call as part of the message history as well.

> **Project: chat-rsc-langchain**
>
> The code for this example project is in the ch06/chat-rsc-langchain folder. You can use that example by running this command in the root folder:
>
> ```
> $ npm run dev -w ch06/chat-rsc-langchain
> ```
>
> You'll need an OpenAI API key to access their REST API or a Google API key for Google services. For details on setting up and creating API keys, refer to the appendix.
>
> ```
> // .env
>
> OPENAI_API_KEY=<SECRET_KEY>
> GEMINI_API_KEY=<YOUR_GEMINI_API_KEY>
> ```

WARNING Make sure that your Google/Open API key is valid to avoid any problems during the installation process. Remember, this secret key should be kept confidential and not shared publicly.

Now start the application and try to ask a few trivia questions. You will see that the response format matches the prompt instructions we required when we defined the prompt template. Figure 6.3 showcases an example interaction.

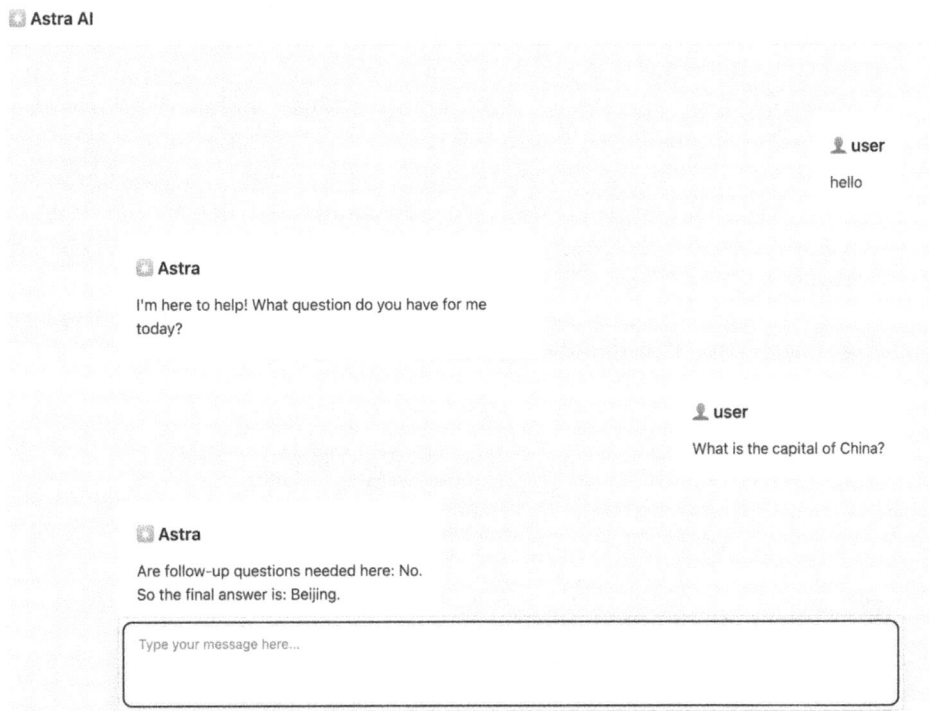

Figure 6.3   Sample interaction with our AI agent that formats the answers based on the examples provided. Behind the scenes, it utilized the `FewShotPromptTemplate` class from the LangChain.js project.

The main benefit of using a `PromptTemplate` is flexibility: if we need to change the style or tone or add more examples later, we can update the template in one place without refactoring the entire project. This makes the system more maintainable, easier to scale, and capable of producing higher-quality, more predictable responses.

INTEGRATING CHAIN CALLS

To integrate chain calls and stream the results back to the UI, it's important to note that we cannot currently use the `streamUI` function from the Vercel AI SDK in conjunction with the LangChain.js chain. This limitation arises because LangChain does not provide an adapter for the AI SDK's language model specification. Therefore, we need to separate these functionalities. So instead of using

```
import { google } from '@ai-sdk/google';
import { openai } from '@ai-sdk/openai';
```

176 CHAPTER 6 *Building AI workflows with LangChain.js*

We will be using

```
import { ChatGoogleGenerativeAI } from "@langchain/google-genai";
// import { ChatOpenAI } from '@langchain/openai';
```

Then, to integrate chain calls and stream the results back to the UI, we'll utilize the `createStreamableUI` function from the Vercel AI SDK and a new function, `getChainStream`, that returns a stream of the chain results as generated from the LLM.

Recall that the `createStreamableUI` returns an object that allows us to manage the UI updates dynamically. When we create a runnable chain using the `RunnableLambda.from` method, we can initiate a stream by calling `chain.stream()`. This setup enables us to push updates to the UI via the update methods and subsequently return the stream values. The rest is up to the Next.js server to render the components to the UI in real time.

Figure 6.4 showcases the steps of this workflow. The main idea is to feed the result of the first stream (the LangChain stream object) to the input of the `createStreambleUI` stream so that the UI will update in real time.

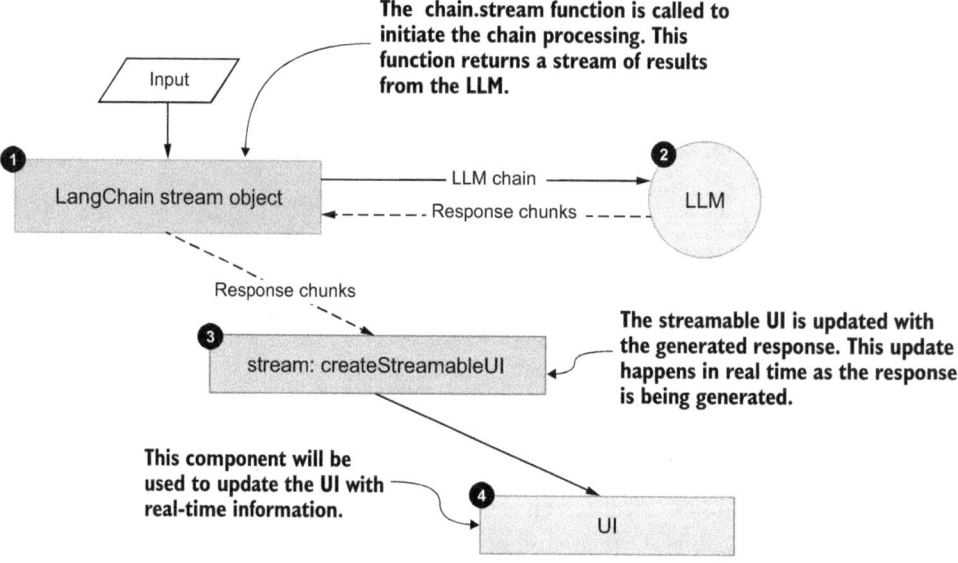

Figure 6.4 Step-by-step integration of the LangChain stream results with the `createStreambleUI` object. Every time there is an update, we push it to the UI stream, which in turn updates the UI in real time.

Here are the main steps to integrating chain calls:

1. The user provides an input prompt.
2. The `chain.stream` function is called to initiate the chain processing. This function utilizes the LangChain runnables that include calls to the LLM API and

returns a stream of results. For example, inside the chain, the `fetchWeatherData` function is called to fetch the weather data for the given city. The language model generates a response based on the processed weather data.

3 The `createStreamableUI` function is called to create a streamable UI component. This component will be used to update the UI with real-time information.

4 The streamable UI and the message history are returned, providing the user with the generated response and the updated UI.

> **Project: chat-rsc-langchain-chains**
>
> The code for this example project is in the ch06/chat-rsc-langchain-chains folder. You can use that example by running this command in the root folder:
>
> ```
> $ npm run dev -w ch06/chat-rsc-langchain-chains
> // .env
>
> OPENAI_API_KEY=<SECRET_KEY>
> GEMINI_API_KEY=<YOUR_GEMINI_API_KEY>
> ```
>
> For details on setting up and creating API keys, refer to the appendix.

Listing 6.4 shows the new changes we must add to the actions.jsx file that implements the functionality for asking the LLM for a weather report of a particular location. The LLM will respond in a particular format to the user. It's worth mentioning that the rest of the code stays the same without modifications. To see this in action, launch your Astra AI application and try entering a specific weather prompt like "What's the weather like in Galway, Ireland?" Astra AI will process your request and respond with a detailed weather report for the specified location, demonstrating its new capability to provide structured information.

Listing 6.4 Integrating the chain into the conversation chain

```
export async function getChainStream(city) {
  const chain = RunnableLambda.from(fetchWeatherData)    ◀── Builds a chain from
                              .pipe(promptTemplate)          weather data → prompt
                              .pipe(llm)                     → LLM → parser
                              .pipe(new StringOutputParser());

  const stream = await chain.stream({ city });    ◀── Starts streaming
  return stream;                                      results from the chain
}

export async function continueConversation(input) {
  const aiState = getMutableAIState();
  const stream = createStreamableUI();    ◀── Creates a live UI
                                              stream for updates

  stream.update(<div>Processing your request...</div>);
```

```
  const aiResponseStream = await getChainStream(input);
  let textContent = '';
  for await (const item of aiResponseStream) {        ◄─── Appends and displays
    textContent += item;                                    chunks as they arrive
    stream.update(<ChatBubble role="assistant"
text={textContent} className={`mr-auto border-none`} />);
  }
  stream.done();
  aiState.done({              ◄─── Saves the final response
    ...aiState.get(),              to conversation history
    messages: [
      ...aiState.get().messages,
      {
        id: generateId(),
        role: 'assistant',
        content: textContent,
      },
    ],
  });

  return {
    id: generateId(),
    display: stream.value,
    role: 'assistant',
  };
}
```

This setup chains multiple steps like data fetching, prompting, LLM processing, and parsing into one pipeline. By streaming, results flow to the UI piece by piece instead of waiting for completion, keeping the app responsive. The modular design also makes it easy to extend without rewriting the flow. This approach improves both flexibility and user experience.

Before we move on, there are a few caveats you need to be aware of when working with the two streams:

- *Closing the streams*—Close the streams after you finish working with them. In the provided code, this is done using `stream.done()` and `aiState.done()`.
- *Accumulating response*—Each item received from `aiResponseStream` represents a chunk of new data. To maintain a complete response, you must keep track of the current message using an accumulator like `textContent`.
- *Order of the chain and input variables*—Pay attention to the order of the chain and the input variables in the functions. In the provided example, the `city` variable in `chain.stream({ city })` is passed to `fetchWeatherData`, and the resulting object is then passed to the prompt template, which expects the rest of the template arguments. If an argument is missing, the LLM will likely complain.

6.2 Preparing and storing documents for retrieval using LangChain

With a basic integration of LangChain and the Vercel AI SDK in place, our focus now shifts to how we can prepare and store document embeddings for information retrieval. Although we've explored this scenario in the preceding chapter, the implementation part was very basic and manual. With LangChain, we can use the chaining functionality of the framework to create composable and reusable pipelines that create embeddings for our documents. The process of preparing documents for retrieval involves several key steps, as shown in figure 6.5.

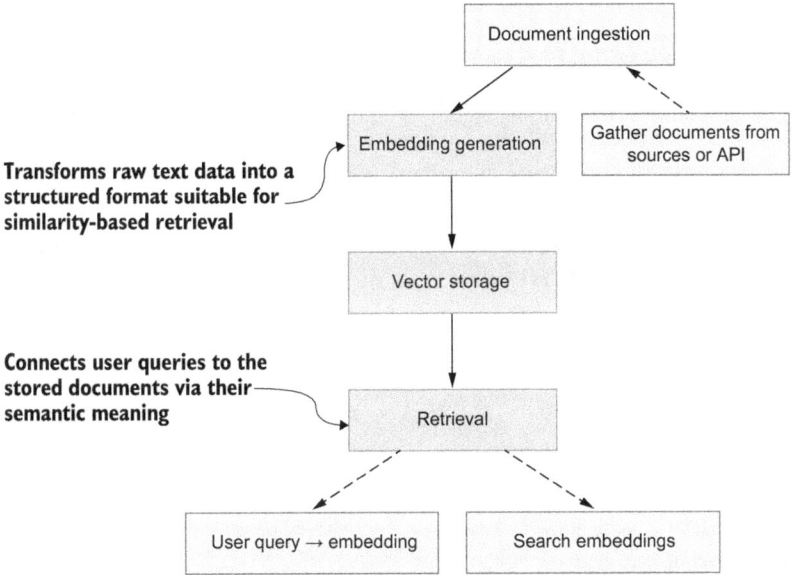

Figure 6.5 The process of document embedding preparation and retrieval. It starts with document ingestion from various sources, followed by embedding generation using LangChain to create semantic vectors. These embeddings are stored in a vector database, enabling efficient similarity-based querying during the information retrieval stage.

The main steps for preparing and retrieval of documents are

- *Document ingestion*—First, we need to gather our documents, which may come from various sources such as databases, APIs, or local files. We also expose an API endpoint to allow the user to upload their own documents from the UI.
- *Embedding generation*—Once the documents are ingested, we can use LangChain to generate embeddings for each document. These embeddings are vector representations that capture the semantic meaning of the content, allowing for effective similarity comparisons during retrieval.
- *Vector storage*—After generating embeddings, we need to store them in a suitable database or vector store. This storage solution should support efficient querying capabilities to allow quick access to the most relevant documents based on user input.

- *Information retrieval*—Finally, we create an instance of a `Retrieval` object available from the LangChain package that takes user queries, converts them into embeddings, and searches against the stored document embeddings to find the most relevant matches. This process can involve techniques like searching for the nearest neighbor or other similarity measures.

Let's see how each of these steps works and how we can accomplish them using LangChain.

6.2.1 Document ingestion using text splitters

The goal of text splitting is to transform documents into smaller, manageable chunks. This process helps ensure that the text fits within the model's context window and maintains semantic coherence. LangChain provides various built-in document splitters that simplify this task, allowing you to manipulate documents effectively. The *text splitters* take input data and transform it into output data suitable for storage. LangChain offers several types of text splitters, as shown in table 6.2.

Table 6.2 LangChain text splitters

Name	Splits	Adds metadata?	Description/use case
Recursive	Specific character	Yes	Recursively splits text while keeping related pieces together; recommended for initial splitting
HTML	HTML characters	Yes	Splits text based on HTML tags and structures
Markdown	Markdown syntax	Yes	Splits text according to Markdown syntax
Code	Code-specific characters	Yes	Splits code based on syntax specific to various programming languages
Token	A token	No	Splits text on tokens, with various methods available for token measurement
Character	A single user-defined character	No	Simple splitting based on a specified character

All of these text splitters work by first splitting the text into small, semantically meaningful units (often sentences). These units are then combined into larger chunks until a specified size limit is reached. Once the size limit is hit, that chunk becomes a standalone piece of text and a new chunk begins, with some overlap to maintain context between chunks.

The `RecursiveCharacterTextSplitter` is LangChain's recommended splitter. It is a highly flexible tool that can be adapted to various types of documents and the specific requirements of your project. It can split text recursively based on a list of separators, starting with newlines and progressing to smaller separators. This approach helps preserve the semantic structure of the text as much as possible.

The following listing shows how to create and use a `RecursiveCharacterTextSplitter` instance to split a text document into a list of chunks ready for ingestion in the vector storage.

Listing 6.5 Splitting a text into a list of chunks for retrieval

```
const splitter = new RecursiveCharacterTextSplitter({
  chunkSize: 100,
  chunkOverlap: 20,
});
const output = await splitter.createDocuments([text]);

/* Example output structure:
[
  Document {
    pageContent: "Artificial Intelligence (AI) is intelligence",
    metadata: { id: 2 }
  },
  Document {
    ...
  },
  ...
]
*/
```

- Sets the size of each text chunk to 100 characters
- Defines a 20-character overlap between chunks to maintain context continuity
- Splits the input text into a list of Document objects based on the configuration

The `RecursiveCharacterTextSplitter` takes two key parameters. First, `chunkSize` defines the maximum number of characters in each chunk. Second, `chunkOverlap` specifies how many characters should overlap between chunks to maintain context. The `createDocuments` method processes the text and returns a list of `Document` instances. Each `Document` contains a chunk of text and its metadata, making it ready for tasks like generating embeddings or storing in a vector database.

Once you have prepared the list of documents, the next step is to ingest them into a database optimized for storing embeddings. This task is handled by vector stores.

6.2.2 Introducing vector stores

Vector stores are specialized databases designed to store and efficiently query high-dimensional vector data. In the context of natural language processing and AI applications, these vectors typically represent embeddings of text documents or chunks of text.

In the previous chapter, we learned that embeddings are floating-point numbers that represent an encoded value of a prompt that can be used in a specific model. With these numbers, we can perform various operations, such as similarity searches, clustering, and classification. Vector stores provide several advantages here. They contribute to efficient similarity search by allowing for quick retrieval of documents that are similar to a given query vector; they can handle large numbers of vectors and perform fast searches even as the dataset grows; and they can seamlessly integrate with machine learning models, allowing for real-time updates and retrievals based on model output.

Since we are working with LangChain, we can use the various adapters that interface with open source vector databases like Supabase, Pinecone, or Chroma. The official website page at https://mng.bz/qRq6 provides a long list of supported vector stores. For simplicity, we will use the `MemoryVectorStore`, which uses an in-memory, ephemeral vector store and does not need additional configuration to employ.

Vector stores serve two primary functions: they ingest and encode documents into a searchable format, and they perform semantic searches to retrieve relevant documents based on their meaning. Let's see how to create and use a `MemoryVectorStore` instance to store documents and then perform a similarity search with it. The following listing shows the two key aspects of information retrieval: embedding generation (with `OpenAIEmbeddings`) and vector storage (via the `MemoryVectorStore.fromTexts` call).

Listing 6.6 Performing similarity search

```
MemoryVectorStore.fromTexts(
    ["Hello world", "Bye bye", "hello nice world"],
    [{ id: 2 }, { id: 1 }, { id: 3 }],
    new OpenAIEmbeddings({apiKey})
);

console.log(
await vectorStore.similaritySearch("hello world", 1));

/* Example output:
[
Document {
    pageContent: "Hello world",
    metadata: { id: 2 }
}
]
*/
```

- List of document texts to be stored
- Array of metadata objects corresponding to each text
- Instance of OpenAI embeddings generator for vector conversion
- Searches for documents similar to "hello world", limiting to one result

Once you have the list of documents stored in a vector store that is suitable for similarity search, you can query the database (via prompting) to answer specific questions or retrieve relevant information based on the context provided. This capability allows you to use the power of semantic search to find precise answers quickly and efficiently. This is the job of the `Retrieval` objects in LangChain.

6.2.3 Document retrieval

Document retrieval is the process of finding and returning the most relevant documents from our vector store based on a given query. Given an instance of a vector storage class, we can ask for the `Retriever` instance (using the `asRetriever` method).

The retrievers allow us to chain the process of retrieving the relevant documents with LangChain in a composable way and let us create robust and flexible query pipelines. The following listing shows how to create the `Retriever` instance and to include it in a prompt chain that performs a chat-like experience regarding the information included in the documents.

Listing 6.7 Calling a retriever with a prompt message

```
import { StringOutputParser }
from "@langchain/core/output_parsers";
import { formatDocumentsAsString } from "langchain/util/document";
import {
  RunnablePassthrough,
  RunnableSequence,
} from "@langchain/core/runnables";

const retriever = vectorStore.asRetriever();
const chain = RunnableSequence.from([
  {
    context: retriever.pipe(formatDocumentsAsString),
    question: new RunnablePassthrough(),
  },
  prompt,
  module,
  new StringOutputParser(),
]);
const answer = await chain.invoke({
question: "What is artificial intelligence?" });
/*
' Artificial Intelligence (AI) is basically intelligence shown by machines...
*/
```

- Imports the StringOutputParser for formatting output as strings
- Converts the vector store into a retriever, allowing for document retrieval based on queries
- Creates a sequence of runnable tasks to process input and generate an output
- Sets up the context by retrieving documents and formatting them as strings

Let's consider what is happening here. First, we create a retriever from a vector store using `vectorStore.asRetriever()`. This retriever is responsible for fetching relevant documents based on the input query.

We use a `RunnableSequence`, which defines a pipeline of operations. Within this sequence, we use the retriever in combination with `formatDocumentsAsString` to convert all the `Document` instances to a list of strings. The `RunnablePassthrough` is used to pass the original question through the chain unmodified (think of it as an identity function).

The chain also includes a prompt, the language model itself, and a `StringOutputParser` to format the output. When invoked, this chain takes a question as input, retrieves relevant context, formats it along with the question into a prompt, sends it to the language model, and then parses the response.

There are a few things you must consider when working with chains that include a combination of retrievers:

- *The order of chain events is important.* Each component in the chain must receive the expected inputs from the previous step. For example, if a prompt expects both context and a question, these must be provided by the preceding chain elements.
- *Perform argument matching.* It's essential to ensure that the outputs of one chain component match the expected inputs of the next. Mismatches can lead to errors like the one mentioned here: "Error: (f-string) Missing value for input context."

■ *Use the respective embeddings generator.* Use the appropriate embeddings constructor corresponding to the specific model you are working with. For example, when generating embeddings for the OpenAI model, utilize the `OpenAIEmbeddings` constructor.

6.2.4 Full example of preparing and storing documents with LangChain

This expanded example builds upon the previous retrieval-based chain by introducing an intermediate step to convert user questions into standalone questions. This addition aims to improve the accuracy of retrieving the answer.

> **Files: retrieval.openai.js, retrieval.google.js**
>
> The code for this example project is in a single file in the ch06 folder. You can use that example by running this command in the source folder if using Google:
>
> ```
> $ node retrieval.google.js
> ```
>
> If you are using Open AI, there is a separate file named retrieval.google.js in the same folder:
>
> ```
> $ node retrieval.openai.js
> ```
>
> You'll need an OpenAI API key to access their REST API or a Google API key for Google services. The appendix provides instructions for setting up a secret key for OpenAI and other providers:
>
> ```
> // .env
>
> OPENAI_API_KEY=<SECRET_KEY>
> GEMINI_API_KEY=<YOUR_GEMINI_API_KEY>
> ```

Let's call out the key differences and enhancements in this code. First, it introduces a `standaloneQuestionChain` that transforms the user's input into a concise standalone question. This step helps to remove ambiguity and context-dependent elements from the original query. Then the overall chain structure is more complex. It first generates a standalone question. Then it uses this standalone question for retrieval. Finally, it combines the original question and retrieved context and generates an answer. The retriever is now part of a more sophisticated chain (`retrieverChain`) that takes the standalone question as input, retrieves relevant documents, and formats them as a string. The example also shows multiple queries, with two invocations of the chain: one with a question about AI (which should be answerable from the context) and another that is out of scope.

Feel free to use additional queries to test the performance of the chain and to explore how well it retrieves information based on different types of questions. You can experiment to see how effectively the system handles both straightforward and ambiguous questions.

6.3 Using memory components in LangChain to remember conversation history

So far we have kept the history of messages in memory by using the `getMutableAIState` to keep the AI state in sync. But this approach lacks persistence and does not provide mechanisms for querying different conversational sessions, leaving it up to the developer to implement a suitable solution.

To be fair, the Vercel AI SDK provides an alternative method for storing and retrieving conversation history through callbacks. Specifically, it includes the `onFinish` callback of the `generateText` or `streamText` functions. This callback is triggered after the model's response and all tool executions are complete, providing access to the final text, tool calls, tool results, and usage information. This makes it an ideal point to store chat history in a database. Despite this helpful feature, developers still need to implement their own integration with a storage solution to manage conversation history effectively.

Using LangChain, developers have access to a set of tools to manage conversation history with proper abstractions and tools to verify the semantic meaning of them. Figure 6.6 shows how to implement conversational memory components using LangChain.

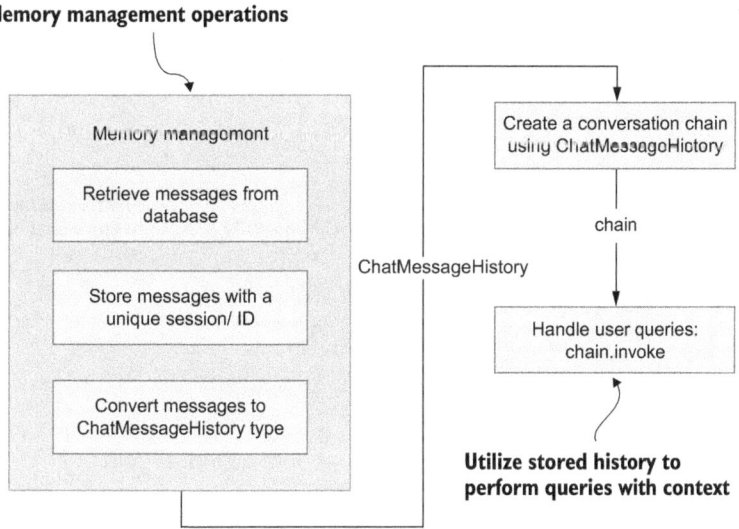

Figure 6.6 Managing user messages to improve conversation accuracy. Messages are retrieved from a database, stored with a unique session ID, and converted into a `ChatMessageHistory` format. This history is used to create a `ConversationChain` that handles user queries, using stored context to enhance response accuracy. The history is integrated into other prompts to refine the model's performance.

As you can see, the process starts by fetching previous conversation messages from a database or any storage solution you are using. This message retrieval will provide the context needed for the current interaction. Messages can be stored using a unique identifier for each session, and each user might have one or more sessions stored (like how ChatGPT and other services offer a way to select previous chat histories).

Once you have the past messages, convert them into instances of `ChatMessageHistory`. This allows you to manage and utilize the conversation history effectively. Next, create a chain out of `ChatMessageHistory`. Use the `ConversationChain` class provided, passing in the language model and the memory instance. This chain will handle interactions while maintaining context from previous messages.

Then you can perform queries based on conversation history. With everything set up, you can invoke the `ConversationChain` to handle user queries, using the stored conversation history for context. You can also include the chain in the context of other prompts to improve the accuracy of the results. These steps can be executed with just a few lines of code, as shown in the following listing.

Listing 6.8 Performing queries with a conversation memory

```js
import { SystemMessage, HumanMessage, AIMessage } from "@langchain/core/messages";
import { ChatMessageHistory } from "langchain/stores/message/in_memory";
```
Imports message classes for system, human, and AI interactions

```js
const llm = new ChatGoogleGenerativeAI({ apiKey });
const pastMessages = [];
pastMessages.push(new SystemMessage("You are a helpful assistant. Answer all questions to the best of your ability."));
pastMessages.push(new HumanMessage("Hi! I'm Jim."));

const memory = new BufferMemory({
    chatHistory: new ChatMessageHistory(pastMessages),
});
```
Initializes a memory buffer to store chat history

```js
const res1 = await chain.invoke({
input: "Can you give me an example of AI?" });
console.log({ res1 });
/*
Expected Output:
{
  res1: {
    text: "Sure! An example of AI is a virtual assistant like Google Assistant."
  }
}
*/

const res2 = await chain.invoke({ input: "What did I just ask you?" });
console.log({ res2 });
```
Logs the response from the assistant regarding the previous question

```
/*
Expected Output:
{
  res2: {
    text: "You just asked for an example of artificial intelligence."
  }
}
*/
```

Once you create an instance of the `ConversationChain` component, you can integrate it into other chains and perform more complex queries. This highlights the power of functional composability that the LangChain project provides.

Regarding the first step of retrieving past messages from a database, LangChain offers reference integrations for popular databases, enabling you to store and retrieve messages in a format that is human readable and easily indexable for searching. You can find the official list of supported integrations on the LangChain documentation page (https://js.langchain.com/docs/integrations/memory).

> **Files: memory.openai.js, memory.google.js**
>
> The code for the project, showing conversational memory in LangChain, is in the ch06 folder in the repository. You can use that example by running this command in the source folder if using OpenAI:
>
> `$ node memory.openai.js`
>
> If you are using Google AI, there is a separate file named memory.google.js in the same folder:
>
> `$ node memory.google.js`
>
> You'll need an OpenAI API key to access their REST API or a Google API key for Google services. For details on creating API keys, see the appendix:
>
> `// .env`
>
> `OPENAI_API_KEY=<SECRET_KEY>`
> `GEMINI_API_KEY=<YOUR_GEMINI_API_KEY>`

When implementing conversation memory in LangChain.js, keep the following in mind:

- *Prompt configuration*—If you wish to customize the prompt of the chain, you need to override the `prompt` parameter in the `ConversationChain` constructor. Ensure that you include the relevant variables for {history} and {input} in your prompt to maintain context effectively; otherwise, your requests will fail to complete.

- *Message transformation*—To transform messages into specific types such as `System-Message`, `HumanMessage`, or `AIMessage`, use their respective classes. This ensures that messages are correctly formatted for processing within the chain.
- *Unique memory instances*—Be cautious not to share the same history or memory instance between different chains, as this can lead to confusion and inaccuracies in conversation history. Use a dedicated chain for handling the history to keep interactions straightforward and organized.

We now have a comprehensive toolkit to ingest, store, and manage information related to generative AI content. It would be helpful if we could use LLMs to effectively manage these tools, determining which ones to use and continuously invoking reasoning prompts. That's what agents can help us do.

6.4 Utilizing agents in LangChain.js

LangChain agents are abstractions that use LLMs as reasoning engines to determine and execute actions. Unlike standalone LLMs that simply generate text based on prompts, agents can interact with their environment, make decisions, and take actions based on those decisions. Think of agents as pieces of software that have a coded set of end goals and a list of tools that can be used to reach those goals. This capability makes them ideal for complex, multistep tasks that require reasoning and interaction with external tools or APIs.

For instance, a database-querying agent can respond to user inquiries like "What are the top three products in sales this month?" by querying a local database for sales data, analyzing the results to identify the highest-selling products, and returning the relevant details to the user. Similarly, a web search agent can handle questions such as "What are the latest advancements in AI?" by utilizing a search engine API to perform a query, retrieving and summarizing recent articles or papers on the topic, and presenting this information back to the user in a concise format.

Once you create an instance of an agent and provide all the necessary context and tools to achieve their goal, the agent software will follow a heuristic path to accomplish their goals while tracking each step of their progress for transparency.

We saw examples of tool calling using the Vercel AI SDK in chapter 4, but their simplicity is also their drawback. LangChain agents offer a more sophisticated abstraction. They build upon the concepts introduced by Vercel, such as tool composition and application context, but provide a more flexible and powerful framework for creating intelligent, action-oriented systems. LangChain agents improve upon the Vercel AI SDK's multistep design by offering a more dynamic decision-making process and providing built-in support for a wide range of tools and APIs out of the box. They also allow for more complex reasoning chains and iterative problem solving (by utilizing techniques like synergizing reasoning and acting in language models [ReAct, a prompting framework]).

Given the complexity of agents and intelligent workflow automation, our focus here will be on practical methods for creating agents with LangChain and integrating them into web applications.

6.4.1 How LangChain agents work

Figure 6.7 illustrates the iterative workflow of LangChain agents, showing how they reason, act, and observe in a continuous loop until a final response is generated.

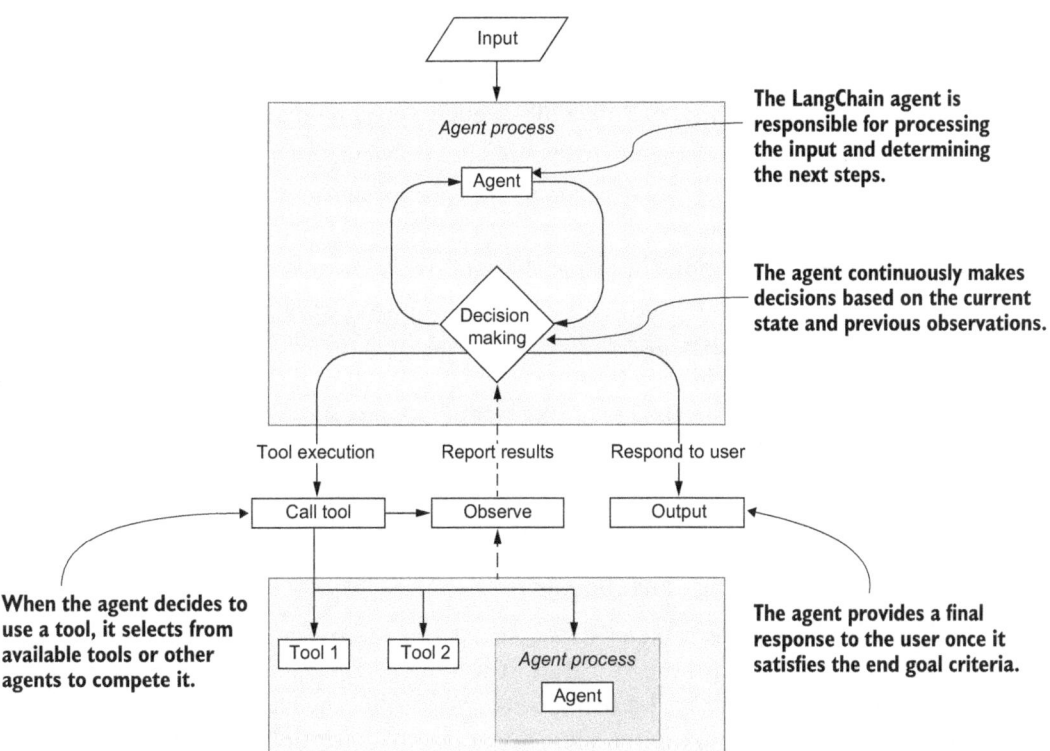

Figure 6.7 The iterative decision-making process of a LangChain agent. Starting with user input, the agent cycles through decision making, tool execution, and observation phases. The agent can utilize multiple tools (represented as tool 1, tool 2, or other agents) as needed. This process continues until the agent determines it can provide a final response to the user.

To see a better picture of this process, let's look at an example interaction for an agent that plans vacations. We start with the user prompt "Plan a seven-day vacation to Japan for a family of four with a budget of $5000." Here are the iterative steps that the agent will follow (with the tools used in italics):

1. The LangChain *agent* processes this request and begins its decision-making process.
2. The *agent* determines it needs more information and decides to use a *research* tool.
3. The *research* tool also contains a list of tools to facilitate planning. It contains a *web search* tool to gather information about travel to Japan, family-friendly activities, and typical costs.

4   The *agent* processes the search results, noting key information about flights, accommodations, and attractions.
5   The *agent* returns to the decision-making phase. It may decide it needs more specific information and choose to use a flight price comparison tool.
6   The *agent* uses the *flight comparison* tool to find suitable flights within the budget.
7   The *agent* notes the flight options and prices.
8   This process continues with the *agent* attempting to use other tools, such as
    – A *hotel booking* tool to find family-friendly accommodations
    – A *currency conversion* tool to ensure budget calculations are accurate
    – A *weather forecast* tool to recommend appropriate activities based on projected weather reports
9   After several iterations of using tools and making observations, the *agent* determines it has enough information to create a vacation plan.
10 The *agent* compiles all the gathered information into a coherent seven-day itinerary, including flight details, hotel recommendations, daily activities, and a budget breakdown. This final plan is presented to the user.

With all the information presented to the user, they will be able to ask additional queries to improve the results, which may also trigger additional iterations on the *agent* side. But as far as the user is concerned, the AI interface is abstracted from them.

6.4.2 Creating an agent using LangChain.js

Let's now look at an example of how to create an agent using LangChain and then how to integrate this with the Vercel AI SDK into our application. To create an agent capable of calling tools to achieve a specific goal, follow the basic steps outlined here. In LangChain, agents are essentially chains, as they are instances of the `Runnable` abstract class. This design allows them to be integrated into other chain compositions seamlessly.

To successfully create an agent, you will need the following three components:

- *A list of tools*—This includes the various tools your agent can utilize to perform tasks.
- *The AI model*—Specify which AI model your agent will use for processing and decision making.
- *The system prompt*—Define the system prompt that guides the agent's behavior and responses.

Having already covered how to define a system prompt and select an AI model, the next step is to establish your list of tools.

To create a tool, you can either use a list of available community tools from https://js.langchain.com/docs/integrations/tools/ or define a custom tool using the `tool` function from the `@langchain/core/tools` package. Once you have configured your tools, you can proceed to create an instance of your agent. The following listing shows how to instantiate an agent for integration into other chains.

Listing 6.9 Integrating an agent into the conversation chain

```
const tools = [new WikipediaQueryRun({
  topKResults: 3,
  maxDocContentLength: 4000,
  handleValidationError: (error) =>
console.error('Search validation error:', error)
})];
```
Initializes an array of tools with a WikipediaSearch instance that limits results to a maximum of the top three results

```
const AGENT_SYSTEM_TEMPLATE = `You are a helpful AI assistant
specializing in technical queries and web technologies.
When using WikipediaQueryRun for searches:
Prioritize technical documentation and standards
Cross-reference information from multiple sources
Format code examples using markdown
Example interaction: User: Explain WordPress webhook architecture
Action: WikipediaQueryRun(search="WordPress webhook system")
Response: WordPress webhooks use... [technical details]`;
```
Defines a template string for the agent's system message

```
const prompt = ChatPromptTemplate.fromMessages([
  ['system', AGENT_SYSTEM_TEMPLATE],
  ['human', '{input}'],
  new MessagesPlaceholder('agent_scratchpad'),
]);

const agent = createReactAgent({
  llm: model,
  tools,
  prompt,
});
```
Creates a new agent instance using the specified language model, tools, and prompt

```
const output = await agent.invoke({
  messages: [new HumanMessage("Everest")],
});
```
Invokes the agent with a specific input message and awaits its response

An agent in LangChain combines three key parts: a system prompt that defines behavior, a set of tools for taking actions, and a language model for reasoning. The createReactAgent function implements the ReAct framework, where the model not only generates answers but also decides when to use tools like Wikipedia search. This design matters because it transforms a static model into a dynamic problem solver—able to reason step by step, call external tools, and incorporate fresh, relevant information. Currently, ReAct is the main agent type supported in LangChain, but the framework may expand with new approaches in the future.

> **Files: agents.google.js, agents.google.js**
>
> The code for this example project is in the ch06 folder, including the code creating agents in LangChain. You can use that example by running this command in the source folder if using OpenAI :
>
> ```
> $ node agents.openai.js
> ```

> *(continued)*
>
> If you are using Google AI, there is a separate file named agents.google.js in the same folder:
>
> ```
> $ node agents.google.js
> ```
>
> You'll need an OpenAI API key to access their REST API or a Google API key for Google services. For details on setting up and creating API keys, see the appendix.
>
> ```
> // .env
>
> OPENAI_API_KEY=<SECRET_KEY>
> GEMINI_API_KEY=<YOUR_GEMINI_API_KEY>
> ```

In the provided code, we create an instance of a retriever, which is then transformed into a tool using the `createRetrieverTool` function from LangChain. By doing this, we can seamlessly integrate the existing retrieval functionality into our agent creation process.

The `createRetrieverTool` function allows us to define a specific name and description for the tool, enhancing its usability and clarity when interacting with the AI model. The agent will try to use this tool description as a hint about whether it needs to call this tool and based on the predefined system prompt message that it follows.

The rest of the code is like the one shown in figure 6.7. I've also included code that shows how to stream the results back to the console.

Two things can affect the effectiveness and usability of these agents. First are *context length limitations*. The number of tools you can incorporate into a LangChain agent is constrained by the context length of the language model being used. Each tool's name, description, and arguments contribute to the total token count in the prompt, so if you have many tools with different contexts, you might see problems with maximum context window limits.

Second, there are *delays* and *propagation effects. Propagation* refers to the way information flows through the various components of the agent. In a typical LangChain setup, data must be passed through multiple layers—such as retrievers, tools, and language models—before reaching the final output. Each step in this chain can introduce additional latency and make our application respond slower. There are several ways to improve the efficiency of the LLM responses, including minimizing unnecessary computations and using caching mechanisms where appropriate. In chapter 8, we will explore best practices and advanced techniques to address these challenges.

6.4.3 Agent integration with the Vercel AI SDK

Once we have an instance of an agent configured, we can integrate this with the Vercel AI SDK in a manner similar to the way we streamed the chaining calls for the weather tool earlier in this chapter.

Utilizing agents in LangChain.js

In this example, we employ an agent that uses the Wikipedia search tool available at https://mng.bz/7QN7, which allows the AI to answer a wide range of questions by searching the Wikipedia website in real time. The system now uses a ReAct agent, which can reason about its actions to gather information. The LLM responses are streamed, and the UI is updated in real time to show the agent's thought process, including when it's performing searches and generating responses. Again, we keep the same basic functionality intact: the UI elements stay the same, and we are using the createStreamableUI to push UI updates directly to the client as ReAct components.

> **Project: chat-rsc-langchain-agents**
>
> The code for this example project is in the ch06/chat-rsc-langchain-agents folder. You can use that example by running this command in the root folder:
>
> ```
> $ npm run dev -w ch06/chat-rsc-langchain-agents
> ```
>
> The appendix provides instructions on how to create a secret key for OpenAI and other providers:
>
> ```
> // .env
>
> OPENAI_API_KEY=<SECRET_KEY>
> GEMINI_API_KEY=<YOUR_GEMINI_API_KEY>
> ```

Now start the application and ask a question. The agent in the background will try to use the Wikipedia search tool to retrieve information and present this to the user. Since we configured the tool to fetch only a single result, the UI will list the first one found (figure 6.8).

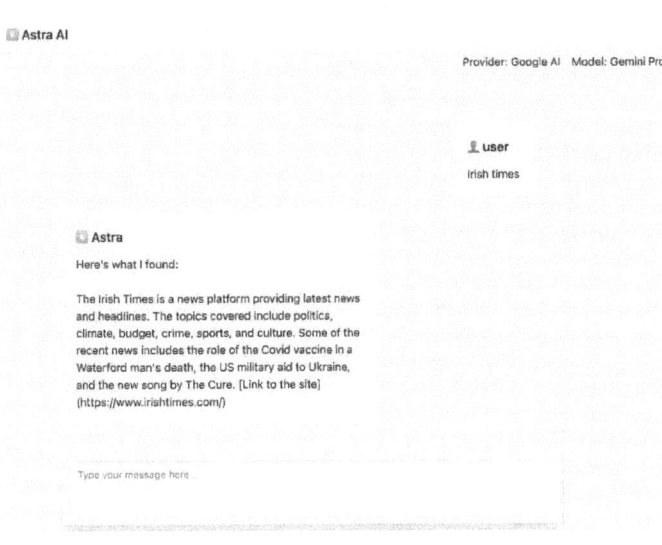

Figure 6.8 Sample interaction with our AI agent that uses `WikipediaQueryRun` to return a search result and display it to the user. Behind the scenes, the agent performs one or more calls to the provided tool to reach its end goals as instructed by the system prompt.

Feel free to review the code in the actions.jsx file, which contains the core logic of this functionality. The composable nature of LangChain runnables offers a nice way to swap implementation details on the fly while keeping the rest of the application intact.

6.4.4 Overview of LangChain.js modules

We've seen how to use some of the modules available in the LangChain.js library. Table 6.3 summarizes these, and the main modules provide helpers and functions that work together to allow us to develop complex generative AI chains.

Table 6.3 The main modules available from the LangChain.js library

Module	Description
langchain/prompts	Manages prompt templates and input variables
langchain/agents	Implements autonomous agents that can use tools and make decisions
langchain/chains	Combines multiple components into reusable pipelines
@langchain/core	Core package that exposes many common utilities and functions
@langchain/community	Community packages
langchain/vectorstores	Various vector database store integrations
langchain/storage	Provides abstractions for storing data in memory or in databases
langchain/document_loaders	Provides helpers for loading documents from various sources
@langchain/openai, @langchain/anthropic, ...	Provides LLM integration classes with various providers
langchain/output_parsers	Exposes classes that transform outputs from LLMs into a more suitable format

6.5 Going deeper with LangChain.js

Two advanced LangChain.js features, the LCEL and LangGraph, provide greater control and flexibility for designing complex chains and workflows. They're not essential, but I'll introduce them here in case you want to look into them. LCEL provides a declarative, streamlined approach to building and optimizing chains for linear workflows, while LangGraph offers a more advanced, graph-based framework for creating stateful, multistep agentic applications with conditional logic and loops.

6.5.1 LangChain Expression Language

The LCEL is a declarative approach to building chains from existing Runnables. This means you describe the desired workflow, and LangChain optimizes the execution

for you. A chain built with LCEL is itself a runnable, meaning it implements the full
`Runnable` interface and can be used like any other component.

COMPOSITION PRIMITIVES
LCEL chains are built by composing existing `Runnables`. The two primary composition
primitives are `RunnableSequence` and `RunnableParallel`:

- `RunnableSequence`—Chains `Runnables` sequentially, where the output of one runnable becomes the input for the next:

```
const chain = new RunnableSequence({
first: runnable1,
last: runnable2,
});
```

- `RunnableParallel`—Runs multiple `Runnables` concurrently with the same input. The output is an object with keys corresponding to the `Runnables` and values as their respective outputs:

```
const chain = new RunnableParallel({
   key1: runnable1,
   key2: runnable2,
});
```

- `RunnableLambda`—A special primitive that allows you to define generic JavaScript functions as runnables, making it easy to incorporate custom logic into your chains:

```
const someFunc = RunnableLambda.from((input) => {
return input;
});
const chain = someFunc.pipe(runnable1);
```

The best part is that all of the chains you've already built with runnables are compatible with LCEL, so you can start using it to improve performance, enhance observability, and increase the readability of your code.

6.5.2 LangGraph

LangGraph (https://langchain-ai.github.io/langgraphjs/) is an open source library built on top of LangChain that allows you to create stateful, multiactor applications with LLMs. Unlike the linear, chain-based approach of the LCEL, LangGraph uses a graph-based architecture to model workflows with loops and conditional logic. This makes it an ideal tool for building complex, dynamic systems like autonomous agents.

LANGGRAPH VS. LCEL
While LangGraph is built on LangChain's foundation and uses its components, it's designed for a different type of workflow:

- *LCEL*—Best for directed acyclic graphs or linear workflows where a specific sequence of steps is known in advance. A simple retrieval-augmented generation pipeline—where you fetch documents, summarize them, and answer a question—is a perfect example of a straightforward, one-way process that doesn't need to loop back.
- *LangGraph*—Better for *cyclical graphs* and *stateful applications* that require more control and adaptive behavior. This is crucial for agents that need to decide what to do next based on an evolving situation, like a chatbot that needs to rephrase a query after a failed search or a system that needs to ask for clarification from a user.

In short, LCEL is a great orchestration tool for simpler chains, but when you need to build complex, multiagent systems with loops, conditional logic, and persistent memory, LangGraph is the more powerful and flexible choice.

Summary

- LangChain.js provides a framework for building context-aware AI applications, integrating features like agents, memory, and chains to enhance user interactions.
- The framework allows for effective prompt management using tools like `PromptTemplate` and few-shot learning strategies, enabling developers to create more accurate and relevant AI responses.
- The modular design of LangChain.js includes various packages that simplify different aspects of development, such as document loading, vector storage, and output parsing.
- Runnables in LangChain enable flexible and composable workflows by allowing developers to chain multiple operations for processing data efficiently.
- The use of memory in LangChain enables applications to retain conversation history and enhance the contextual understanding of ongoing interactions with users.
- Integration with the Vercel AI SDK allows developers to combine the strengths of both platforms, using LangChain's advanced features while utilizing Vercel's efficient UI updates and structured data handling.
- Agents in LangChain can utilize both community-driven and custom-made tools for real-time information retrieval, providing dynamic responses that enhance user experience.

Document summarization and RAG with LangChain.js

This chapter covers

- Building a document summarization app
- Implementing retrieval-augmented generation
- Providing grounding support for AI outputs
- Processing documents with advanced techniques

Let's put the tools and techniques we've learned into action with two more sophisticated web apps. First, we'll create a document summarization web application capable of handling two document formats (PDFs and DOCX) implementing advanced semantic chunking strategies and generating meaningful summaries. The application will also show us how to overcome some limitations of document summarization, such as prompt compression and k-means clustering to improve context retention and summary quality.

The second project uses retrieval-augmented generation (RAG) to create a system that dynamically retrieves and synthesizes information based on a list of documents. By combining hybrid search strategies, multistep document processing, and prompt engineering, we will develop a web application that can answer queries about the data we provide. The application will use techniques like grounding to ensure the generated responses remain faithful to the source documents, enhancing the accuracy and reliability of the AI-generated content.

You should be comfortable with the Vercel AI SDK (chapters 3–4) and LangChain.js workflows (chapter 6). Familiarity with prompt engineering techniques (chapter 5) will help you implement effective summarization and RAG strategies.

7.1 Building a document summarization web application with LangChain.js

We've used the Vercel AI SDK to create reactive UIs powered by large language models (LLMs), and LangChain.js to develop scalable conversational platforms capable of complex data processing. Now we will use that know-how to build a web application that uses generative AI to take complex documents and produce concise, meaningful summaries. This app features a user-friendly web interface that accepts user-submitted documents, such as Word (DOCX) files or PDFs. Some of the challenges we'll face include addressing inaccuracies, managing large documents that exceed the LLM's context window, and ensuring the quality of summaries.

7.1.1 Summarization app project requirements

The application we are going to build has these key elements:

- *Web interface for document submission*—A user-friendly interface that allows users to upload documents, such as Word files or PDFs, for summarization.
- *Document-processing pipeline*—An architecture that includes steps for document loading, text extraction, chunking, and semantic embedding to prepare the content for summarization.
- *Summarization workflow*—Implementation of various summarization techniques using LangChain.js and LLMs, enabling the generation of concise summaries from the processed documents.
- *Integration with the Vercel AI SDK*—We will utilize server actions to provide a nice user experience while summarizing documents.

7.1.2 Architecture and workflow

Before writing any code, we want to establish the components and technologies that will bring this web application to life. This overview will help us define the scope and determine which libraries and tools to use.

In this document summarization service, the web application architecture follows a pipeline approach. Each document moves through various processing stages from upload to summary generation, creating a streamlined workflow. We'll use a set of familiar technologies that we've already explored:

- *Next.js*—Provides a framework for building responsive web interfaces using synergizing reasoning and acting in language models (ReAct)
- *Vercel AI SDK*—Responsible for connecting the AI and UI state components and streaming components to the UI
- *LangChain.js*—Powers the backend document-processing pipelines, which enables prompt management and handling of multistep workflows
- *LLMs*—Drive the generative AI capabilities, performing summarization from user input

Figure 7.1 provides a visual representation of the typical workflow for this application.

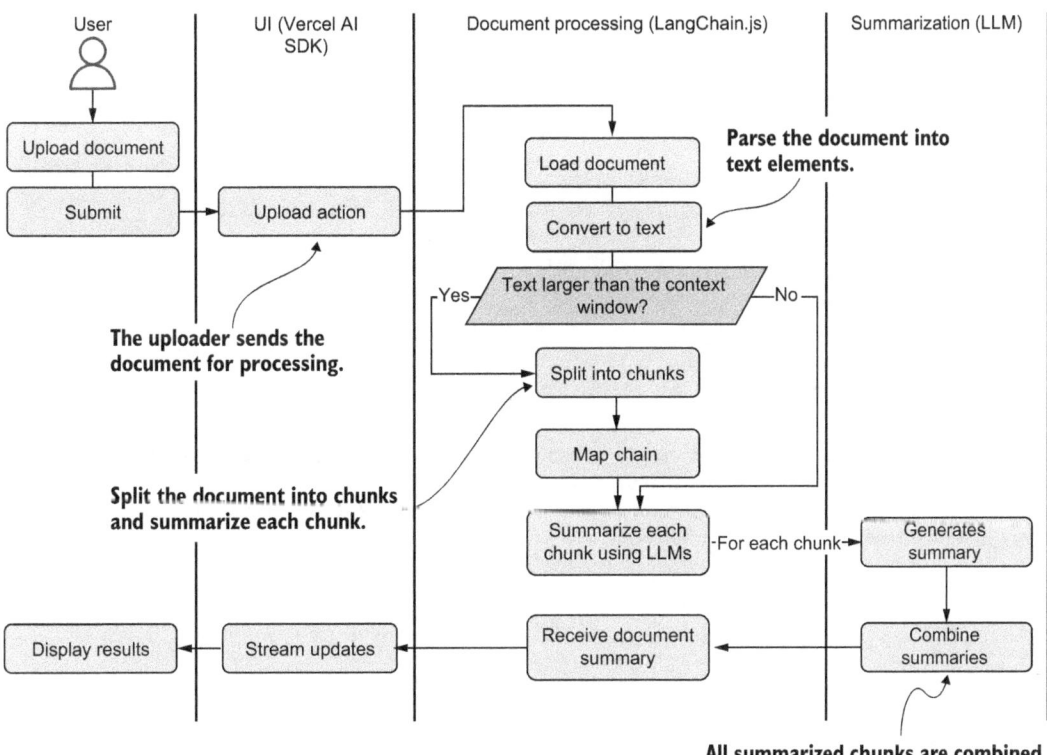

Figure 7.1 The architecture of a document summarization system integrating LangChain.js and the Vercel AI SDK. The user uploads a document, which is processed by LangChain.js; it checks if the document exceeds the context window, splits it into chunks, and summarizes each chunk using LLMs. The individual summaries are then combined by the summarization (LLM) component, which is displayed to the user through the UI.

The summarization step illustrates one approach to processing a large document into manageable chunks using the *MapReduce* method. This technique involves breaking down the document into smaller sections, summarizing each chunk independently, and then aggregating these summaries into an overview. This multistage process is particularly effective for handling extensive texts, as it allows for parallelization of tasks. Figure 7.2 shows this approach close up.

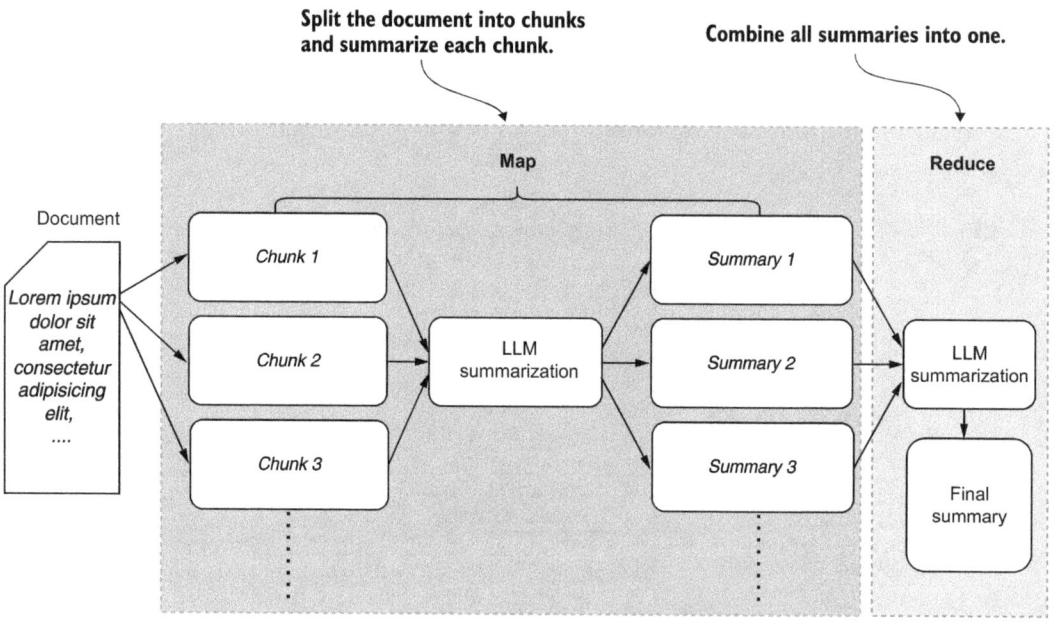

Figure 7.2 The MapReduce summarization pattern, behind the scenes. The input document is divided into smaller chunks. Each chunk is then processed independently by the map function, generating intermediate summary pairs. These pairs are subsequently organized and are grouped together. The reduce step is then applied to these grouped pairs, aggregating the values to produce a final summary.

Here's a breakdown of the steps:

1 *Split document into chunks*—The first step is to split the original document into smaller "chunks" or sections.
2 *Summarize each chunk*—For each chunk, a summarization process is applied to generate a summary of the content in that chunk.
3 *Map*—The summaries of each chunk are then "mapped" to an intermediate representation inside a data structure that keeps track of the individual summaries.
4 *LLM summarization*—The intermediate representation of the individual chunk summaries is then passed through an LLM summarization process. This step takes the individual chunk summaries and combines them into a high-level summary.
5 *Reduce*—The final step is to "reduce" the LLM-generated summaries into a single, combined summary that represents the overall document.

MapReduce is not the only option available within LangChain. The framework also supports other summarization strategies through the `loadSummarizationChain` function, including the stuffing and refine methods.

The *stuffing* method involves passing the entire document to the language model in a single call. It "stuffs" the text into the prompt as context, allowing the model to generate a summary based on all available information at once. This is the preferred choice for shorter documents that fit inside the context window.

The *refine* method operates by first generating an initial summary from a small chunk of data. Subsequent chunks are then processed, with this initial output being refined based on new information. This is the preferred choice for larger documents where context from previous outputs is used to improve the final output. Figure 7.3 demonstrates how the refine summarization process works.

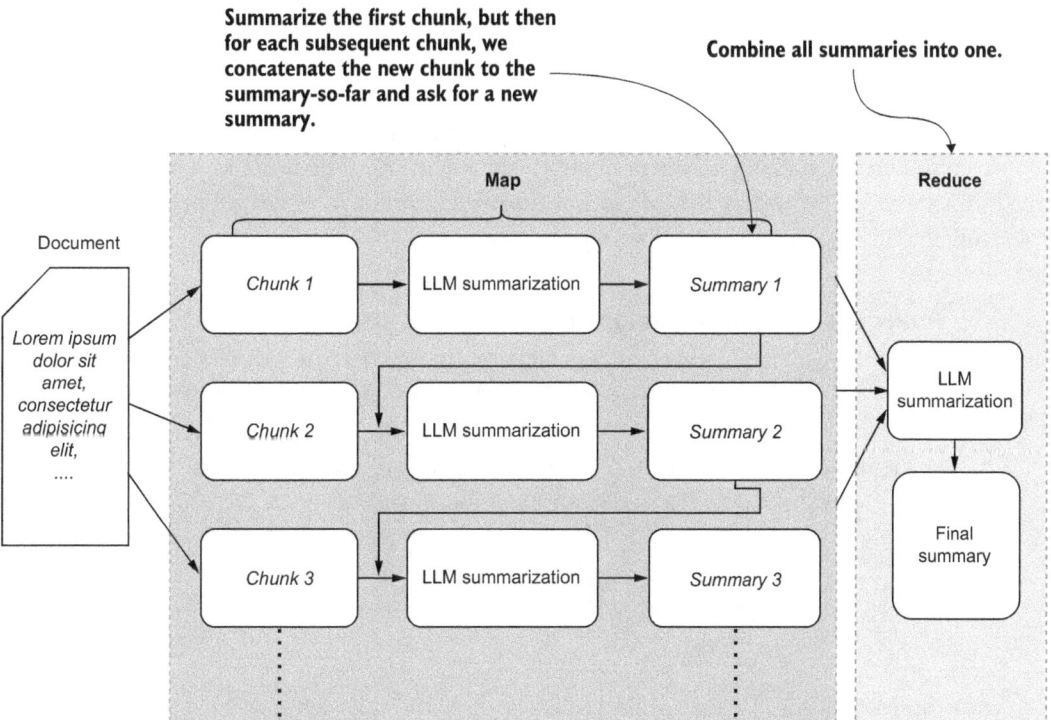

Figure 7.3 How the refine summarization method operates behind the scenes. This method enhances summarization quality by iteratively updating the summary with each new chunk of text. Initially, the first chunk is summarized, and for each subsequent chunk, it is concatenated to the existing summary. A new summary is generated based on this updated text, repeating the process until all chunks have been processed.

Each of these two methods has its advantages and tradeoffs, which you will need to consider when you expose any application that uses them to the public. For example, the stuffing method struggles with longer or more complex documents, while the refine method is more complex and may propagate errors if early summaries are of poor quality.

As we address the challenges that come from increased complexity, we also need to consider problems that may arise from integrating these new elements into our established app. In particular, we will encounter limitations related to performance and overall user experience. What happens if a user uploads a large document? Will our application be able to handle it without losing accuracy? Could the design of our processing pipelines lead to poor performance?

7.1.3 Building the document summarization web application

The summarization app kicks into gear when a user uploads either a PDF document or a Word document through the user interface. This action triggers a server-side process that handles the uploaded document. The server action uses LangChain.js to summarize the document. After summarizing the document, the server streams the summarized text back to the user in their preferred format—either as a paragraph or as bullet points—based on their prompt preferences. For simplicity, we will not keep the original document itself in context after processing.

The main challenges here are ensuring accurate summarization across various document types, managing context effectively during user interactions, and optimizing performance to provide timely responses during summarization tasks. Let's start with the main code that handles the document processing.

> **Project code: Summarization-examples**
>
> The code for this project is available at https://github.com/Generative-AI-Web-Apps/Code/tree/main/ch07/summarization-examples in the ch07/summarization-examples folder.
>
> You'll also need either the OpenAI API or the Google API keys to access their REST API. For details on creating API keys, refer to the appendix:
>
> ```
> // .env
> OPENAI_API_KEY=<OPEN_AI_SECRET_KEY>
> GEMINI_API_KEY=<GOOGLE_AI_SECRET_KEY>
> ```

NOTE The core LangChain.js library is implemented in TypeScript/JavaScript and does not require Python to be installed on your system. It runs natively in Node.js or browser environments. However, some community integrations or example projects may depend on Python tools or libraries and thus require a Python environment.

LOADING AND PREPROCESSING THE DOCUMENT

Ideally, we want the document chunks to contain relevant data ready to be used in an LLM prompt. Listing 7.1 shows a script that captures the core piece of this functionality.

The main idea is to parse the document and detect its type. Then, it loads documents (PDF or DOCX) using the LangChain.js community packages, specifically `PDFLoader` and `DocxLoader`. Those are convenient functions that parse a document and return a list of `Document` types, which we can further use for splitting it up into chunks for summarization.

Listing 7.1 Loading different document types

```
import { PDFLoader } from "@langchain/community/document_loaders/fs/pdf";
import { DocxLoader } from "@langchain/community/document_loaders/fs/docx";
import path from "path";

const loaders = {
  pdf: PDFLoader,
  docx: DocxLoader,
};

const loadDocumentFromFile = async (filePath) => {
  const fileExtension = path.extname(filePath)
.substring(1).toLowerCase();
  const LoaderClass = loaders[fileExtension];

  if (!LoaderClass) {
    console.error(`No loader found for file extension: ${fileExtension}`);
    return null;
  }

  const loader = new LoaderClass(filePath);
  return await loader.load();
};

loadDocumentFromFile("./data/aesops-fables.pdf")
  .then((documents) => {
    console.log(`Loaded ${documents.length} documents.`);
  })
  .catch((error) => {
    console.error("Error loading documents:", error);
  });
```

- Imports the PDFLoader class from the LangChain community package to handle PDF documents
- Imports the DocxLoader class for handling DOCX files
- Functions to load a document from a specified file path
- Calls the loadDocumentFromFile function with a specific PDF file path

Once we have the parsed documents, we need to split them into chunks that will be used for summarization and for fitting the context window that many LLMs impose limits on.

> **NOTE** The `PDFLoader` from LangChain.js serves as a reasonable middle ground for parsing PDF documents for LLMs, but it's not perfect. The analysis of PDF content using these advanced models remains an ongoing area of study aiming to improve reliability.

SPLITTING THE DOCUMENT INTO MANAGEABLE CHUNKS

Before processing large documents, it's important to split them into smaller, manageable chunks. This ensures that the language model can handle the content efficiently without losing context. LangChain provides two common approaches:

RecursiveCharacterTextSplitter and TokenTextSplitter. Here we use, Recursive-CharacterTextSplitter because it splits text by characters while maintaining a small overlap between chunks. This overlap preserves context across chunk boundaries, which is essential for tasks like summarization or information retrieval. Once the document is split into chunks, each piece can be processed individually, allowing strategies like MapReduce to summarize or analyze the content effectively.

The code that performs this task is just a couple of lines long:

```
const splitter = new RecursiveCharacterTextSplitter({
    chunkSize: 1500,
    chunkOverlap: 200,
});

const documentChunks = await splitter.splitDocuments(documents);
```

Once we have all the splits of the text, we can perform the summarization strategies we introduced using the MapReduce method.

APPLYING THE SUMMARIZATION CHAIN AND DISPLAYING TO THE USER

The core process of facilitating the summarization of large documents by using various techniques, including the MapReduce method, is encapsulated within the loadSummarizationChain function in LangChain.js. This function takes an instance of an LLM and an options object that specifies the desired summarization type, such as "map_reduce", "refine", or "stuff". The following listing shows the code that we use to perform the summarization using MapReduce.

Listing 7.2 Performing summarization using MapReduce

```
import { loadSummarizationChain } from "langchain/chains";

const chain = loadSummarizationChain(model, {          ◀── Initializes the summarization chain by
  type: "map_reduce",                                       calling loadSummarizationChain with
  verbose: true,                                            the specified map_reduce type
});

// Call the summarization chain
const res = await chain.invoke({                       ◀── Invokes the summarization chain
  input_documents: docs,                                    asynchronously with the input documents
});                                                         (docs) to generate a summary

console.log("Summarization Result: ", res);
/*
Summarization Result:  {
  text: `Hadley Wickham's "Tidy Data" advocates for a
standardized data structure—each variable in a column,
each observation in a row, each unit in a table—to simplify
 data analysis.  This "tidy data" framework, illustrated
through numerous examples and contrasted with messy data
formats, improves data cleaning, manipulation, and
visualization, especially within R's vectorized environment.
  While acknowledging limitations and ongoing challenges
```

```
in data cleaning, the paper promotes tidy data as a
crucial step towards more efficient and accessible
statistical analysis.\n`
}
*/
```

In this listing, the `loadSummarizationChain` function takes the model as the first argument and an options object as the second argument, where the `type` is set to `"map_reduce"` and `verbose` is set to `true` to enable verbose logging.

The returned object then is used to invoke the summarization chain by calling the `invoke` method, passing in an object with the `input_documents` property, which contains the documents to be summarized.

Once the process is complete (which, depending on the length of the document and the network connection, could take a few seconds), the final result is printed to the console.

> **NOTE** I've added another example using the refine methodology in the file located at summarize-refine.js inside the ch07/summarization-examples folder.

> **WARNING** Summarizing large documents will cost you credits. We provide an example folder with some PDF documents that are fairly small, but if you want to summarize larger documents, you should be aware of the cost implications. Using the GPT-3.5 Turbo model is generally cheaper than using GPT-4 or later models. Additionally, I found that the Google AI provider is often more reliable and generous in terms of summarizing text compared to the OpenAI provider. Be sure to keep track of your credit usage when summarizing longer documents using either the MapReduce or the refine methods. You can typically monitor your usage and spending directly through the respective AI provider's online dashboard (e.g., OpenAI's Usage Dashboard, Google Cloud's billing section for Gemini API).

Before we showcase the application, we spend some time explaining the main challenges and limitations when it comes to document summarization using LLMs.

7.1.4 Caveats and limitations of document summarization

While our current examples of summarizing documents are effective for relatively small texts, there are several nuances to consider when addressing edge cases.

PARSING AND CLEANING UP DOCUMENTS

The initial step of parsing documents can be entangled with difficulties, especially when dealing with complex formats like PDFs or DOCX files. Text may be scattered across different sections, embedded in images, or poorly formatted, leading to incomplete or inaccurate data extraction. For instance, in PDFs, text can be encoded in various ways, making it challenging to extract the content accurately. Elements like tables, footnotes, and annotations can complicate the parsing process further.

We normalize the document content to improve summarization accuracy by ensuring the summarization algorithm focuses on the core substance of the documents and to reduce computational processing costs by performing upfront content-cleaning steps.

Here are three remedies to try:

- *Removing headers and footers*—During or after parsing of the documents, you can preprocess the results to remove extraneous content such as headers, footers, page numbers, and watermarks that do not contribute to the main text. Bear in mind, though, that this process is harder to do for PDFs compared to DOCX documents since headers and footers are simply text elements in a page.
- *Removing stopwords*—Another important aspect of cleaning up documents is the removal of stopwords—common words that do not carry significant meaning (like "and," "the," "is"). By filtering out these words, you can reduce noise in the data and reduce the number of tokens that you use for summarization.
- *Extracting images*—The current implementation of the `PDFLoader` does not recognize or extract images from PDF files, resulting in these visual elements being overlooked during the parsing process. To enhance the functionality of the loader, an alternative solution involves extracting images from the PDF and marking their locations within the document. Once the images are extracted, you can utilize optical character recognition software or an external LLM to generate descriptive text for each image. This text can then be attached to the corresponding document instance as metadata.

These solutions aim to address the current limitations that you may face when processing documents for summarization and analysis. I've also included a helper function, `normalizeDocuments`, in the summarization application folder (ch07/summarization-examples). This function streamlines the normalization of document content by implementing various cleaning techniques, and you are free to extend it as you see fit. The following listing shows its main functions.

Listing 7.3 Normalization of document content

```
function normalizeDocuments(docs) {
  return docs.map((doc) => {
    let pageContent;
    if (typeof doc.pageContent === "string") {         // Consolidates the page
      pageContent = doc.pageContent;                   // content if it's stored as an
    } else if (Array.isArray(doc.pageContent)) {       // array of strings, by joining
      pageContent = doc.pageContent.join("\n");        // the array elements with
    }                                                  // newline characters
    if (pageContent) {

                                                       // Removes any leading or trailing
      pageContent = pageContent.trim();                // whitespace from the page content

      // Remove unwanted characters (e.g., figure references)
      pageContent = pageContent.replace(/Figure \d+:.*?\n/g, '').replace(/-\
  d+\n/g, '');
```

Building a document summarization web application with LangChain.js

```
        // Normalize spaces
        pageContent = pageContent.replace(/\s+/g, ' ');          ◄── Removes empty
        pageContent = pageContent.replace(/(\s*l\s*){2,}/g, ' ');     spaces and
                                                                     irregular
        // Filter out non-content lines                              characters
        const filteredDocument = pageContent.split('\n').filter(line =>
          !line.includes('References') && !line.includes('Acknowledgments')
        )[0];                                        ◄──
        doc.pageContent = filteredDocument;              Filters out any lines that contain
        return doc;                                      the words "References" or
      }                                                  "Acknowledgments," as these are
                                                         likely not part of the main content
      return null;
    }).filter(doc => doc.content !== null);
// Filter out any null entries from the result
}
```

MEASURING THE COST OF MULTIPLE LLM CALLS

One of the key challenges when using LLMs in an application like the summarization tool is the cost management aspect, particularly when dealing with large documents.

The problem arises because LLMs have a limited context window; they can only process a certain amount of text in a single API call. When the input document exceeds this context window, we are forced to make multiple calls to the LLM to process the full content. Each of these API calls incurs a cost, which can quickly ramp up, especially for applications that need to process large volumes of text.

To help manage these costs, LangChain.js provides a built-in mechanism for tracking token usage during LLM calls using callback functions. This allows you to gain insights about the number of tokens used on each call. The following listing shows an example of how you can set up this token usage tracking.

Listing 7.4 Tracking usage of tokens

```
import TokenTracker from "./TokenTracker.js";        ◄── Imports the TokenTracker class
const tokenTracker = new TokenTracker();                 from the TokenTracker.js file to
const model = new ChatGoogleGenerativeAI({               manage token usage
  apiKey: apiKey,
  model: "gemini-2.0-flash",
  streaming: false,                                  Callback function triggered
  callbacks: [                                       when an LLM call completes
    {
      handleLLMEnd: (output) => {        ◄──
        const { message } = output.generations[0][0];   Updates the token tracker
        tokenTracker.                                   with usage metadata from
updateTokens(message.usage_metadata);                   the message
        console.log('Current Token Usage:', tokenTracker.getCurrentUsage()); ◄──
        console.log('Token Differences:', tokenTracker.getTokenDiff());
      },                                                     Logs the current
    },                                                       token usage statistics
  ],                                                         to the console
});
```

The `TokenTracker` class is a custom implementation to monitor and manage the token usage during interactions with the language model. This class tracks the tokens used in the current session but can also be extended to export these token metrics to an analytics service if needed.

The provided code creates an instance of `TokenTracker` to monitor the number of tokens used in the current session. When an API call to the language model completes, the `handleLLMEnd` callback function is triggered, extracting the message object from the output. It then updates the token tracker with usage metadata from the message, which includes details about input and output tokens.

> **NOTE** While this implementation captures token usage effectively through message metadata, there is an alternative method for counting tokens using `output.llmOutput?.tokenUsage`, but it is limited to certain models and may not be reliable across different providers. For example, since it uses js-tiktoken, it can only currently support counting tokens for OpenAI models and not Google Gemini models.

What can we do with this addition? For one, it allows us to gain precise insights into how many tokens are consumed during each API call, enabling better cost management and optimization of resources. Monitoring the token usage is crucial since it will allow us to refine our prompts to minimize unnecessary token usage.

Let's move on to the UI part of the application and showcase the first usable demo of the whole web application.

7.1.5 Demonstrating the app

As we develop the application to handle the goals we aim to achieve, we need to make some small adjustments to the UI we have been using so far to accommodate this new feature. These changes will improve the user experience and ensure that users can efficiently interact with the summarization functionality.

First, we will implement a single input field that allows users to either paste text directly or upload a document for summarization. While the user waits for the summarization to complete, we will include a message to keep them informed that their request is being processed. Finally, once the summary is generated, it will be displayed in a message format within the UI.

> **NOTE** The source code for the examples in this chapter is available at https://github.com/Generative-AI-Web-Apps/Code/tree/main/ch07/summarization-web-app.

> **Project code: summarization-web-app**
>
> The code for this example project is in the ch07/summarization-web-app folder. You can use that example by running this command in the root folder of the project repository:

```
$ npm run dev -w ch07/summarization-web-app
```

You'll also need either the OpenAI API or the Google API keys to access their REST API. For details on setting up API keys, refer to the appendix.

```
// .env
OPENAI_API_KEY=<OPEN_AI_SECRET_KEY>
GEMINI_API_KEY=<GOOGLE_AI_SECRET_KEY>
```

NOTE The core LangChain.js library is implemented in TypeScript/JavaScript and does not require Python to be installed on your system. It runs natively in Node.js or browser environments. However, some community integrations or example projects may depend on Python tools or libraries and thus require a Python environment.

The following figures are screenshots of the new UI when running the application. In the first use case (figure 7.4), the user uploads either a PDF or a DOCX document, and the AI provides a summary of this document.

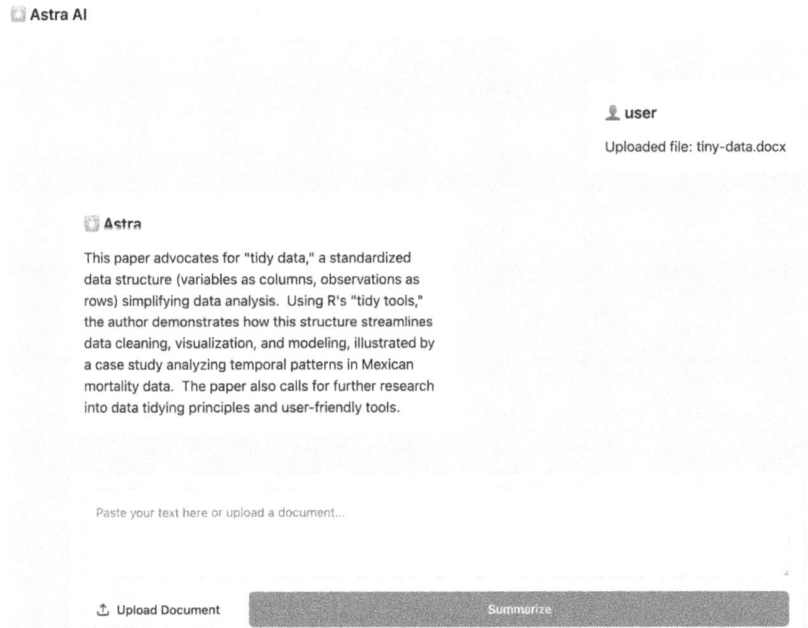

Figure 7.4   How the web application uses a MapReduce summarization technique to generate a concise summary from a large document through the UI. The application then sends the input to the backend service, which uses the LangChain.js library to split the document into manageable chunks, process them through the summarization model, and return the final summary to be displayed in the user interface.

In the second use case (figure 7.5), the user pastes some text in the message box instead of the file upload, and the AI web app again provides a summary of that text. Feel free to run the application locally and explore its functionality.

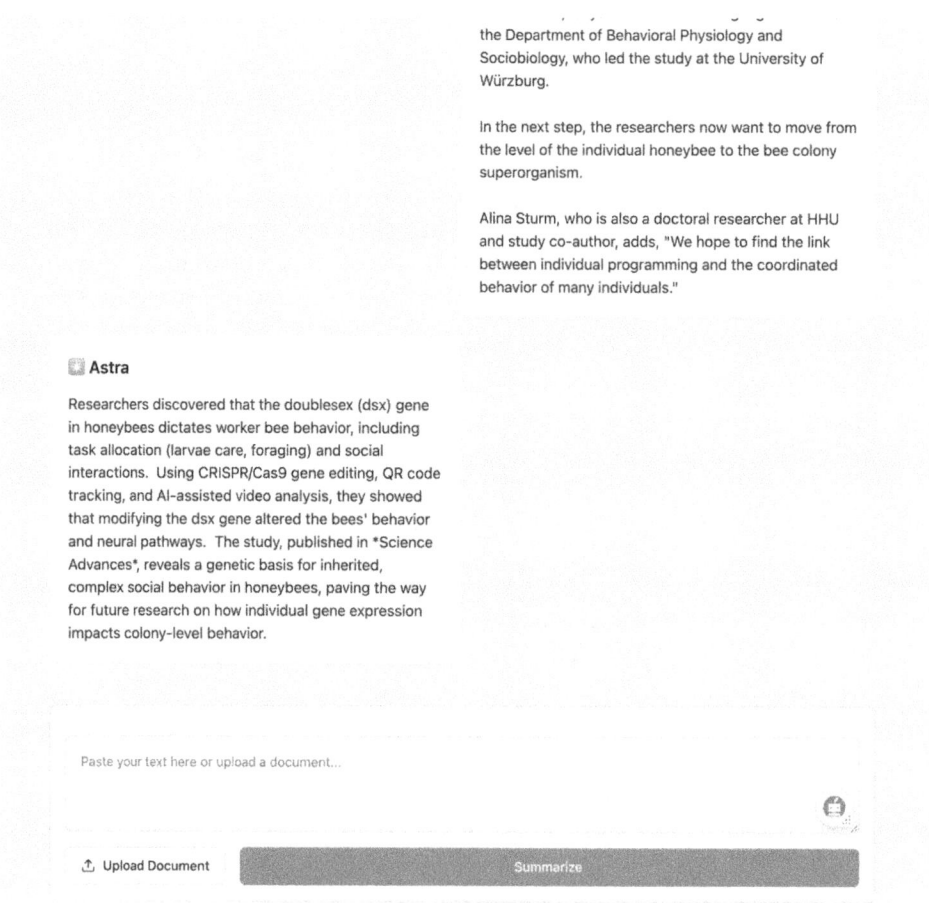

Figure 7.5 The user in this case can directly paste long-form text that utilizes the same service to summarize it.

Now let's take a closer look at the key pieces of code that run within the server actions file. The main idea of this new input is to submit either the text or the binary format of the file upload using a server action. Next.js will make sure to transfer the binary file from the UI to the backend service seamlessly. Then, in the `continueConversation` action, we check if the input was a file or text and process the input accordingly.

We are only highlighting the important parts related to handling text and file-based summarization input, since the rest of the codebase remains the same.

Listing 7.5 Integrating the summarization action based on the input

```
const summarizeText = async (text) => {
  return summarizeDocs([text]);
};
export async function continueConversation(input) {
  const aiState = getMutableAIState();

  try {
    let summary;
    if (input instanceof FormData) {
      const file = input.get('file');
      summary = await processFile(file, file.type);
    } else {
      summary = await summarizeText(input);
    }
    ...
```

- The summarizeText function is responsible for handling text summarization.
- Checks if the input is an instance of FormData. This indicates that the user has uploaded a file for summarization.
- If the input is a file, we extract the file from the FormData object and call the processFile function, passing the file and its MIME type.

The continueConversation function orchestrates the overall process by checking if the input is a file or text and calling either the summarizeText or the processFile.

Both functions call the summarizeDocs function that is a wrapper of the code in listing 7.2, with some small adjustments to include the normalizeDocuments function introduced in listing 7.3. The output of the summarizeDocs function is a string that contains the summary of the list of documents.

Regarding the changes to the UI, it's important to note the modifications made to the handleSubmit function within page.js. When a user uploads a document, we encapsulate the selected file in a FormData object. This approach ensures that the continueConversation function can accurately check the type of input being processed. The relevant code snippet initializes a new FormData instance and appends the uploaded file and then calls the continueConversation.

Listing 7.6 Uploading a document file to summarization

```
    ...
    const formData = new FormData();
    formData.append('file', selectedFile);

    setConversation((currentConversation) => [
      ...currentConversation,
      { id: generateId(), role: 'user',
        display: `Uploaded file: ${selectedFile.name}` },
    ]);

    response = await continueConversation(formData);
```

- Creates a new FormData object to hold form data, including file uploads
- Adds a new message entry indicating the uploaded file
- Calls the continueConversation function with the FormData object to process the uploaded file and continue the conversation

Now that we have covered a basic web application capable of summarizing documents, we can focus on enhancing its reliability and performance.

7.1.6 Additional considerations for summarizing documents

There are two problems that frequently arise when summarizing documents. First, PDF semantic chunking is difficult. One challenge with PDF documents is that they often lack a clear separation into logical chunks or sections. Unlike web pages or word-processing documents, the content in PDFs may not have well-defined structural elements like headings, paragraphs, or sections. This can make it difficult to identify the most important parts of the document and extract relevant information for summarization. DOCX files, on the other hand, are easier to parse and can be grouped into logical sections more readily.

Then there's the fact that large prompts are slow and expensive for very large documents. When summarizing lengthy documents, the input prompt can become extremely large, often exceeding the token limits of LLMs. This can lead to increased processing times and higher computational costs. Techniques like MapReduce and refine can help, but they essentially involve looping over all chunks, which can still be inefficient for exceptionally large documents. To address some of the concerns about prompt size and cost effectiveness, we can explore two techniques that have shown good prospects.

Prompt compression can significantly reduce the length of the input prompt while preserving the essential information. There is active research into tools, such as LLMLingua, developed by Microsoft, that compress prompts. The main idea is to use for the compression process a small local LLM that is fast and uses different types of compression techniques to reduce the prompt size while maintaining the same prompt information. As illustrated in figure 7.6, this adds an intermediary step before sending the prompt to the LLM for processing.

By compressing the original prompt, the number of tokens is reduced, achieving 2.5× compression for standard prompts, up to 10× for conversation history, and 20× for highly repetitive content. This allows for faster turnaround times when processing the prompt through the LLM.

> **NOTE** *LLMLingua* is currently available as a plugin to the LangChain Python library and is not yet integrated into the LangChain.js framework.

Merging similar chunks together using k-mean clustering is another approach to representing the semantic content of large documents, such as document embeddings. These representations can then be used as the input for the summarization model rather than relying solely on the raw text. This can be particularly useful for summarizing long or complex documents where simply extracting and compressing the text may not be sufficient. The key steps in this process are

1 *Sentence splitting and chunking*—First we split and chunk the text using `Recursive-CharacterTextSplitter` since it is designed to divide large texts into manageable chunks while preserving semantic overlaps.

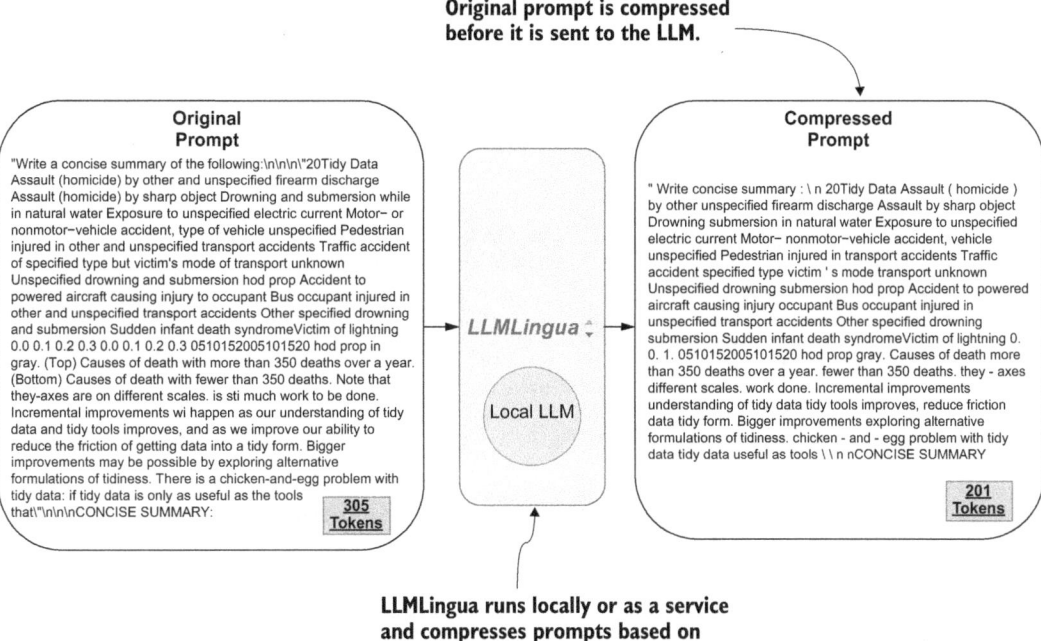

Figure 7.6 The process of compressing a prompt before sending it to an LLM using LLMLingua. The original prompt is compressed into a more concise version, which is then passed to the LLM for processing.

2   *Embedding computation*—We then use a language model to compute embeddings for each chunk. This allows you to represent the semantic content of each chunk as a vector.

3   *Applying k-means clustering*—After creating the chunks, we can apply k-means clustering to group them based on their semantic similarity, which allows us to complete the following optimization step.

4   *Chunk merging*—We then compare the embeddings between chunks and merge any chunks that are deemed semantically similar, based on a distance threshold in the embedding space. This groups the text into semantically coherent sections.

Figure 7.7 shows these steps, and there is also a sample reference JavaScript implementation in the k-means-summarization file inside the ch07/summarization-examples folder.

The document-clustering process is a more complex approach to organizing and preparing text for efficient summarization of large documents. At its core, the `cluster-Documents` function orchestrates three main steps: embedding computation, k-means clustering, and cluster merging. Listing 7.7 focuses on the details of this function.

214 CHAPTER 7 *Document summarization and RAG with LangChain.js*

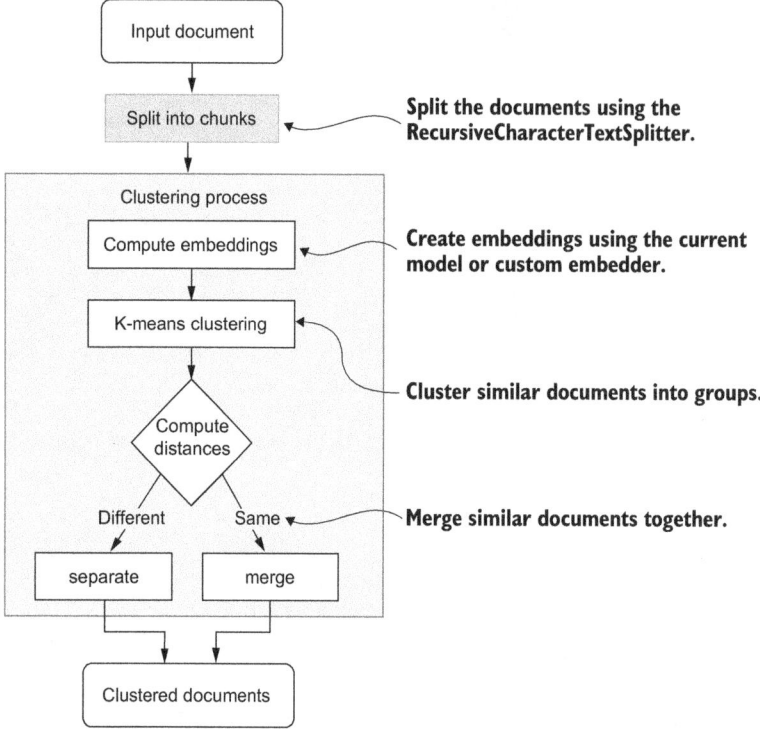

Figure 7.7 The sequential process of document clustering using the k-means algorithm. The input text is first split into chunks using `RecursiveCharacterTextSplitter`, which preserves semantic context. These chunks are then transformed into vector embeddings to capture their semantic meaning. The k-means clustering algorithm groups similar chunks based on their vector representations. A distance-based comparison determines whether chunks should be merged or kept separate, ultimately producing semantically coherent sections.

Listing 7.7 Clustering documents for summarization

```
import { kmeans } from 'ml-kmeans';
import { pipeline } from '@huggingface/transformers';
```
Imports the k-means clustering algorithm from ml-kmeans library for document clustering

```
async function clusterDocuments(documentChunks, similarityThreshold = 0.8) {
  const extractor = await pipeline('feature-extraction',
'Xenova/all-MiniLM-L6-v2');
  const chunkEmbeddings = await Promise.all(
documentChunks.map((chunk) => extractor(chunk)));
  const flattenedEmbeddings = chunkEmbeddings.map(
(embedding) => embedding[0][0].data);
```
Initializes feature extraction pipeline using the MiniLM model for generating document embeddings

```
  const numChunks = flattenedEmbeddings.length;
  if (numChunks === 0) {
    throw new Error('No document chunks available for clustering.');
  }
```

```
  const optimalClusters = Math.max(1, Math.min(Math.ceil(
Math.sqrt(numChunks / 2)), numChunks - 1));

  console.log('Number of document chunks:', numChunks);
  console.log('Optimal number of clusters:', optimalClusters);

  const kmeansResult =
kmeans(flattenedEmbeddings, optimalClusters);
  const mergedChunks =
mergeSimilarClusters(documentChunks, kmeansResult.clusters,
similarityThreshold);

  return mergedChunks;
}
```

- Calculates the optimal number of clusters using the square root of half the number of chunks, bounded between 1 and numChunks - 1
- Applies k-means clustering to the document embeddings using the calculated optimal number of clusters
- Merges similar chunks within each cluster based on the similarity threshold to create coherent document sections

First, the input document is split into manageable chunks using `RecursiveCharacterTextSplitter` with a chunk size of 10,000 characters and an overlap of 250 characters. The `clusterDocuments` function then employs the Hugging Face pipeline with the `Xenova/all-MiniLM-L6-v2` model for feature extraction, converting each text chunk into a dense vector representation. The algorithm next determines the optimal number of clusters, using a heuristic formula based on the document size.

Finally, `clusterDocuments` implements a similarity threshold to merge clusters that are semantically related. This merging step is handled by the helper function `mergeSimilarClusters`, which combines chunks from the same cluster.

> **Implementation tips**
>
> While this code demonstrates a more complex document-clustering approach using k-means, users don't need to deeply understand all the internal mechanics. The key aspects are
>
> - The algorithm provided to compute K is a practical heuristic formula that takes the square root of half the number of chunks. The formula isn't magical—it's a practical compromise that works well for document clustering while scaling reasonably with document size.
> - The embedding and clustering process is abstracted away behind easy-to-use functions.
> - The similarity threshold (0.8 by default) is the main parameter users might want to adjust where higher values create tighter, more similar clusters while lower values allow more diversity.

NOTE While using techniques like sentence splitting and k-means clustering can help in organizing and summarizing large documents, there will inevitably be some information loss. This is particularly relevant to how the k-means clustering algorithm is configured and tuned, as different settings can significantly affect the granularity and coherence of the resulting clusters.

Both prompt compression and k-means clustering offer unique advantages for document summarization, but a balanced approach is recommended. A hybrid strategy, combining both, can enhance performance and robustness while testing and accepting feedback to help address any shortcomings and improve outcomes. The code examples should give you a good overview of how to implement these summarization techniques in your own projects.

7.2 Building a RAG web application with LangChain.js

Let's move on to our second project, which makes use of retrieval-augmented generation (RAG) techniques. RAG is an advanced natural language processing technique that enhances LLMs by retrieving relevant information from external knowledge bases before generating a response. In simple terms, it injects real-time information retrieval into the workflow so the model can answer queries with fresh, topic-specific context. By supplying the LLM with this retrieved context for each query, RAG significantly increases the accuracy and relevance of its responses. Instead of relying solely on pre-trained, potentially outdated knowledge, the model can incorporate the latest data, facts, and insights that are directly related to the user's inquiry.

7.2.1 RAG app project requirements

This app uses RAG to enhance the accuracy and relevance of generated responses by integrating real-time information retrieval with generative capabilities.

Here's what we'll be building:

- *User interface*—We will create a user-friendly interface using Next.js and the Vercel AI SDK to facilitate user interactions.
- *Document processing*—We will implement the LangChain.js library to process and manage documents, ensuring they are properly sanitized and chunked for efficient retrieval.
- *Query processing*—Using LangChain.js, we will develop a robust query-processing mechanism that includes input handling, document retrieval, and ranking of relevant information.
- *Augmentation layer*—We will integrate the retrieved context with user queries through LangChain.js, preparing an enriched prompt for the generation engine.
- *Response generation*—Finally, we will utilize the capabilities of LLMs to generate coherent and contextually relevant responses based on the augmented prompts. We will be presenting this into the familiar UI interface for the user to interact with.

Once we implement these steps, we will create a comprehensive RAG system that effectively combines document retrieval and generation capabilities. Before we look at the technical requirements of the project, let's learn a bit more about RAG and its key architectural components.

7.2.2 Key architectural components of RAG

Figure 7.8 illustrates the general architecture of a typical RAG system that surfaces knowledge from a list of documents and allows users to query information using a chat-like environment.

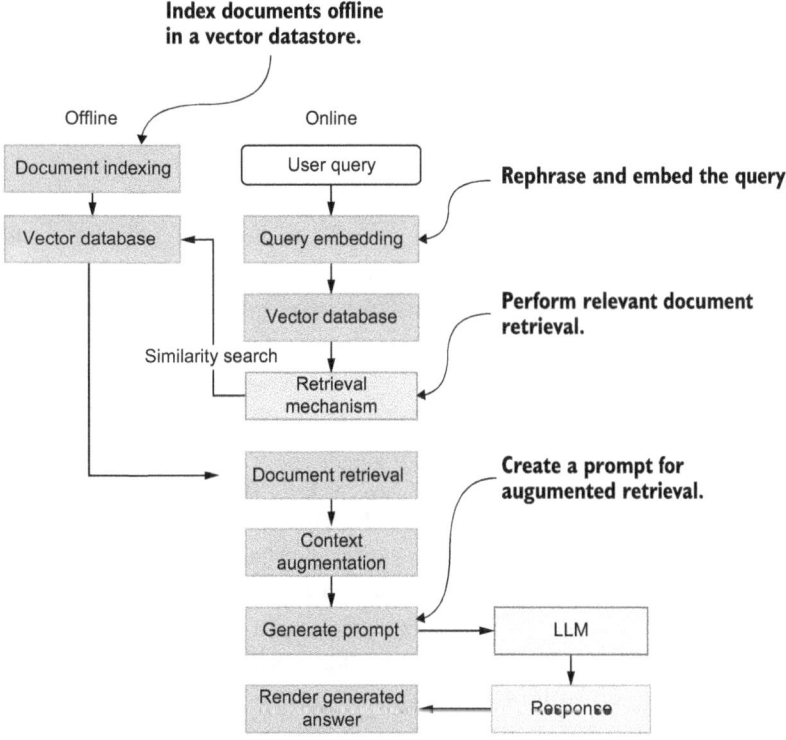

Figure 7.8 Architecture of a RAG system. The system first indexes a collection of documents offline into a vector database, enabling efficient semantic search. When a user query is received, the system embeds the query, searches the vector database for relevant documents, and retrieves the most relevant contexts. These contexts are then used to augment the original query, creating an enriched prompt that is passed to a large language model to generate a final response.

The key architectural components of a RAG system are

- *Document indexing*—We need to populate the knowledge base by indexing. Indexing transforms raw text into a machine-readable format by converting documents into high-dimensional vector embeddings. This vectorization process captures the semantic elements of the text and makes it easier to search using semantic queries.
- *Retrieval mechanism*—The "R" in RAG is the retrieval mechanism, which employs advanced vector similarity techniques to identify and rank the most relevant documents for a given query.

- *Augmentation layer*—The "A" in RAG is the augmentation layer. This layer combines the most relevant retrieved contexts with the original user query, carefully preparing an enhanced prompt that provides the language model with comprehensive background information while ensuring everything fits within the context window.
- *Generation engine*—The "G" in RAG is the generation engine. This engine uses LLMs to transform the augmented context and query into coherent responses. This engine uses the intricacies of the targeted LLM to maintain high relevance, accuracy, and coherence with the original information sources.

While these components form the core of this approach, there are several ongoing research directions and variations of RAG systems that aim to improve their capabilities.

One variation is *MultiHop-RAG*, where the system recursively retrieves additional relevant contexts based on the initial results and reinforcement learning–based retrieval. The latter is used to learn to optimize the retrieval process for specific task objectives that require reasoning over multiple pieces of supporting evidence.

Another variation is *hypothetical document embedding* (HyDE). The idea is to go beyond simply indexing and retrieving real-world documents. Instead, the system could generate synthetic document representations that do not correspond to any existing text but are designed to complement and enhance the information retrieval process across various tasks (e.g. web search, Q/A, and so on).

For the sake of simplicity, we will focus on implementing this core RAG with a grounding system. The key components will include document indexing, a retrieval mechanism, a grounding layer to identify noticeable facts and relationships, and an augmented generation process that incorporates the grounded information.

In chapter 11, we will explore a more realistic and complex example that uses RAG for a real-world application scenario. This will allow us to dive deeper into the nuances and advanced techniques within the RAG paradigm, building upon the foundational knowledge established in this chapter.

7.2.3 Technical architecture overview

Similar to the summarization web application, the RAG service utilizes relevant libraries and frameworks. The key difference is the inclusion of additional procedures to enable the RAG workflow. Here is the list of technologies that we are using:

- *Frontend*—ReAct
- *Backend*—Next.js
- *Vector database*—HNSWLib
- *Embedding model*—GoogleAI
- *LLM integration*—GoogleAI
- *Grounding*—Google grounding AI

Grounding is basically a form of verification check. It helps verify the factual accuracy of the generated responses by cross-checking them against a corpus of reliable information. This reduces the risk of hallucinations, where the language model produces plausible-sounding but factually incorrect output.

For the grounding component in our RAG system, we will use the Google Geminilog probabilities support, which allows us to assess the confidence and uncertainty of the system's responses. In the next sections, we'll implement a step-by-step RAG web application using LangChain.js, demonstrating how to create a robust, context-aware generative system.

> **NOTE** The source code for the examples in this chapter is available at https://github.com/Generative-AI-Web-Apps/Code/tree/main/ch07/rag-web-app.

> **Project code: rag-web-app**
>
> The code for this example project is in the ch07/rag-web-app folder. You can use that example by running this command in the root folder of the project repository:
>
> ```
> $ npm run dev -w ch07/rag-web-app
> ```
>
> For details on setting up and creating API keys, refer to the appendix:
>
> ```
> // .env
> OPENAI_API_KEY=<OPEN_AI_SECRET_KEY>
> GEMINI_API_KEY=<GOOGLE_AI_SECRET_KEY>
> ```

7.2.4 RAG system components

Since there is quite a bit of code involved when explaining the key components of a RAG system, we will look at the important bits of each component while focusing on the bigger picture. Let's start with the document-indexing process.

> **Note for running the example script**
>
> To test the RAG implementation described in this chapter, first navigate to the script's directory and then run it:
>
> ```
> $ cd ch07/summarization-examples
> $ node rag.js
> ```
>
> This script provides a practical example of the RAG workflow we've just discussed, allowing you to experiment with the code and see the RAG system in action.

DOCUMENT INDEXING

Document indexing transforms raw text documents into a machine-readable, semantically searchable format. This important first step in the RAG workflow involves converting unstructured documents into high-dimensional vectors.

The process begins by collecting documents from a specified directory and converting them into manageable chunks that preserve contextual information. Since we've already explained how to do this step in the summarization web application for a single document, we can now extend this to perform over a list of documents.

Next, those chunks are transformed using an embedding model, which converts text into dense vector representations. Once vectorized, the document chunks are stored in a vector database like HNSWLib, which enables efficient semantic search. Each vector is accompanied by metadata such as the source document, page number, and processing timestamp, providing additional context for later retrieval.

We saw a similar example in the previous chapter using a MemoryVectorStore class. However, now we need to be able to store the indexes in a more permanent solution so that our web application can perform semantic retrieval. The HNSWLib vector store, which is part of the LangChain.js community, is a perfect solution for our needs. HNSWLib is a portable and easy-to-use store that saves the indexes in the filesystem, which can be loaded later on for similarity searching.

The following listing shows the key section of the indexing algorithm that processes each document from a directory and indexes them using the HNSWLib vector store.

Listing 7.8 Indexing documents using a vector store

```
import { HNSWLib } from '@langchain/community/vectorstores/hnswlib';
async indexDocumentsFromDirectory(documentDirectory) {
    const documents = [];

    // Find all PDF files in the directory
    const pdfFiles = fs
      .readdirSync(documentDirectory)
      .filter((file) =>
path.extname(file).toLowerCase() === '.pdf')
      .map((file) =>
path.join(documentDirectory, file));    // Finds all PDF files in the directory

    // Process each PDF document                // Processes each PDF document
    for (const filePath of pdfFiles) {
      const processedDocs = await this.processDocument(filePath);
      documents.push(...processedDocs);
    }

    // Create vector store from processed documents
    const vectorStore =
await HNSWLib.fromDocuments(documents, this.embeddings);   // Creates vector store from processed documents

    console.log(`Indexed ${documents.length}
document chunks from ${pdfFiles.length} documents`);

    return vectorStore;
  }
```

Here, the new part is the `HNSWLib` import that uses the `fromDocuments` method to convert the processed text chunks into a vector representation, utilizing the predefined embedding model. This vector store can then be used for semantic search, enabling the RAG system to retrieve relevant information based on user queries.

To perform the indexing of documents effectively, it is best to conduct this process offline, especially when dealing with a large volume of documents. For convenience, a script has been provided that you can run alongside a sample list of documents located in the scripts folder within the `rag-web-app` example.

To index the documents, you must first navigate to the ch07/rag-web-app directory and then execute the following command in your terminal:

```
$ cd ch07/rag-web-app
$ node scripts/indexDocuments.google.js -d corpus
```

This command will initiate the indexing process using the specified corpus of documents. The script is designed to handle the indexing efficiently, ensuring that all documents are processed and stored correctly. I've prepopulated this folder with example documents from the KG-RAG datasets repository (https://github.com/docugami/KG-RAG-datasets) containing several aviation accident reports in PDF form, but feel free to use your own set of data instead.

> **NOTE** This script uses Google Gemini embeddings and requires an active Google Gemini API key to generate vector representations of documents. The API key must be set in the .env file as `GEMINI_API_KEY`.

The script will process your documents, creating vector embeddings that enable semantic search capabilities. Be aware that running this script will incur costs associated with OpenAI's API usage for embedding generation.

If you prefer to use an alternative embedding provider like OpenAI, the companion script `indexDocuments.openai.js` is available, which requires a `OpenAI_API_KEY` instead.

RETRIEVAL

The retrieval process is a critical component of the RAG system, responsible for finding the most relevant documents in response to a user's query. In our implementation, the retrieval uses LangChain's `asRetriever` method, which we explored in the previous chapter.

When loading a previously indexed vector store, the system creates a retriever instance that can efficiently search through the semantic vector representations. In this implementation, the retriever is configured to return the top six most similar document chunks, providing a comprehensive yet focused set of contextually relevant information.

The `asRetriever` method essentially transforms our vector store into a sophisticated search engine. Here is the code snippet that provides this feature:

```
async loadIndex(path) {
    this.vectorStore = await HNSWLib.load(path, this.embeddings);
    this.retriever = this.vectorStore.asRetriever({
      k: 6,
    });
    console.log('Vector store loaded successfully');
}
```

This code snippet demonstrates the simplicity of creating a retriever. We load the previously saved vector store and apply the `asRetriever` method, which we can use to perform semantic search operations.

In the subsequent augmentation and generation layers, these retrieved document chunks will be integrated with the original query to provide prompts to the language model. Let's explore the details.

AUGMENTATION AND GENERATION

The augmentation and generation phases represent the final, transformative steps in the RAG workflow. This process combines the retrieved contextual documents with the original query to generate a precise, context-aware response using an LLM.

To perform this, we simply craft a prompt that instructs the LLM and then use the retriever to ask the LLM to generate a response based on the prompt instruction.

Listing 7.9 Performing augmentation of the response

```
async performRAG(query) {
    const prompt = ChatPromptTemplate         ◄── Creates a chat prompt template that
.fromTemplate(`                                   instructs the model to answer based
        Answer the question based only on the context provided.
                                                  only on provided context

        Context: {context}

        Question: {question}`);

    const chain = RunnableSequence.from([    ◄── Creates a processing pipeline
      {                                          that retrieves, formats, and
        context: this.retriever.pipe(formatDocs),  generates a response
        question: new RunnablePassthrough(),
      },
      prompt,
      this.llm,AQ:
      new StringOutputParser(),
    ]);

    const response = await chain.invoke(query);   ◄── Generates the final response
    const sourceDocuments =
await this.retriever.invoke(query);    ◄── Tracks the source documents
    return {                                      used in the generation
      answer: response,
      sourceDocuments,
    };
}
```

This code shows how to combine retrieval, prompt engineering, and language model generation using the LangChain.js chain system—a system that creates a lot of the nuances for the developer.

The provided `performRAG` method creates a chat prompt template that instructs the language model to answer questions based solely on the provided context. It then uses the retriever to fetch and format relevant documents according to the input query, accepts the question as input, and generates a response using an LLM. The function invokes this processing chain to generate the final response while also retrieving the source documents used for reference. Ultimately, it returns an object containing both the generated answer and the corresponding source documents.

With all the essential components of a RAG system in place, the next step is to create a user interface that allows users to perform queries based on the provided documents.

7.2.5 Web app demonstration

The web application uses our existing UI components with a key enhancement: integrating a RAG system. The core functionality remains unchanged, but we've added a sophisticated document retrieval and context-aware response generation mechanism.

RAG INDEX CONFIGURATION

To enable the RAG functionality, you must specify the absolute path to your vector index. This is done by setting the `RAG_INDEX_PATH` environment variable in the .env file:

```
RAG_INDEX_PATH=/absolute/path/to/your/rag_index
```

If you run the `indexDocuments.js` script inside the scripts folder, it will create a folder in the project directory that contains the embeddings. Provide the absolute path of this folder for the application to load them for retrieval.

KEY CODE CHANGES

The following listing shows the important code snippet that initializes the RAG system in the actions.jsx file.

Listing 7.10 Initializing the RAG system on the server

```
import { RAG } from '@/lib/RAG';
import { getAbsoluteRAGIndexPath } from '@/lib/utils';
export async function initializeRAG() {
  if (!ragSystem) {
    ragSystem = new RAG(apiKey);
    const indexPath = getAbsoluteRAGIndexPath();
    await ragSystem.loadIndex(indexPath);
  }
  return ragSystem;
}

export async function continueConversation(input) {
  const aiState = getMutableAIState();

  try {
```

- Imports the RAG class, which encapsulates the RAG system functionality
- Defines an async function to initialize the RAG system

```
    // Ensure RAG system is initialized
    const rag = await initializeRAG();        ◄──── Calls the initialization function
                                                    to get the RAG system
    // Perform RAG query
    const result = await rag.performRAG(input);  ◄──── Performs a RAG query
                                                       with the input
    const message = {
      id: generateId(),
      role: 'assistant',
      content: result.answer,
    };

    // ... rest of the implementation
  }
}
```

The `initializeRAG()` function is a critical component of our RAG implementation. It creates a singleton instance of the RAG system. When `continueConversation()` is called, it checks if the RAG system is initialized, loads the index from the specified path, and then performs a retrieval-augmented query.

DEMO

Figure 7.9 shows the web interface with a RAG-generated response, demonstrating the integration of the new functionality. The user has submitted a query about the Reims

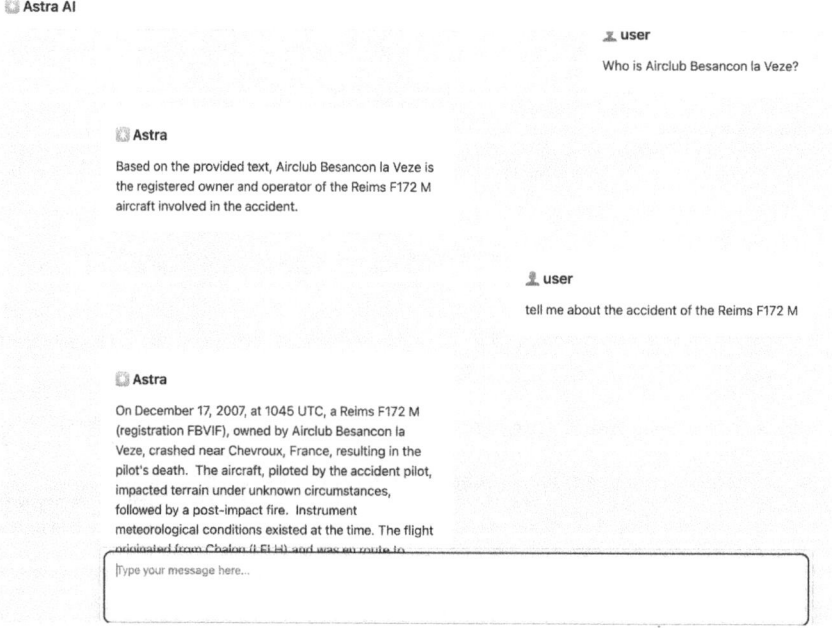

Figure 7.9 Screenshot of an Astra AI conversation interface where the user asks questions regarding the indexed list of documents using RAG

F172 M aircraft involved in an accident, and the application has generated a detailed, context-rich response.

With the RAG system in place, users can explore the indexed corpus, obtain detailed information, and gain a deeper understanding of the topics covered. This lays the foundation for the last piece of the web application, which is the introduction of grounding support.

7.2.6 Adding grounding support

Grounding is a valuable technique in generative AI that ensures AI-generated responses are validated by reliable, factual information sources. Essentially, grounding provides another layer of verification. Traditional AI without grounding resembles a student who relies entirely on their own memory to answer a question, potentially mixing up or fabricating information with no way to verify its accuracy. With grounding, you have something more like a very smart librarian who doesn't just answer questions from memory but always checks multiple reference books before giving an answer.

Technically, the grounding process can be visualized as a sequential flow: the user poses a question, which triggers a search through relevant documents. The system extracts precise information, generates a response that incorporates these verified sources, annotates the answer with its origins, and then delivers a verified response. Figure 7.10 shows the pieces of this process.

GROUNDING TYPES

There are five main types of grounding. Each method serves a unique purpose in integrating external knowledge while maintaining consistency:

- *Retrieval-augmented grounding*—Retrieves relevant information from external sources and integrates it into the generation process, which reduces the chance of inaccuracies. As an example, Google recently added grounding support on a limited basis using Google search or via your own data.
- *Knowledge base grounding*—Uses curated, validated information repositories to constrain responses to specific, trusted domains.
- *Citation-based grounding*—Generates responses with explicit source references, allowing users to verify the credibility of the information. For example, in academic writing or research-focused AI applications, when an AI generates a summary or analysis, it may include citations from peer-reviewed journals or other databases.
- *Contextual grounding*—Adapts responses based on previous interactions and modifies the output to the user's specific needs. For instance, if a user previously asked about a specific product, the chatbot can reference that interaction in future conversations.
- *Log probability grounding*—Uses log probabilities to assess the confidence of a language model's responses. By calculating the probability of each token

226 CHAPTER 7 *Document summarization and RAG with LangChain.js*

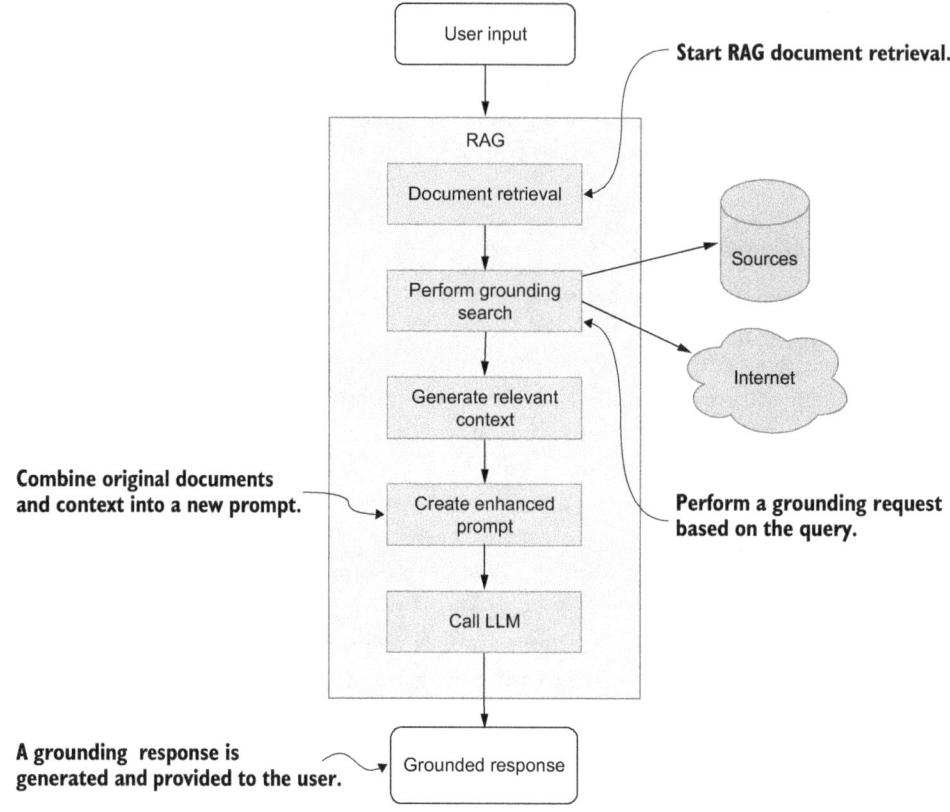

Figure 7.10 RAG approach for grounding LLMs with relevant information. The system performs a grounding search to extract the most relevant context, which is combined with the original user input to create an enhanced prompt. This prompt is then passed to the LLM, which generates the final grounded response that is provided to the user.

generated, the model can indicate how certain it is about its answers. For instance, when a model responds to a query, it can provide a log probability score for the first token, reflecting its confidence in having enough information to answer the question accurately. This approach allows for more refined decision making, as users can gauge the reliability of the information based on these confidence scores.

WARNING Per-token log probabilities are now supported by newer models like Gemini 2.0 Flash and Gemini 1.5 Flash, but they are not yet fully standardized as a first-class feature within the LangChain.js ChatGoogleGenerativeAI integration. Google AI provides a dedicated grounding API within its Vertex AI platform at https://mng.bz/QwK1. Please note that the availability of Vertex AI generative AI features, including the grounding API, may vary by region or country.

GROUNDING WITH LOG PROBABILITIES

OpenAI's API includes a feature that enables models to return log probabilities for each token generated, providing valuable insights into how confident the model is about its answers. To utilize this feature effectively, you need to pass additional configuration options when initializing the API request. This allows the model to also evaluate the likelihood of each token it produces, which can be particularly useful for assessing the reliability of the information provided.

Here is a quick example of how to set this up when you create an instance of the `ChatOpenAI` class:

```
const openAI = await new ChatOpenAI({
    model: 'gpt-3.5-turbo',
    apiKey: OpenAIKey,
    logprobs: true,
    topLogprobs: 3,
});
```

Two additional options when we instantiate the OpenAI client are

- `logprobs`—Enables the return of log probabilities for each token
- `top_logprobs`—Specifies that the top three probable tokens should be returned along with their probabilities

A response might look like the following when querying about a specific topic, such as "What are the benefits of exercise?":

```
"logprobs": {
        "tokens": ["Regular", "exercise", "improves",
"physical", "health", ",", "boosts", "mental",
"well-being", ",", "and", "enhances", "overall",
"quality", "of", "life", "."],
        "token_logprobs": [-0.5, -0.7, -0.6, -0.8,
-0.9, -1.0, -0.4, -0.5, -0.6, -0.7, -0.8, -0.9, -1.0,
-1.1, -1.2, -1.3],
        "top_logprobs": [
          {"token": "Regular", "logprob": -0.5},
          {"token": "Consistent", "logprob": -0.6},
          {"token": "Daily", "logprob": -0.7},
          {"token": "exercise", "logprob": -0.7},
          {"token": "activity", "logprob": -0.8},
          {"token": "workout", "logprob": -0.9}
        ]
    }
```

> **NOTE** Not all LLMs offer support for log probabilities in their public API methods. While this feature is available in OpenAI's API, the implementation and response formats may differ between platforms. Carefully review the documentation for each API to understand how log probabilities are handled and how they can be utilized effectively in their applications.

How can we utilize those numbers to perform grounding? In very simple terms, we can analyze the log probabilities associated with each token and determine how confident the model is in its answers, which helps us decide whether to trust those answers or seek additional information.

We first establish thresholds for these log probabilities to determine when a response is reliable enough to be considered "grounded." For example, if the log probability for a particular response is above a certain threshold (e.g., −1.0), we might decide that it's trustworthy. On the other hand, if the model indicates low confidence in its answer (e.g., log probabilities suggest uncertainty), we can either

- Prompt the model to provide an alternative answer.
- Use external data sources to supplement or verify the information.
- Ask the user for more context to improve response accuracy.

The following listing shows how to use log probability grounding in the existing RAG application we've developed so far.

Listing 7.11 Integrating log probability grounding

```
// import { RAG } from '@/lib/RAG';
import { LogProbsRag as RAG }
from '@/lib/LogPropsRag';

export async function continueConversation(input) {
  const aiState = getMutableAIState();

  try {
    // Ensure RAG system is initialized
    const rag = await initializeRAG();

    // Perform enhanced RAG query
    const result = await rag.performEnhancedRAG(
      input,
      {
        confidenceThreshold: 85,
        fallbackStrategy: 'ask_user'
      }
    );

    // Log confidence metrics if available
    if (result.confidenceMetrics) {
      console.log('Confidence Metrics:', result.confidenceMetrics);
      console.log('Results:', result);
    }
    // rest of code
  } catch (error) {
    console.error('Error in continuing conversation:', error);
  }
}
```

- Comments this out as it shows the original import statement for the RAG class
- Uncomments this class to use the updated RAG with log probabilities
- Calls the performEnhancedRAG method on the RAG instance, which executes a query with enhanced capabilities
- Sets a confidence threshold of 85% for determining if the response is reliable
- Specifies a fallback strategy to ask the user for more context if confidence is low

To utilize this implementation, you need to modify the import statement in ch07/rag-web-app/src/app/(chat)/actions.jsx to

```
import { LogProbsRag as RAG } from '@/lib/LogPropsRag';
```

This adjustment enables the use of the new `performEnhancedRAG` method, which incorporates log probability grounding for improved response accuracy and reliability. The details of the `LogPropsRag` file are not shown here, but essentially it uses an AI-powered confidence evaluation process. This evaluation examines whether the retrieved context contains sufficient information to comprehensively answer the user's question. When the confidence level is high, the method proceeds with generating a response using the retrieved documents. However, if the confidence falls below a specified threshold, the method activates a fallback strategy. In that case, it will ask the user to rephrase or provide more context about their query.

> **WARNING** Grounding support can significantly increase the number of API requests made during interactions with AI models. When grounding is enabled, each query may trigger additional requests to retrieve relevant external data, such as information from Google Search or requesting log probabilities. This can lead to higher usage costs and potential rate limiting if the API has a daily query limit. Additionally, grounding may create challenges with large context windows, as incorporating extensive external data could exceed the model's input size limitations.

With those changes in place, we can now rerun the application and try to ask the RAG system a question that does not have a valid answer because it's not part of the knowledge base. Let's examine how the AI's responses differ when it encounters questions about topics outside its knowledge base, both with and without proper grounding context. Figure 7.11 shows the importance of context in preventing hallucination and ensuring accurate responses.

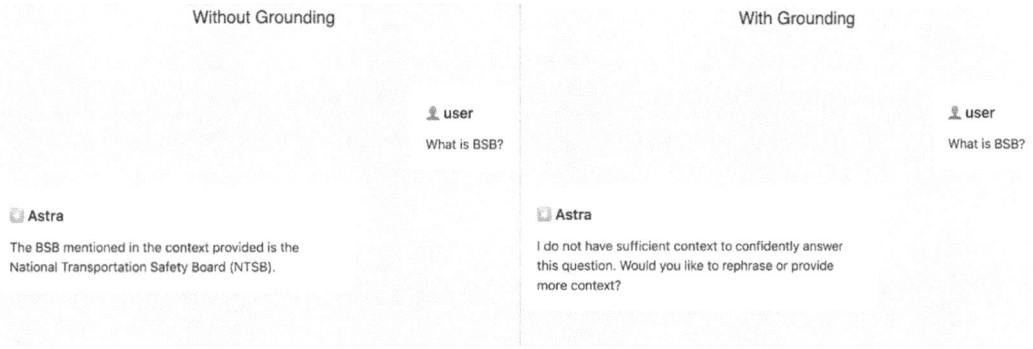

Figure 7.11 Comparison of AI responses with and without grounding context. The left panel shows the AI's response without grounding, while the right panel shows the AI's response when provided with additional contextual information to ground its understanding.

Without the grounding information, shown in the left panel, the AI simply provides a response stating that the "BSB" mentioned in the context is the National Transportation Safety Board. This response is not technically correct, and the AI lacks the necessary context to fully understand the user's intent and provide a meaningful answer.

In contrast, when the user asks, "What is BSB?" and the system has the additional grounding information, the AI recognizes that the available context is insufficient to provide a confident answer. Instead of guessing, it politely asks the user to clarify or provide more context, preventing misinformation.

By explicitly evaluating confidence, the system transparently communicates its uncertainty, reducing hallucinations and improving reliability. This approach ensures that responses are both accurate and trustworthy while also guiding the user to supply the necessary information for meaningful answers.

Summary

- Building a document summarization web application involves creating a user-friendly interface for uploading documents and generating concise summaries using advanced techniques.
- Implementing RAG allows for dynamic information retrieval, enhancing the accuracy of responses by integrating real-time data with generated content.
- Developing reliable RAG web applications requires a thoughtful approach and combines a plethora of tools and techniques. Incorporating a grounding evaluation mechanism is a very useful step to ensure the system provides transparent and trustworthy outputs.
- Providing grounding support for AI outputs ensures that generated summaries are anchored to the source documents, improving reliability and reducing inaccuracies.
- Advanced document-processing techniques, such as semantic chunking and k-means clustering, enhance context retention and summary quality in large documents.
- Handling various document formats, including PDFs and DOCX files, requires specialized loaders to extract text effectively for summarization.
- Utilizing the MapReduce method for summarization allows for parallel processing of document chunks, improving efficiency and enabling the handling of extensive texts.
- The `RecursiveCharacterTextSplitter` and `TokenTextSplitter` methods facilitate effective chunking of text, preserving context while managing LLM input limitations.
- The integration of LangChain.js with the Vercel AI SDK streamlines the document-processing pipeline, providing a seamless user experience during summarization tasks.

- Addressing challenges related to performance and user experience is crucial when implementing large-scale document summarization applications.
- Exploring different summarization strategies, such as the stuffing and refine methods, provides flexibility in how summaries are generated based on document complexity.

Testing and debugging techniques

This chapter covers
- Debugging methods for identifying problems in Next.js applications
- Troubleshooting the Vercel AI SDK
- Debugging techniques in LangChain.js
- Mocking frameworks that allow for controlled testing environments
- Best practices for integrating testing and testing strategies for AI web applications

Writing reliable software is a tricky business. There are a lot of intricacies to consider, and it is especially easy to make mistakes if you are not familiar with the technologies you are using. Take the technologies we have discussed in this book: each one of them is a potential candidate for error. With Next.js, for example, the use of server components requires developers to change some of their typical patterns, which can lead to unexpected behavior if not handled correctly. It's especially important to understand the nuances of server components and server actions. The

Vercel AI SDK abstraction layer simplifies interactions with AI models but can introduce risks if developers are not fully aware of its underlying mechanics. Misconfiguration or incorrect assumptions about SDK behavior can lead to errors. The LangChain.js framework comes with its own set of challenges. The fast code iterations and changes of this library mean that best practices are continually changing, so developers must keep up with the new norms.

As always, we can improve the stability and security of our software by adhering to good engineering practices and implementing thorough testing and debugging strategies. Here we will explore essential testing and debugging techniques specifically tailored for the technologies we use in this book. You can, of course, apply the key concepts to any framework or software.

This chapter assumes familiarity with the technologies introduced in previous chapters (Next.js, Vercel AI SDK, LangChain.js) and experience implementing AI-driven features. You should be comfortable navigating React and server-side code, understanding SDK interactions, and integrating AI workflows.

8.1 Debugging Next.js AI applications

Next.js is a powerful full-stack framework for building React applications. When integrating AI—whether through direct large language model (LLM) APIs or the Vercel AI SDK—we introduce unique debugging challenges due to the complex architecture that involves server-side AI processing, streaming responses, and nontrivial state management.

While no universal debugging strategy applies to all scenarios, we can develop a systematic approach based on identifying and analyzing symptoms. For instance, when a user submits a prompt and encounters an error, we can follow a structured debugging process to pinpoint the root cause and implement an appropriate solution.

The three main problem areas for Next.js are rendering, state management, and performance. Figure 8.1 outlines key steps to debugging these kinds of problems. Let's go through the problems and solutions represented in the figure.

8.1.1 Debugging common Next.js rendering issues

By default, Next.js provides some excellent debugging features out of the box. If the React component code logic is wrong or throws an error, it will produce an overlay that covers the page and highlights the error. Figure 8.2 shows an example of this overlay.

> **NOTE** The source code for the examples in this chapter is available at https://github.com/Generative-AI-Web-Apps/Code/tree/main/ch08/chat-rendering-troubleshooting.

When an error is thrown during the rendering cycle, Next.js presents an overlay containing the call stack as soon as the page is loaded.

234 CHAPTER 8 *Testing and debugging techniques*

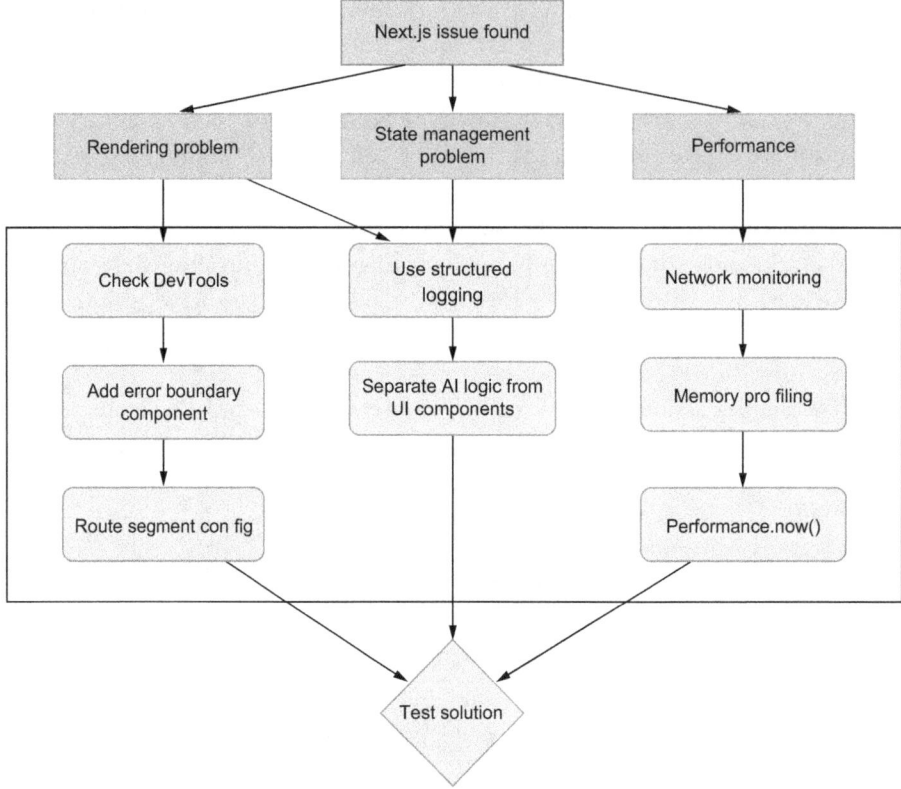

Figure 8.1 The three main categories of Next.js problems (rendering, state management, and performance) and their corresponding debugging strategies. Each branch shows specific diagnostic steps and tools, ultimately leading to a test solution phase.

Figure 8.2
An error overlay shows whenever there is an error thrown in Next.js development mode. This helps catch problems early when developing the web application.

> **Project code: chat-rendering-troubleshooting**
>
> The code for this example project is in the ch08/chat-rendering-troubleshooting folder. You can use that example by running this command in the root folder of the project repository:
>
> ```
> $ npm run dev -w ch08/chat-rendering-troubleshooting
> ```
>
> You'll also need either the OpenAI API or the Google API keys to access their REST API. For details on creating API keys, refer to the appendix:
>
> ```
> // .env
> OPENAI_API_KEY=<OPEN_AI_SECRET_KEY>
> GEMINI_API_KEY=<GOOGLE_AI_SECRET_KEY>
> ```

In production environments, you won't have access to the development error overlay, so it's best to use an *error boundary* component, as this will allow users to see meaningful error messages instead of blank screens and will present them with a list of recovery call-to-action buttons. Instructions on how to create an error boundary component are listed in detail in the official React reference docs (https://mng.bz/mZqW).

After handling basic application setup, you will often encounter challenges related to UI rendering, particularly when dealing with asynchronous responses from server handlers. These problems are especially prevalent in AI applications due to streaming responses and dynamic content updates. Let's look at the main categories of problems and their solutions.

SCROLL BEHAVIOR PROBLEMS

Automatic scrolling happens when new messages arrive and get rendered on the screen and the app scrolls down to the last message. While I covered the basic implementation in chapter 2, several things can affect automatic scrolling behavior in AI chat applications.

Note that the placement of the scroll anchor element is crucial. Moving it outside the message list container or in a different order can break the scrolling behavior:

```
{
conversation.length > 0 && <ChatList
messages={conversation} isLoading={isLoading} />}
      <div ref={messageEndRef} />
```

Another problem you might find is that while the UI scrolls to the last message, it's still not scrolling down enough for the user to see the last sentence. This happens because there should be a gap at the bottom of the list to allow for the message box to appear. For instance, if a user sends a lengthy message that fills up the chat window, the last part of that message might be obscured by the input field at the bottom, making it difficult for the user to read. Alternatively, you could also restructure the chat message container so it has its own fixed height and position within the page.

Tailwind.css has some convenient utility classes that you can use to add padding in containers:

- `p-4`—Applies padding of `1rem` on all sides
- `px-8 py--4`—Applies horizontal padding of `2rem` and vertical padding of `1rem`
- `p-0`—Sets no padding at all

In our example projects, we used `py-24`, which adds a `6rem` padding to the vertical axis, giving us space for the message box form.

Another challenge is that while the application scrolls on some messages, it does not scroll on some of the longer messages when streaming the content back to the user. This might happen because of how React triggers the `scrollToBottom` callback in the `useEffect` hook. If the conversation object reference does not change, React won't be able to trigger this effect:

```
useEffect(() => {
    scrollToBottom();
}, [conversation]);
```

If you are using streaming responses, ensure that each new chunk of data is treated as a separate update to the conversation state. This can be achieved by updating the state in such a way that it creates a new reference each time new data is received:

```
setConversation(prev => [...prev, newMessage]);
```

Even a small feature, such as scrolling behavior, can have many moving parts that can go wrong. Spending time learning about these intricacies, side effects, and edge cases will pay off significantly when building the application or debugging some of the unexpected behaviors. But this is part of being a developer.

STREAMING-RESPONSES PROBLEMS

Streaming is working properly when set up correctly in a Next.js application. For streaming to work with the Next.js app router, you need to ensure that caching is disabled for the page. This can be accomplished by using the following configuration at the top of the page.jsx component that corresponds to the route segment configuration:

```
// Force the page to be dynamic and allow
// streaming responses up to 30 seconds
export const dynamic = 'force-dynamic';
export const maxDuration = 30;
```

Another reason that streaming may not work depends on where you deploy the application. For example, when deploying on Vercel, you may encounter problems with caching that prevent streaming from functioning correctly. To address this, you can use the `unstable_noStore` function from the `next/cache` module. This function allows you to opt out of caching at the component level, ensuring that your component always fetches fresh data. Here's how to implement it:

```
import { unstable_noStore as noStore } from 'next/cache';

export default async function Component() {
  noStore();
  const result = await streamText({...});
  ...
}
```

Of course, each deployment provider might have its own nuances and workarounds regarding potential problems with streaming or other considerations. In such cases, I recommend following their open issues and documentation for further insights.

8.1.2 Debugging client-server problems

Understanding the boundary between server and client components is crucial when developing web applications. In Next.js, components can be designated as either server or client components. Server components are rendered on the server and can fetch data directly, while client components are rendered in the browser and can handle user interactions.

It is essential to be able to detect any problems that happen between those boundaries. Fortunately, there are many industry-standard development tools that can help us identify and resolve problems:

- *React DevTools extension*—This powerful browser extension allows developers to inspect the React component tree, view props and state, and analyze component performance.
- *Live debuggers*—The Node.js Inspector provides a way to debug your Node.js applications using Chrome DevTools. This allows you to set breakpoints, step through code, and inspect variables in real time.
- *Console logs*—Console logging remains a fundamental debugging technique. It allows developers to output values and messages to the console, helping track the flow of execution and identify errors.

These tools should be a staple in every developer's toolkit and are essential first steps when building web apps. But not all tools are 100% bulletproof, especially when it comes to the differences in deployment providers.

Certain providers, like Vercel, do offer different Node.js runtimes as listed at their official documentation site (https://vercel.com/docs/functions/runtimes). It's no surprise that while you may be able to run your Next.js application locally without any problems, you may encounter challenges when deploying it on Vercel. For example, in its support on streaming, Vercel's documentation says:

In addition, Serverless Functions have a maximum duration, meaning that it isn't possible to stream indefinitely. Edge Functions do not have a maximum duration, but you must send an initial response within 25 seconds. You can continue streaming a response beyond that time.

So choosing an appropriate runtime will affect the reliability of your services. If you configure and respect the streaming limits, then streaming will work as expected.

Still, the best strategy is to add structured logging in key places on your app and then review and filter those logs to detect what is going wrong. Is it your code that is misbehaving, or is it the AI provider that is not responding to requests? Is your deployment configuration missing some important elements so that at run time you encounter critical errors? All those questions can be answered if you have access to detailed error reporting or relevant error logs.

To implement structured logging in a Next.js application, I suggest starting with a dedicated logging library such as the Pino logging library. In any file where you want to log messages, import the logger and create a child logger as needed. This allows you to set attributes that will appear on every log line, making it easier to identify the source of logs. The following listing shows a simple logger you can use.

Listing 8.1 Creating a Pino logger instance

```
import pino from 'pino';

export const logger =
  process.env.NODE_ENV === 'production'
    ? pino({ level: 'warn' })
    : pino({
        transport: {
          target: 'pino-pretty',
          options: {
            colorize: true,
          },
        },
        level: 'debug',
      })
```

`import pino from 'pino';` — Imports the Pino logging library for structured logging

`target: 'pino-pretty'` — Uses 'pino-pretty' for formatted console output during development

For your convenience, I've included several logger calls in both the client and server actions codebase, which you can inspect when running a few queries (see figure 8.3).

Logging in general is universal and can help you uncover and understand problems that stem from various aspects of application development. It is highly recommended to include log statements as a first step in key areas of the code (such as API responses, before and after state changes) that you are working on.

8.1.3 Handling state management

State management problems in Next.js happen because there are often complex interactions between client and server state, component lifecycles, and data flow patterns. For these, use *logging* and remember to *keep the AI logic separate from UI components*.

```
GET / 200 in 48ms
GET /_next/static/webpack/fe0b867b46ccd463.webpack.hot-update.json 404 in 331ms
GET / 200 in 19ms
[12:21:43.266] INFO (2661): Continuing conversation
[12:21:43.267] DEBUG (2661): Supported model determined
[12:21:44.390] INFO (2661): Conversation continued successfully
POST / 200 in 1912ms
[12:21:45.152] INFO (2661): Streaming completed for input

User submitted input  ▼ Object i
                          inputValue: "tell me a poem"
                        ▶ [[Prototype]]: Object
Assistant response received  ▼ Object i
                        ▼ assistantMessage:
                          ▶ display: {$$typeof: Symbol(react.element), type: Symbol(react.suspense), key: null, ref: null, props: {…}, …}
                            id: "aoxUpvLfKU5YCcRm"
                            role: "assistant"
                          ▶ [[Prototype]]: Object
                        ▶ [[Prototype]]: Object
```

Figure 8.3   Console and server log statements in a structured format help us understand how the client and server communication works.

As we've seen, we can use logging to track state changes and component behavior. This helps identify where and when state mutations occur and can reveal unexpected state transitions.

We've also discussed the importance of maintaining a clear separation of concerns by extracting AI-related logic from UI components. This practice makes the state flow more predictable and easier to debug while also improving code maintainability. For example, in chapter 4, we configured Vercel AI SDK UI and AI state management components to help us achieve this separation effectively.

Ultimately, the primary consideration in state management is understanding where your data resides within the application and how it is being updated. Once you have complete visibility into both aspects, it becomes easier to pinpoint problems that may affect your web application's behavior.

8.1.4   Performance monitoring

Some performance challenges emerge from the complexity of data handling, API interactions, and state management in Next.js applications that utilize generative AI. The asynchronous nature of interactions with AI providers means that requests can take several seconds to complete. This delay can lead to a perception of sluggishness in the application, especially if errors occur behind the scenes or the application retries some request. Since each retry adds to the overall response time, it can significantly affect user experience.

To mitigate performance problems, we need to implement effective performance optimization techniques. Let's look at three key strategies for monitoring performance of your Next.js applications: network monitoring, memory profiling, and the `Performance.now()` API.

NETWORK MONITORING

The network tab in your browser provides tools for monitoring network activity, allowing you to track API calls and data-fetching patterns and identify potential bottlenecks in network requests. HTTP proxies can capture traffic between server and client, providing better visibility into data transfer. It's best to combine this with the structured logging to correlate important network events like request/response data or status.

MEMORY PROFILING

Memory leaks can become significant factors when using streaming or manipulating long lists of messages in memory without proper cleanup procedures. For instance, you might inadvertently create dangling references through forgotten timers or callbacks while trying to update AI message thread histories. This can lead to increased memory consumption and slower application performance, especially when message histories become very elongated. You may experience this with ChatGPT, for example, which becomes really slow when your message thread becomes large (some providers like Claude just impose a limit to the thread window). Utilize built-in browser memory-profiling tools to identify memory leaks, track component memory usage, and optimize resource allocation. Regularly profiling your application helps ensure that it remains responsive over time.

With memory profiling, problems can also occur on the server side (Node.js). One helpful facility the Node ecosystem offers is the ability to create a heap profile. Start your Next.js build with the following command:

```
node --heap-prof node_modules/next/dist/bin/next dev
```

This will create a `.heapprofile` file at the end of the build, which you can load into Chrome DevTools Memory tab for analysis. Figure 8.4 is a screenshot of the profile, which shows the memory usage per function.

Self size		Total size		Function	
12.6 MB	30.33 %	12.6 MB	30.33 %	▶ readFileSync	node:fs:434
3.3 MB	7.89 %	3.3 MB	7.89 %	▶ wrapSafe	node:internal/m...js/loader:1596
1.2 MB	2.81 %	2.3 MB	5.50 %	▶ requireWithFakeGlobalScope	/Users/theo.des...ves/load.js:40
1.1 MB	2.54 %	1.1 MB	2.54 %	▶ test	
1.0 MB	2.52 %	1.0 MB	2.52 %	▶ (anonymous)	/Users/theo.des...bundle.js:1871
1.0 MB	2.52 %	14.2 MB	34.23 %	▶ __webpack_require__	/Users/theo.des.../bundle5.js:28
831 kB	2.00 %	831 kB	2.00 %	▶ slice	node:buffer:636
592 kB	1.42 %	6.7 MB	16.17 %	▶ __require	
534 kB	1.28 %	2.6 MB	6.33 %	▶ analyze	/Users/theo.des...nft/index.js:1
529 kB	1.27 %	529 kB	1.27 %	▶ (anonymous)	
527 kB	1.27 %	527 kB	1.27 %	▶ 4117	/Users/theo.des...el/bundle.js:1

Figure 8.4 Chrome DevTools Memory Profiler view with a heap snapshot. It displays memory allocation statistics for various functions and components in a Node.js application.

Typically, for better results, you want to run the application for some time and perform several interactions so that you can accumulate instances of functions that pose heavy memory usage. This approach allows you to observe how the application behaves under typical usage patterns, helping to identify specific areas where memory consumption spikes.

PERFORMANCE.NOW()

The `Performance.now()` API provides high-resolution timestamps that let you measure the time taken by specific operations in your application. This precision is useful for benchmarking performance-critical sections of your code. In the example project, we have an example profiler that uses this function to capture some important performance metrics like duration of calls, streaming metrics, and average latency. Here is an example usage:

```
import { Profiler } from '@/lib/profiler';
   const profiler = new AIPerformanceProfiler();
   profiler.startOperation('initialAIRequest');
   // Call API
   const finalMetrics = profiler.endOperation('completeAIRequest');
   console.log('Performance Metrics:', {
       totalDuration: finalMetrics.duration,
       apiLatency: finalMetrics.duration,
       streamingMetrics: finalMetrics.streamMetrics,
       averageChunkLatency: finalMetrics.streamMetrics.avgChunkLatency
   });
```

The main idea here is to capture performance metrics of costly operations to help optimize the entire pipeline from the initial request to final token delivery. Once you measure important metrics, you can set up a tracker that captures improvements or degradations in performance over time. This allows for continuous monitoring and evaluation of your application's efficiency and an understanding of where optimizations are needed.

8.2 Vercel AI SDK troubleshooting

Many potential problems with the Vercel AI SDK arise because the library relies on external APIs, which can have differences between them. Additionally, major updates to this SDK introduce deprecations and changes to the recommended classes or functions. For example, during the authoring of this book, there has been two major version changes in this SDK, which required me to review existing code to verify its functionality. When developing software that depends on external tools and SDKs, you will need to adopt a similar approach to ensure secure and up-to-date dependencies.

Despite these challenges, we can still follow a methodical approach to identifying and resolving problems related to this library. Figure 8.5 shows some common troubleshooting workflows that can guide you through the process.

242 CHAPTER 8 *Testing and debugging techniques*

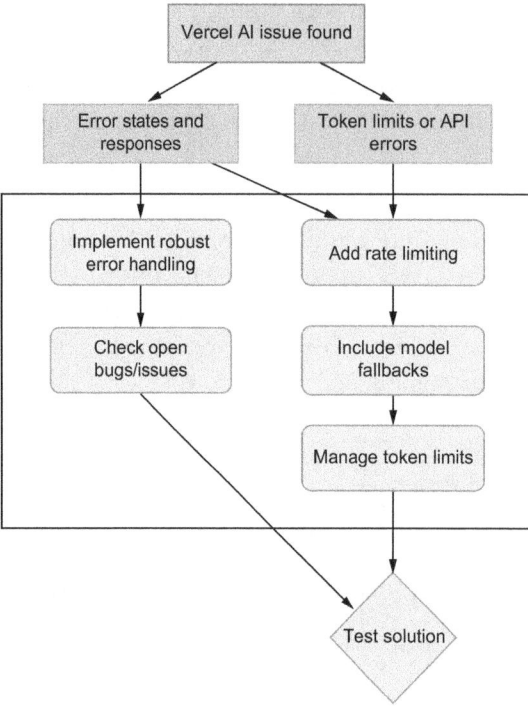

Figure 8.5 Troubleshooting strategies for Vercel AI SDK problems. There are two main paths: error states/responses and token limits/API errors. Each path shows specific steps for resolution, including implementing error handling, rate limiting, model fallbacks, and token management.

You can use this figure as a starting point when debugging problems with Vercel AI SDK implementation and relevant backend services. Let's explore the two main paths: errors states and responses, and token limits and API errors.

8.2.1 Handling error states in AI-generated content

When working with AI models through the Vercel AI SDK, the most frequent problems come from the misalignment between what providers advertise and what they support. Their API can change, but they do not inform the endpoint consumers about the implications of those changes. Of course, this challenge might not exist at all if you self-host your own LLM, but it can appear when there are intermediate errors that break the normal flows.

PROVIDER COMPATIBILITY PROBLEMS

The following is a comprehensive breakdown of common error states you may find when working with AI providers. The most prevalent source of errors occurs when AI providers make unannounced changes or have undocumented limitations:

- Sudden API changes without warning (especially common with OpenAI and Anthropic)
- Regional restrictions that aren't clearly documented (e.g., Azure OpenAI Services not being available in certain regions)

- Feature gaps between documentation and actual implementation
- Inconsistent behavior between different model versions from the same provider

MODEL CAPABILITY MISMATCHES

Many errors occur when attempting to use features that aren't supported:

- Image analysis capabilities might be mentioned in docs but not enabled for your tier.
- Audio transcription features may be region locked or require special access.
- Function calling might work differently than documented or be completely unavailable.
- Streaming responses might not be supported for certain model types.

COMMON RUN-TIME ERRORS

Several types of errors typically manifest during normal operation:

- Empty responses when the model fails silently
- Max token limits enforced differently than documented
- Unclear error messages for content policy violations

So how do you mitigate those kinds of errors? Some of them, like region-locked features, can be verified by simply executing workflows and reviewing the responses for any relevant error messages. However, since there could be a variety of types of errors that can be thrown at any given interaction, it's important to at least implement a robust error-handling mechanism in key areas of your application logic and provide options for the user to recover or retry the request.

IMPLEMENTING ROBUST ERROR HANDLING WITH USER-FACING FALLBACKS

The simplest way to handle errors is to extend your existing `try-catch` block in server actions.jsx to catch potential errors. You can detect instances of an error either by using `instanceof` operators or by checking the error message contents.

> **NOTE** The source code for the examples in this chapter is available at https://github.com/Generative-AI-Web-Apps/Code/tree/main/ch08/chat-vercel-troubleshooting.

> **Project code: chat-vercel-troubleshooting**
>
> The code for the example project can be found in the ch08/chat-vercel-troubleshooting folder. You can use that example by running this command in the root folder of the project repository:
>
> ```
> $ npm run dev -w ch08/chat-vercel-troubleshooting
> ```
>
> You'll also need either the OpenAI API or the Google API keys to access their REST API. For details on creating API keys, refer to the appendix:

(continued)
```
// .env
OPENAI_API_KEY=<OPEN_AI_SECRET_KEY>
GEMINI_API_KEY=<GOOGLE_AI_SECRET_KEY>
```

The following listing shows how we implemented this in the example project.

> **Listing 8.2 Integrating error tracking into the application**

```
import { AIErrorTracker } from '@/lib/error-tracking';    ◄── Imports the custom AIErrorTracker module
                                                              for tracking errors related to AI interactions
export async function continueConversation(input, provider, model) {
    ...
} catch (error) {
    const errorData =
await AIErrorTracker.trackError(error, {    ◄── Tracks the error using
    provider,                                   AIErrorTracker, passing
    model,                                      relevant context data
    input,
});

    const userError =                                    ◄── Creates a user-friendly
AIErrorTracker.createUserFacingError(errorData);          error message based on
    return {                                               the tracked error data
        id: userError.requestId,
        role: 'assistant',         Prepares the display content
        display: (            ◄──  for rendering an error
          <ChatBubble              message in the chat interface
            role="error"
            text={`${userError.message} (Request ID: ${userError.requestId})`}
            className="mr-auto border-none error"
          />
        ),
    };
}
```

I've created an example `AIErrorTracker` class, located in the error-tracking.js file within the lib folder, which encapsulates all the supported error types you may encounter when dealing with an AI provider, along with corresponding error messages that can be displayed to the user. This approach to error handling allows easier management of errors in a consistent manner. You can add more checks by extending the `ErrorType` and `ERROR_PATTERNS` constants within the `AIErrorTracker` class to cover additional error types.

Another benefit of this approach is that for certain errors, like network errors, you might want to prompt users to check their internet connection or try again later. Conversely, if an authentication error arises, you could display a message asking users to log in again or verify their credentials. Here is a snippet of code that adds a retry server action in the display message as an example:

```
<ChatBubble
    role="error"
    text={userError.message}
    className="mr-auto border-none error"

>
    {userError.requestId && (
      <button onClick={retryAction}>Retry</button>
    )}
</ChatBubble>
```

Since React server components are streamable functions, we use this abstraction as much as possible, making it easier for developers to add robust error-handling mechanisms with relevant call-to-action components.

CHECKING THE OFFICIAL VERCEL AI SDK ISSUE TRACKER

Remember to stay informed about existing bugs and their workarounds. The SDK is actively maintained, but like any software, it can have problems that affect your implementation. The primary source for known problems is the GitHub repository's bug tracker. (https://github.com/vercel/ai/labels/bug), shown in figure 8.6. Make sure you review this tracker if you encounter an unknown problem to see if someone else has experienced it before.

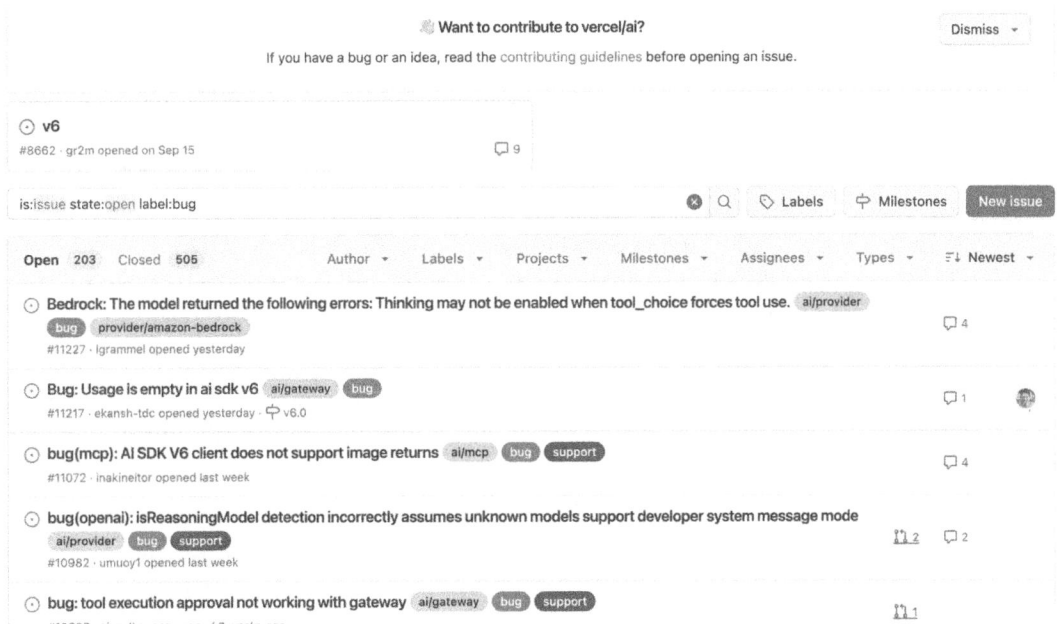

Figure 8.6 Check the current list of open bugs/issues on the official Vercel AI SDK repository to get insight into a potentially relevant problem that you've encountered.

Keeping the dependency versions of all relevant libraries (like @ai-sdk/*, ai, and Next.js) up to date is an additional step in ensuring the reliability and performance of your application. Make sure to regularly update dependencies to take advantage of new features, performance improvements, and security patches.

8.2.2 Managing token limits and rate limiting

When working with AI providers, sooner or later, you will encounter problems; managing token limits and implementing rate limiting are key aspects to check so that your application runs smoothly and efficiently. If you run out of quota limits or you don't control the flow of requests, your services might get bogged down and stop working efficiently.

Here is a quick overview of some particular problems:

- *Token limits*—Token limits refer to the maximum number of tokens that can be processed within a given timeframe. Each AI provider has specific limits on the number of tokens that can be sent or received in requests, which can vary based on the pricing tier or plan. For example, Azure OpenAI API has defined limits such as requests per minute, requests per day, tokens per minute, and tokens per day. Exceeding these limits can result in errors or throttled responses.
- *Rate limiting*—Rate limiting is a technique used to control the number of incoming requests to an API within a specified timeframe. Each provider has its own rate limits imposed in its public-facing API. In addition, when exposing API endpoints in your own apps, adding rate limiting helps prevent abuse and ensures fair usage among all users.
- *Model fallbacks*—Model fallbacks are mechanisms that allow applications to switch between different AI models or providers when one becomes unavailable or encounters problems. This is to ensure that users will be served by an available service provider.

Since both token/rate limits and fallbacks have different meanings and recovery mechanisms compared to traditional error handling, it's important to create specific abstractions that manage both cases in your web application.

MANAGING TOKEN LIMITS

Token management should be a proactive process in general since we know that sent tokens that exceed the specified AI provider limits will be automatically rejected. We have a variety of strategies to prevent reaching those limits:

- *Use of* maxTokens *parameter*—The maxTokens parameter allows you to specify the maximum number of tokens for each response. This helps ensure that the generated output does not exceed the allowed token count according to the provider's constraints:

```
const response = await streamText({
  model: supportedModel,
```

```
  prompt: "Write a poem about love.",
  maxTokens: 100, // Limit response to 100 tokens
});
```

Imposing a `maxTokens` value lets you control the size of the generated responses, which could allow you to pack more conversations within a context window without losing valuable information.

- *Rolling conversation context*—With rolling context, we send only a limited number of past messages (e.g., the last 10), so you can ensure that your application stays within token limits while still providing relevant context:

```
while (messageHistory.length > 10) {
  messageHistory.shift(); // Remove the oldest message
}
```

Pairing the token limit with the `maxTokens` parameter enables you to calculate the length of the `messageHistory` allowed for each conversation thread. By selecting a round number that is divisible by the provider's token limits, you can ensure that your application operates within the boundaries.

- *Token count monitoring*—You can implement a monitoring mechanism to track the total number of tokens being used in your conversation history. To achieve this, you can utilize libraries like js-tiktoken, which allows you to encode messages and calculate their token counts accurately. However, it's important to note that js-tiktoken may not support all AI models, so you might need to develop a custom solution for those that are not covered.

Even when you have abstractions to measure the number of tokens you send with each request, your application might get an influx of incoming responses that would fail. For that use case, you want to have an option to perform retries. However, it's important to understand that retries should primarily be for transient errors (e.g., network glitches, temporary service unavailability, or rate limiting) and generally not for persistent problems like exceeding your API quota. The following section explains how to configure this option.

RETRYING FAILED REQUESTS

The `maxRetries` parameter from each of `streamText`, `generateText`, `streamUI`, and the related family of functions allows you to specify the maximum number of times a request should be retried if it fails due to transient errors, such as rate limiting or server problems.

While it may seem counterintuitive to retry a Too Many Requests (HTTP 429) error, this type of error is indeed retryable, because rate limits are typically temporary and time-based. A 429 indicates that you've exceeded a request threshold within a brief window; it's not a permanent block. For example, you can set `maxRetries` when making API calls:

```
const response = await streamText({
  model: supportedModel,
  prompt: "Generate a summary of the latest news.",
  maxRetries: 3, // Retry up to 3 times on failure
});
```

In this case, if the request fails due to a retryable error (like a 429), the SDK will automatically attempt to resend the request up to the specified number of retries before ultimately failing.

If the LLM provider is down or unavailable, you can also consider using a fallback model.

MODEL FALLBACKS

A package like the ai-fallback library is a good candidate that offers model fallbacks. This library provides a structured way to implement model fallback mechanisms when interacting with AI models. Specifically, if an AI provider becomes unavailable, the fallback mechanism will automatically trigger and reroute the request to an alternative provider. Here's how to set it up:

1 Install the ai-fallback library. Add the npm package to your project dependencies list:

```
$ npm install ai-fallback
```

2 Create a fallback model. You can create a fallback model that will automatically switch between different AI providers when errors occur, such as hitting token limits or experiencing rate limiting. In our example, we just use Open AI, with Google AI as a fallback.

Listing 8.3 Creating a fallback model

```
import { createFallback } from 'ai-fallback';        ◄── Imports the
import { createOpenAI } from '@ai-sdk/openai';            createFallback
import { createGoogleGenerativeAI } from '@ai-sdk/google';  function from the
                                                          ai-fallback library
const openAPIKey = process.env.OPENAI_API_KEY;            to create a fallback
const googleAPIKey = process.env.GEMINI_API_KEY;          model for AI
                                                          interactions
// Create a fallback model instance
const supportedModel = createFallback({       ◄── Creates an instance of a fallback model that
  models: [                                        can switch between different AI models
    createGoogleGenerativeAI(
{ apiKey: googleAPIKey })('models/gemini-2.0-flash'),
    createOpenAI({ apiKey: openAPIKey })('gpt-3.5-turbo'),
  ],
  onError: (error, modelId) => {
    console.error(`Error with model ${modelId}:`, error);
  },
  modelResetInterval: 60000,    ◄── Sets the interval (in milliseconds) for resetting
});                                  back to the primary model after an error occurs
```

3   Handle retry conditions (optional). Configure the `shouldRetryThisError` option for retrying requests when specific errors occur. You can customize the behavior by specifying which errors should trigger a retry:

```
const retryableStatusCodes = [429, 500];
const supportedModel = createFallback({
  models: [
  ...
  ],
  shouldRetryThisError: (error) => {
    retryableStatusCodes.includes(error.statusCode)
  },
});
```

The code specifies a list of retryable status codes, such as 429 and 500 (Internal Server Error), which indicate conditions under which requests should be retried. Of course, you are free to modify the logic based on a specific error code or response type.

> **Reviewing the ai-fallback implementation**
>
> While you are setting up this feature, it's also important to review the existing code of the library's main class to see how it works behind the scenes. The code defines a `FallbackModel` class that implements the `LanguageModelV1` interface, allowing for seamless switching between multiple AI models based on their performance and availability:
>
> ```
> export class FallbackModel implements LanguageModelV1 {
>     readonly specificationVersion = 'v1'
>     // rest of code here
> }
> ```
>
> The `LanguageModelV1` interface is essentially an extension to the language specification model that I explained in chapter 3. This examination will provide valuable insights into how to implement similar extensions effectively in the future.

Retry logic, fallback, and token limit mechanisms are all effective solutions for addressing problems that arise when an AI provider becomes unavailable or stops functioning. These strategies help ensure that customers receive uninterrupted service by providing alternative options when primary models fail. However, relying on these mechanisms is only one part of the equation; you still need to actively monitor the health and reliability of the AI services being utilized. Usually this involves using an external service provider.

We won't go into detail about which providers to use for logging and monitoring web applications, but there are two popular options:

- *Sentry*—A free tier is available for error tracking and performance monitoring. Sentry helps developers identify and fix problems in real time by capturing exceptions and performance data.

- *Elastic Stack*—While the Elastic Stack (Elasticsearch, Logstash, Kibana) can be used as an open source solution, managed services like Elastic Cloud provide additional support and features at a cost. This stack is excellent for searching, analyzing, and visualizing log data.

8.3 Troubleshooting LangChain.js

LangChain.js serves as an abstraction designed to simplify the development of applications utilizing LLMs in a composable manner. However, this added layer of abstraction can increase complexity and introduce new challenges when attempting to resolve unexpected errors.

> **NOTE** The source code for the examples in this chapter is available at https://github.com/Generative-AI-Web-Apps/Code/tree/main/ch08/chat-langchain-troubleshooting.

> **Project code: chat-langchain-troubleshooting**
>
> The code for this example project is in the ch08/chat-langchain-troubleshooting folder. You can use that example by running this command in the root folder of the project repository:
>
> ```
> $ npm run dev -w ch08/chat-langchain-troubleshooting
> ```
>
> You'll also need either the OpenAI API or the Google API keys to access their REST API. The appendix offers instructions on how to set up a secret key for OpenAI and other providers:
>
> ```
> // .env
> OPENAI_API_KEY=<OPEN_AI_SECRET_KEY>
> GEMINI_API_KEY=<GOOGLE_AI_SECRET_KEY>
> ```

> **NOTE** The core LangChain.js library is implemented in TypeScript/JavaScript and does not require Python to be installed on your system. It runs natively in Node.js or browser environments. However, some community integrations or example projects may depend on Python tools or libraries and thus require a Python environment.

Figure 8.7 illustrates the two main troubleshooting paths when working with LangChain.js: chain execution problems and model integration problems.

> **TIP** To troubleshoot problems with frameworks like Next.js, the Vercel AI SDK, and LangChain.js, combine technical knowledge, intuition, and hands-on experimentation. Problems often originate from multiple layers of the stack. Start by documenting your current state, reproducing the problem

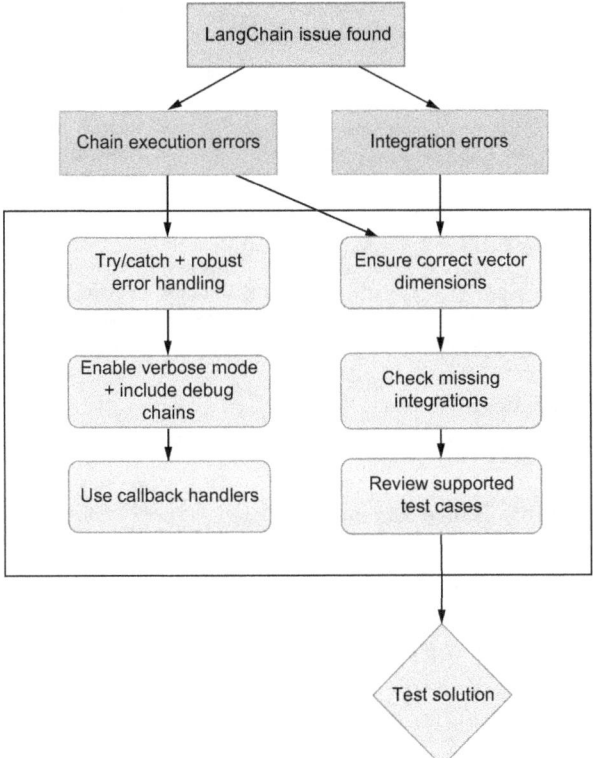

Figure 8.7 LangChain.js problems and their respective debugging and resolution steps

reliably, and testing potential solutions systematically. The more experience you gain from working with active services, the more efficient you will be at detecting and resolving production errors.

8.3.1 Chain execution errors

The most common error you will encounter when working with LangChain is chain execution errors. These occur when there's a problem in the flow of your chain execution.

Many things related to chain execution can significantly affect the reliability and performance of applications. One is undefined outputs, which often occur when required inputs are missing, leading to incomplete or erroneous results. Additionally, incorrect data propagation disrupts the flow of information between different components of the chain, resulting in unexpected behaviors. Finally, unexpected chain termination happens when unhandled errors occur during execution.

WRAPPING EXECUTION WITH TRY/CATCH STATEMENTS

One way to tackle potential errors, with respect to the way that you normally compose chains, is to wrap the execution chain into a try/catch statement. The following listing shows an example.

Listing 8.4 Catching execution errors in runnable chains

```
const chainGoogle = RunnableSequence.from([
  {
    standalone_question: standaloneQuestionChainGoogle,
    original_input: new RunnablePassthrough(),
  },
]);
const executeChain = async (input) => {
  try {
    const result = await chainGoogle.invoke(
{ question: input });
    console.log('Result:', result);
  } catch (error) {
    console.error('Chain execution failed:', error);
  }
};

executeChain("What is artificial intelligence?");
```

- Creates the sequence with an array of runnables that will be executed in order
- Invokes the chain sequence with an object containing the input question within a try/catch block
- Executes the chain while catching any errors

This will catch the execution part of the flow, which typically is used to invoke the LLM to generate responses.

To observe the try/catch in action, you can intentionally trigger an API error: simply locate the apiKey variable in your execution-error-handling.js script and temporarily change its value to an invalid string—for example, const apiKey = 'INVALID_KEY_FOR_TESTING'. Then run the script again from the ch08/chat-langchain-troubleshooting directory using node execution-error-handling.js, and you will see the chain-execution-failed message logged by your catch block:

```
% node execution-error-handling.js (main !) file:///Users/theo.despoudis/
workspace/Generative-AI-Web-Apps/node_modules/@langchain/google-genai/dist/
embeddings.js:89        throw new Error("Please set an API key
for Google GenerativeAI " + ^
Error: Please set an API key for Google
GenerativeAI in the environmentb variable
GOOGLE_API_KEY or in the apiKey field of the
 GoogleGenerativeAIEmbeddings constructor
```

ENABLING VERBOSE MODE IN MODELS OR TOOLS

When initializing a model like ChatGoogleGenerativeAI or a tool like DuckDuckGoSearch, you can enable verbose logging as follows:

```
const googleModel = new ChatGoogleGenerativeAI({ apiKey, verbose: true });
```

By setting verbose: true, all interactions with this model or tool will log detailed information about the inputs it receives and the outputs it generates. One potential negative is that this could be overly verbose if there are multiple requests happening, so you want to configure your terminal to allow for a larger log history for easier searching.

ADDING DEBUG CHAINS FOR MONITORING EXECUTION STEPS

Monitoring chain events allows us to track the execution flow and performance of their chains. This includes logging inputs and outputs at various stages, which is helpful for debugging and introspection purposes. The following listing shows the simplest way to add this to an existing chain.

Listing 8.5 Integrating debug information into the runnable chain

```
import { RunnableSequence } from "@langchain/core/runnables";
const debugChain = (input) => {
  console.log("Current Execution Context:", input);    ◄── This function is intended to log the current execution context for debugging purposes.
  return input;
};

const finalChain = RunnableSequence.from([
  debugChain,
  chainGoogle,    ◄── Add this chain to the sequence, which will log the input before passing it to the next runnable.
]);

(async () => {
  await finalChain.invoke(
{ question: "What is artificial intelligence?" });    ◄── Invokes the finalChain with an object containing a question
})();
```

Using the debug chain in your LangChain.js application provides a straightforward mechanism for logging the arguments or current context at specific points during the execution of your chain.

Note that the order of the operations matters here. Each runnable is executed in the sequence in which it is defined, which means that any changes made by earlier runnables will affect the inputs passed to subsequent ones.

UTILIZING CALLBACK HANDLERS

Callbacks provide valuable insights into the execution flow and can be customized further based on your application's requirements. These handlers allow us to hook into various stages of the application, enabling functionalities such as logging, monitoring, and error handling.

The following is an example of how to use the built-in `ConsoleCallbackHandler` in a LangChain.js application. This handler will log all calls made with this LLM:

```
import { ConsoleCallbackHandler } from "@langchain/core/tracers/console";
const handler = new ConsoleCallbackHandler();
const googleModel =
new ChatGoogleGenerativeAI({ apiKey, callbacks: [handler] } );
```

The `callbacks` option is basically a list of objects that has a predefined list of keys corresponding to an associated event type. Table 8.1 shows a short list of events together with their associated methods (as object property names).

Table 8.1 Common callback handlers in LangChain.js

Event	Trigger	Method
Chain start	When a chain starts running	handleChainStart
Chain end	When a chain ends	handleChainEnd
Chain error	When a chain errors	handleChainError
LLM start	When an LLM starts	handleLlmStart
LLM new token	When an LLM or chat model emits a new token	handleLlmNewToken
LLM end	When an LLM or chat model ends	handleLlmEnd
LLM errors	When an LLM or chat model encounters an error	handleLlmError

Callback handlers in LangChain.js can be injected not only within the LLM provider calls but also within individual invoke-method calls, providing a more fine-grained tracing capability. Here is an example:

```
console.log(await finalChain.invoke(
{ question: 'What is artificial intelligence?' },
{callbacks: [handler]}));
```

All available options to capture traces and logs from your chain execution processes are extremely helpful for debugging purposes, and you should utilize them in full when working with LangChain.js.

8.3.2 *Troubleshooting model integration problems*

Model integration problems typically arise when setting up and configuring language models within LangChain.js. These problems can lead to unexpected behaviors, errors, and inefficiencies in how models interact with other components of the system. There are many situations when LangChain.js chains will fail to run effectively, so be sure to set up a reliable logging system to capture any errors.

VECTOR DIMENSIONS MISMATCH

This problem arises when the dimensions of the embeddings produced by a model do not match the expected dimensions in the vector store. For example, if a vector store is configured for 1,024-dimensional embeddings but receives 8,192-dimensional vectors, it will throw an error. This mismatch can arise from two reasons:

- *Incompatible models*—Using a model that produces embeddings with dimensions different than those expected by the vector store can lead to integration failures.
- *Incorrect configuration*—Misconfigurations in either the embedding model or the vector store setup can result in dimension mismatches.

We can reproduce vector dimension mismatch by reviewing the code we discussed in the previous chapter when parsing the PDF documents into the HNSWLib vector store.

If you later attempt to load or query this vector store using a different embedding model that produces vectors of a different dimension, you will encounter problems.

Listing 8.6 Reproducing a vector dimension mismatch

```
const createVectorStore = async (documents) => {
  const splitter = new RecursiveCharacterTextSplitter({
    chunkSize: 1500,
    chunkOverlap: 200,
  });
  const documentChunks = await splitter.splitDocuments(documents);

  const embeddings =
new GoogleGenerativeAIEmbeddings({ apiKey,
model: ' gemini-embedding-exp-03-07' });        ◀── Creates embeddings using
  return HNSWLib.fromDocuments(                       Google generative AI with a
    documentChunks,                                   specific model for saving
    embeddings
  );
};
                                                         Initializes a
                                                         different
const loadVectorStoreWithDifferentEmbeddings = async () => {   embedding
  const differentEmbeddings =                            model for
new GoogleGenerativeAIEmbeddings(                        loading
{ apiKey, model: ' models/embedding-001' });     ◀──
  const vectorStore = await HNSWLib.load(VECTOR_STORE_INDEX, differentEmbeddings);

  const results =                                  The query here fails with
await vectorStore.similaritySearch('query', 5);  ◀── "Error: Query vector must have
};                                                   the same length as the number
                                                     of dimensions (0)."
```

To run this example, you must first navigate to the correct directory and then execute the script:

```
$ cd ch08/chat-langchain-troubleshooting
$ node embeddings-error-handling.js
```

The challenge here is that the two models may produce vectors of different dimensions, which results in compatibility problems during queries. For instance, the error message "Query vector must have the same length as the number of dimensions (0)" indicates that the dimensions of the query vector do not match what the vector store expects. To avoid this, you must ensure you use the same embeddings model in both retrieval and storage operations.

MISSING INTEGRATION PROBLEMS

Often, certain features may not be supported by specific models or integrations, leading to runtime errors. For example, a common error you may find is when you want to generate structured outputs with JSON objects. Some providers do not support this feature, so the relevant calls will fail:

```
const modelWithParser = model.withStructuredOutput(format, {
  method: 'jsonMode',
});
const result = await modelWithParser.invoke('Tell me a poem');
Error: ChatGoogleGenerativeAI only supports "functionCalling" as a method.
```

This error indicates that the `ChatGoogleGenerativeAI` model does not support JSON mode for structured outputs and can only operate with the function calling method. The fix here is to just remove the config option for `method: 'jsonMode'`. To arrive at that conclusion, we had to review the implementation of the `ChatGoogleGenerativeAI` class.

When faced with such errors, it can be challenging to determine the exact capabilities of each provider. Therefore, a practical approach is to verify the implementation details of the provider by examining the actual API calls made within the code. This allows you to understand what features are supported and how to work around limitations effectively.

For further verification, you may need to explore the examples provided in the LangChain.js repository. The examples folder contains dozens of working implementations that demonstrate correct usage of each provider and reference function call. This is all expected, since there are many ways of utilizing LangChain.js, and not all of them are properly documented on the official documentation site, so experimentation is necessary.

Of course, sometimes certain features are not entirely supported for a specific model, whether it is intentional or not, and you will have to provide alternatives.

8.4 Testing strategies for AI applications

There are four areas to consider when testing AI-powered web apps: unit and integration testing, mocking LLM responses, and testing Vercel AI SDK and LangChain.js responses, shown in figure 8.8.

8.4.1 Unit and integration testing in React and Next.js

In web applications built with React and Next.js that use generative AI, we write tests to ensure both the individual components and the overall system function correctly. There are two main testing methods: unit testing and integration testing.

> **Project code: chat-testing**
>
> The code for this example project is in the ch08/chat-testing folder. You can run the test cases of this example by running this command in the root folder of the project repository:
>
> ```
> $ npm run test -w ch08/chat-testing
> ```
>
> You won't need either the OpenAI API or the Google API keys since the code listed is for testing purposes.

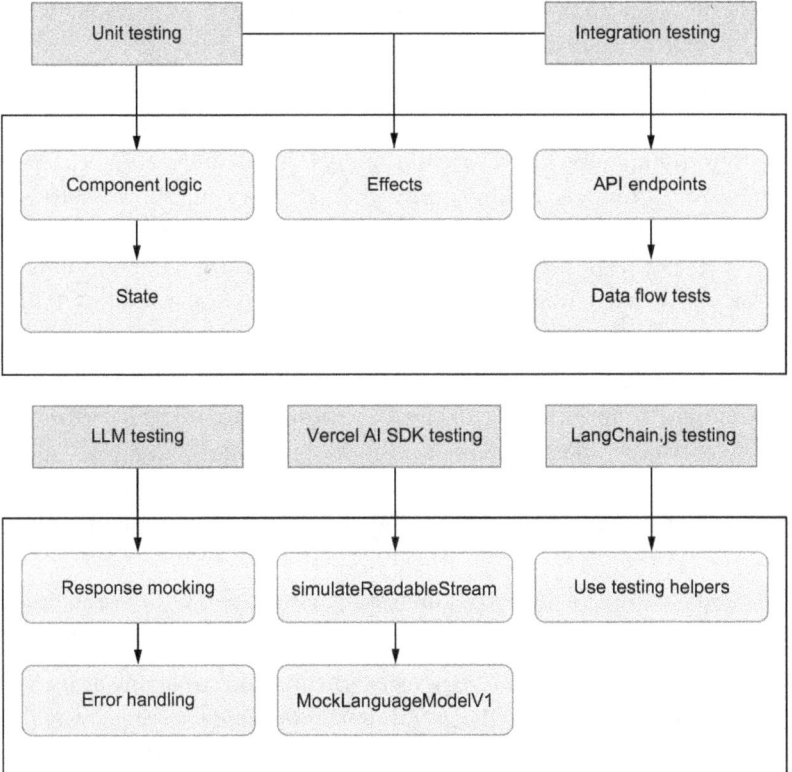

Figure 8.8 The various testing methods used in the software development process. Unit testing, integration testing, LLM testing, Vercel AI SDK testing, and LangChain.js testing are all employed to validate different aspects of the software, including component logic, effects, API endpoints, state, data flows, response mocking, readability stream simulation, error handling, and language model integration.

UNIT TESTING

Unit testing focuses on verifying the functionality of individual components in isolation. For instance, using frameworks like Jest and React Testing Library, developers can create tests that check whether a component renders correctly with given props or handles user interactions as expected.

Setting up a unit testing infrastructure is a straightforward process with the current tools available, so I won't dive into the specifics. What is important, however, is to establish criteria for what is being tested. Developers should focus on key aspects such as component rendering under various conditions, state management, event handling, and lifecycle methods. With component logic, unit tests focus on verifying the logic of individual components. This involves checking that functions and methods behave as expected when given specific inputs. For state management, unit tests can verify that state updates occur correctly in response to user actions or lifecycle events, ensuring the component maintains the expected behavior throughout its cycle. Unit tests can also assess whether event handlers trigger the correct responses, such as clicks or form submissions, and produce the desired outcomes.

INTEGRATION TESTING

Integration testing examines how different parts of the application work together. This includes testing interactions between components, API routes, and external services such as generative AI models. For example, when an API route is called to generate a response from an LLM, integration tests can verify that the application correctly sends requests and handles responses. Developers should focus on API endpoints and handlers, how the data flows between boundary systems, and component integration:

- *API endpoints*—Integration tests evaluate how well the application interacts with external APIs. This includes testing whether API calls return the expected data and whether the application can handle various response scenarios effectively.
- *Data flow*—These tests ensure that data flows correctly between components and services within the application. They validate that data passed from one component to another is accurate and that any transformations applied to the data are performed correctly.
- *Component integration*—Integration testing checks how different components work together as a unit as they perform interactions with each other.

Overall, this type of testing is more expensive to run, both in terms of infrastructure and running speed. By employing both unit and integration testing strategies, developers can achieve a robust testing framework that ensures a stable delivery of new features.

8.4.2 Mocking LLM responses

Mocking is a testing technique where you replace real system dependencies with simulated objects that mimic the behavior of the real components. These controlled environments allow you to test various scenarios without the added costs of real model interactions. In LLM testing, mocking involves creating artificial responses that simulate what an LLM would return, without calling the LLM API.

Mocking LLM responses is useful for several practical reasons. Real LLM API calls are expensive and slow, making frequent testing costly and time consuming. LLMs are nondeterministic and return different responses to identical prompts, which makes writing reliable tests more difficult. Mocking allows you to isolate your code logic from external dependencies so that tests focus on your application rather than the LLM service's behavior.

CHALLENGES AND CONCERNS OF MOCKING

Mocking LLM responses presents several significant challenges. The authenticity of the mocked responses is particularly obvious when dealing with context-dependent tasks such as a response to a carefully crafted prompt. A mock might return a simple predefined response for a sentiment analysis task, while a real LLM would consider more intricate factors to determine the output.

This problem becomes even more apparent when models receive updates. For instance, if OpenAI improves GPT coding capabilities, all your mocked coding responses might become outdated.

The core question then becomes, what are you truly testing? Are you assessing the model's performance or the system's behavior based on a fixed set of predefined responses? Mocking is useful for testing system logic and error handling, but it falls short when evaluating tasks that rely on the model's evolving capabilities. This brings us to the following topic of discussion.

WHAT TO MOCK VS. WHAT NOT TO MOCK

Deciding what to mock in testing LLM applications is a debatable topic. Mock components are best used for simpler, predictable tasks such as input sanitization, response processing, error handling, and basic flow control, as these do not require the complexity of real model interactions and allow for faster testing cycles. However, tasks like complex sentiment analysis, performance characteristics, and model reliability should not be mocked, as they require real model outputs for accurate validation. Additionally, when working with external LLM providers, testing can become more challenging since you lack control over their performance. Therefore, you need to find a balance when utilizing mocking for testing LLM responses.

CAVEAT: MOCKING EXPOSES IMPLEMENTATION DETAILS

Mocking LLM responses often requires you as a developer to make assumptions about the internal structure and behavior of the LLM system, which can lead to tightly coupled and brittle tests. When you create mocks, you essentially encode specific implementation details about how the LLM service works, rather than testing the actual behavior your application needs. Consider this example:

```
const mockLLMResponse = {
  choices: [{
    text: "Hello world",
    finish_reason: "stop",
    logprobs: {
      tokens: ["Hello", "world"],
      token_logprobs: [-0.22, -0.2]
    },
    model_version: "gpt-3.5-turbo"
  }],
};
const simplifiedMockResponse = {
  text: "Hello world",
  isComplete: true
};
```

The level of detail in the first `mockLLMResponse` can lead to tests that are overly reliant on the specific structure of the mocked response, making them fragile and difficult to maintain if the real model's output format changes. The `simplifiedMockResponse`, on the other hand, strips away unnecessary details and focuses on just the essential information needed for testing: the generated text and whether the response is complete. Ideally, you want to balance detail and simplicity in the mock responses to ensure effective testing without compromising flexibility.

8.4.3 Testing Vercel AI SDK responses

Let's now focus on how to test Vercel AI SDK functuality. The SDK provides tools that facilitate effective testing of applications using generative AI. It includes mock providers and test helpers that allow developers to simulate model behavior, at least with a predefined list of responses.

The key helpers that the framework exposes for testing are `MockLanguageModelV1`, a mock language model that allows you to define custom responses for testing, and `simulateReadableStream`, a helper function that simulates streaming responses so you can test streaming functionalities. Both helpers are useful for creating reliable and efficient tests that ensure the application behaves as expected under different conditions without using actual calls to an API.

> **Running the unit tests**
>
> To run these unit tests, navigate to the ch08/chat-testing directory in your terminal (where where the package.json file, which defines the test script, is located) and execute the `npm run test` command:
>
> ```
> cd ch08/chat-testing
> $ npm run test
> ```

MOCKLANGUAGEMODELV1

The `MockLanguageModelV1` is a mock provider included in the Vercel AI SDK that allows developers to simulate the behavior of a language model during testing. By using this mock, developers can define specific responses to test various scenarios without calling the provider API. When you need to mock one of the AI generator functions (`generateText, generateObject`) without calling the actual AI provider, you just need to create a mock instance of a model using the `MockLanguageModelV1` class with the dummy content as a response. The following listing shows the simplest use case.

Listing 8.7 Testing with `MockLanguageModelV1`

```
import { generateText } from 'ai';
import { MockLanguageModelV1 } from 'ai/test';
describe('Text Generation Tests', () => {
  test('should return predefined text from mock model', async () => {
    const result = await generateText({
      model: new MockLanguageModelV1({
```

◁── Imports the MockLanguageModelV1 to simulate a language model for testing purposes

◁── Creates a new instance of MockLanguageModelV1 to simulate a language model's behavior

```
      doGenerate: async () => ({
        rawCall: { rawPrompt: null, rawSettings: {} },
        finishReason: 'stop',
        usage: { promptTokens: 10, completionTokens: 20 },
        text: `Hello, world!`,
      }),
    }),
    prompt: 'Hello, test!',
  });

  expect(result.text).toBe('Hello, world!');
});
});
```

Defines the behavior of the mock model when generating text

Asserts that the returned text matches the expected output

The `MockLanguageModelV1` is instantiated to simulate a language model's behavior, where its `doGenerate` method is overridden to return a controlled response without making live calls. To test this code, you must first navigate to the ch08/chat-testing directory. Then, you can simply run the provided npm task named `test:vercel:ai`:

```
$ cd ch08/chat-testing
$ npm run test:vercel:ai


> chat-testing@0.0.0 test:vercel:ai
> jest --testPathPattern=vercel-ai

PASS __tests__/test-vercel-ai.js
  Text Generation Tests
    ✓ should return predefined text from mock model (2 ms)
    ✓ should return a predefined object from mock model (2 ms)
```

Just as we used `generateText` to test strings, we can use `generateObject` with a schema and verify the output using `expect(result.object).toEqual()` by reviewing the implementation details in the same test file.

SIMULATEREADABLESTREAM

The helper function `simulateReadableStream` simulates streaming responses and is useful for testing the `streamObject` or `streamText` versions of the SDK. It basically enables developers to mimic the behavior of live data streams in a controlled environment.

To test streaming, you need to use both `MockLanguageModelV1` to create a mock instance of a model and then the `simulateReadableStream` to return a simulated stream of text in chunks. The following example code snippet shows how to define this instance:

```
const result = streamText({
    model: new MockLanguageModelV1({
        doStream: async () => ({
            stream: simulateReadableStream({
                chunks: [
                    { type: 'text-delta', textDelta: 'This is ' },
```

```
        { type: 'text-delta', textDelta: 'a test ' },
        { type: 'text-delta', textDelta: 'of streaming.' },
        {
          type: 'finish',
          finishReason: 'stop',
          logprobs: undefined,
          usage: { completionTokens: 15, promptTokens: 5 },
        },
      ],
    }),
      rawCall: { rawPrompt: null, rawSettings: {} },
    }),
  }),
  prompt: 'Start streaming!',
});
```

The result object exposes a textStream property, which we can call repeatedly until the stream is closed (exhausted). After all chunks are received, we can join them into a single string and assert that the complete output matches the expected string.

The complete unit test for this streaming example, including the streamText and simulateReadableStream usage, is located at ch08/chat-testing/tests/test-vercel-ai.js.

TESTING THE CONTINUECONVERSATION SERVER ACTION

Now let's get more practical. Let's say we want to test the continueConversation function from the chapter 3's code, where we introduced the React server component actions. Here is the snippet:

```
export async function continueConversation(input, history, provider, model) {
  'use server';
  const supportedModel = getSupportedModel(provider, model);
  const result = await generateText({
    system: "I'm happy to assist you in any way I can.
How can I be of service today?",
    prompt: input,
    model: supportedModel,
    maxTokens: 512,
  });
  return {
    messages: history,
    newMessage: result.text,
  };
}
```

To effectively test this function, we will utilize mocking to simulate the behavior of the AI model and ensure that our function behaves as expected under various scenarios.

In our testing strategy, we can use the logic within the getSupportedModel function. By mocking this function, we can return an instance of the MockLanguageModelV1 class instead of a real model. This enables us to focus on testing the core functionality of continueConversation without being affected by external factors such as network latency or API changes. The following listing presents the full test case for this function, which covers various aspects of its behavior.

> **Listing 8.8 Unit testing the model return values**

```
import { continueConversation } from '../src/actions';
import { getSupportedModel } from '../src/utils';
import { MockLanguageModelV1 } from 'ai/test';

jest.mock('../src/utils', () => ({        ◀── Mocks the utils module to control
  getSupportedModel: jest.fn(),                its behavior during testing
}));

describe('continueConversation', () => {
  it('should return messages and the new message
generated by the model', async () => {
    const history = [];
    const provider = 'someProvider';
    const model = 'someModel';
    const mockGeneratedText = 'Hello, world!';      Mocks the return value of
    getSupportedModel.mockReturnValue(              getSupportedModel to return an
new MockLanguageModelV1({                    ◀──    instance of MockLanguageModelV1
      doGenerate: async () => ({
        rawCall: { rawPrompt: null, rawSettings: {} },
        finishReason: 'stop',
        usage: { promptTokens: 10, completionTokens: 20 },
        text: mockGeneratedText,
      }),
    }));                                            Asserts that getSupportedModel
    const response =                                was called with correct arguments
await continueConversation("Hello", history, provider, model);
    expect(getSupportedModel).toHaveBeenCalledWith(provider, model);  ◀──
    expect(response.messages).toEqual(history);
    expect(response.newMessage).toEqual(mockGeneratedText);
  });
});
```

While both helpers (simulateReadableStream, MockLanguageModelV1) are very useful for testing certain parts of generative AI web applications, remember that there are important caveats to consider when using mocking techniques.

Note that while the code example in the provided listing demonstrates the use of mocking techniques, another approach could be to utilize environment variables to create a mock model for testing purposes. This can help reduce the reliance on mocking techniques.

For example, you could set an environment variable NODE_ENV to a specific value (e.g., "testing") and then use that value to determine the appropriate model to use in your tests. This approach can provide a more realistic testing environment while still allowing for controlled testing of specific scenarios.

One significant concern is that overreliance on mocks may result in a false sense of confidence; while they can speed up testing and isolate application logic, they do not accurately reflect the unpredictable nature of real model outputs. After all, the developer crafts the actual responses instead of the generative AI model. There is an option to set up a small LLM for local testing, but in that case our tests would be considered more like integration tests instead of unit tests, so our expectations would change.

It is also essential to remember that mocking code under your control can obscure problems within your own implementation. What you should do instead is focus on mocking external dependencies or components that are not the primary focus of the test. Be aware of these considerations when writing unit tests so that the quality of your test cases won't degrade as you develop your applications further.

8.4.4 Testing LangChain.js

When working with LangChain.js, testing the responses from language models and the behavior of chains helps ensure your application functions as intended. There are many considerations, but they basically boil down to the type of code we have introduced as part of using LangChain.js. To test relevant functionality effectively, use mocking to simulate the behavior of AI models and ensure that your functions behave as expected under various scenarios. Here's how we can approach testing each part of the code:

- *Mocking dependencies*—Use mocking to simulate the behavior of external libraries and APIs, such as `ChatGoogleGenerativeAI`, `PDFLoader`, and `DocxLoader`. This allows us to isolate the logic of our application from external dependencies since it's not our responsibility to cover unit tests of external libraries.
- *Unit testing functions*—Each function can be tested individually to ensure it performs its tasks correctly. For instance, we can test that functions like `normalizeDocuments` correctly format document content or that `processFile` correctly handles different file types.
- *Integration testing*—For functions that involve multiple components or chains, such as `summarizeDocs`, integration tests can verify that these components work together as expected.

Let's test a few functions and helpers we used in the previous chapters that included LangChain.js.

TESTING HELPERS FROM LANGCHAIN

LangChain provides several testing helpers, summarized in table 8.2, to simulate the behavior of language models, loaders, retrievers, and other components. This allows developers to create test cases without relying on actual API calls or external dependencies.

Let's see how to create unit tests for the `performRAG` method in the `RAGSystem` class that we created in chapter 7, utilizing the `FakeLLM` and `FakeRetriever` classes from LangChain (see listing 8.9). We will ensure that the `performRAG` method behaves correctly under various scenarios by simulating the behavior of the language model and retriever. To do that, we replace the inner properties of this class with the respective `FakeLLM` and `FakeRetriever` instances.

Table 8.2 Common testing handlers in LangChain.js

Helper Class	Description
FakeLLM	Simulates a language model's behavior, allowing you to specify predefined responses or errors for testing purposes.
FakeStreamingLLM	Similar to FakeLLM but designed for scenarios where streaming responses are expected. It yields responses over time.
FakeChatModel	Simulates chat interactions by overriding the _generate method to return fixed messages based on input.
FakeStreamingChatModel	Extends FakeChatModel to support streaming responses, yielding messages over time while simulating chat behavior.
FakeRetriever	Simulates a retriever that returns a fixed set of documents when queried, useful for testing retrieval logic.
FakeRunnable	A fake runnable that can return input as output or options based on configuration, useful for testing runnable logic.
FakeSplitIntoListParser	Parses comma-separated values from text and returns them as an array, useful for testing parsing logic.
FakeListChatModel	A fake chat model that returns a predefined list of responses, useful for simulating sequential chat interactions.
FakeEmbeddings	Provides fake embeddings by overriding methods to return fixed values, useful for testing embedding-related functionality.
FakeTracer	A mock tracer that collects run data during tests, allowing you to verify tracing behavior without actual execution.
FakeChatMessageHistory	Simulates chat message history management, allowing you to test how your application handles message storage and retrieval.
FakeListChatMessageHistory	Similar to FakeChatMessageHistory but designed for list-based message management in chat applications.
FakeTool	A mock tool that can be used in testing scenarios to simulate tool behavior and validate interactions with tools.

Listing 8.9 Unit testing the RAG class methods using FakeLLM

```
describe('RAGSystem', () => {
  let ragSystem;

  beforeEach(() => {
    const apiKey = 'test_api_key';
    ragSystem = new RAGSystem(apiKey);

    const retriever = new FakeRetriever({
      output: [
        { pageContent: 'This is some context about AI.' },
        { pageContent: 'This is another context about machine learning.' },
      ],
    });
```

Initializes a new **RAGSystem** instance with a test API key for each test case

Creates a **FakeRetriever** instance with predefined output documents to simulate document retrieval

```javascript
    const llm = new FakeLLM({
      response: 'The answer based on the provided context.',
    });                                                              // Sets up a FakeLLM with a fixed response
                                                                     // to simulate AI-generated answers
    ragSystem.retriever = retriever;
    ragSystem.llm = llm;
  });
                                                                     // Tests the error handling
                                                                     // when the retriever is not
  it('should throw an error if retriever is not                      // initialized, ensuring the
initialized', async () => {                                          // system behaves correctly
    ragSystem.retriever = null;

    await expect(ragSystem.performRAG('What is AI?')).rejects.
toThrow('Retriever not initialized.
Run indexDocuments first.');
  });                                                                // Tests the main functionality of
                                                                     // the RAG system, verifying that
  it('should return an answer and source documents',                 // it returns the expected answer
async () => {                                                        // and source documents
    const query = 'What is AI?';

    const result = await ragSystem.performRAG(query);

    expect(result.answer).toEqual('The answer based
on the provided context.');
    expect(result.sourceDocuments).toEqual([
      { pageContent: 'This is some context about AI.' },
      { pageContent: 'This is another context about machine learning.' },
    ]);
  });
});
```

Here, the code creates mock instances of `FakeRetriever` and `FakeLLM`, which simulate document retrieval and AI responses, respectively. The first test case verifies that an error is thrown when the retriever is not initialized, ensuring proper error handling. The second test case checks that the `performRAG` method returns the expected answer and source documents when given a valid query.

Given that the class `RAGSystem` that we created contains instances of a retriever and LLM as properties, can we refactor our code so it's easier to test? The answer is, of course, yes—if it makes sense to make your code more testable and composable in nature and it's a valuable testing strategy. One way to refactor this is to use dependency injection. By injecting dependencies such as the retriever and LLM into the class rather than hardcoding them as properties, we can create a more flexible and modular design. This approach allows for easier substitution of real implementations with mock objects during testing.

The following is a short code snippet demonstrating how to refactor the `RAGSystem` class to use dependency injection:

```javascript
class RAGSystem {
  constructor(apiKey, retriever, llm) {
```

```
    if (!apiKey) {
      throw new Error('Google API Key is required');
    }
    this.apiKey = apiKey;
    this.embeddings = new GoogleGenerativeAIEmbeddings({ apiKey });
    this.retriever = retriever; // Injected dependency
    this.llm = llm; // Injected dependency
  }
  ...
}
```

In this refactored version of `RAGSystem`, both the retriever and the LLM are passed as parameters to the constructor. This design pattern enhances testability because, during unit tests, you can easily inject mock instances of `FakeRetriever` and `FakeLLM` to enable controlled testing environments where you can simulate various behaviors and responses.

I encourage you to review your existing code and refactor it to enhance testability without compromising readability or usability. Refactoring for testability not only simplifies the testing process but also ensures that your code remains modular and easy to maintain.

Summary

- When troubleshooting, developers should
  - Check that mock responses match expected formats and content.
  - Verify error handling by simulating various error conditions.
  - Ensure asynchronous operations are properly handled in tests.
  - Validate that streaming behaviors work as intended.
  - Confirm that custom events are properly emitted and handled.
- Effective debugging of AI web applications requires a systematic and investigative approach.
- Mocking external dependencies in AI application tests allows for controlled, reproducible test environments that are important for maintaining code reliability.
- Unit testing individual components of AI systems, such as document processing and text summarization, ensures each part functions correctly in isolation.
- Integration testing of AI chains and workflows verifies that multiple components work together as expected, simulating real-world usage scenarios.
- Robust testing frameworks for AI applications should include checks for error handling, edge cases, and varying AI model outputs to ensure stability.
- Testing LangChain.js-powered applications involves simulating AI model responses and document retrieval using functions like `FakeLLM` and `FakeRetriever` testing helpers.

Deployment and security

This chapter covers

- Mitigating prompt injection and API abuse
- Securing API keys and managing rate limits
- Maintaining GDPR and CCPA compliance
- Monitoring and observing AI workflows
- Deploying on hosted or self-hosted systems
- Detecting injections and applying privacy controls

Deploying AI applications introduces risks that traditional software also faces. A single misconfigured API endpoint could expose sensitive user data to adversarial prompts, while unmonitored large language model (LLM) usage might lead to astronomical costs or regulatory violations. This is no different from using any other paid service provider, where you must abide by their code of conduct.

Consider again the stack technologies we've been utilizing, and some of their unique challenges:

- *Next.js*—Server-side rendering and API routes require rigorous input validation to prevent prompt injection attacks targeting AI models. For example, a poorly secured /api/chat endpoint could become an attack vector for malicious actors.

- *Vercel AI SDK*—While simplifying LLM interactions, its abstraction layer demands careful configuration to avoid credential leaks or unintended model behavior. A missing rate limit could let attackers drain API credits in minutes. Additionally, API management policies should also be considered to ensure accountability.
- *LangChain.js*—Rapid iterations in AI frameworks mean security best practices evolve weekly. Out-of-date plugins and integrations require you to constantly review the code for potential breaking changes or misconfigurations that could increase the chances of runtime failures. When integrating external data sources, verify their reliability to avoid exposure to harmful or misleading content.

This chapter provides battle-tested strategies to secure AI applications without sacrificing scalability. You'll implement Redis-based rate limiting, audit logging, and privacy-preserving data masking while optimizing deployment pipelines for both Vercel and self-managed infrastructures.

This chapter assumes familiarity with previous chapters, including AI workflows, Next.js API routes, and integrating LangChain.js and the Vercel AI SDK. You should be comfortable managing server-side code and API keys and ready to apply security best practices in production.

9.1 Building a secure foundation with input validation, rate limits, and middleware

So far, we've been developing our web applications on local machines for development purposes, utilizing local resources without safety credentials, operating under the assumption that we are the sole users of the application features. This approach may work well in a controlled environment, but it falls flat when we consider exposing our application to the internet via a public IP address.

To transition from a local development environment to a publicly accessible application, we must dedicate an entire section to securing our application against various risks. This includes protecting our API keys from abuse, which could exhaust our credits if we rely on a commercial LLM provider like OpenAI. Additionally, we must ensure confidentiality and privacy regarding any user information processed by our application.

When exposing the application online, you must consider multiple aspects of security. Authentication and authorization mechanisms become crucial in controlling access to sensitive features and data. Furthermore, effective API key management is vital to prevent unauthorized use of our services. Implementing robust strategies in these areas is critically important to avoid major incidents. Figure 9.1 illustrates the key areas to focus on when doing multilayered security checks.

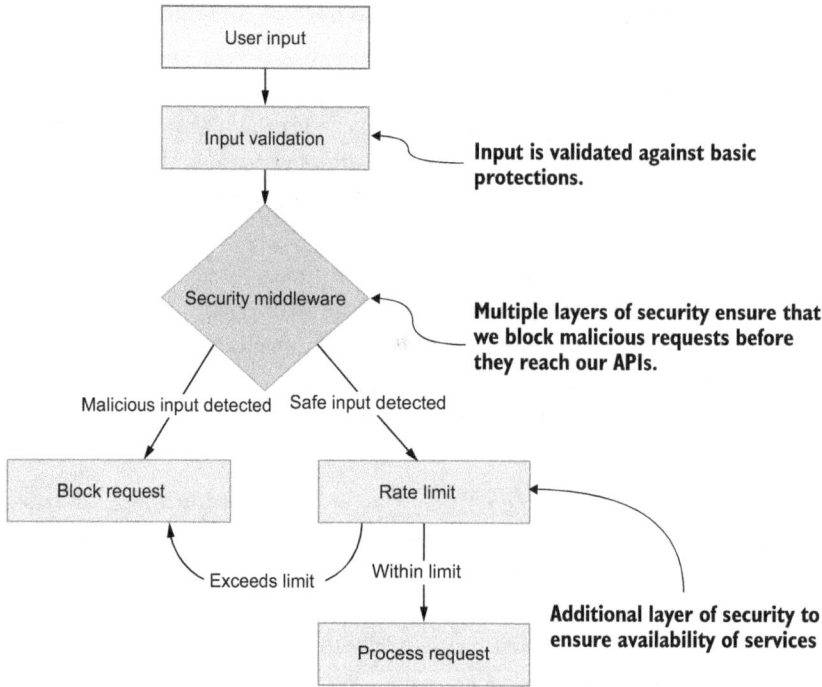

Figure 9.1 The multilayered security checks from user input validation through request processing, showcasing multiple defensive layers including input validation, security middleware, and rate-limiting mechanisms

Generally, security should follow a multilayered approach like the one shown in figure 9.1, where each request flows through progressively more sophisticated security checks. Only requests that successfully navigate all these security layers proceed to final processing, creating a robust defense system that both protects our AI resources and maintains service quality for legitimate users.

9.1.1 Input validation

Input validation ensures that user inputs conform to expected formats and constraints. With input validation, we can significantly reduce the risk of processing malicious data that could lead to security vulnerabilities, such as prompt injection attacks or excessive data usage. Before we even consider what to validate, we need to do some work to establish our web application's threat model.

ESTABLISHING A THREAT MODEL

A threat model is a process to help identify potential vulnerabilities and assess which components of the application are most at risk. This process involves analyzing various aspects of an application, including

- *Public endpoints*—Identify all public endpoints that external users can access. These are the primary entry points into your application and are often targeted by malicious actors.
- *User input points*—Determine where user input is accepted, such as forms or API requests. Understanding these points will help you focus on areas that require stringent validation.
- *Data sensitivity*—Evaluate the sensitivity of the data being processed. Inputs that could lead to exposure of sensitive information should be prioritized in your validation strategy. Important personal details like emails, passwords, IPs, or special identifiers are all classified as personal data.

Take, for example, our React server–component Next.js applications, where we often invoke POST requests to the current page at the following request URL:

```
http://localhost:3000/
```

In contrast, when we did not use React server components (in chapter 3, for example), the endpoint typically resided in the API routes at

```
http://localhost:3000/api
```

It is crucial to monitor all public endpoints, since they represent the main entry points for your applications. Once you do that, you can start securing all data that flows in or out of the application.

SERVER VS. CLIENT VALIDATION

When implementing input validation, it's important to distinguish between server and client validation. Here are their main differences:

- *Server validation*—This occurs on the server after data has been submitted. It is important because it ensures that even if client validation is bypassed (which can happen easily), the server still checks for valid input before processing it. Server validation should always be performed on each client request.
- *Client validation*—This occurs in the browser before data is sent to the server. While it can enhance user experience by providing immediate feedback, it should never be relied on as the sole method of validation. Malicious users can manipulate client code and bypass these checks.

Always assume that any data coming from the client can be tampered with: server validation must be the source of truth.

EXAMPLE: INPUT VALIDATION OF NEXT.JS API HANDLER

As an example, say we want to filter the user input prompt so it will not exceed 1,000 characters in length. We can implement Zod within the API handler.

> **Project code: chat-validation**
>
> The code for this example project is in the ch09/chat-validation folder. You can use that example by running this command in the root folder of the project repository:
>
> ```
> $ npm run dev -w ch09/chat-validation
> ```
>
> You'll need either the OpenAI API or the Google API keys to access their REST API. You'll also need Upstash Redis REST URL and the Upstash Redis REST token as well. The appendix offers instructions on how to set up and create a secret key for OpenAI and other providers:
>
> ```
> // .env
> GEMINI_API_KEY=<GEMINI_AI_SECRET_KEY>
> UPSTASH_REDIS_REST_URL=<UPSTASH_REDIS_REST_URL>
> UPSTASH_REDIS_REST_TOKEN=<UPSTASH_REDIS_REST_TOKEN>
> ```
>
> Instructions on how to set up and create secret keys for Google and Upstash Redis are also provided in the appendix.

The following listing shows how to validate incoming requests using Zod.

Listing 9.1 Validating incoming requests using Zod

```
import { z } from 'zod';                         // Imports the Zod schema validation library

const promptSchema = z.object({                  // Defines a Zod schema for validating
  prompt: z.string().min(1).max(1000),           // the structure of incoming data
});

export default async function POST(req, res) {
  try {
    const validatedData =                        // Attempts to validate the
promptSchema.parse(req.body);                    // incoming request body against
                                                 // the defined Zod schema
    const response =
await process(validatedData.prompt);             // After successful validation, this line
    res.status(200).json({ response });          // processes the validated prompt.
  } catch (error) {
    return res.status(400).json({ error: error.errors });
  }
}
```

With this check, if a user submits a POST request with more than 1,000 characters, then the server would reject the request altogether. Additional surface-level checks can also be implemented at this point to ensure some basic sanity tests for your inputs.

In addition to server validation, ensure that the UI also limits user input for the prompt to a maximum of 1,000 characters. This provides immediate feedback to the user and prevents them from submitting prompts that exceed the limit:

```
<textarea maxLength={1000} ... />
```

Of course, input validation is only a first step in securing your web application, as it must be part of a broader security strategy. Establishing reasonable defaults for input validation helps mitigate common vulnerabilities, but additional layers of security controls are essential.

9.1.2 Security middleware layer

The security middleware layer acts as a pivotal decision point in your application, analyzing incoming requests to determine their safety. This intermediate layer functions as a security system that employs multiple security controls and algorithms to detect potential threats. The middleware performs several key functions:

- *Analyzes request patterns*—It examines the frequency and nature of incoming requests to identify any unusual patterns that may indicate malicious activity, such as brute-force attacks or denial-of-service attempts.
- *Checks for known attack signatures*—The middleware utilizes a database of known attack signatures (such as SQL injection patterns or cross-site scripting attempts) to flag requests that match these signatures.
- *Validates authentication tokens*—If you employ authorization or authentication frameworks, it verifies the authenticity of tokens (like JWTs) included in requests to ensure that users are who they claim to be and have the necessary permissions.
- *Examines request headers and metadata*—The middleware inspects headers and metadata for anomalies, such as unusual user agents or IP addresses, which might suggest a spoofing attempt.
- *Applies machine learning models for threat detection*—By using machine learning algorithms, the middleware can identify emerging threats based on historical data and adapt to new attack vectors over time.
- *Rate limits requests*—Stops excessive requests that can flood your backend services.

The middleware ultimately makes a binary decision, either flagging the input as malicious or marking it as safe for further processing. It should be part of your overall security model and be scalable enough to handle the incoming load of requests from your clients.

> **NOTE** For optimal effectiveness, the security middleware layer should be positioned at the very beginning of your request-processing pipeline. This placement ensures that all incoming requests are intercepted and analyzed before they reach any part of your application's core logic. When deploying Next.js applications on platforms like Vercel, for example, these middleware functions

can run on the edge network, which are geographically located servers. This means the security checks are performed closer to the user to improve the overall performance and security of your web application.

Listing 9.2 shows a typical middleware pipeline that encapsulates some of the aforementioned security controls and filters. This code is a reference implementation of a composable middleware function you can use.

Listing 9.2 Composable middleware

```
import { NextResponse } from 'next/server';
const composeMiddleware = (middlewares) => {     ◀── Takes an array of middleware
  return async (request) => {                        functions as input and returns
    let response = NextResponse.next();              a single, composed
                                                     middleware function
    for (const middleware of middlewares) {
      try {
        const result =
 await middleware(request, response);           ◀── Executes middleware
        if (result.response) return result.response;   and handles results
        if (result.continue === false) break;
      } catch (error) {
        console.error('Middleware error:', error);
        return NextResponse.json(
          { error: 'Internal Server Error' },
          { status: 500 }
        );
      }
    }

    return response;
  };
};
const middlewareChain = composeMiddleware([      ◀── Composes all
  handleCORS,                                        middleware functions
  rateLimit,
  authenticate,
  securityHeaders,
]);

export async function middleware(request) {      ◀── The main middleware
  return await middlewareChain(request);             function that Next.js will
}                                                    execute for matching routes

export const config = {          ◀── Defines the paths that the
  matcher: '/api/:path*',             middleware should be applied to
};
```

Here the composeMiddleware function takes an array of individual middleware functions (handleCORS, rateLimit, etc.) and creates a single, composed middleware function. This composed function then iterates through each middleware in the provided array, executing them sequentially. Each middleware can modify the response, short-circuit the chain by returning a response, or halt further processing. Error handling is included to prevent a single failing middleware from crashing the entire request.

Most importantly, this pattern makes it easy to add middleware that interfaces with external APIs or security services. For example, you could integrate with a threat intelligence platform to identify and block malicious requests or use a third-party service to perform advanced authentication or authorization checks.

9.2 Building a core security and data protection pipeline

Once we have some security elements in place, the next list of security considerations is related to strengthening the security model of the whole application. That includes how we allow users to interact with our application. If we are using external AI providers like OpenAI, we must implement fair and robust security controls to prevent overuse of our API credits. This means allowing very limited interactions with visitors (such as unauthenticated users) and then prompting them to authenticate so that users are enrolled with a quoted plan. This strategy helps you control costs, prevent abuse, and ensure fair access to your application's resources.

It's also crucial to manage API keys and secrets securely, considering all the potential threats. Anti-patterns like hardcoding API keys in the application code are one of those things that can hurt the overall security model.

Data management and compliance are of utmost importance if you are dealing with personally identifiable information (PII). Nowadays, many developers choose to offload authentication to dedicated providers like Google, but even if you are only storing information like emails or passwords, you must ensure they are handled with the highest levels of security. In short, to build a robust security and compliance pipeline for your AI web applications in production, pay attention to authentication/authorization, API key management, rate limiting, and data security (figure 9.2).

Let's start by discussing how to establish a secure authentication and authorization framework for your AI web application.

9.3 Setting up authentication and authorization

Given the computational resources and API costs associated with AI models, implementing robust authentication and authorization is crucial to controlling access and preventing abuse. We definitely don't want to allow every visitor on the site to abuse the AI interactions by spamming messages, and even if they do log in, we definitely want to impose quotas and reasonable limits. Remember that most commercial LLMs cost money and are quite expensive compared to traditional services if you don't carefully manage their usage.

How do we implement robust authentication and authorization controls? First, let's clarify what these are. *Authentication* is determining a user's identity. *Authorization* is determining what a user is allowed to do—in other words, what is this user allowed to access, or how many messages are they allowed to send to the AI web application?

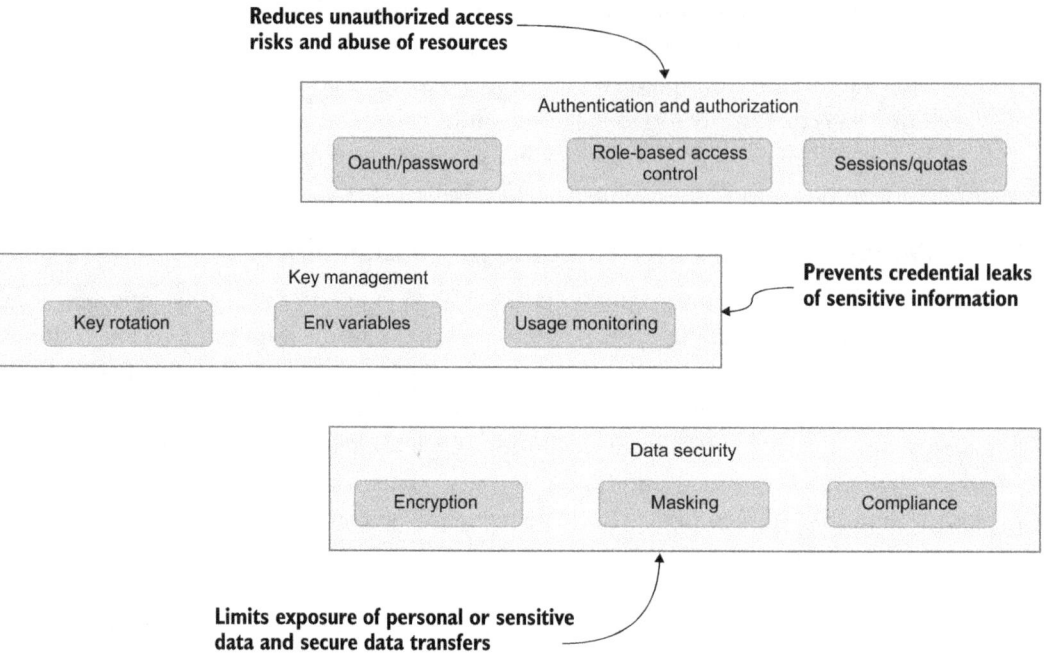

Figure 9.2 A layered approach covering secure development practices, authentication and authorization, API key management, data protection, and compliance to ensure robust security and threat prevention

For authentication, we have several options:

- *Username/password*—The simplest approach is to register users with a username and a password. While basic and widely recognized, handling passwords securely is complex, demanding a robust implementation of password policies that enforce sufficient length, complexity, and regular updates. This method is mostly not recommended in the current era due to the difficulty in implementing and maintaining user information securely.
- *OAuth 2.0/social login*—By using OAuth 2.0, users of an application can allow limited access to their resources on another site without exposing their credentials. Allowing users to authenticate using existing accounts such as Google or Facebook simplifies the login process and uses the robust security infrastructure of these established providers. With social login, it's crucial to carefully review the permissions being requested by the third-party application and avoid excessive permission requests; otherwise, users might not agree to share their data with your platform. This method is highly recommended if you provide mechanisms for users to unlink their social accounts and delete their data.
- *Passwordless authentication*—Passwordless authentication offers a modern approach to verifying users by using email or SMS verification codes, eliminating the need for them to create or remember passwords.

- *Multifactor authentication (MFA)*—MFA adds an extra layer of security by prompting users for a secondary method like a one-time password using authenticator apps. This is the most secure method to authenticate your users, but it requires some additional setup to implement.

Which of these options you commit to depends on your use case and how much is at stake. If your web application is small and uses local LLMs without storing any sensitive information, then either the basic username/password or social login options are reasonable starting points. The choice often comes down to ease of implementation versus user convenience.

However, if you are building a platform that stores more than just simple emails or you are accepting payments, then MFA with a robust third-party authentication provider is mandatory. The added complexity of MFA significantly reduces the risk of account compromise by offloading most of the compliance requirements to a third party in exchange for commercial support.

In our case, I present a recommended approach using an external authorization provider that is robust and free for development. Since we are using Next.js, we'll use the NextAuth.js package, which provides a flexible and secure way to implement authentication in Next.js applications. It allows you to easily integrate authentication logic into your serverless functions or API routes.

As for the external authorization provider, we have several great options:

- Clerk.js
- Google Firebase Authentication
- Auth0
- AWS Cognito

Here we focus on Clerk.js. Clerk offers a comprehensive user management and authentication solution that streamlines user onboarding, provides built-in MFA, and handles complex authentication flows. Its generous free tier makes it an excellent choice for development and experimentation.

9.3.1 Simple authentication with Clerk.js and Next.js

The following are the key steps required to configure authentication with Clerk and Next.js:

1. Ensure all users are authenticated before they can use the web app. Upon landing on the index path, they will be redirected to the sign-in page.
2. Redirect authenticated users to the /chat endpoint, which is protected.
3. Limit authenticated users to a maximum of 10 messages per day using Upstash Redis.

NOTE This tutorial presents one approach to implementing authentication and authorization using Clerk.js in a Next.js application. There are many ways to structure your authentication flow, and the best approach depends on the specific requirements of your application. Detailed instructions for configuring Clerk using this approach are located in the appendix.

I've established these policies to mirror real-world use cases and provide a baseline for securing your AI web application. However, feel free to adjust the policy limits, the message quota, allowed authentication methods, or specific route protections. Consider factors such as the cost of your AI resources or the anticipated usage patterns of your users when making these adjustments.

> **Project code: chat-authentication**
>
> The code for this example project is in the ch09/chat-authentication folder. You can use that example by running this command in the root folder of the project repository:
>
> ```
> $ npm run dev -w ch09/chat-authentication
> ```
>
> You'll need the Google API key, the existing Upstash keys and the new Clerk.js authentication keys to access their respective REST APIs. These are configured as environment variables:
>
> ```
> // .env
> GEMINI_API_KEY=<GEMINI_AI_SECRET_KEY>
> UPSTASH_REDIS_REST_URL=<UPSTASH_REDIS_REST_URL>
> UPSTASH_REDIS_REST_TOKEN=<UPSTASH_REDIS_REST_TOKEN>
> NEXT_PUBLIC_CLERK_PUBLISHABLE_KEY=<NEXT_PUBLIC_CLERK_PUBLISHABLE_KEY>
> CLERK_SECRET_KEY=<CLERK_SECRET_KEY>
> ```
>
> Instructions on how to set up and create secret keys and necessary credentials for Google AI and Upstash Redis, as well as how to retrieve your Clerk API keys, are provided in the appendix.

CLERK PROJECT SETUP

Create a new Clerk project at the Clerk.js website. Configure the desired authentication methods (e.g., username/password). At the end of setup, you must populate the following .env variables for Clerk to work:

```
CLERK_SECRET_KEY=
NEXT_PUBLIC_CLERK_PUBLISHABLE_KEY=
```

MIDDLEWARE CONFIGURATION

Next, we need to configure the authentication middleware in Next.js. Install the necessary Clerk packages in your Next.js project `@clerk/nextjs` using npm or Yarn. Then create a middleware.js file in the root of your project (or in the /src directory if you're using one).

Listing 9.3 Configuring Clerk middleware

```
import { clerkMiddleware, createRouteMatcher } from "@clerk/nextjs/server";
```
← The main middleware function allows you to protect routes in your application based on authentication status.

```
const isProtectedRoute =
createRouteMatcher(["/chat(.*)"]);
```
← We are using a route matcher; if it matches, the auth.protect() method will be invoked.

```
export default clerkMiddleware(async (auth, req) => {
  if (isProtectedRoute(req)) await auth.protect();

  const corsResponse = handleCORS(req);
  if (corsResponse instanceof NextResponse) {
    return corsResponse;
  }
  const rateLimitResponse = rateLimit(req);
  if (rateLimitResponse instanceof NextResponse) {
    return rateLimitResponse;
  }
  return NextResponse.next();
});

export const config = {
  matcher: [
    // Skip Next.js internals and all static files, unless found in search params
    '/((?!_next|[^?]*\\.(?:html?|css|js(?!on)|jpe?g|webp|png|gif|svg|ttf|woff2?|ico|csv|docx?|xlsx?|zip|webmanifest)).*)',
    // Always run for API routes
    '/(api|trpc)(.*)',
  ]
};
```

With this middleware in place, Clerk.js will protect all routes under the /chat endpoint (including the chat/api routes) from unauthenticated requests. The last step is to make a redirect to the sign-in page whenever a user lands on our site.

CREATING THE SIGN-IN PAGE AND UNAUTHENTICATED REDIRECTS

To manage the initial user experience, we'll implement a redirect on the index page. The goal is to check if the user is authenticated. If not, we'll redirect them to the /sign-in page. If they are authenticated, we'll redirect them to the /chat page.

Listing 9.4 Redirecting to authentication page if not signed in

```
'use client';
import { useUser } from "@clerk/nextjs";
import { useRouter } from 'next/navigation'; // Changed import
import { useEffect } from 'react';

export default function IndexPage() {
```

```
  const { isSignedIn } = useUser();          ◀── The useUser hook from @clerk/nextjs
  const router = useRouter();                 ◀── gets the current user.

  useEffect(() => {                           ◀── Imports the useRouter hook from next/
    if (!isSignedIn) {                            navigation to perform redirects
      router.push('/sign-in');
    } else {                                  Uses the isSignedIn property from the
      router.push('/chat')                    useUser hook to redirect to the sign-in
    }                                         page if the user is not authenticated
  }, [isSignedIn, router]);

  return (
    <div>
        Loading...
    </div>
  );
}
```

At this point, feel free to test out this interaction with the provided project. This is located at ch09/chat-authentication in the source code of this book:

```
$ npm install
$ npm run dev
```

Access the application at `http://localhost:3000`. After running the application, check that the flow works as expected:

- If you visit /, you should be redirected to the Clerk-hosted /sign-in page.
- After signing in, you should be redirected to the /chat page.

Now, with all the previous steps completed, the only task remaining is to set up a message quota limit for each authenticated user. In the next part, we'll walk through the steps to implement this quota using Upstash Redis.

> **NOTE** If you encounter a "New sign-ups are currently restricted" error when trying to sign in with Clerk, you will need to access your Clerk Dashboard at https://dashboard.clerk.com/, navigate to your application's settings, and adjust the Sign-Up Strategy to allow new users or add your specific email address to the list of allowed emails. For example, I added my Google email to the list of users, and then I was able to log in.

9.3.2 Practical security control: Rate limiting

Rate limiting is crucial for protecting APIs from abuse by setting a maximum threshold on the number of requests a client can make within a specified time. This is especially important when utilizing external LLMs, since they also have their own rate-limiting policies. To prevent your application from being rate limited or banned from those services, you must also limit the number of requests per second you send to the APIs.

Taking a look at the middleware code provided earlier, let's see how we can implement rate limiting, particularly in the context of the Vercel AI SDK.

Listing 9.5 Integrating a rate limiter in middleware

```javascript
import { Ratelimit } from "@upstash/ratelimit";     // Imports the rate limit library from upstash
import { Redis } from "@upstash/redis";

const redis = new Redis({                            // Creates a new Redis client instance
  url: process.env.UPSTASH_REDIS_REST_URL,
  token: process.env.UPSTASH_REDIS_REST_TOKEN,
});

const ratelimit = new Ratelimit({                    // Creates a rate limiter using a sliding window algorithm, allowing 5 requests every 10 seconds
  redis: redis,
  limiter: Ratelimit.slidingWindow(5, "10 s")
});


const rateLimit = async (request, response) => {
  const identifier = request.ip || '127.0.0.1';      // Sets the identifier to the request IP or localhost

  try {
    const { success, limit, reset, remaining } =
await ratelimit.limit(identifier);                   // Calls the limit method of the Ratelimit instance to check if the client has exceeded the rate limit

    if (!success) {
      console.log("Rate limit exceeded");
      return {
        response: NextResponse.json(
{ message: "Too many requests" }, { status: 429 }),
        continue: false,
      };
    }

    return { continue: true };

  } catch (error) {
    console.error("Rate limiting error:", error);
    return {
      response: NextResponse.json(
{ error: "Internal Server Error" }, { status: 500 }),
      continue: false,
    };
  }
};
```

The provided code implements rate limiting using Upstash Redis and the @upstash/ratelimit library. It's not the only library in existence, but the rate limiter is stable enough to be used in production. One benefit is that Upstash offers a free serverless Redis database with low latency and durable storage for development purposes if you join via their website.

Now let's simulate reaching the rate limit. I have provided a Bash script named `load-test.sh` that you can run inside the project folder ch09/chat-validation/ to generate load:

```
%./load-test.sh
{"message":"Too many requests"}....
```

As a rule, using external rate-limiting services like Cloudflare, AWS WAF, or a dedicated Redis cluster is recommended; they provide two crucial advantages. First, they handle requests before they reach your application servers, meaning that malicious traffic or denial-of-service attempts are stopped before consuming your application resources. Second, these services are distributed and highly available, making them resilient against targeted attacks and highly expensive for attackers to bring down.

With a practical understanding of security controls, we can now apply similar principles to manage resource usage more directly. Let's implement a message quota for authenticated users to control API credit consumption and ensure fair access.

MESSAGE QUOTA IMPLEMENTATION

The message quota is enforced on the backend, specifically within the API route that handles user messages (/api/chat in our case). Here's a breakdown of the process:

1 *User identification*—When a user sends a message, the API route identifies the user using their Clerk user ID, obtained from the getAuth function from @clerk/nextjs/server.
2 *Quota check*—The API route then checks the user's message count for the current day in Upstash Redis.
3 *Increment count*—If the user hasn't exceeded their quota, the message count is incremented in Redis.
4 *Quota exceeded*—If the user has exceeded their quota, an error is returned, preventing the message from being processed.

Figure 9.3 illustrates this simple logic for checking and incrementing the message quota for a user.

How should we implement this? Ideally, we want to place it in our middleware section, but we can also add this check directly to the API handler. The following listing shows how to do it.

Listing 9.6 Integrating message quota limits

```
import { getAuth } from '@clerk/nextjs/server';
const checkMessageQuota = async (userId) => {
  const now = new Date();
  const today = now.toISOString().split('T')[0];
  const key = `message_count:${userId}:${today}`;
```

⬅ Imports getAuth from Clerk to retrieve user authentication details

⬅ Constructs a Redis key to track daily message counts for a specific user

```
  const count = await redis.incr(key);          ◀──── Increments the message count in
  if (count === 1) {                                  Redis; initializes to 1 if it doesn't exist
    await redis.expire(key, 24 * 60 * 60);
  }

  if (count > 10) {         ◀──── Checks if the count exceeds the limit
    return false;                  (10 messages); returns false if it does
  }

  return true;
};

export async function POST(req) {
  try {
    // rest of the code
const { userId } = getAuth(req);
    const quotaAvailable = await checkMessageQuota(userId);
    if (!quotaAvailable) {
      return new Response(JSON.stringify(           ◀──── Handles the case where a user
{ error: 'Message quota exceeded.                         has exceeded their message
You can only send 10 messages per day.' }), {             quota by returning a response
        status: 429,                                      with an error message
        headers: {
          'Content-Type': 'application/json',
        },
      });
    }
// rest of the code
}
```

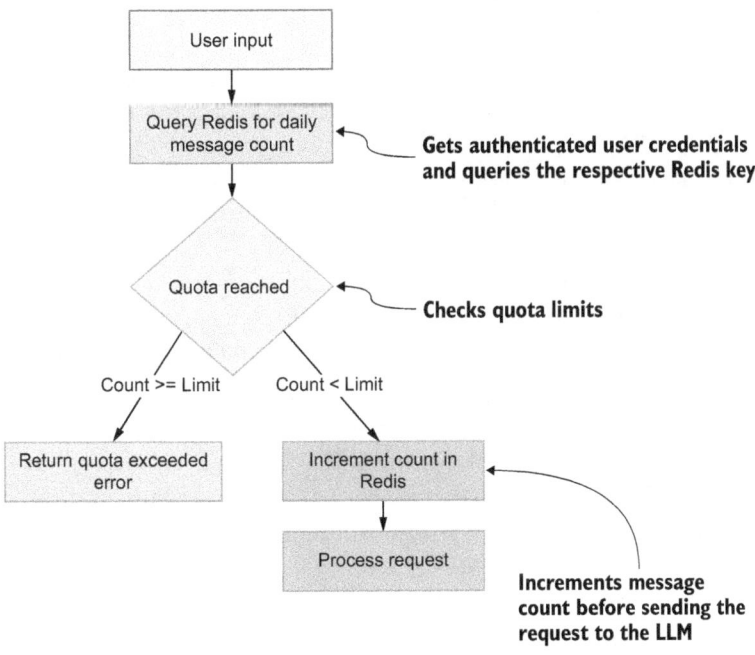

Figure 9.3 The server quota enforcement process, where user requests are authenticated via Clerk, checked against Redis-stored daily limits, and either processed or rejected based on quota status

When a user sends a message, the system first checks if the user exists in the Upstash Redis database. If the user does not exist, a new entry is created with a message count of 1. If the user exists, the system increments the message count. If the message count exceeds the quota limit (e.g., 10), the message is rejected. Otherwise, the message is allowed, and the updated message count is stored in Upstash Redis.

> **Redis key format and management considerations**
>
> In this example, we used the format for the Redis key as follows:
>
> ```
> const key = `message_count:${userId}:${today}`;
> ```
>
> However, there are other ways to define this key format that can enhance data management. For instance, incorporating a date prefix can be beneficial as well:
>
> ```
> const key = `${today}:message_count:${userId}`;
> ```
>
> This structure allows for easier searching and targeted cleanup of old keys based on their date. For example, to delete all keys related to a specific day, you can filter by the date prefix. This allows you to clean up old keys and reduce the size of the database.
>
> Next, notice that in the code we always increase the Redis count even if the count exceeds the message limit. We can improve this by implementing strategies to prevent abuse of the Redis store, especially when users can send multiple requests quickly:
>
> - Implement rate limiting to restrict the number of requests a user can make within a defined timeframe so that the count does not get increased often. This means that we need to include the quota check after a rate limit middleware to ensure this feature is not abused.
> - Introduce cooldown periods and enforce cooldowns after a user sends a message to limit immediate subsequent requests. This can prevent users from rapidly sending messages in succession.
>
> Those additional security controls should safeguard your Redis store from abuse.

You can verify that this works by sending several messages to the AI application and then checking the Upstash dashboard. In the Data Browser section, you should see a Redis key with the format `message_count:{userId}:{YYYY-MM-DD}`. The corresponding value will be the number of messages sent by that user on that day. Once the message count reaches 10, any further interactions with the application on the same day will result in a 429 Too Many Requests status code. The UI can then display a message to the user, informing them that they have reached their message limit and can try again tomorrow. Figure 9.4 shows the message quote implementation.

Currently, the UI does not provide an indicator to inform users when they have exceeded their daily message limit. However, I encourage you to consider this as an exercise to further improve the application experience.

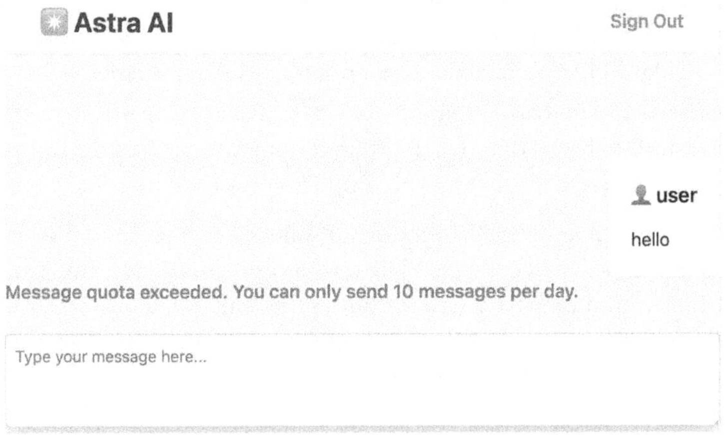

> **Astra AI**   Sign Out
>
>   user
>   hello
>
> Message quota exceeded. You can only send 10 messages per day.
>
> [Type your message here...]

Figure 9.4 Overview of the message quota implementation. The top part displays the Upstash Data Browser, showing the Redis key and value tracking the number of messages sent by a user on a given day. The bottom part shows the API response, indicating a 429 Too Many Requests status code when the user exceeds their daily message limit of 10 messages.

> **WARNING** While implementing message limiting helps manage user interactions, determined individuals may exploit disposable email services to create multiple accounts and bypass these limits. To enhance the security of registered users, implement invitation-only registration to restrict access and reduce the risk of abuse from disposable emails. Utilize unique invitation codes, require email verification, and monitor registration patterns to detect suspicious activity. Consider requiring business email addresses for registration and using CAPTCHA to deter automated submissions. This will help you avoid excessive use of API credits.

Now that we have some good practices in place for managing message quotas and Redis keys, we turn our attention to another critical aspect of application security: API key and secrets management.

9.4 API key and secrets management

Managing API keys and secrets securely is very important for any Next.js application, especially when working with services like OpenAI. Having poor secrets management can lead to costly security breaches, leaked credentials, and compromised user data. Clearly, we need to be familiar with best practices and common pitfalls in handling sensitive credentials.

9.4.1 Understanding Next.js environment variables

So far, we've been placing our secrets and environment variables into an .env file. However, Next.js provides two different ways to define them, with each serving different purposes:

- *Private environment variables*—These are accessed only on the server, prefixed with NEXT_PRIVATE_ or without the NEXT_PUBLIC_ prefix. These should store sensitive information like API keys, database credentials, and other secrets.
- *Public environment variables*—Prefixed with NEXT_PUBLIC_, these are exposed to the browser and embedded in the client JavaScript bundle. This means that they will be visible to anyone inspecting your application's source code.

The best practice for managing environment variables is to inject them at run time using a deployment provider like Vercel. Thus, we do not hardcode any variables in the repo or any file, even if they have default values. Instead, we allow them to be configured in the Vercel dashboard, ensuring that sensitive information is not hardcoded in your source files. The steps involved are discussed later in this chapter when we talk about deployments.

Now, to clarify the need for API key management and how to control keys. There are two strategies here for managing the API keys: application-level API keys and user-provided API keys.

9.4.2 Application-level API keys

Store application-level API keys, such as those used for OpenAI, in private environment variables to prevent hardcoding them into your source code. Additionally, make authenticated requests through server routes instead of exposing keys to the client, which minimizes the risk of unauthorized access.

Next.js facilitates this process with the use server directive, which designates a function or file to be executed on the server. This allows developers to securely handle sensitive operations without exposing API keys or other critical information to the client.

For instance, consider the example with the Redis client. The following code runs exclusively on the server, and sensitive information like the API tokens is never exposed to the client:

```
'use server';
import { Redis } from '@upstash/redis';

const redis = new Redis({
  url: process.env.UPSTASH_REDIS_REST_URL,
  token: process.env.UPSTASH_REDIS_REST_TOKEN,
});
```

Here, the Redis client operates on the server, and any interactions with the Redis database are conducted securely without ever revealing connection details to users.

9.4.3 User-provided API keys

For user-provided API keys, such as those from users accessing their OpenAI accounts, there are two primary approaches: server storage and client storage. When using server storage, encrypt user-provided API keys and store them in a secure database. This means that user-provided keys are treated as passwords, and it requires you to implement server routes that act as intermediaries between user requests and external APIs.

While allowing client storage of API keys can reduce server load and simplify implementation, it poses significant risks that cannot be overlooked. One of the primary concerns is the exposure of sensitive information through browser vulnerabilities. When API keys are embedded in client code, they become accessible to anyone who inspects the web application using developer tools. Some providers, like OpenAI, have built-in detection and may automatically disable any API key that has been exposed in that way.

Moreover, relying on client API calls lacks usage control and monitoring capabilities. Without a server intermediary, it becomes challenging to track how the API keys are being used, making it difficult to identify and mitigate abuse. This lack of oversight can result in unexpected charges if the keys are exploited for excessive usage, which will anger your users.

Additionally, implementing this approach is not trivial. It requires the client to import all necessary SDKs to perform API calls directly from the client. This not only complicates the setup but also necessitates exposing some internal logging, like internal prompt queries and processing pipelines, to make it work effectively.

For all the reasons mentioned, it is preferable to manage your own organization's API keys when exposing a service to the public. This approach ensures that you have ultimate responsibility and control over API usage, which is critical for maintaining security and compliance.

Many providers, like OpenAI or Google AI, offer robust API usage-monitoring capabilities through their platforms. For example, Google Cloud's Vertex AI allows users to monitor API usage effectively, particularly for the Gemini API. OpenAI has a Usage tab, showing how its API and models are used from within the organization (figure 9.5).

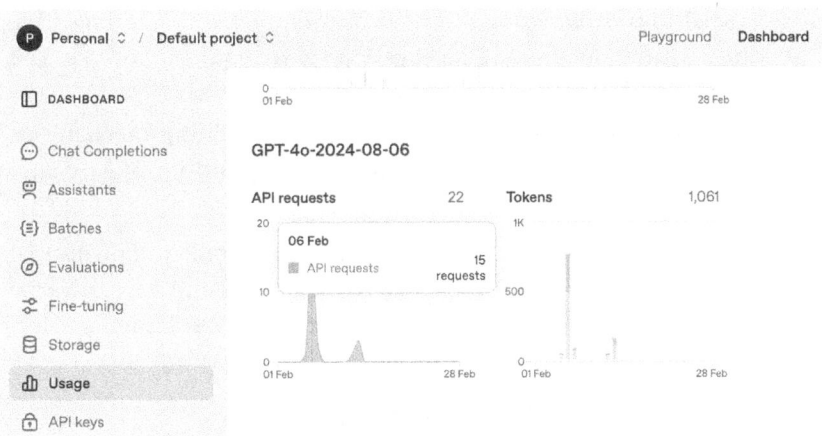

Figure 9.5 OpenAI API usage dashboard displaying metrics for a GPT-4 model instance, showing API requests and total token usage. The dashboard interface includes a navigation sidebar with options for monitoring various aspects of the API deployment.

9.5 Data protection and compliance

As we build applications that store data, we need to carefully consider the implications of using AI technologies while adhering to data protection regulations and compliance with laws such as the General Data Protection Regulation (GDPR) for EU markets and others. Failing to prioritize data protection can lead to significant legal repercussions, including costly lawsuits and regulatory fines. When it comes to general data protection and compliance with AI web applications, we need to be aware of several key considerations:

- *Sensitivity of chat data*—Evaluate the content of your chat histories. Do they contain PII? Financial details? Medical information? The more sensitive the data, the stronger your security measures need to be.
- *Encryption*—When storing chat histories, consider the sensitivity of the data. If the chat history contains sensitive information, such as PII or financial details, it is crucial to implement encryption measures using industry-standard algorithms like AES.
- *Access control*—Who can access or view user chat histories? Employ the principle of least privilege, granting access only to those roles or individuals who absolutely need it. Consider using impersonator users for specific scenarios to ensure qualified users can review another user's history. Ensure that impersonation actions are strictly logged, limited in scope, and granted only temporary access.
- *Data retention policies*—How long do you need to retain chat histories? Consider both legal requirements and business needs. Once the retention period expires, ensure the data is securely and permanently deleted. Make sure your users are aware of the data retention policies and have ways to download their chat history.
- *Anonymization/pseudonymization*—Explore opportunities to anonymize or pseudonymize chat histories, especially if using the data for model training or analysis. It's crucial to prevent storing any PII in prompt queries and avoid logging or sending sensitive details to LLMs that don't share your PII policies. This protects user privacy and complies with data protection regulations.
- *Logging and auditing*—Implement logging and auditing mechanisms to track access to chat histories. This can help you detect and investigate any unauthorized access or security breaches.

Each of these areas requires a suitable solution or set of policy controls that must be established within the code itself to guarantee data safety and user privacy. We don't have room to go over all of them, so here we'll focus on practical methods for performing anonymization and pseudonymization of user messages.

9.5.1 Example: Adding anonymization to our chat messages

In the context of data protection and privacy, anonymizing chat histories for compliance reasons is important. For example, storing sensitive information such as emails and Social Security numbers in chat histories poses significant risks, especially when these histories may be exposed to external LLMs. If chat histories containing sensitive information are inadvertently sent to LLMs, there is a potential for the data to be leaked or misused, leading to severe consequences such as identity theft, financial fraud, and privacy violations.

> **NOTE** This example uses `redact-pii`, a simple JavaScript library for redacting PII from user messages. However, for production environments, it's strongly recommended to use `@google-cloud/dlp` for more comprehensive and robust PII detection and anonymization, especially for non-English data or sensitive applications. Also, consider implementing the anonymization logic in your middleware for optimal performance.

Here's how to modify the existing chat API handler to include the client library:

1. Install the `redact-pii` library. You can do this by running

   ```
   $ npm install redact-pii
   ```

2. Import and initialize the Redactor class:

   ```
   import { SyncRedactor } from 'redact-pii';
   const redactor = new SyncRedactor();
   ```

3. Create a function for anonymization. Implement a function that uses the SyncRedactor to anonymize user messages.

The following listing gives the full code.

Listing 9.7 Anonymizing prompt input data

```
import { SyncRedactor } from 'redact-pii';
const redactor = new SyncRedactor();
function anonymizeText(text) {
  return redactor.redact(text);    ◀── Identifies and replaces sensitive
}                                       information (PII) within the text

export async function POST(req) {
  try {
    const body = await req.json();
    const validatedData = promptSchema.parse(body);

    const { userId } = await auth();
    if (!userId) {
      return new Response('Unauthorized', { status: 401 });
    }
    const anonymizedInput =
anonymizeText(validatedData.text);    ◀── The result of the anonymizeText is
// rest of the code                       used as the prompt sent to the LLM.
  }
}
```

This code simply includes another step in the API handler that redacts any sensitive information from the incoming user message before it is stored in the message history. If the contents are safe, they will pass unchanged. If the content contains sensitive data, it will be replaced by a placeholder text.

Now load up the web application, and after login, you can try to send a message that includes potentially sensitive information. Then inspect the logs and the LLM response to see if any of the information is leaked. Figure 9.6 is an example interaction.

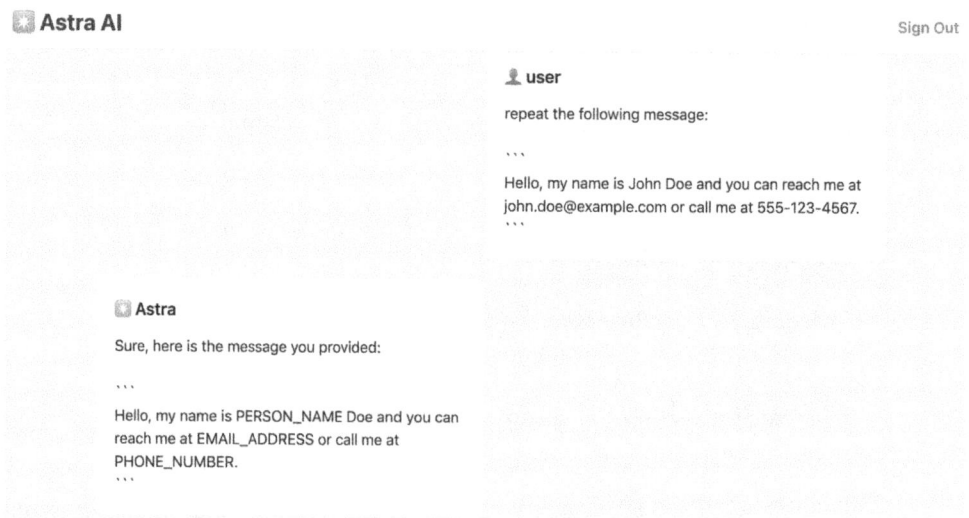

Figure 9.6   Simple data anonymization feature in action. The user provides a message containing personal information (name, email address, and phone number), and the system responds by replacing the sensitive data with generic placeholders: PERSON_NAME, EMAIL_ADDRESS, and PHONE_NUMBER.

The most important thing to understand here is that the LLM sees only the redacted input. If the logging is set up correctly, there's no way for the original text with PII to reach the LLM unless it bypasses the filter.

If your server logs show that redacted input is correctly anonymized but your UI shows the LLM is responding as if it saw the PII, then you have a problem somewhere in how you're handling or displaying the LLM's response, not in the anonymization itself. Double-check the UI code.

If the server logs show that redacted input isn't anonymized, then you have a problem with the redact library configuration or the anonymization function itself.

As you can see, part of the process of building web applications is understanding how data flows into, across components, and out of your application. As we prepare to deploy our full-stack Next.js application, we have to keep all these considerations in mind.

9.6 Deployment considerations for AI web applications

Deploying AI web applications involves unique considerations beyond traditional web applications. The integration of LLMs introduces complexities such as cost management, data privacy, and latency that must be carefully addressed. Let's look at our options.

9.6.1 Deployment options

Deploying an AI web application to a production environment involves exposing it to the public internet at a designated URL address. But this process encompasses more than just the application itself. If your application provides data—such as chat histories or user-generated content—you will also need to configure databases for production use. Additionally, if you are utilizing external services like Clerk.js for authentication or Upstash for rate limiting, you need to configure these services appropriately for a production environment. Essentially, everything your application relies on must be reconfigured to ensure scalability and security.

There are several options available for hosting your application online.

DEDICATED PROVIDERS (VERCEL)

Dedicated platforms like Vercel offer streamlined deployment workflows specifically designed for modern web applications, particularly those built with Next.js. Vercel provides a comprehensive suite of tools and infrastructure optimized for web applications, including AI web applications.

One of the reasons I frequently mention Vercel is its out-of-the-box experience that addresses many components of the production checklist we will discuss in the next section, such as content delivery network (CDN) integration, monitoring capabilities, and automated backups. For those just starting their journey with AI and Next.js, deploying on Vercel is highly recommended. It allows you to focus on development without getting bogged down in infrastructure management—at least until your application scales beyond what Vercel can accommodate. At that point, you may need to migrate some components or services outside of Vercel to meet your growing demands.

CONTAINERIZATION (DOCKER) AND ORCHESTRATION (KUBERNETES)

For more advanced deployment needs, Docker and Kubernetes are powerful tools that facilitate the deployment of AI models while ensuring consistency across different environments. Docker allows you to package your applications into self-contained packages, which encapsulate all necessary dependencies and configurations. This approach guarantees that your application runs consistently regardless of where it is deployed.

Kubernetes, on the other hand, is basically a system that manages those containers at scale. It automates critical tasks such as load balancing, scaling based on demand, and rolling updates to ensure high availability and reliability.

SELF-HOSTING

If you prefer not to use Vercel or have a preferred server-hosting provider, you can self-host your AI systems, which offers unmatched flexibility and customization. While self-hosting provides greater control over your environment, it also demands a higher level of technical knowledge and ongoing maintenance efforts. You will have to take a more hands-on approach with deploying and delivering your app to users and make sure that the operating systems that host your code are configured as well.

Overall, when considering deployment options for your AI web application, it's essential to weigh the pros and cons of each approach. Each project is unique, with varying requirements based on factors such as scale, budget, technical expertise, and specific use cases. Therefore, there is no one-size-fits-all solution. Certainly, though, you need to define your priorities regarding security, compliance, and reliability. This can be achieved by establishing a production checklist.

9.6.2 Production deployment checklist

Before deploying any web application to a production environment, it's crucial to have a production checklist in place. This checklist ensures all necessary steps are accounted for and executed effectively. Scalability requirements vary significantly based on the anticipated traffic volume, and what works for a small-scale application won't suffice for a large-scale, high-traffic system. We'll start with the requirements based on expected traffic.

TRAFFIC-BASED REQUIREMENTS

Your approach to deployment should be driven by the expected load on your application. For example, let's examine three distinct tiers, each with its unique requirements for monitoring, scaling, security, and backup procedures:

- *Tier 1: Small-scale applications (<10,000 requests/day)*—For applications with a relatively low traffic volume, the focus is on establishing a reliable and secure foundation. At this tier, you should implement
  - *Basic monitoring and alerting*—Set up fundamental monitoring tools to track the application's uptime and response times. Typically, those are provided by a hosting provider like Vercel.
  - *Simple horizontal scaling*—Ensure that you can easily add more instances of your application to handle increased load.
  - *Standard security measures*—Implement essential security practices such as HTTPS, input validation, and protection against common web vulnerabilities.
  - *Daily backups with a short retention policy*—Regularly back up your application's data and configuration to prevent data loss in case of a failure.
  - *Basic error tracking*—Use error-tracking tools to identify and resolve problems promptly, ensuring a stable user experience.
- *Tier 2: Medium-scale applications (10,000–100,000 requests/day)*—As traffic increases, you'll need more sophisticated measures to ensure optimal performance and reliability. At this tier, you should enhance your infrastructure with
  - *Basic CDN implementation*—Use a CDN like Cloudflare to distribute static assets and reduce latency for users across different geographic regions. Some

providers like Vercel always put their assets on a CDN by default, so you may not have to do a lot of work here.

- *Enhanced security measures*—Implement advanced security measures, such as intrusion detection systems, web application firewalls, and regular security audits, to protect against more sophisticated threats. This means that you must employ additional services like Vercel Firewall to cover such scenarios.
- *Comprehensive error tracking and logging*—Set up detailed logging and error tracking to capture all relevant information for debugging and auditing, which will allow you to quickly identify and resolve problems. You may have to utilize an external provider like Sentry or Datadog to provide a more customizable experience.

- *Tier 3: Large-scale applications (>100,000 requests/day)*—For high-traffic applications, you'll need enterprise-grade solutions to handle the immense load and ensure maximum uptime. At this tier, you should deploy higher-grade (thus more expensive) solutions to accommodate those policies, including
  - *Distributed logging and observability*—Include a distributed logging system that aggregates logs from all components of your application, which will provide a centralized view for troubleshooting and analysis.
  - *Geographic distribution*—Distribute your application across multiple geographic regions to minimize latency for users around the world and improve resilience in the face of regional outages. You may have to store content close to your customers and run application instances in regions close to your data.

Once you have a rough estimate of the amount of traffic you are expecting on your web application, create a checklist that covers the basic requirements to ensure a successful production deployment.

> **NOTE** It's fine to include scaling strategies from other levels, like CDNs and firewalls, even if your application's traffic doesn't yet require a higher tier. Implementing these measures early can prepare your infrastructure for future growth and enhance overall reliability.

PRODUCTION DEPLOYMENT CHECKLIST FOR AI WEB APPLICATIONS

The following is a checklist of good practices:

- Cost management
  - Understand pricing models of LLM providers.
  - Monitor and optimize API calls to reduce costs.
- Data privacy
  - Evaluate privacy policies of LLM providers.

- Ensure compliance with relevant regulations (e.g., GDPR, HIPAA).
- Encrypt sensitive data at rest and in transit.
- Anonymize or pseudonymize data where possible.
- Security
  - Implement secure coding practices.
  - Protect against cyberattacks (e.g., rate limiting, firewalls).
  - Regularly audit API key usage.
  - Rotate API keys periodically.
  - Never commit secrets to version control.
- Performance and latency
  - Assess the effect of network latency and mitigate delays.
  - Implement local caching where applicable.
  - Optimize API calls and data retrieval for efficiency.
- Scalability and reliability
  - Implement CI/CD pipelines for automated deployment.
  - Ensure high availability with redundancy and failover strategies.
- Monitoring and logging
  - Set up real-time monitoring and alerting.
  - Implement detailed logging for debugging and auditing.
- Compliance
  - Understand and adhere to data policies.
  - Ensure compliance with industry regulations and security standards.
- Deployment strategy
  - Choose the right deployment platform (e.g., AWS, GCP, Azure).
  - Use deployment strategies to minimize downtime (e.g., blue-green, canary, rolling updates).

Many of the checklist items mentioned have been discussed in the current and previous chapters, so you may find some familiar concepts. However, there are certain aspects that we have not covered, which primarily fall outside the scope of this book.

9.6.3 *Example deployment to Vercel*

Let's use our deployment checklist to deploy our simple chat application with the security controls we've discussed.

> **NOTE** The source code for the example in this chapter is available at https://github.com/Generative-AI-Web-Apps/Code/tree/main/ch09/chat-deployment.

> **Project code: chat-deployment**
>
> The code for this example project is in the ch09/chat-deployment folder. You can use that example by running this command in the root folder of the project repository:
>
> ```
> $ npm run dev -w ch09/chat-deployment
> ```
>
> You'll need the Google API key, the existing Upstash keys, and also the Clerk.js authentication keys to access their respective REST APIs. These are configured as environment variables:
>
> ```
> // .env
> GEMINI_API_KEY=<GEMINI_AI_SECRET_KEY>
> UPSTASH_REDIS_REST_URL=<UPSTASH_REDIS_REST_URL>
> UPSTASH_REDIS_REST_TOKEN=<UPSTASH_REDIS_REST_TOKEN>
> NEXT_PUBLIC_CLERK_PUBLISHABLE_KEY=<NEXT_PUBLIC_CLERK_PUBLISHABLE_KEY>
> CLERK_SECRET_KEY=<CLERK_SECRET_KEY>
> ```
>
> Instructions on how to set up and create secret keys for Google, obtain the necessary credentials for Google AI and Upstash Redis, as well as how to retrieve your Clerk API keys are provided in the appendix.

Since we will be deploying to Vercel, we can check many items from the list regarding security and quality of service items, including

- *Encrypting sensitive data at rest and in transit*—Vercel deployments are served under HTTPS, and we use external providers for authentication, like Clerk, which securely encrypts user data at rest.
- *Monitoring and logging*—Vercel offers detailed monitoring features even in its free plan, allowing us to keep track of application performance and problems.
- *Implementing CI/CD pipelines*—Vercel integrates seamlessly with Git, enabling automated CI/CD pipelines through its deployment and build tools.
- *API keys*—Vercel provides a secure way to manage and inject environment variables into your applications, ensuring sensitive information is protected.
- *Cost management*—We will limit interactions with the model to 10 messages per day per user. Additionally, access will be restricted to select users for testing purposes only.

Before we deploy to Vercel, you need to first create an account and enter your business or personal details. You can sign up by visiting the Vercel website at https://vercel.com/ and choosing your preferred plan.

To create an account, simply enter your email address to receive a six-digit one-time password, or you can sign up using a supported Git provider for easier integration. After registration, you'll need to verify your email address to complete the setup.

Next, follow the steps to ensure a successful deployment to Vercel. Pay attention to the following.

PREDEPLOYMENT CONFIGURATION

This section outlines key steps for a successful deployment to Vercel. While these steps are specific to the Vercel platform, it's crucial to note certain practices, such as ensuring successful local builds and providing necessary environment variables:

- *Create a new Vercel project and add environment variables.* On the Vercel dashboard, create a new, empty project to house your application. Add all necessary environment variables to the project settings on Vercel, as in figure 9.7. This ensures that your application has access to the required configuration during deployment and run time.

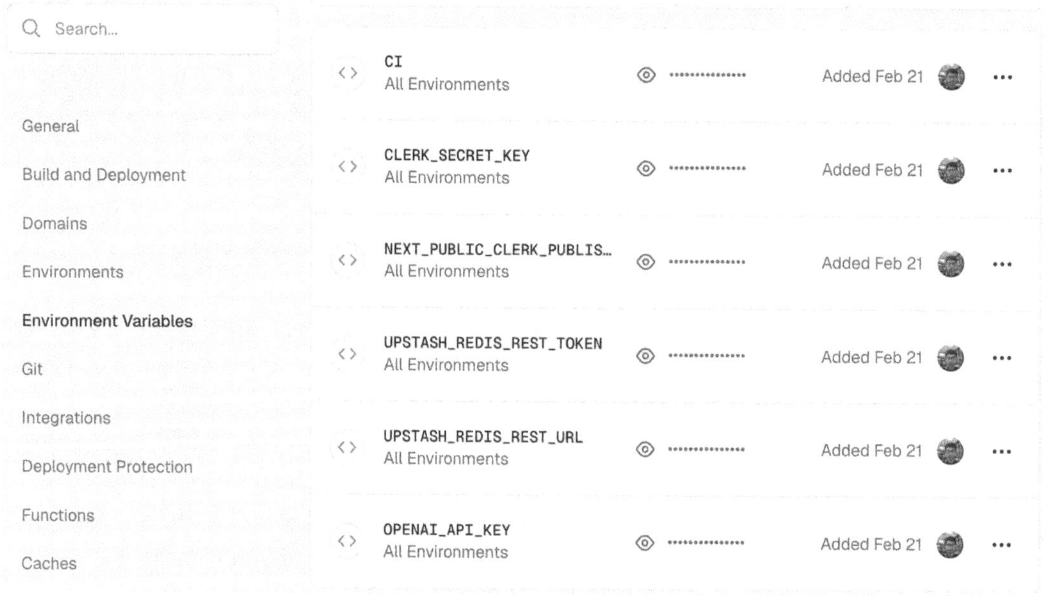

Figure 9.7 Configuration interface for project environment variables on the Vercel dashboard, displaying several masked API keys and authentication tokens

- *Ensure correct Node version.* Vercel supports specific Node.js versions, and using a compatible version is crucial for a successful deployment. Before deploying, check the Node.js version your project requires in the Build and Deployment options section of the project settings, shown in figure 9.8.
- *Verify local build success.* Before deploying to Vercel, ensure that your `npm run build` command executes successfully in your local environment. If that command fails locally, the deployment to Vercel will also fail.

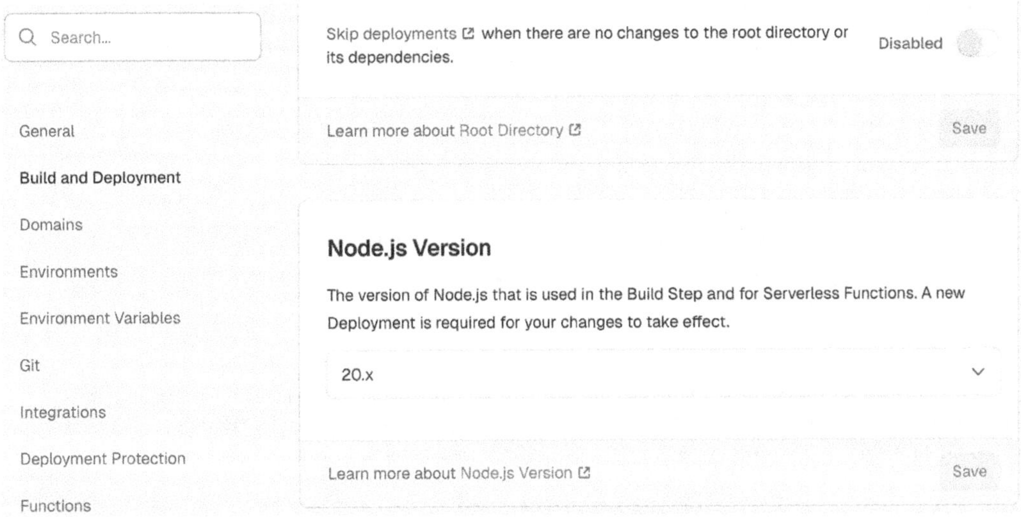

Figure 9.8 Vercel dashboard build configuration settings screen showing where we set the Node.js version to 18.x for both the build step and serverless functions

DEPLOYMENT INSTRUCTIONS USING THE VERCEL CLI

The following instructions show how to use the Vercel CLI tool to deploy the web application from your command line to the platform project:

1 Install Vercel CLI. Install the Vercel CLI globally using `npm`:

```
$ npm install -g vercel
```

2 Deploy to Vercel. Run the `vercel` command in your project directory:

```
$ vercel
```

If you are not logged in, the tool will ask you to log in first. Once this is completed, the build process will commence. You will be able to inspect the console logs about the status of the deployment. On success, you will be presented with a unique deployment URL where you can inspect the application (figure 9.9).

```
% vercel
         (main !?)
Vercel CLI 41.1.4
🔍  Inspect: https://vercel.com/theo-despoudis-projects/chat-deployment/GVqi96r8xCSjsJP5SXWE5FZW7
LUP [2s]
✅  Preview: https://chat-deployment-geasjmyb1-theo-despoudis-projects.vercel.app [2s]
```

Figure 9.9 Terminal output showing successful Vercel CLI deployment of a chat application. The deployment shows both the project dashboard URL and the preview domain, along with instructions for promoting to production using the `vercel --prod` command.

Upon visiting the URL, you should be able to review the app functionality. If there was an error with the build process, then you will be presented with instructions on what happened and how to inspect the error logs (figure 9.10).

```
⊚ % vercel
                    (main x!)
Vercel CLI 41.1.4
🔍  Inspect: https://vercel.com/theo-despoudis-projects/chat-deployment/3bBRf1PEoNVGWbFt573jNQ1oeCYc [2s]
✅  Preview: https://chat-deployment-eyjb518cu-theo-despoudis-projects.vercel.app [2s]
Error: Command "yarn run build" exited with 1
Error: Check your logs at https://chat-deployment-eyjb518cu-theo-despoudis-projects.vercel.app/_logs
or run `vercel logs chat-deployment-eyjb518cu-theo-despoudis-projects.vercel.app`
```

Figure 9.10 Terminal output showing a failed Vercel deployment attempt with error messages. The output includes links to the deployment dashboard and preview URLs, along with instructions for viewing detailed error logs either through the web interface or via the `vercel logs` CLI command.

TROUBLESHOOTING DEPLOYMENT PROBLEMS

A lot of things can go wrong when deploying the web application to a server, so it's important to follow a methodical approach to troubleshooting the problems. Here are some useful tips that will help you fix certain problems:

- *Invalidate build cache*—Vercel caches some of the framework files and folders to speed up subsequent deployment. If some errors persist, try redeploying without using the existing cache. You can do this by using the `vercel --force` command.
- *Build errors*—If the `npm run build` command fails, check for any syntax errors or missing dependencies in your project. Ensure that all necessary packages are installed by running `npm install` or `yarn install` depending on your package manager. Then you can use Vercel's Build and Deployment settings page to change the build command that will run when pushing code changes.
- *Package manager problems*—If the `npm` command fails to deploy, try switching to `yarn` or `pnpm` in the Vercel Build and Deployment settings page. This can sometimes resolve problems related to package installation.
- *Check official discussions for any relevant problems*—It's highly recommended to consult the official Vercel discussions page at https://github.com/vercel/vercel/discussions. This is to check if deployment problems have likely been encountered and resolved by others and to ask specific questions related to your deployment challenges.

By following these steps, you should be able to deploy your web application to Vercel. If you encounter any problems, refer to the troubleshooting tips provided earlier or explore the Vercel discussions page for community insights.

POSTDEPLOYMENT EFFORT

After successfully deploying the web application to the public, you should monitor how it's being used by external users. To do this effectively, you need sophisticated tooling that tracks all incoming traffic and captures application logs. You should be notified about any problems that arise affecting site availability and performance. Let's look at the key components of that effort:

- *Traffic monitoring*—We can use Vercel's built-in analytics with real-time insights into page views, unique visitors, and performance metrics. However, if you prefer more comprehensive traffic analysis, you can integrate external tools like Google Analytics or Plausible for additional insights. To do this, you want to go to the Analytics page on the Vercel dashboard and enable this for your project.
- *Log management*—For starters, you can use Vercel's detailed logs that allow you to view, search, and inspect logs across different environments. For more advanced log analysis, use external tools like New Relic or Datadog to gain deeper insights into application behavior. This is on the Logs page of the project dashboard.
- *Alerting and notifications*—While Vercel has monitoring features, it does not offer alerting. In that case, you can enhance alerting capabilities by integrating with external services like PagerDuty or Sentry for real-time notifications about critical challenges.
- *Setting up firewall rules*—Vercel offers a simple yet effective web application firewall solution on all plans and can be enhanced by custom rules. For example, you can add a custom rule to log, deny, challenge, bypass, or rate limit traffic to your site. This feature is on the Firewall page of the project dashboard.

Utilizing the basic security and monitoring offerings from Vercel is a very affordable way to ensure your web application remains secure and performant. You get the essentials like HTTPS encryption, detailed monitoring, and automated pipelines all in their free plan. That said, as your app grows, you might want to look beyond Vercel, mainly to have extra eyes on your app's performance and to avoid putting all your eggs in one basket.

Next, for readers interested in exploring different hosting and deployment workflows, we include the details for deploying to Netlify and Hugging Face. Those who are deploying elsewhere or not focusing on deployment details can skip these sections without missing any core content.

9.6.4 Alternative deployments: Netlify

Netlify is a prominent choice for deploying modern web applications. Similar to Vercel, Netlify provides a platform optimized for static sites and serverless functions, offering a seamless and fast deployment experience.

While you can use the Netlify CLI to automate deployments directly from your terminal, the most intuitive way to set up your initial deployment is by using their UI. The web interface guides you through connecting your Git repository (e.g., GitHub, GitLab, or Bitbucket) and configuring your build settings, which is often a more straightforward process for new projects (see figure 9.11).

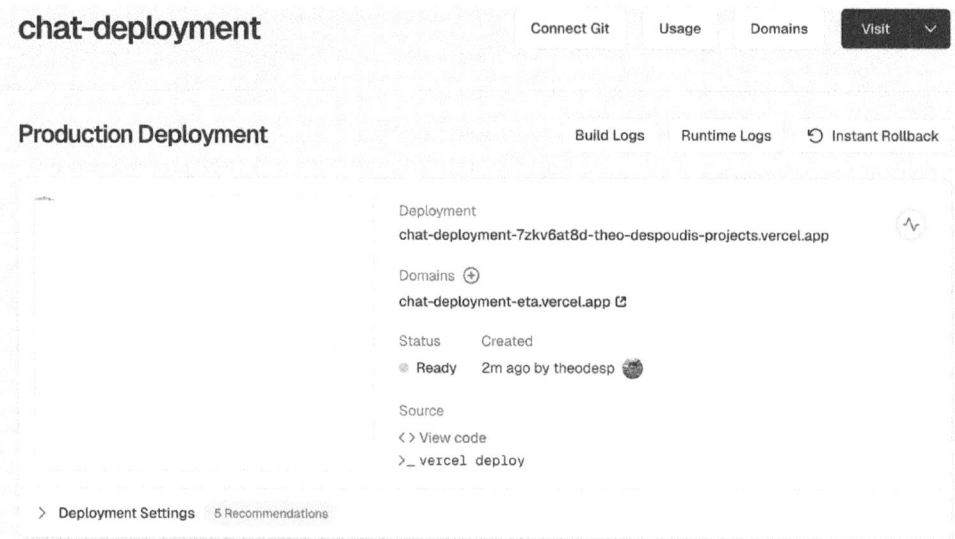

Figure 9.11 The Netlify UI dashboard for a successful deployment, showing the `chat-deployment.netlify.app` project overview, with a Production Deploys section

You can find more detailed information and guides in their official documentation:

- *Netlify documentation*—https://docs.netlify.com/
- *Netlify CLI documentation*—https://mng.bz/64Ep

9.6.5 Alternative deployments: Hugging Face Spaces

Another viable option for deploying your application is Hugging Face Spaces. This platform is a great fit for projects that are specifically focused on machine learning and AI models, as it's designed to host and share these types of applications. It offers a variety of deployment options, including static sites, Gradio apps, and Docker-based deployments.

Unlike Vercel and Netlify, Hugging Face does not offer a CLI for deployment at this time. All project configuration and file uploads must be handled through the Hugging Face Spaces UI. This means you'll need to create your space, configure its settings, and manually upload your project files or link to a Git repository directly within the web interface:

- *Hugging Face documentation*—https://huggingface.co/docs/hub/spaces-overview
- *Getting started with Hugging Face Spaces*—https://huggingface.co/docs/hub/spaces

9.6.6 Next steps

After deploying your app and ensuring it is safe and protected, what comes next? It depends on your end goals and overall objectives for your web application:

- *Personalization*—You can integrate AI-driven personalization to customize the user experience based on user behavior and preferences.
- *Chat histories*—Consider adding a chat history feature. This allows users to view past conversations, providing context and continuity in their interactions. For that, you want to use a database like MySQL or MongoDB so you can retrieve them by ID. This would involve adding a chat list or a button to view past conversations.
- *Accessibility features*—We can ensure the application is accessible by implementing features like text-to-speech, high-contrast mode, and keyboard navigation.
- *Integrate more AI models*—Consider integrating additional AI models to enhance functionality. For example, consider hosting your own `deepseek-r1` model for a more affordable way to use generative AI in certain interactions.

Remember that for each new feature that you add, you need to include integration tests to ensure that the new feature works well with other parts of the application. This means testing how different components interact with each other.

It's helpful to include scoped logging as it allows you to track specific parts of your application's behavior by logging events within a defined scope. Here is a quick example with Pino:

```
const userLogger= logger.child({ scope: 'user-interaction' });
const aiModelLogger = logger.child({ scope: 'ai-model' });
userLogger.info('User submitted a query');
aiModelLogger.info('AI model generated a response');
```

As you add more features, it's useful to include scoped loggers for those features to make them easier to track. This is just a small part of the overall improvements you can make to your application as you develop it over time.

Summary

- AI-powered applications face unique security threats like prompt injection, model manipulation, and API abuse, requiring specialized security measures beyond traditional software practices.
- Securing AI applications involves a multilayered approach, starting with input validation to prevent malicious data from reaching the AI models.
- Establishing a threat model is crucial for identifying potential vulnerabilities in your application, including public endpoints, user input points, and the sensitivity of the data being processed.
- Server validation is essential to ensure data integrity and security, as it cannot be bypassed by malicious users, unlike client validation, which primarily enhances user experience.
- A security middleware layer acts as a central decision point, analyzing incoming requests for potential threats using various techniques, rate limiting, signature matching, token validation, and machine learning models.

- Effective security middleware should be positioned at the beginning of the request-processing pipeline to intercept and analyze all incoming requests before they reach the application's core logic.
- Rate limiting is a crucial security control for protecting APIs from abuse by setting a maximum threshold on the number of requests allowed within a specific timeframe.
- User-provided API keys can be stored on the server (encrypted in a database) or on the client, but server storage is recommended for better security and control.
- Prioritizing data protection and compliance with regulations like GDPR is critical when building AI applications that store user data.
- Anonymizing or pseudonymizing chat histories helps protect user privacy and comply with data protection regulations, especially when using the data for model training.
- Deploying AI web applications requires careful consideration of cost management, data privacy, and latency.
- Deployment involves not only the application itself but also the configuration of databases and external services (e.g., authentication, rate limiting) for production use.
- Dedicated providers like Vercel offer streamlined deployment workflows specifically designed for Next.js applications, including CDN integration, monitoring, and firewalls.
- For more advanced deployment needs, Docker and Kubernetes are powerful tools for containerization and orchestration.

Part 3

Hands-on projects

You've built a strong theoretical foundation in generative AI and mastered advanced techniques with the Vercel AI SDK and LangChain.js. Now it's time to bridge the gap between learning and production by exploring complete, functional, generative AI web applications. This part is dedicated to providing you with real-world codebases so you can see how all the pieces fit together in a practical context.

I'll provide the full code for two significant projects: an AI interview assistant and an AI retrieval-augmented generation agent. For each project, we'll go beyond simply presenting the code. Instead, we'll explore its key features, dissect the architectural decisions, and delve into crucial development considerations, including best practices for performance, scalability, and maintainability. This process will give you the practical insights needed to understand, adapt, and build your own complex generative AI web applications.

Building an AI interview assistant: Project walk-through

This chapter covers

- Building an AI interview assistant covering UX and technical implementation
- Configuring chat, text-to-speech, and feedback features
- Architecting the app with Next.js, the Vercel AI SDK, and Redis
- Managing conversations, data persistence, and AI responses
- Securing user data and preventing system abuse

In this chapter, we'll take a comprehensive tour through our AI interview assistant application, examining both its user-facing features and the technical decisions to make during development. We'll explore the architecture, which is built on all the fundamental tools and technologies that we've been working with: Next.js, the Vercel AI SDK, and Upstash Redis for data management. The full code for this project is in the project repository.

10.1 Overview of the application

Our AI interview assistant is designed to help job seekers prepare for interviews by simulating realistic interview scenarios with a large language model (LLM)–powered interviewer. The application provides personalized practice, immediate feedback, and the ability to review past performances. We'll start by looking at the core features that define the user experience.

> **Project code: interview-assistant**
>
> The code for this example project is in the ch10/interview-assistant folder. You can use that example by running this command in the root folder of the project repository:
>
> ```
> $ npm run dev -w ch10/interview-assistant
> ```
>
> You'll need the Google API key, Upstash Redis REST URL, Upstash Redis REST token, and Clerk.js authentication credentials to access their respective REST APIs. These are configured as environment variables:
>
> ```
> // .env
> GEMINI_API_KEY=<GOOGLE_AI_SECRET_KEY>
> UPSTASH_REDIS_REST_URL=<UPSTASH_REDIS_REST_URL>
> UPSTASH_REDIS_REST_TOKEN=<UPSTASH_REDIS_REST_TOKEN>
> NEXT_PUBLIC_CLERK_PUBLISHABLE_KEY=<CLERK_PUBLIC_KEY>
> CLERK_SECRET_KEY=<CLERK_PRIVATE_KEY>
> ```
>
> Instructions on how to set up and create secret keys for Google AI and Upstash Redis are provided in the appendix.

10.1.1 Key features

Let's explore the key features of this application.

AUTHENTICATION WITH CLERK

Users must authenticate with Clerk.js before accessing the interview application. This ensures user session data is securely stored in Redis and allows for control over API credit usage. We require all users to authenticate to the application before they use its features. Figure 10.1 shows a screenshot of the login page.

CHOOSING AN INTERVIEW TYPE

Once logged in, users begin their experience by selecting an interview type. The application offers two primary paths:

- *Custom interview*—This option allows users to tailor the interview experience to their specific needs by submitting a custom title and job description that will be used in preparing the interview questions. Figure 10.2 shows the UI of the main interview preparation page, where users can customize the job description.

Overview of the application 307

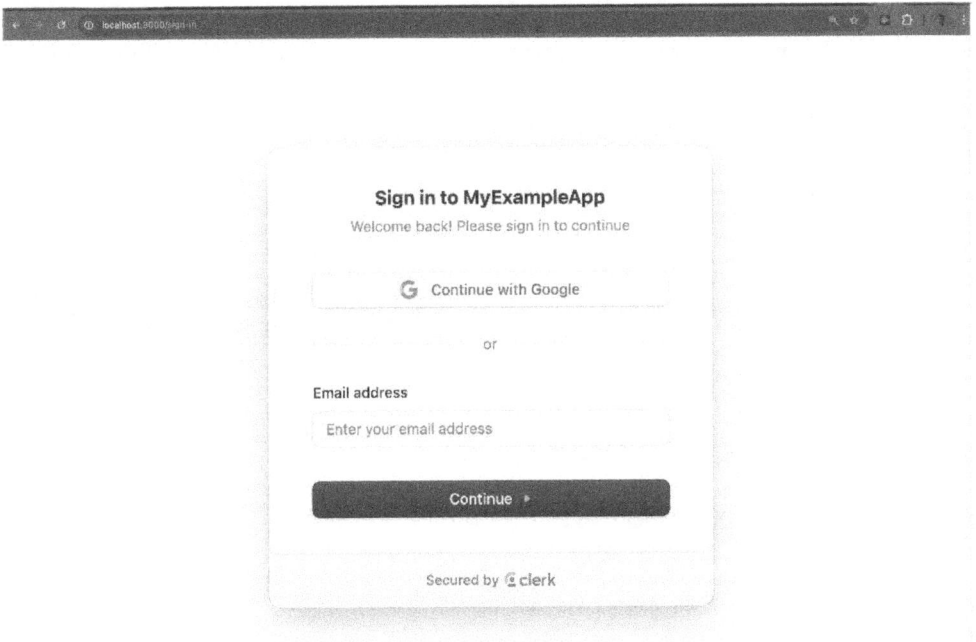

Figure 10.1 Sign-in page of the interview assistant application. Users can log in via Google or using their email address.

Figure 10.2 The main front page asks the user to submit a custom job title or use a predefined software engineer role.

- *Predefined template*—For users seeking immediate practice, we offer predefined templates, with the software engineer interview as a predefined option. See figure 10.3.

Figure 10.3 The predefined template for a typical software engineer job. You are free to modify as well.

INTERVIEW PARAMETERS CONFIGURATION

After selecting an interview type, users can fine-tune additional parameters, including

- *Number of questions*—Users can specify how many questions they want to tackle in a session, allowing for both quick practice sessions and more comprehensive mock interviews.
- *Difficulty level*—The difficulty setting adjusts the complexity of questions, enabling users to gradually increase the challenge as they improve.
- *Question types*—Users can select either behavioral, technical, or mixed question types.

Figure 10.4 shows a screenshot of the interview configuration section.

INTERACTIVE CHAT-BASED INTERVIEW UI

The interview interface itself is designed around a familiar chat-based UI. It has two key features:

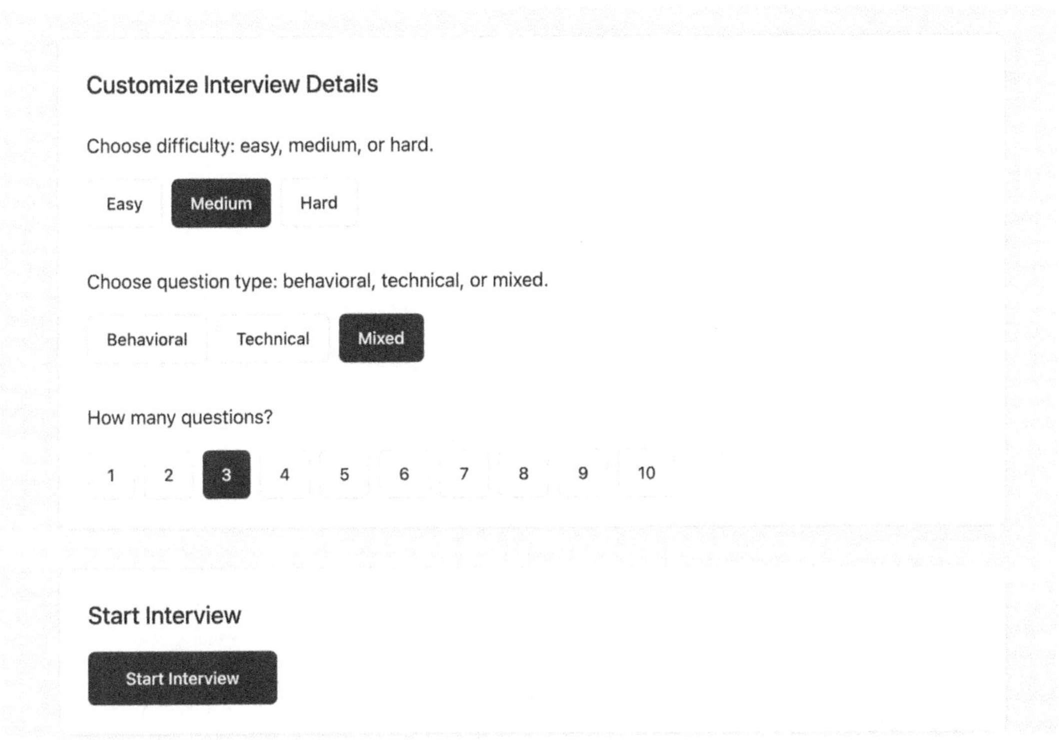

Customize Interview Details

Choose difficulty: easy, medium, or hard.

[Easy] [**Medium**] [Hard]

Choose question type: behavioral, technical, or mixed.

[Behavioral] [Technical] [**Mixed**]

How many questions?

[1] [2] [**3**] [4] [5] [6] [7] [8] [9] [10]

Start Interview

[**Start Interview**]

Figure 10.4 After the job description section, the user can configure the simulated interview experience with some options. They can change the difficulty, question types, and number of questions. Starting the interview will redirect them to the main chat UI page.

- *Conversational flow*—The interview progresses naturally through a chat interface, with the AI interviewer asking questions and responding to user answers with follow-ups when appropriate.
- *Context awareness*—The AI maintains awareness of previous questions and answers, allowing for a coherent interview narrative rather than disconnected questions.

In addition to the text-based interaction, the application exposes a way to conduct the interview via a microphone using text-to-speech. Users can enable text-to-speech functionality to hear questions spoken aloud using Google Cloud text-to-speech APIs. Users can enable or disable this functionality on demand by clicking the relevant sound icon. Figure 10.5 shows a screenshot of the chat page.

INTERVIEW CLOSING AND SUMMARY

Upon completion of all questions, users have access to these features:

- *Session close*—Users can close the interview session, locking further interactions with the agent.

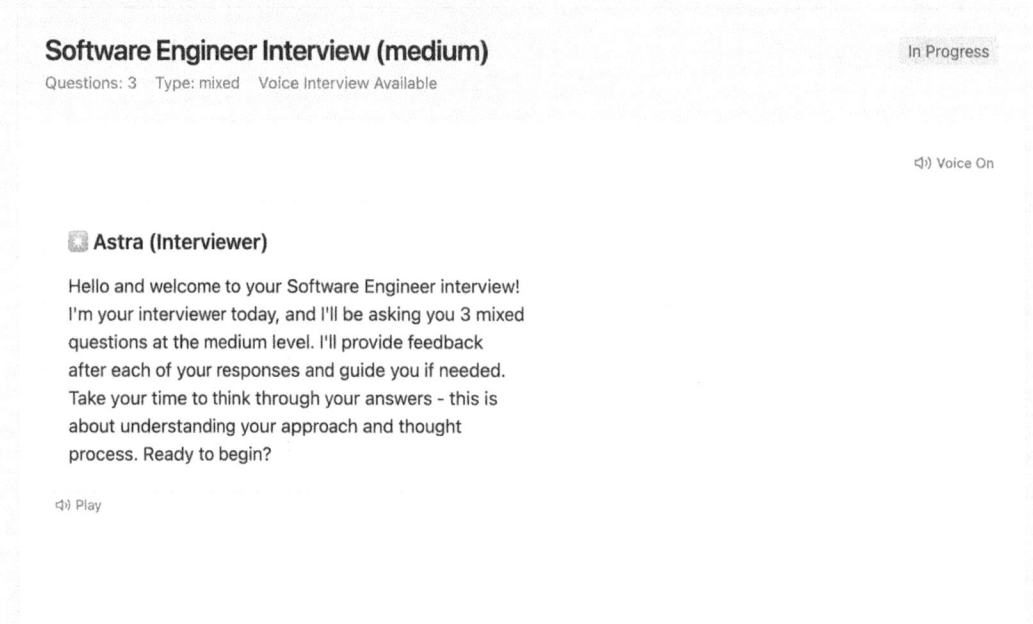

Figure 10.5 Once the interview starts, the user will be able to start answering the AI interviewer's questions. Additionally, the user can close the interview session, preventing any further interactions.

- *Quick summary and feedback*—The LLM analyzes the entire interview conversation to generate detailed feedback. Users receive an immediate overview of their performance, highlighting strengths and potential improvement areas.
- *Manual completion*—The user can click the "Complete interview" button to close the interview session and thus prevent any further modifications to the thread.

NOTE I intentionally did not allow the LLM agent to close the interview automatically once the question quota was reached. This decision was made to ensure users retain control over the session's closure.

PAST INTERVIEW SESSION REVIEW

Users can access a chronological list of all past interview sessions by selecting a session from the sidebar on the right-hand side. Initially, the sidebar session list for the current user will be empty, but once at least one interview session has been created, both current and past sessions will be listed there (see figure 10.6).

NOTE A missing feature in the current implementation is the ability to delete past sessions. I intentionally left this out to allow you to consider how such a feature might be implemented.

Now that we've previewed the application features, let's discuss the technologies used and their technical considerations.

10.1.2 Technical implementation

The web application uses the key components for building conversational UI web applications that we've discussed in this book, with some additions.

10.1.3 Technology stack overview

Our AI interview assistant is built on a stack of technologies explored in this book, using the strengths of several key tools:

- *Next.js framework*—Next.js provides a versatile environment for building dynamic web applications, supporting both server-side rendering and static site generation.
- *Vercel AI SDK*—Manages LLM and conversational state capabilities, including streaming responses and seamless integration with Next.js server components.

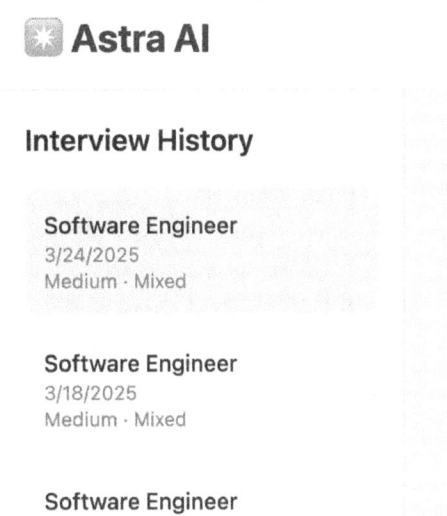

Figure 10.6 The sidebar section will be filled with the current and past interview sessions. Clicking on a session link will load the message history for review.

- *Upstash Redis*—For external data storage, we employ Upstash Redis as a simple yet performant solution. This choice meets our intermediate data needs while allowing for easy scalability to a relational database like PostgreSQL if required.
- *Clerk.js*—For authentication, we utilize Clerk.js, which effectively externalizes the risk associated with managing and handling user authentication and authorization for us.

This combination of technologies enables us to create an initial project that can be further extended with additional features.

APPLICATION ARCHITECTURE

The application follows a modular architecture, including a frontend layer consisting of React components with Tailwind CSS for a responsive UI. It uses the shadcn component library for the common components like buttons, alerts, and textboxes.

Now let's look at the individual features and how they are implemented.

CHATTHREAD

This component handles the core chat interface. It displays messages, manages UI interactions, and includes controls for enabling/disabling text-to-speech.

FEEDBACK PAGE

This page retrieves messages from a session and requests comprehensive feedback from the LLM. To improve efficiency and reduce latency, the feedback is cached in Redis under the key `feedback:${sessionId}` to prevent regeneration on subsequent visits.

INTERVIEWSIDEBAR

This component lists all interview sessions for a logged-in user. It uses the `fetchInterviewSessions` server action to fetch session data from Redis. It then displays session details like job type, date, difficulty, and question type. The following listing shows the contents of this function.

> **Listing 10.1 Function to retrieve all the past interview sessions**

```
export async function fetchInterviewSessions(userId) {
  const sessionIds =
    await redis.smembers(`user:sessions:${userId}`);
  const sessions = await Promise.all(
    sessionIds.map(async (sessionId) => {
      const session = await redis.hgetall(`session:${sessionId}`);
      return { ...session, id: sessionId };
    }),
  );
  sessions.sort((a, b) => b.createdAt - a.createdAt);
  return sessions;
}
```

Annotations:
- Retrieves all session IDs associated with a given user from Redis
- Iterates over each session ID, fetching the session details from Redis in parallel
- Sorts the sessions in descending order based on the createdAt timestamp. This ensures the most recent sessions are displayed first.

In the given code, `user:sessions:${userId}` is a Redis key used to store a set of session IDs associated with a specific user. A Redis set is used here due to uniqueness, since we don't want duplicate session IDs for a user.

The `redis.smembers(user:sessions:${userId})` command connects to the Redis server and executes the SMEMBERS command. SMEMBERS retrieves all members of the set stored at the specified key. The result, `sessionIds`, will be an array of strings, where each string is a session ID. Then, for each `sessionId`, we fetch the session details. The result is then sorted by date in descending order, thus bringing the most recent sessions first in the list.

TEXT-TO-SPEECH API ROUTE

The `/api/tts` API route uses the Google Cloud Text-to-Speech API to convert text into natural-sounding audio. This route streams the audio content back to the client for playback. We opt for an API route over a server action to showcase the flexibility of the framework. A feature flag, controlled by the `NEXT_PUBLIC_FEATURE_TTS_ENABLED` environment variable, enables or disables the entire text-to-speech functionality, including the audio controls in the user interface.

10.2 Security measures implemented

The AI interview assistant incorporates several security measures to protect user data and prevent system abuse. These measures are implemented in a middleware.js function to ensure that all incoming requests are validated and secured before they reach the application's core logic:

- *Authentication*—As mentioned before, we use Clerk.js to ensure that all users are authenticated before accessing the interview application. This helps control the application's use and stores user session data securely in Redis.
- *Cross-origin resource sharing (CORS) handling*—We use a middleware function to configure CORS and to allow requests from specific origins while blocking others. This prevents unauthorized access to the application's resources from malicious websites.
- *Rate limiting*—Implemented using Upstash Redis, the `rateLimit` function limits the number of requests a user can make within a specific time frame. This prevents abuse by malicious actors who might try to overload the server with excessive requests.
- *Security headers*—The `securityHeaders` middleware function sets several HTTP headers to enhance security.

Of course, these security measures only serve as a minimum requirement when implementing publicly available web applications. Try to maintain a proactive mindset when considering the security of your platform and stay informed about emerging threats and vulnerabilities.

10.3 Challenges during development

During the development of the AI interview assistant, I encountered several challenges and applied innovative solutions to overcome them.

10.3.1 State management considerations

Managing the state of the conversation, including the history of questions and answers, and maintaining context awareness for the AI interviewer proved difficult. We aim to enable users to seamlessly retrieve their session data for each past interview and quickly switch between threads without any problem.

To solve this, I opted to use Upstash Redis for storing session data, including the conversation history and user-specific settings. Redis's speed and efficiency make it ideal for managing real-time conversation data. However, this required establishing a simple ad hoc correlation between session IDs and session messages using a key-value database. While Redis is not inherently designed for complex relational models, we can make it work by creating and programmatically maintaining these straightforward pairings. Ideally, of course, you want to use SQL since it supports transactions on the persistence layer.

10.3.2 Text-to-speech integration

Integrating external services like Google Text-to-Speech requires an understanding of the technology and its integration into the application. Minimizing the latency of the text-to-speech functionality to provide a seamless user experience is also a key priority. As part of the solution, we implement a protected API route (/api/tts) that streams the audio content back to the client. This approach not only simplifies the feature delivery to the UI but also offloads the processing to the server.

We also use a simple feature flag support using the env variable to enable this feature, but it would be a more reasonable solution to have an external API or service that better controls those features. While using environment variables for feature flags provides a quick and straightforward way to toggle the text-to-speech functionality, this approach lacks the flexibility and control needed for more complex scenarios. In a production environment, a dedicated feature management service offers significant advantages, such as the ability to enable or disable features for specific user-facing segments.

10.3.3 Generating feedback

We use a simple prompt to guide the agent in providing feedback based on the interview thread:

```
const prompt = `
Please provide comprehensive feedback for this interview.
    The session contains the following messages:
    ${messages.map((message) => `${message.role}: ${message.content}`).join('\n')}

    Provide a structured feedback summary covering these points:
    - Overall performance: Assess the candidate's overall performance.
    - Strengths: Highlight the candidate's
strengths demonstrated during the interview.
    - Areas for improvement: Suggest areas where the candidate could improve.
    - Technical skills: Evaluate the candidate's
technical skills based on their responses.
    - Communication skills: Assess the candidate's communication skills.
    - Recommendations: Provide specific recommendations for the candidate.
`;
```

While this approach works well in ideal scenarios, improvements could be made to enhance the feedback's depth, conciseness, and focus.

Specifically, the agent could be guided to provide more detailed and targeted feedback while also being trained to ignore irrelevant parts of the conversation to ensure a more streamlined and relevant assessment, implementing a more guided process. There are many opportunities for improvement here, including

- *Incorporating a knowledge base*—Provide the AI with access to a knowledge base of best practices, common interview questions, and expected answers for the specific role. This will allow the AI to provide more accurate and relevant feedback.

- *Implementing a fact-checking tool*—You can instruct the AI to use tools based on the question type to perform fact verification. For example, you might cross-reference the extracted keywords against a knowledge base to verify accuracy and identify potential misconceptions.
- *Implementing a custom scoring system*—You might devise a scoring system that quantifies the candidate's performance in different areas (technical skills, communication, problem solving, etc.). This will make the feedback more objective and easier to understand.

Of course, the idea here is to provide the AI with the right amount of context and precise prompt instructions to deliver a valid and fair review of the candidate's performance. Using prompt engineering techniques, as discussed in chapter 5, and experimenting with a variety of configurations will significantly enhance the system's value.

10.4 Additional considerations and improvements

At this point, I urge you to try out the web application and see how it behaves. Here are some aspects to review and potential improvements:

- *Text-to-speech integration*—The application effectively uses text-to-speech functionality to provide audio feedback.
- *Feedback generation*—The feedback page offers comprehensive insights based on the interview session.

On the other hand, some pieces are missing, and these would be nice additions to the existing application:

- *Speech-to-text interactions*—Currently, users cannot interact with the AI using voice commands. Implementing speech-to-text functionality would allow users to speak to the AI agent, like how text-to-speech is used. You can reference examples like Google's Speech-to-Text API for inspiration.
- *Follow-up interviews/multiround interviews*—The feedback page could be enhanced to facilitate follow-up interviews based on previous feedback. This would help users track progress over time.
- *Graphical visualization*—Providing a graphical representation of technical performance points could make feedback more engaging and easier to understand. This could include charts or graphs to highlight areas of improvement.
- *Personalized practice plans*—Generating individual practice plans based on low performance points would offer users actionable steps to improve. This could involve AI-driven analysis to tailor recommendations.

Summary

- Implementing robust security measures is crucial for protecting user data and preventing system abuse in web applications. This includes using authentication services like Clerk.js, handling CORS requests, implementing rate limiting, and setting security headers to enhance the application's security stance.
- Effective state management is essential for maintaining context awareness in conversational AI applications. You can use key-value databases like Redis, although more complex relational models may prove better in the long run.
- Integrating external services, such as Google Text-to-Speech, requires careful consideration of latency and user experience.
- Feature flag management is used for controlling the rollout of new features. While environment variables can be used for simple toggles, more sophisticated solutions involving external APIs or services provide greater flexibility and control.
- Use prompt engineering techniques to significantly enhance the value of AI-generated responses like feedback or reviews by tailoring them to specific needs and areas of improvement.

Building an AI RAG agent: Project walk-through

This chapter covers

- Building RAG apps with Next.js, Clerk, and LangChain.js
- Securing documents and isolating user data
- Using Upstash Redis and Vector for search and state
- Designing chat interfaces with text-to-speech
- Optimizing databases and prompt engineering
- Solving state sync and document-parsing issues

This project is a more complex full-stack generative AI web application: a retrieval-augmented generation (RAG) app designed to manage multiple knowledge bases. The app uses the Vercel AI SDK and LangChain.js libraries to enable users to upload documents, organize them into knowledge bases, and interact with these knowledge bases via conversational AI. The application also integrates modern authentication, persistence, and vector search technologies to ensure a more robust experience.

We start with the features and how the application behaves and then go over the technical decisions. I conclude this chapter with some important next steps to your learning path for building robust, full-stack, AI-powered web applications.

11.1 Overview of the application

Our RAG web app allows users to create, manage, and query knowledge bases composed of multiple documents (PDFs and DOCX supported). Each user can securely authenticate, create or delete knowledge bases, upload new documents to them, and chat with an AI assistant that answers questions based on the knowledge within the selected knowledge base.

This is useful when you want to build, for example, a corporate knowledge base for your employees or customers to chat with using a conversational agent.

11.1.1 Key features

In the first iteration of the project, I provide a basic set of features that accomplish the task. Along with the methods and techniques we already know, we'll add some new, unique features.

AUTHENTICATION WITH CLERK

User authentication happens with Clerk.js, like the previous applications. Clerk.js is a solid choice since it provides secure and fine-grained control of the user logins and user information storage. We require all users to authenticate to the application before they gain access to the chat interface.

MAIN DASHBOARD PAGE

Once logged in, users begin their experience by navigating to the main dashboard page. This page contains an overview of the existing knowledge base and useful links and shortcuts to access key application features. Figure 11.1 shows the UI of the main dashboard page.

If you have existing knowledge bases created, they will be listed here, and you can begin chatting. Clicking View All Links when you don't have a knowledge base created will prompt the user to create one instead. Figure 11.2 shows the UI part of this as well.

CREATING A NEW KNOWLEDGE BASE

To create a new knowledge base, click the New Knowledge Base button. This action takes you to a form where you can configure your knowledge base by providing the necessary details. The form requires the following inputs:

- *Name of the knowledge base*
- *Description*—An optional field where you can add a brief explanation or purpose of the knowledge base

Figure 11.3 shows a screenshot of the form with the fields completed.

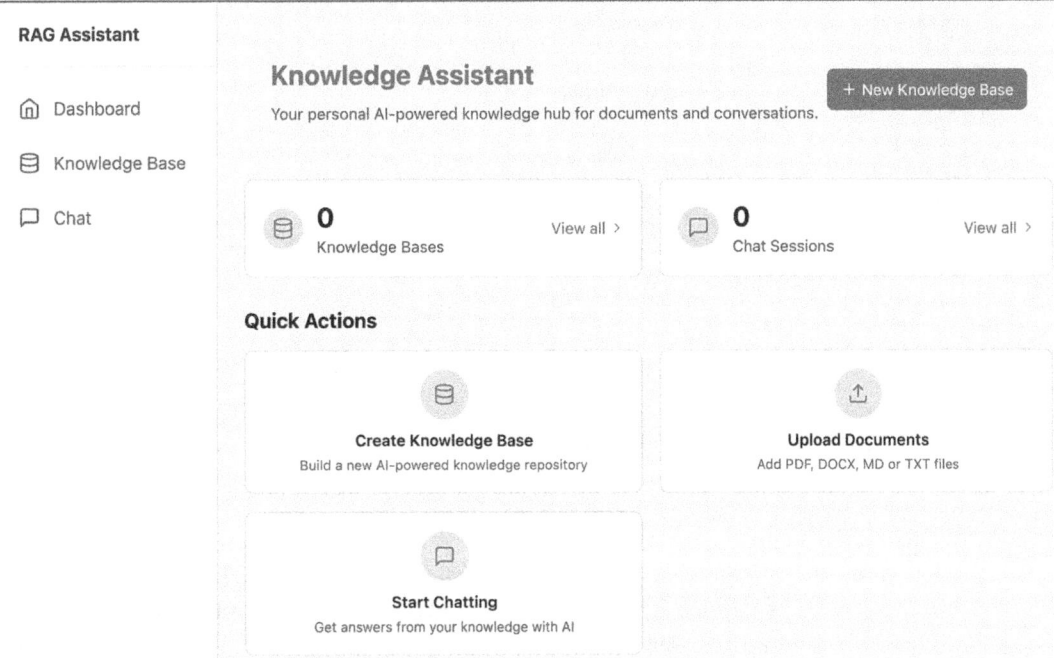

Figure 11.1 The main dashboard page contains a button to create a new knowledge base and useful quick action buttons.

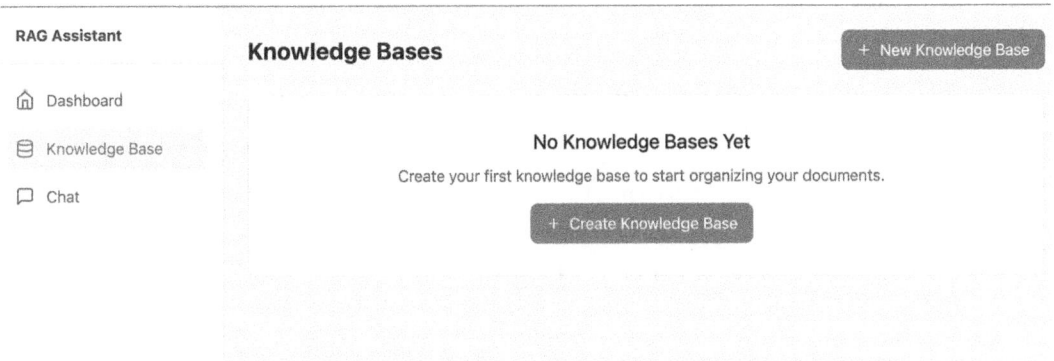

Figure 11.2 When the user clicks to review existing knowledge bases when none have been created, the application will inform the user that they need to create one first.

DOCUMENT UPLOADING

After creating a new knowledge base, users need to upload documents to enable conversational interactions with their content. The knowledge base details page provides an overview of the knowledge base along with a list of uploaded documents.

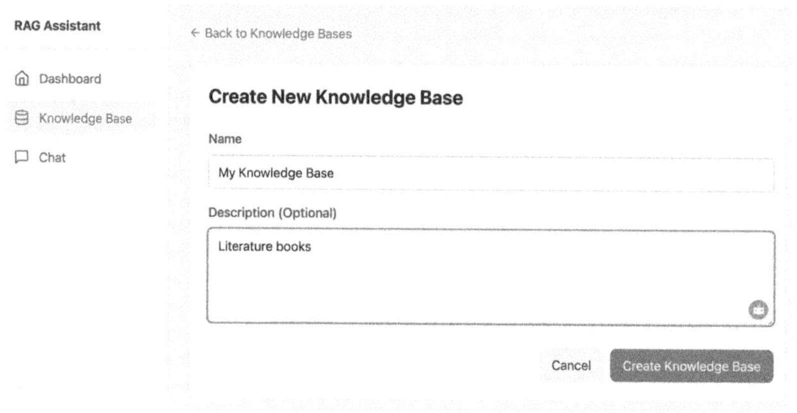

Figure 11.3 Users need to fill in a name and optionally a description to create a new knowledge base.

By clicking the Upload Document button, users are directed to a page containing instructions on how to upload files. Users can select a document from their local filesystem—supported formats include PDF and DOCX—and submit it to the application.

Once uploaded, the application parses and analyzes the document, converting its content into vector embeddings. These embeddings are then stored in the Upstash Vector database, enabling efficient similarity search. This process allows users to chat with the document content in real time through the conversational AI agent. Figure 11.4 shows a screenshot of the upload page showcasing the user interface.

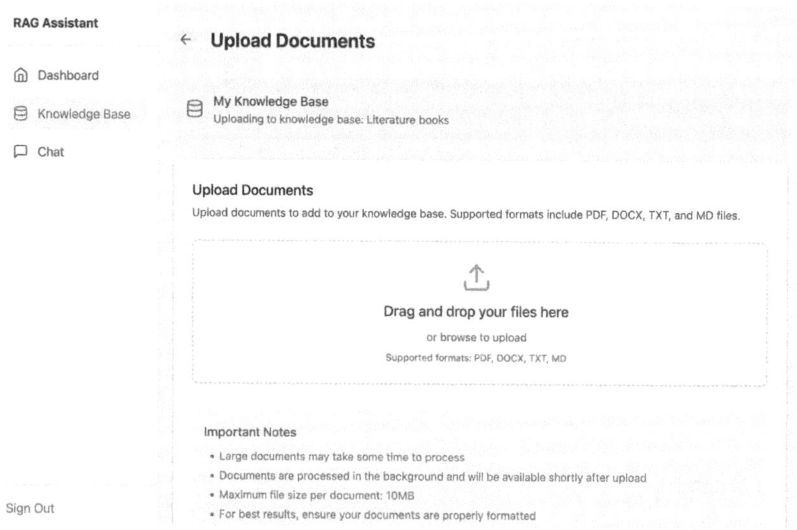

Figure 11.4 The upload documents page allows users to submit documents that can be used for chat-like interactions.

CHATTING WITH A KNOWLEDGE BASE DOCUMENT

Once you have uploaded at least one document to a knowledge base, you can start interacting with the content through a conversational AI agent. Users can ask questions and receive answers grounded in the document data, enabling a natural, dialogue-based exploration of the knowledge base.

This functionality builds upon the retrieval techniques discussed in the previous chapter, where we created and utilized informational retrievers with LangChain.js. Unlike the local filesystem storage used earlier, here the vector embeddings are stored externally in Upstash Vector, allowing for a scalable and efficient similarity search.

When a user submits a query, the application embeds the question, performs a vector search to find the most relevant document chunks, and then uses the Vercel AI SDK to generate a context-aware response. Figure 11.5 shows a screenshot of a sample interaction where the uploaded document is *To Kill a Mockingbird* by Harper Lee.

Figure 11.5   Once the knowledge base contains a few documents, users can start chatting with them conversationally.

OTHER FUNCTIONALITIES

Beyond the core features discussed earlier, the application includes some new ones. First, users can permanently delete a knowledge base, along with its associated documents and vector embeddings, via the Delete Knowledge Base button on the knowledge base details page. Second, individual documents can be removed from a knowledge base, which removes all document chunks that are associated with the deleted document.

To encourage experimentation and learning, we also deliberately omitted two features: the ability to edit existing knowledge bases and to review past chat sessions. Instead, we leave these as exercises for readers to implement using the codebase as a foundation.

11.1.2 Technical implementation

The web application uses the key components for building conversational UI web applications discussed in this book, with some additions.

> **Project code: rag**
>
> The code for this example project is in the ch11/rag folder. You can use that example by running this command in the root folder of the project repository:
>
> ```
> $ npm run dev -w ch11/rag
> ```
>
> You'll need the following API keys for this to work, as the application uses services from different vendors: the Gemini API key, the Upstash Redis and Vector REST URLs, the Upstash Redis and Vector REST Tokens, and the Clerk.js authentication credentials. These are configured as environment variables:
>
> ```
> // .env
> GEMINI_API_KEY=<GEMINI_API_SECRET_KEY>
> UPSTASH_REDIS_REST_URL=<UPSTASH_REDIS_REST_URL>
> UPSTASH_REDIS_REST_TOKEN=<UPSTASH_REDIS_REST_TOKEN>
> UPSTASH_VECTOR_REST_URL=<UPSTASH_REDIS_REST_URL>
> UPSTASH_VECTOR_REST_TOKEN=<UPSTASH_REDIS_REST_TOKEN>
>
> NEXT_PUBLIC_CLERK_PUBLISHABLE_KEY=<CLERK_PUBLIC_KEY>
> CLERK_SECRET_KEY=<CLERK_PRIVATE_KEY
> ```
>
> Instructions on how to set up and create secret keys for Gemini AI and Upstash Redis are provided in the appendix.

11.1.3 Technology stack overview

Our RAG web application is built on a stack of technologies explored in this book, using the strengths of several key tools:

- *Next.js framework*—Next.js provides a versatile environment for building dynamic web applications, supporting both server-side rendering and static site generation.
- *Vercel AI SDK*—The Vercel AI SDK is utilized to manage AI and conversational state capabilities, including streaming responses and seamless integration with Next.js server components. This integration enhances our application's ability to handle complex AI-driven interactions efficiently.

- *LangChain.js*—LangChain.js is used for prompt management, document parsing, and vectorization. We use the community-supported `UpstashVectorStore` package to interface with the vector database, enabling semantic search through retrievers that match user queries with relevant document chunks.
- *Upstash Redis*—For external data storage, we employ Upstash Redis as a simple yet performant solution. This choice meets our intermediate data needs while allowing for easy scalability to a relational database like PostgreSQL if required.
- *Upstash Vector*—Upstash Vector serves as our dedicated vector database, optimized for storing and searching vectorized document embeddings. We create a separate client with secure access credentials to interact with this service for enabling efficient similarity search operations suitable for RAG workflows. We utilize a Vector index with 768 output dimensions to match the Google AI embedding model requirements.
- *Clerk.js*—Authentication and user management are handled by Clerk.js, which offloads the complexity and security risks of managing authentication flows.

All the technologies used in this project have been explored in previous chapters, except for the Upstash Vector store. But thanks to LangChain.js's modular retriever interface, integrating Upstash Vector is straightforward. LangChain treats Upstash Vector like any other retrieval service, so it allows seamless management of vector embeddings and semantic search capabilities.

APPLICATION ARCHITECTURE

The application follows a modular architecture. The frontend layer consists of React components with Tailwind CSS for a responsive UI. It uses the shadcn component library for the common components like buttons, alerts, and textboxes. Now let's explore in detail the individual features and how they are implemented.

DOCUMENTUPLOADER

The `DocumentUploader` component provides an intuitive drag-and-drop interface for users to upload documents into a selected knowledge base. It supports multiple file types, including PDF and DOCX. Users can also browse their local files, preview selected documents, remove any before uploading, and receive status updates during the upload process.

KNOWLEDGE BASE UPLOAD PAGE

The knowledge base upload page integrates the `DocumentUploader` within the context of a specific knowledge base. It allows users to manage document uploads tied to that knowledge base and view an overview of uploaded documents. This page acts as the gateway for preparing knowledge bases for conversational AI interactions.

API ROUTES

The application backend is structured using Next.js API routes, organized under the `/api` directory to handle various operations:

- *Knowledge base routes* (`/api/knowledgebase`)—These routes handle CRUD operations for knowledge bases, including creating new knowledge bases, retrieving all or individual knowledge bases, and deleting them. For example, the POST route validates input and creates a knowledge base record in Upstash Redis.

> **Listing 11.1 Creating a new knowledge base route**

```
import { NextResponse } from 'next/server';
import { createKnowledgeBase,
getAllKnowledgeBases } from '@/lib/database';     ◄── Imports the
                                                      createKnowledgeBase
export async function POST(request) {                 and getAllKnowledgeBases
  try {                                               functions from the
    const body = await request.json();                database utility module
    const { name, description } = body;

    if (!name) {
      return NextResponse.json({ error: 'Name is required' }, { status: 400 });
    }

    const knowledgeBase =
await createKnowledgeBase({          ◄── Calls the createKnowledgeBase
        name,                            function with the provided name and
        description: description || '',  optional description to create a new
    });                                  knowledge base record in the database

    return NextResponse.json(knowledgeBase);     ◄── Returns a JSON
  } catch (error) {                                  response
    console.error('Error creating knowledge base:', error);   containing the
    return NextResponse.json(                       newly created
      { error: 'Failed to create knowledge base' }, knowledge base
      { status: 500 }                               data with a 200 OK
    );                                              status
  }
}
```

- *Document routes* (`[knowledgebaseId]/document/[id]`)—These routes manage document-specific actions such as uploading, fetching, and deleting documents within a knowledge base. Uploaded documents are processed and parsed, and their vector embeddings are stored for retrieval.
- *Upload route* (`/api/upload`)—This endpoint receives file uploads from the frontend, associates them with the correct knowledge base, and triggers document processing and vectorization workflows.
- *Chat routes* (`/api/chat/[knowledgebaseId]`)—These routes facilitate the conversational interface, handling user queries, retrieving relevant document chunks from the vector store, and generating AI responses.

KNOWLEDGEBASE CHAT PAGE

The Knowledgebase Chat Page is the core user interface where users interact with the AI assistant to ask questions about the documents stored within a selected knowledge base. This React component is built using Next.js's app router with client-side interactivity and uses the Vercel AI SDK's hooks for managing conversational state.

With the core components and services thoroughly explained, we now shift our focus to the key challenges and critical considerations encountered during the development of this web application, along with proposed future improvements and architectural enhancements aimed at ensuring scalability, security, and maintainability.

11.2 Challenges during development

Building this RAG web application introduced a range of challenges, some similar to those faced in the AI interview assistant, and others unique to the complexities of managing multiple knowledge bases, documents, and vector search.

11.2.1 Shared vs. dedicated user data in vector stores

When storing vectorized document embeddings, a fundamental architectural decision is whether to provision a dedicated vector store instance for each user or to consolidate all users' embeddings within a shared database. This choice directly affects data isolation, query performance, operational complexity, and cost.

In our application, we chose to use a shared Upstash Vector database with strict namespacing and metadata filtering based on the knowledge base and user identifiers. This approach optimizes resource utilization and simplifies infrastructure management while maintaining logical data isolation through query-level filters.

However, in ideal scenarios, especially where stringent security or regulatory compliance is required, the customer data should be physically separated. Provisioning isolated vector databases per user or tenant enhances data privacy and reduces risk but with increased operational overhead and cost.

Implementing fine-grained access control policies at the vector store layer is crucial as well. These controls prevent cross-user data leakage by enforcing strict authorization on all vector search and storage operations.

11.2.2 Security considerations around document management and heavy workloads

Uploading, parsing, and vectorizing documents are resource-intensive operations that also carry potential security risks due to the sensitive nature of document contents. Ensuring the secure handling of files and protecting backend services from abuse is therefore critical.

To address this, we integrated Clerk.js for authentication, ensuring that only authorized users can upload or access documents. File uploads undergo validation on both the client and server sides to enforce allowed file types and size limits. Document processing (parsing and chunking) occurs securely on the server with error handling to prevent crashes and maintain system stability.

However, these measures are only the beginning. To further enhance security and reliability, several improvements should be considered:

- *API rate limiting and upload quotas*—Implementing rate limits and quotas helps prevent abuse and denial-of-service attacks by restricting excessive or malicious upload attempts.
- *Malware scanning*—Integrating malware detection tools for uploaded files is essential to prevent the storage of infected or malicious content that could compromise the system.
- *Background processing*—Offloading heavy tasks like document parsing and vector embedding to background workers or serverless functions improves responsiveness, scalability, and fault tolerance.
- *Encrypted storage*—Storing documents and their vector embeddings in encrypted form protects data at rest, reducing the risk of unauthorized access. Alternatively, documents can be securely discarded after processing if retention is not required.

11.2.3 API design and URL structure to minimize information exposure

You may have noticed that our application employs multiple API routes to facilitate backend operations. Designing these API endpoints to expose minimal sensitive information while maintaining clear, intuitive, and RESTful URL structures is vital for both security and maintainability.

We organized our API routes hierarchically under paths like /api/knowledgebase/[knowledgebaseId] and /api/chat/[knowledgebaseId] to clearly scope operations within the context of specific knowledge bases. Every data access is gated by authentication to prevent unauthorized usage. Additionally, we used secure ID generation methods (such as UUIDs) to avoid predictable or guessable identifiers.

However, there is room for improvement in API security and documentation. For instance, adopting a formal API specification standard like OpenAPI would enhance clarity, facilitate automated documentation, and improve client–server contract enforcement.

Furthermore, integrating a dedicated API gateway with features such as centralized authentication, rate limiting, throttling, and logging would offload these concerns from the main application. This separation helps keep the core codebase lean, easier to maintain, and more secure.

These architectural and operational considerations require careful evaluation and proactive planning when building feature-rich web applications. Neglecting them can result in bloated, fragile, and difficult-to-secure codebases that make future development difficult and expose vulnerabilities.

Since our example RAG web application is primarily intended for educational purposes, we have opted for a minimal viable product approach that delivers core functionality within a single, unified codebase. This design keeps the project simple and accessible for learning and experimentation. But as you prepare to bring your application into production and scale it to support more users and workloads, it becomes essential to consider decomposing the application into dedicated, modular services.

This is what we call a shift from a monolithic codebase to a microservices approach, which is a complex topic worthy of an entire book. The core principle, though, is that both monolithic and microservices architectures serve their purposes depending on the current requirements and context.

11.3 Additional thoughts on AI and the future of web development

As you've seen throughout this book, the landscape of AI-powered web development is evolving at an extremely fast pace. I urge you to continuously invest time and effort in learning and experimenting with these technologies to keep up with the changing tools, libraries, and best practices. The libraries and SDKs we use here are under constant development, and by the time you reach this section, the example codebases may require updates to dependencies or APIs.

What remains constant, however, are the fundamental concepts of web development and the importance of understanding how to use AI effectively. AI is becoming deeply integrated into the core of web technologies, enabling smarter, more personalized, and adaptive user experiences. Trends for 2026 focus on autonomous AI agents performing cross-platform tasks, edge-based inference for near-instant privacy-preserving intelligence, and multimodal optimization as the new standard for accessibility. The future of web development is a transition from "building for the user" to "building environments where AI works for the user." Success belongs to the developers who master these autonomous patterns while maintaining the core pillars of security and performance.

For a final practical example of this forward-thinking approach, the final chapter delves into a real-world integration that prepares your applications for the future of AI.

Summary

- A RAG web application enables users to create, organize, and interact with multiple knowledge bases, each containing uploaded documents such as PDFs and DOCX files.
- The chat interfaces allow users to ask questions and receive answers grounded in the content of their knowledge bases, using LangChain.js retrievers and the Vercel AI SDK for conversational AI.
- Key architectural decisions include considering shared versus dedicated vector stores for user data, implementing secure document handling, and planning for future scalability and modularization.
- The project highlights the importance of designing for security, maintainability, and extensibility. To improve on this basic functionality, consider adding API rate limiting, malware scanning, background processing, and adhering to formal API specifications.

Part 4

Advanced integrations and the future of AI

You've now built a solid foundation for creating AI-powered web applications. You've mastered the fundamentals of prompt engineering, learned to orchestrate complex tasks with frameworks like the Vercel AI SDK and LangChain.js, and explored how embeddings give AI a deeper sense of meaning.

But as the landscape of generative AI evolves, so do the ways we build with it. This final part of the book moves beyond the current best practices to look at what's next. We'll dive into the *Model Context Protocol*, an emerging standard designed to create more seamless, secure, and interoperable connections between your applications and various AI models.

By understanding how to integrate with these foundational protocols, you'll be equipped to build applications that are not only powerful but also resilient and ready for the future of integrating AI with web apps.

12
Integrating web apps with the Model Context Protocol

This chapter covers
- The Model Context Protocol (MCP) and why it is important for building modern web applications powered by large language models
- Integrating the MCP with the Vercel AI SDK to extend web apps with external capabilities
- Practical examples of building and connecting an MCP server
- Developing a complete end-to-end project to integrate an MCP server
- Introducing the MCP architecture, data flow, and integration patterns

The game-changing Model Context Protocol (MCP) is a new open standard designed to connect AI agents with external tools and data sources in a secure and standardized way.

Designed and open sourced by Anthropic (https://mng.bz/oZqy), the MCP defines a server protocol for exposing tools, prompts, and resources to AI models.

It's rapidly gaining traction because it simplifies the process of extending applications with external functionality and enables interoperability across ecosystems.

Any client that implements this protocol, whether a server application, browser-based web app, or CLI tool, can interact consistently with MCP servers. This means the AI agent, wherever it runs, always knows how to call a tool and handle its outputs, whether that tool accesses an API, a database, or a filesystem. In short, adding MCP capabilities to your applications allows them to tap into the many tools and databases that others create, provided those tools are also MCP compatible.

The MCP also supports scalable architectures, allowing multiple external services to be connected via MCP servers. For instance, our React/Next.js web app can communicate with one or more MCP servers, each providing different tools, without rewriting the assistant's core logic. The MCP can be applied to any client or application/server-side apps, agentic systems, or CLI tools.

In practice, the MCP lets developers define tools once and reuse them across AI systems. This separation of tools from assistants simplifies integration, enforces consistent security and resource management, and makes it easier to scale AI applications

In this chapter, we build and integrate a complete MCP server into a full-stack AI application using the Vercel AI SDK, then see how this pattern can scale to multiple servers working together. The goal is to give you a clear starting point for adopting the MCP in your own projects.

12.1 Why the MCP matters for AI integration

Before we get to the practical examples, let's revisit some of the core concepts we've explored in this book: prompts, tools, and generated resources. These form the foundation of modern AI applications and help us understand why a standard such as the MCP is needed.

Prompts, as you may recall, are the structured inputs we provide to large language models (LLMs). Prompts shape the model's behavior, control its reasoning, and define the context in which the AI operates.

Tools are the external capabilities that extend what an AI model can do beyond generating text—such as file access, database queries, or API calls. Tools can run on the client side (invoked by an AI agent in the application) or the server side (invoked by an LLM or MCP server) or be shared across systems. In more complex setups, multiple agents or models may each access different tools, combining their results into a coordinated workflow.

Generated content is the output created by the model or produced from tool usage. These outputs can be natural language responses, structured data, summaries, or even programmatic results like SQL query outputs.

As we've seen, prompts control AI behavior, tools extend its capabilities, and resources are generated to create value. Each integration requires custom wiring: developers define how tools are exposed, how the AI calls them, and how results flow back. Different frameworks approach this differently: Astra, our browser-based chat app built with React and Next.js, calls tools either from the web server or via LLMs like Gemini or OpenAI, often through LangChain or the Vercel AI SDK. While these libraries can orchestrate tools and models, each system defines integrations in its own way, making reuse difficult.

The MCP simplifies this process by introducing a standardized way for AI applications to discover and invoke external tools and resources. Rather than wiring each tool manually, developers can expose them through MCP servers, while AI applications (or other clients) communicate using a shared protocol.

As AI adoption accelerates, one-off solutions quickly become a problem, since each application reinvents how tools are exposed to AI models. LangChain.js introduced tools and agents, but integrations built there don't easily transfer to other frameworks like LlamaIndex or the Vercel AI SDK. A developer might build a weather API integration for LangChain, but reusing it elsewhere requires starting from scratch because each framework has its own conventions, and assistants face inconsistent approaches to security, permissions, and resource management.

What's been missing is a common protocol—a shared language and structure for how AI systems discover, use, and compose tools. The MCP provides this missing standardization, enabling tools to become plug-and-play across assistants, frameworks, and applications.

Here we will apply the MCP specifically to chat-based web applications like Astra/React interfaces backed by Next.js, though the MCP itself is much broader and supports multiagent and distributed systems.

12.2 MCP architecture

At its core, the MCP establishes a client-server architecture that works as follows:

1 The MCP client (e.g., the AI agent or SDK) requests capabilities and invokes tools.
2 The MCP server exposes those tools, handles execution, and returns results.
3 Both communicate via a well-defined protocol, ensuring interoperability.

Figure 12.1 shows how this is set up.

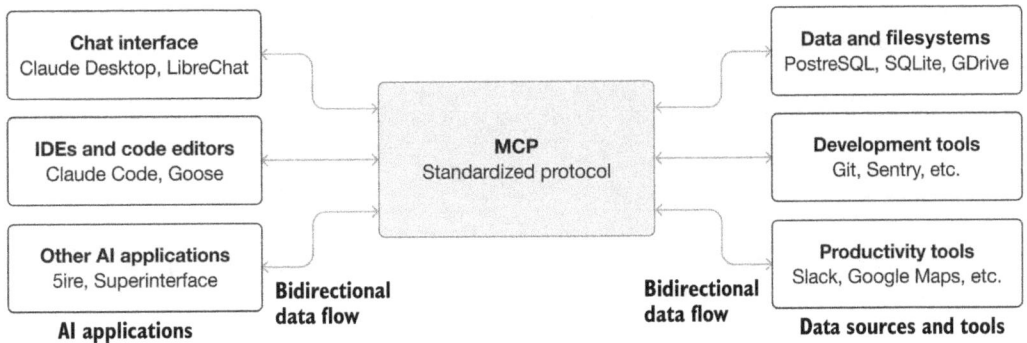

Figure 12.1 The MCP defines a standardized client–server interface that enables communication between web applications powered by LLMs (such as chat interfaces and code editors) and various external data sources and services (like databases, development tools, and productivity software). (Source: https://modelcontextprotocol.io/)

At the core of the MCP is a standardized client–server protocol that defines how web applications, AI assistants, or other systems can connect to external tools and data sources through LLMs. An MCP client handles communication with one or more MCP servers, which expose tools and resources in a consistent, structured format. While an AI agent may use an MCP client as part of its architecture, the two are conceptually distinct, as the client enables protocol-level communication, while the agent handles reasoning and decision making. This architecture supports bidirectional data flow, which allows applications to send requests to tools and receive structured responses that can be incorporated into the AI's reasoning and outputs.

In practice, this means an AI application, whether a chat interface, an IDE, or another AI-powered tool, can interact seamlessly with multiple data sources, such as databases, filesystems, APIs, and productivity tools. The MCP server ensures that these interactions follow a standardized protocol, allowing developers to reuse tools across different AI applications without rewriting code.

12.3 Connecting Next.js and the Vercel AI SDK with the MCP

While the Vercel AI SDK includes experimental support for setting up an MCP server, you aren't limited to that approach. A web app like Astra can act as an *MCP client,* directly connecting to one or more MCP servers to request and process data, or even as an *MCP server* itself, exposing its own tools for use by other agents or applications.

Let's see how we can integrate the Vercel AI SDK to build a simple web application that fetches fun facts using an external API. In this example, we'll use the Chuck Norris Jokes API (https://api.chucknorris.io), a free JSON API that provides random jokes and facts.

You can easily adapt this example to other free public APIs available at https://publicapi.dev/, such as trivia, quotes, and weather services. The same integration pattern applies: the MCP server defines a tool that retrieves data from an external API, and the web application uses that tool to deliver dynamic responses to user prompts.

> **Project code: vercel-ai-sdk-mcp**
>
> The code for this example project can be found in the ch12/vercel-ai-sdk-mcp folder. You can use that example by running this command in the root folder of the project repository:
>
> ```
> $ npm run dev -w ch12/vercel-ai-sdk-mcp
> ```
>
> You'll need the Gemini API key or OpenAI key for this to work as the application uses services from different vendors. These are configured as environment variables:
>
> ```
> // .env
> GOOGLE_API_KEY=<GEMINI_API_SECRET_KEY>
> OPENAI_API_KEY=<OPEN_AI_SECRET_KEY>
> ```

Instructions on how to set up and create secret keys for Google AI and OpenAI are provided in the appendix.

12.3.1 Architecture overview

Figure 12.2 illustrates the high-level architecture of the system. The integration is organized into five logical layers, each playing a distinct role in the flow between the user, the AI, and external data sources:

- *Browser (Client)*—A React-based chat interface built with the Vercel AI SDK. Users type messages, and the SDK manages streaming responses and conversation state.
- *Next.js API route*—Acts as a broker between the frontend and the AI backend. It forwards user messages to the Vercel AI SDK server utilities, which handle the actual model interaction.
- *Vercel AI SDK*—Connects the Next.js API route with the MCP server. This SDK layer interprets model responses, manages tool calls, and coordinates communication between the LLM and MCP servers.

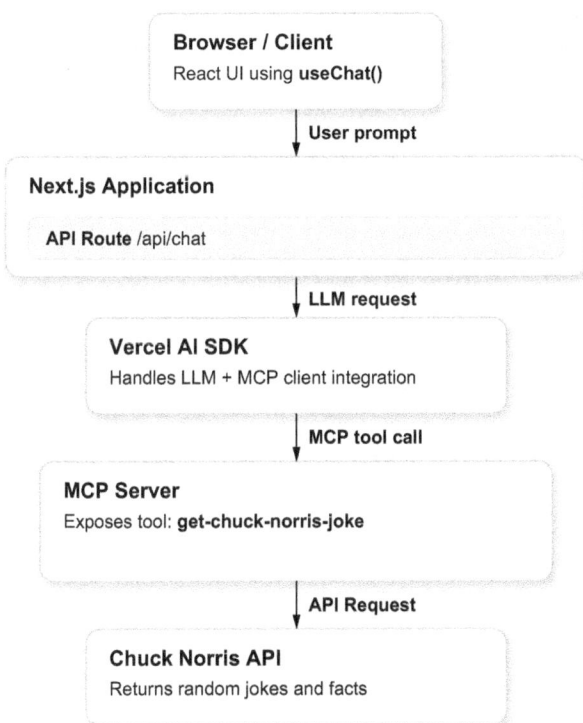

Figure 12.2 High-level architecture showing how a Next.js chat application integrates with the MCP. The Vercel AI SDK communicates with an MCP client, which connects to one or more MCP servers exposing tools. Responses flow back through the client to the API route and are displayed in the chat interface.

- *MCP server*—Runs independently (often over stdio or HTTP) and exposes callable tools. In our example, the MCP server defines the tool get-chuck-joke, which retrieves random facts from an external API.
- *External API or data source*—The Chuck Norris API (https://api.chucknorris.io) serves as our external data source. The MCP server queries it and returns the results to the client through the SDK and API route.

12.3.2 Building an end-to-end integration with the MCP in Next.js

We begin by copying the starter-project folder as the foundation. The main goal is to integrate MCP tools while keeping the AI model isolated from external APIs.

In this example, the MCP server runs locally and is instantiated using the Vercel AI SDK, which provides the infrastructure to expose callable tools to your AI assistant. Communication between the Next.js app and the MCP server is handled via StdioServerTransport, which uses standard input/output streams to send and receive structured messages. This allows the MCP server to run as a separate process on the same machine, making it easy to demonstrate tool integration without relying on network configuration. First is an MCP server implementation, as shown in the following listing.

Listing 12.1 Example MCP server for Chuck Norris jokes

```
import { McpServer } from '@modelcontextprotocol/sdk/server/mcp.js';
import { StdioServerTransport } from '@modelcontextprotocol/sdk/server/stdio.js';
import { z } from 'zod';

const server = new McpServer({          ◄── Initializes a new MCP server
  name: 'chuck-norris-mcp',                  instance with a name and version
  version: '1.0.0',
});
                                        Defines a tool on the MCP server
/ Register joke tool                    with a name, description, input
server.tool(          ◄──               schema, and handler function
  "get-chuck-joke",
  "Fetch a random Chuck Norris joke",
  {},
  async () => {
    try {
      const response = await fetch("https://api.chucknorris.io/jokes/random");
      if (!response.ok) {
        return {
          content: [{ type: "text",
text: `No joke available at the moment.` }],
        };
      }
      const data = await response.json();
      return { content: [{ type: "text", text: data.value }] };
    } catch (err) {
      const message =
```

```
        err instanceof Error ? err.message : "An unknown error occurred";
      return { content:
[{ type: "text", text: `Error fetching joke: ${message}` }] };
    }
  }
);
```
Fetches a Chuck Norris fact from the API and handles errors gracefully

```
async function main() {
  const transport = new StdioServerTransport();
  await server.connect(transport);
  console.log('Chuck Norris MCP Server running on stdio');
}
main()
```
Creates a stdio transport and connects the MCP server so clients can call its tools

In this example, the MCP server is local to the Next.js application. The StdioServerTransport is a local interprocess communication mechanism: it runs the MCP server as a separate Node.js process and communicates over standard input/output (stdio). This means that the MCP server doesn't expose HTTP endpoints itself because it listens for requests via stdio, and the Next.js API route acts as the client that sends requests and receives structured responses.

The server executes the tool logic (e.g., fetching a joke from the Chuck Norris API) and returns the output in an MCP-compliant format. The AI model, here the Gemini model instantiated via the Vercel AI SDK, is completely isolated from direct API calls. The model only "knows" about the tools exposed by the MCP server; it cannot directly query external APIs. This separation ensures that all external API access is mediated by the MCP server, which simplifies security and modularity.

Figure 12.3 shows how the local MCP integration is structured within the Astra chat application. In this setup, the MCP server runs locally alongside the Next.js application. Communication between the API route and the MCP server occurs through standard input/output (stdio), a lightweight interprocess transport mechanism. This means the MCP server does not expose any HTTP endpoints, but instead, the Next.js API route launches and communicates with it directly, invoking tools and receiving structured responses.

The following listing shows the code on the Next.js side; we need to initiate both the server and the client inside the REST API route.

Listing 12.2 API route that serves the MCP server in Next.js

```
import { createGoogleGenerativeAI } from '@ai-sdk/google';
import { streamText, convertToModelMessages,
experimental_createMCPClient } from 'ai';
import { StdioClientTransport } from '@modelcontextprotocol/sdk/client/stdio';

export const maxDuration = 30;

const gemini = createGoogleGenerativeAI({
    apiKey: process.env.GEMINI_API_KEY || '',
});
```

```
export async function POST(req) {                    Configures stdio client
    const { messages } = await req.json();           transport to connect to the
    const transport = new StdioClientTransport({     local MCP server script
        command: 'node',
        args: ['src/stdio/server.js'],
    });

    const mcpClient =                                Initializes the MCP client
await experimental_createMCPClient({ transport });   using the transport
    const tools = await mcpClient.tools();
                                                     Retrieves the available
    const result = streamText({                      tools exposed by the
        model: gemini('gemini-2.5-flash'),           MCP server
        messages: convertToModelMessages(messages),
        tools,
        system: 'You are a helpful assistant that can
call tools when needed.',
        onFinish: async () => {
            await mcpClient.close();
        },
        onError: async () => {
            await mcpClient.close();
        },                                           Streams the AI-generated
    });                                              response to the frontend
    return result.toUIMessageStreamResponse();       in UIMessage format
}
```

`StdioClientTransport` is used to facilitate communication with the MCP server over standard input/output (`stdio`) streams. It allows the application to send requests to the server and receive responses in a reliable, streamable manner without needing a separate network connection. The responses from the server are structured in the Gemini protocol format, which represents messages as a sequence of structured events (such as text, tool outputs, or errors). This format enables the frontend to render the chat dynamically, supporting incremental updates and tool integrations while maintaining compatibility with the user interface. The MCP client is closed after the response finishes or if an error occurs, ensuring proper cleanup and modular tool execution.

The following is the relevant snippet for page.js that uses the `useChat` hook:

```
const { messages, sendMessage, status } = useChat({
  transport: new DefaultChatTransport({
    api: '/api/',
  }),
});
```

This hook connects the React frontend to the API route that streams responses from the Gemini model and MCP tools. `messages` contains the chat history, `sendMessage` sends user input to the server, and `status` indicates the current state of the chat (ready, loading, etc.). The transport ensures all messages go through the `/api/` endpoint, allowing the AI to invoke tools seamlessly.

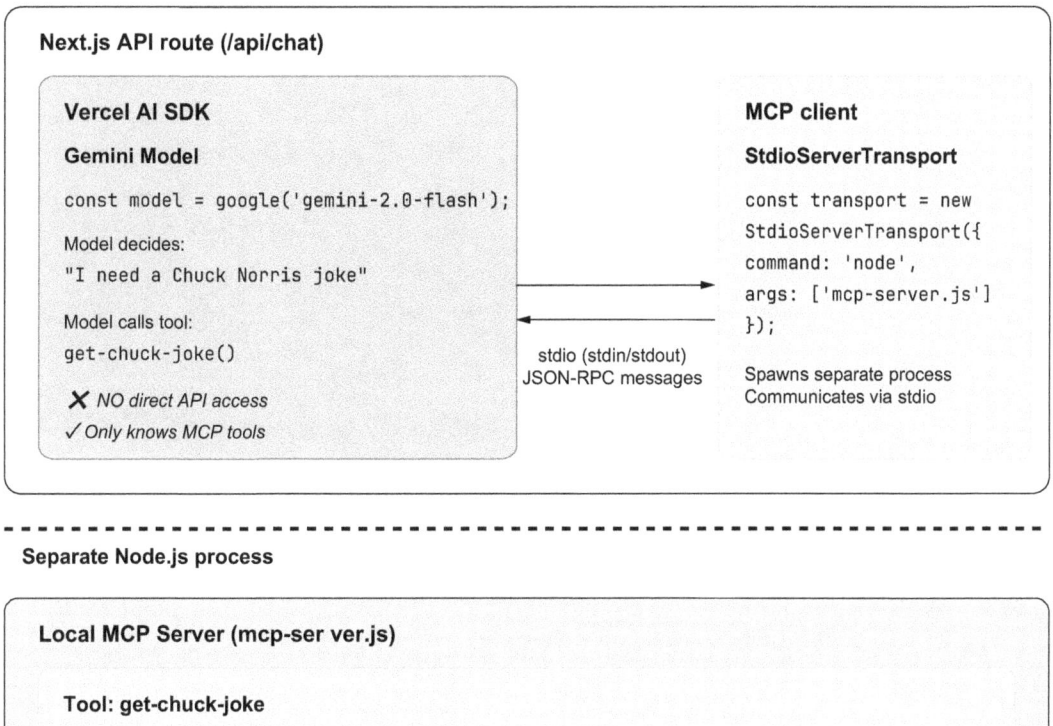
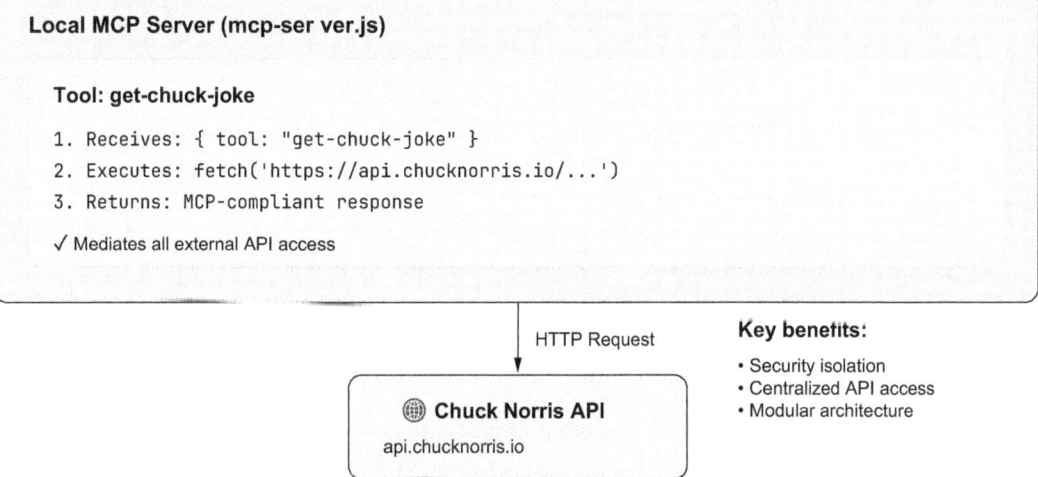

Figure 12.3 How the Vercel AI SDK communicates with a local MCP server through `stdio` transport. The MCP client spawns the server as a separate Node.js process, and they exchange JSON-RPC messages via stdin/stdout. When the model calls a tool like `get-chuck-joke()`, the request flows through stdio to the MCP server, which executes the actual HTTP request and returns the response.

Now start the application from the command line and ask for a few facts about Chuck Norris:

```
$ npm run dev -w ch12/vercel-ai-sdk-mcp
```

Figure 12.4 is a screenshot of the running chat application with MCP tool integration.

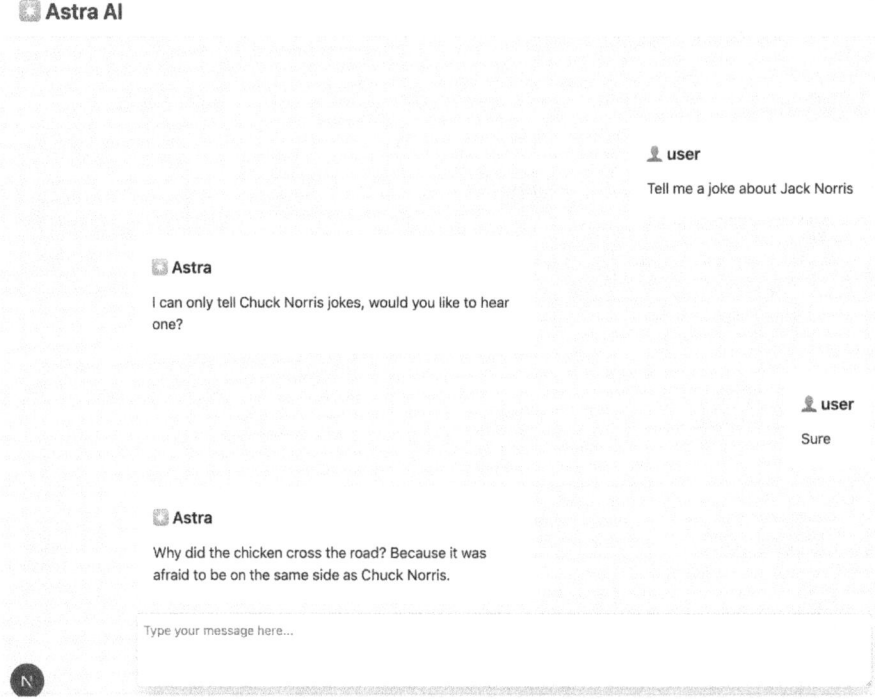

Figure 12.4 Running the Chuck Norris chat application using the Vercel AI SDK with MCP

When the user sends a message, the frontend captures it through the useChat hook and posts it to the /api/ endpoint. The API route streams the input to the Gemini model, providing it access to MCP tools. In this example, the get-norris-fact tool is invoked dynamically when the AI detects a suitable question. The server fetches a fact from the Norris API and returns it as a structured message, and the frontend renders it in the chat history.

12.3.3 Benefits of using the MCP for web applications with LLMs

What is the real advantage of implementing with Next.js and calling the MCP server to provide some data? There are several.

First, it keeps the AI model and external APIs separate. In traditional setups, the AI might need to directly call APIs or handle raw data, which can make the system messy and harder to maintain. With the MCP, the AI only talks to a server that knows how to use the APIs, so everything is cleaner and easier to extend.

Second, it allows the AI to use tools dynamically. Instead of hardcoding every possible API call, the model can decide at run time which tool to invoke. For example, it can call the Chuck Norris API only when the user asks about a random fact, making the assistant smarter and more flexible without extra coding.

Finally, it improves safety and stability. Since the AI never directly accesses external services, your API keys and sensitive logic stay hidden in the MCP server. This separation reduces the risk of leaks or errors, while making it easier to add or update tools without touching the AI itself.

In short, using the MCP with Next.js provides a modular, flexible, and safer integration model for building web applications enhanced by LLMs.

12.4 Inside an MCP server: Extending web applications

Before looking at a more complex integration of MCP servers with LangChain.js, we need to take a closer look at the main components of an MCP server. We've now seen MCP servers in action, but to understand their full potential, we need to look at their core building blocks. An MCP server exposes tools, prompts, and resources to clients or agents. These components form the interface between external systems and the AI model, making the system both extensible and modular.

Figure 12.5 shows the main building blocks of an MCP system and how they relate to applications, clients, servers, and external services. Any application, whether a web UI, CLI tool, or script, acts as a consumer, sending requests to a local or colocated MCP client (also called an agent or SDK). The MCP client discovers and invokes tools, prompts, and resources exposed by an MCP server, which may be local or remote. The MCP server streams responses back through the client to the application, enabling incremental updates and tool integration. Figure 12.5 emphasizes the roles and flows rather than specific deployment locations.

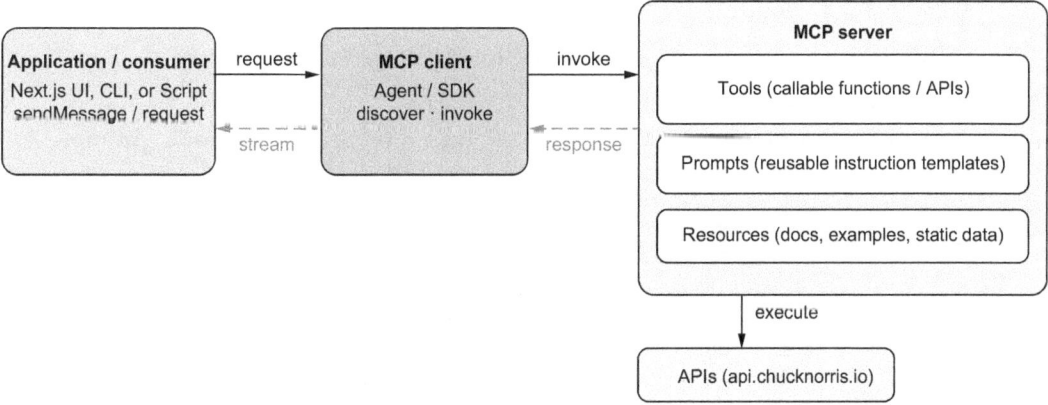

Figure 12.5   MCP server building blocks and how they interact with clients and external services

NOTE The MCP Inspector is a graphical tool that comes with the local MCP server. It allows you to explore the server's available integrations, including tools, prompts, and resources, without needing to go to the MCP website. You can run it locally alongside your MCP server to inspect, debug, and experiment with the system in real time.

> **MCP resources and project code: mcp**
>
> For the most up-to-date reference documentation and specifications of the MCP, see the official MCP site at https://modelcontextprotocol.io/docs/getting-started/intro.
>
> The code for this example project can be found in the ch12/mcp folder. You can use that example by running this command in the root folder of the project repository:
>
> ```
> $ npm run dev -w ch12/mcp
> ```
>
> This launches a local MCP server that you can explore using the MCP Inspector tool. The Inspector provides a graphical interface for inspecting available integrations (tools, prompts, and resources) exposed by the server, which is helpful for debugging and experimentation in web applications.
>
> You'll need the Gemini API key or OpenAI key for this to work, as the application uses services from different vendors. These are configured as environment variables:
>
> ```
> // .env
> GOOGLE_API_KEY=<GEMINI_API_SECRET_KEY>
> OPENAI_API_KEY=<OPEN_AI_SECRET_KEY>
> ```
>
> Instructions on how to set up and create secret keys for Google AI and OpenAI are provided in the appendix.

12.4.1 MCP server structure

Let's break down the structure of the example MCP server step by step.

MCP SERVER INITIALIZATION

First, we need a running MCP server object before registering any tools, prompts, or resources.

Listing 12.3 Initializing an MCP server

```
import { McpServer } from '@modelcontextprotocol/sdk/server/mcp.js';

const server = new McpServer({       ◄─── Creates a new MCP server
  name: 'chuck-norris-mcp',               instance named chuck-norris-mcp
  version: '1.0.0',
});
```

This server instance is the entry point where all tools, prompts, and resources are registered and later exposed to clients or AI SDKs.

DEFINING A TOOL

Tools provide external functionality that the AI model can invoke dynamically, such as fetching data from APIs. We use the `tool` method to provide an implementation of the API call.

Listing 12.4 Registering a tool in an MCP server

```
server.tool(
  "get-chuck-joke",                              ◄── Registers the tool with its name,
  "Fetch a random Chuck Norris joke",                description, and input schema
  {},
  async () => {
    try {
      const response = await fetch("https://api.chucknorris.io/jokes/random");
      if (!response.ok) {
        return {
          content: [{ type: "text", text: `No joke available at the moment.` }],
        };
      }
      const data = await response.json();
      return { content:                          ◄── Returns the fetched
[{ type: "text", text: data.value }] };              Chuck Norris fact
    } catch (err) {
      const message =
err instanceof Error ? err.message : "An unknown error occurred";
      return { content:
[{ type: "text", text: `Error fetching joke: ${message}` }] };
    }
  }
);
```

This tool fetches a random fun or historical fact about Chuck Norris from the API. The AI can call this tool whenever a user mentions *Chuck*.

DEFINING A PROMPT

Prompts define reusable instructions for the AI model. They can standardize responses, summaries, or transformations on data returned by tools. We use the `server.prompt` method to provide the instructions for the AI model.

Listing 12.5 Creating an MCP prompt to summarize a joke

```
server.prompt(                                   ◄──
  "summarize-fact",                                    Registers a prompt
  "Summarize a Chuck Norris joke into a short sentence",   with input schema
  {
    joke: z.string().describe("The joke to summarize"),
  },
  async (args) => {
    const joke = args.joke || "";

    return {                ◄── Returns the user message
      messages: [               for the AI, instructing it to
        {                       summarize the provided joke
          role: 'user',
          content: {
            type: 'text',
```

```
            text: `You can use the get-chuck-joke
or get-chuck-joke-category tools to fetch jokes.
Here is a joke to summarize:\n"${joke}"`
          }
        }
      ]
    };
  }
);
```

This prompt constructs a user message instructing the AI to summarize a joke. The joke itself can be retrieved using the `get-chuck-joke` tool, and the AI generates the concise summary in response.

DEFINING A RESOURCE

Resources provide static or preloaded context that clients or AI models can access directly. This could be a file, a JSON object, or any kind of text.

> **Listing 12.6 Adding a resource to the Chuck Norris MCP server**

```
server.resource(           ◄──── Registers a new resource with the server
  'examples',
  'examples://chuck-norris',  ◄──── Provides a URI so clients and the
  async (uri) => ({                  AI can request this resource
    contents: [{           ◄──── Defines the actual content returned
      uri: uri.href,              when the resource is read
      text: `
# Chuck Norris MCP Server Examples  ...
`
    }]
  })
);
```

This resource contains a Markdown document describing the Chuck Norris MCP server examples, including which tools and prompts are available. It can be used by clients or the AI for reference or context.

RUNNING THE MCP INSPECTOR

The MCP Inspector is the interface for exploring and interacting with resources registered on the Chuck Norris MCP server. To run the inspector for this example, use the following command as mentioned in the sidebar "MCP resources and project code: `mcp`":

```
$ npm run dev -w ch12/mcp
```

The inspector will automatically instantiate the script mcp.js and open a new browser window. It is particularly useful for debugging, testing, and experimenting with the server in real time. Figure 12.6 shows the view of the inspector when we use `get-chuck-joke`.

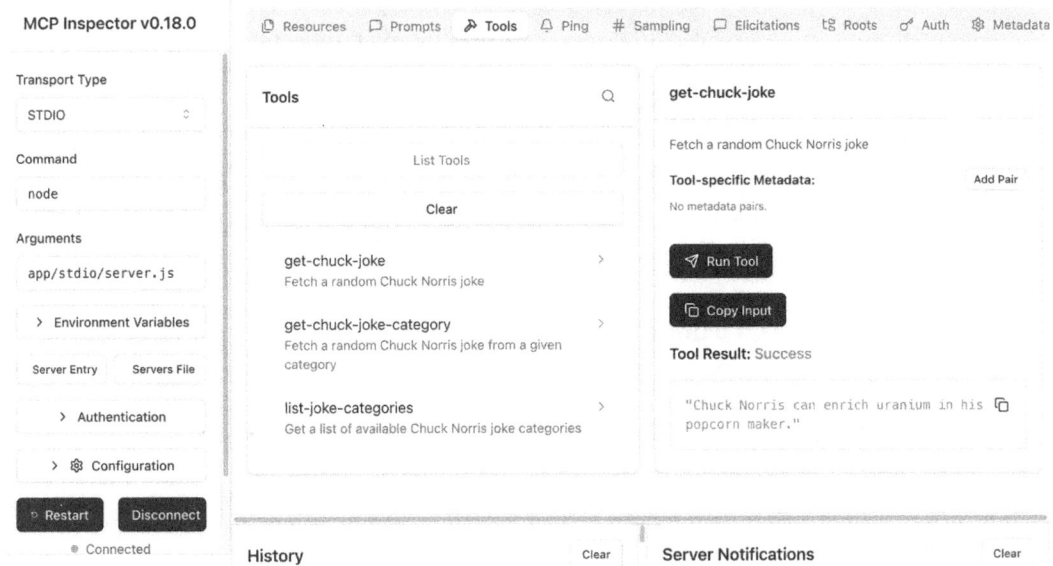

Figure 12.6 Using the MCP Inspector tool to test and debug the server implementation

12.4.2 Additional considerations for MCP servers

When designing and deploying MCP servers, it is useful to reflect on both the current specification of the MCP and its future roadmap. MCP servers function as an additional layer of abstraction designed primarily for web applications that rely on LLMs. They allow clients to explore resources, invoke prompts, and orchestrate tools in a structured way, effectively serving as a bridge between AI models and the underlying data or functionality. Despite this specialized role, MCP servers are still servers in the conventional sense, so standard maintenance, security, and operational practices apply. This includes managing API keys, controlling access, monitoring performance, and ensuring reliable uptime.

The MCP specification emphasizes clear resource registration, structured message formats, and tool integration. Each resource or prompt must have a unique identifier and URI, and its responses should be well structured and predictable, enabling clients to reliably fetch and interact with content.

By keeping both the AI-focused abstraction and the server responsibilities in mind, developers can build MCP servers that are robust, secure, and maintainable while still enabling powerful AI orchestration.

12.5 Integrating MCP servers with LangChain.js

We've integrated the Vercel AI SDK with the MCP to expose external APIs as callable tools. Now let's see how the same MCP server can be integrated into a Next.js application using LangChain.js.

346 CHAPTER 12 *Integrating web apps with the Model Context Protocol*

LangChain provides higher-level abstractions for agents, tool management, and reasoning loops. With its MCP adapters, we can plug MCP tools into LangChain's agent ecosystem with minimal effort. The result is a more flexible orchestration layer where the AI can decide when to invoke tools and how to combine their results.

Let's see an example of how we can integrate LangChain with the Vercel AI SDK and provide a web application that allows users to ask for jokes about Chuck Norris. The jokes will be sourced from the Chuck Norris API (https://api.chucknorris.io/) into our application.

> **Project code: langchain-mcp**
>
> The code for this example project can be found in the ch12/langchain-mcp folder. You can use that example by running this command in the root folder of the project repository:
>
> ```
> $ npm run dev -w ch12/langchain-mcp
> ```
>
> You'll need the Gemini API key or OpenAI key for this to work as the application uses services from different vendors. These are configured as environment variables:
>
> ```
> // .env
> GOOGLE_API_KEY=<GEMINI_API_SECRET_KEY>
> OPENAI_API_KEY=<OPEN_AI_SECRET_KEY>
> ```
>
> Instructions on how to set up and create secret keys for Google AI and OpenAI are provided in the appendix.

12.5.1 Architecture overview

Figure 12.7 shows the overall system design for the LangChain.js with MCP integration.

The architecture layers are like the Vercel AI SDK integration but with some key differences:

- *LangChain agent*—Instead of directly streaming responses from the SDK, LangChain creates an agent that can reason about when to use tools (`createReactAgent`).
- *MCP integration via adapter*—LangChain uses the `MultiServerMCPClient` to fetch MCP tools and expose them as LangChain tools.

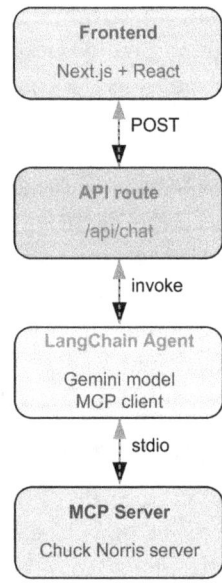

Figure 12.7 High-level architecture of a Next.js chat application using LangChain.js and MCP. The frontend interacts with a Next.js API route. This route constructs a LangChain agent that uses an MCP client. The MCP client connects to the Chuck Norris MCP server over stdio and invokes tools on behalf of the model.

- *Response handling*—Instead of streaming every token, this example transforms results into structured UI messages and displays them in a richer card component.

12.5.2 Building an end-to-end integration with LangChain.js

In this step, we turn to the backend API route. The MCP server implementation remains the same as before—it still exposes the get-norris-joke tool backed by the Chuck Norris API, so there is no need to change it. Our focus now is on the Next.js API route that connects the frontend to LangChain, Gemini, and the MCP server.

Figure 12.7 shows the overall flow of messages through the system. The API route sits in the middle of that flow. Its job is to receive the user's input from the frontend, pass it into a LangChain agent that can use MCP tools, and then stream the agent's output back to the user interface. We will build this in four parts:

1. Create an MCP client to connect to the Chuck Norris MCP server and discover its tools.
2. Initialize the Gemini model.
3. Configure a LangChain React agent that combines the model with the MCP tools.
4. Invoke the agent with the user's message, close the MCP client, and stream the result back to the UI.

Listing 12.3 shows how this comes together in a simplified version of the API route. The full implementation in the repository includes extra helpers for normalizing messages and handling streaming, but here we focus on the core ideas.

Listing 12.3 Next.js API route with LangChain and MCP

```
import { ChatGoogleGenerativeAI } from "@langchain/google-genai";
import { createUIMessageStreamResponse } from "ai";
import { MultiServerMCPClient } from "@langchain/mcp-adapters";
import { createReactAgent } from "@langchain/langgraph/prebuilt";
import { HumanMessage } from "@langchain/core/messages";

async function createMCPClient() {
  const client = new MultiServerMCPClient({         ◀── Creates a MultiServerMCPClient to
    useStandardContentBlocks: true,                      connect to the Chuck Norris MCP
    mcpServers: {                                        server and fetch available tools
      norris: {
        transport: "stdio",
        command: "node",
        args: ["app/stdio/server.js"],
        restart: { enabled: true, maxAttempts: 3, delayMs: 1000 },
      },
    },
  });
  const tools = await client.getTools();
  return { client, tools };
}
```

```
export async function POST(req) {
      const body = await req.json();
  const input = body.input || "";
  const humanMessage = new HumanMessage(input);
  const { client, tools } =
await createMCPClient();
  const model = new ChatGoogleGenerativeAI({
    model: "gemini-2.5-flash",
    apiKey: process.env.GEMINI_API_KEY,
  });
  const agent =
createReactAgent({ llm: model, tools });
  const result = await agent.invoke({ messages: [humanMessage] });
  await client.close();

  // Stream result back in UIMessage format
  return
createUIMessageStreamResponse({stream: result});
}
```

- Initializes the MCP client and tools for the agent
- Configures a LangChain React chain agent with Gemini and the MCP tools
- Invokes the agent, closes the client, and streams the result back to the frontend

> **NOTE** This listing is simplified to reduce size. The full version includes helper functions for normalizing user messages, handling streaming, and writing structured UI events.

The listing implements the four steps outlined previously. It starts with create-MCPClient(), which establishes a connection to the Chuck Norris MCP server via stdio and fetches the tools it provides. In the POST handler, the user's input is wrapped as a HumanMessage. The Gemini model is initialized, and a LangChain React agent is created by combining the model with the MCP tools. When the agent is invoked with the message, it decides whether to use the get-chuck-joke tool. After the agent produces its output, the MCP client is closed, and the result is streamed back in a UI-friendly format to the frontend.

THE FRONTEND

On the frontend, the application uses the useChat hook (from the Vercel AI SDK) to manage chat state and send user input to our /api/chat endpoint. Messages returned from the backend come back as structured UI events. For example, when the agent calls the Chuck Norris MCP tool, the response is rendered with a custom ChuckNorris-FactCard component. This gives the chat a richer feel than plain text and highlights tool outputs in a user-friendly way.

The rest of the frontend is standard Next.js with React: an input box for the user, a chat history display, and conditional rendering of special cards when the backend streams structured tool responses. The important part is that we don't need extra glue code—the backend already formats responses as UI events, and the frontend simply listens and renders. Instead of showing more code here, I give you a feel for the result by showing the application live in figure 12.8.

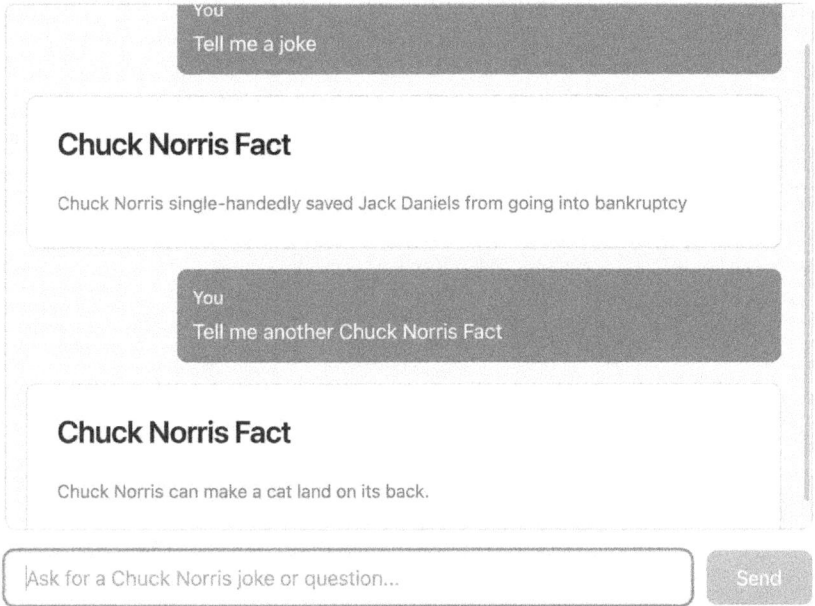

Figure 12.8 The user asks the chat interface for some Chuck Norris facts, and the request flows through the Next.js API to the LangChain agent. The agent uses its MCP client to call the Chuck Norris server via stdio, retrieving a fact from api.chucknorris.io that streams back to update the UI.

The chat interface demonstrates the MCP architecture in action. When a user requests a joke, the message flows from the application through the API route to the LangChain agent. The agent's MCP client communicates with the Chuck Norris MCP server via stdio transport, which calls https://api.chucknorris.io/ to retrieve a random joke or a joke from a specific category. Users can ask for a joke about movies or request a list of available categories. The response then streams back through the same components to update the user interface in real time, as shown in the screenshot.

12.6 The future of the MCP: Gateways, directories, and MCP-as-a-service

The MCP is still in its early stages, but adoption is accelerating. Developers, platform providers, and businesses are experimenting with new layers and services built on top of the MCP. These emerging directions point toward a future where the MCP becomes a foundational layer of the web, much like HTTP or REST once were. Let's take a quick look at three initiatives that guide the next phase of the MCP.

12.6.1 MCP gateways

One problem today is LLM-powered web apps often need many separate integrations (calendars, email, commerce, and CRMs). Each integration is an independent MCP server with its own authorization, format, and state. When an agent tries to use many servers directly, they get duplicated authorization logic, inconsistent state, and fragile orchestration.

An MCP gateway is a single, AI-aware proxy. The LLM app connects to the gateway once. The gateway knows how to talk to every registered MCP server, and it provides a stable, consistent interface back to the agent. Figure 12.9 is a simple visualization of the MCP gateway concept.

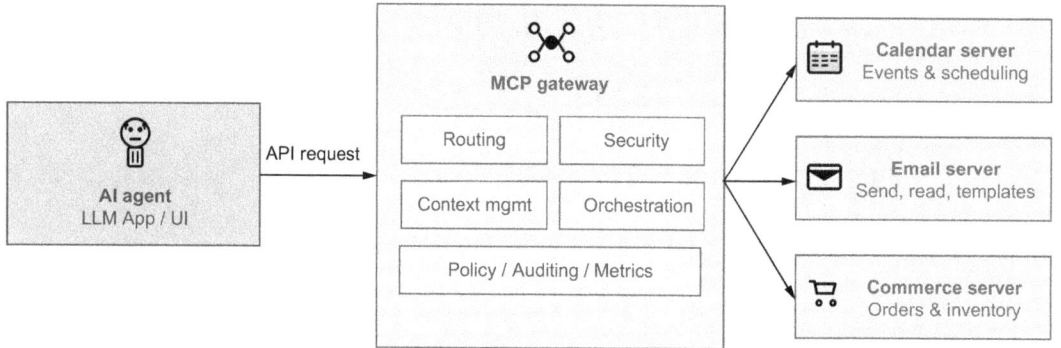

Figure 12.9 An MCP gateway centralizes how an AI agent connects to multiple MCP servers, handling routing, security, and context so that the application sees a single unified interface.

The MCP gateway reduces the complexity that arises when an LLM-powered web app must connect directly to many independent MCP servers. Instead of duplicating authentication and juggling inconsistent states, the application connects once to the gateway, which handles security, routing, and context on its behalf. This allows the app to treat all services as part of a single unified interface. Because the gateway maintains shared context, multistep workflows feel seamless; for example, scheduling a meeting can also trigger an email confirmation and a CRM update without the agent managing each integration separately. In this way, the gateway functions less like a traditional API proxy and more like an AI-aware service mesh, centralizing trust and enabling smoother orchestration across tools.

12.6.2 MCP-as-a-service

MCP-as-a-service is emerging as a natural evolution for businesses looking to integrate with AI assistants. Just as SaaS transformed software delivery by centralizing functionality in the cloud, MCP endpoints allow companies to expose their services directly to LLM-powered applications. Instead of building custom integrations for each AI platform, a business can operate a single MCP server and let users connect it to any compatible assistant.

For example, a local bookstore could run an MCP server at mybookstore.com/mcp. Customers might click a button labeled Add This Store to OpenAI, granting the AI assistant access to check inventory, reserve books, or place orders. Similarly, community forums can expose endpoints like `get_news` or `post_message`, enabling users to interact with site content entirely through conversation.

The key implication is that the MCP may become the new standard: the "Add us to your AI" mechanism. Just as websites once added RSS feeds or apps prompted users to install a mobile client, businesses will increasingly provide MCP endpoints so that their services are directly accessible from chat-based interfaces.

Over time, instead of relying on visual interfaces, users may engage primarily through AI assistants that call MCP-enabled services behind the scenes, streamlining workflows and creating entirely new user experiences.

12.6.3 MCP directories and registries

Discovering useful MCP servers is still a challenge. Right now, developers often rely on community recommendations, forum posts, or small niche catalogs. There isn't yet a single, fully mature directory, so finding the right server for your needs can feel like searching in the early days of the web. Figure 12.10 illustrates the MCP discovery ecosystem, showing how developers find and access MCP servers efficiently.

MCP discovery ecosystem

Problem	Solution	Outcome
Fragmented discovery	Centralized registries	Organized ecosystem
? Forum posts	Official lists	☑ Commerce server
? Niche catalogs	Community catalogs	☑ Calendar server
? Word of mouth	Developer tools	☑ Email & API

Figure 12.10 Developers face fragmented discovery across forums, niche catalogs, and word of mouth. Centralized registries and community catalogs improve access to those services by creating an organized and trusted ecosystem for commerce, calendar, email, and API servers.

Emerging solutions are starting to fill this gap. The official MCP Registry (https://github.com/modelcontextprotocol/registry) provides a centralized listing of available servers, though it is still growing and adding content. Community-curated catalogs, like Glama and Pulse MCP, offer collections of trusted servers. CLI tools such as `mcpreg` (https://github.com/trose/mcp-registry-cli) allow developers to browse, search, and install MCP servers directly from the command line. Even app-based catalogs are appearing, letting users discover and install MCP endpoints with a single click, similar to an app store experience.

This ecosystem is comparable to the pre–search engine stage of the internet. Over time, we can expect richer directories with ratings, categories, reviews, and possibly monetization models, making it easier to discover, trust, and deploy MCP servers in web applications powered by AI.

12.7 Your next steps with MCP servers

Now that we've seen example integrations of MCP servers with the Vercel AI SDK and LangChain, the next step is hands-on exploration and integration. As a developer, you can browse official and community registries to identify MCP servers relevant to your projects and then use CLI tools or app-based catalogs to search, install, and manage these servers efficiently. By experimenting with these integrations and contributing back through adding servers, sharing usage experiences, or providing ratings, you can help strengthen the ecosystem.

Summary

- The MCP provides a common interface for exposing tools, prompts, and resources to AI models, making them reusable across applications and frameworks without rewriting logic.
- The MCP separates AI logic from external APIs, so the AI model never directly calls APIs, which improves security, maintainability, and modularity.
- MCP servers define callable tools (e.g., fetching number facts), prompts to structure AI instructions, and resources for preloaded context or reference material, forming the core building blocks of an integration.
- Client-server architecture allows MCP clients (AI agents or SDKs) to communicate with MCP servers over transports like `stdio`, enabling multiple servers to provide distinct functionalities to a single AI application.
- External APIs may fail, so MCP servers should include graceful error handling and predefined fallback responses to ensure continuous service and predictable outputs.
- Integrating the MCP with frameworks like Next.js, the Vercel AI SDK, or LangChain allows AI assistants to dynamically invoke tools, retrieve structured data, and render rich responses in the frontend.
- Emerging directions such as centralized MCP gateways, public directories, and cloud-based MCP endpoints will simplify tool discovery, orchestrate multiserver workflows, and enable scalable plug-and-play AI applications.

appendix
Running the examples

This book's accompanying code and resources are available in a GitHub repository, making it easy for you to access and run the examples discussed throughout the chapters. The repository can be found at https://github.com/Generative-AI-Web-Apps/Code.

Some of the key features of the repository are

- *Organized by chapters*—I organized each chapter with its own directory, containing the code examples and projects discussed in that chapter. For example, chapter 2 is in the ch02 folder, chapter 3 in ch03, and so on.
- *npm workspaces*—The repository is set up using npm workspaces, allowing for efficient management of multiple projects. This allows us to put several individual projects within the same repo and manage their dependencies in one place.
- *Up-to-date dependencies*—The repository includes the latest tools and dependency information, ensuring compatibility with the most recent versions of the tools and libraries used.

A.1 Running examples

To run a specific example from the book, use the following steps:

1. Before you do anything, make sure you install the npm dependencies for the project. You just need to run the following command in your terminal:

```
$ npm i
```

2 To run a specific example, make sure you use the following command structure:

```
$ npm run dev -w [chapter-folder]/[project-name]
```

For example, to run the chat-client-next project from chapter 2:

```
$ npm run dev -w ch02/chat-client-next
```

This command runs the specified project within the chapter folder using the npm workspace structure.

A lot of projects require an OpenAI API key to access the AI model. I provide instructions on how to set up your key and assign this to a project.

A.2 Accessing OpenAI APIs

To use the OpenAI APIs in the projects, you'll need to create an API key. Here's how to do it:

1 Visit the OpenAI platform: https://platform.openai.com/. If you don't have an account, you will be asked to create one.
2 Navigate to the API keys page: https://platform.openai.com/api-keys. Figure A.1 shows the page that you will see.

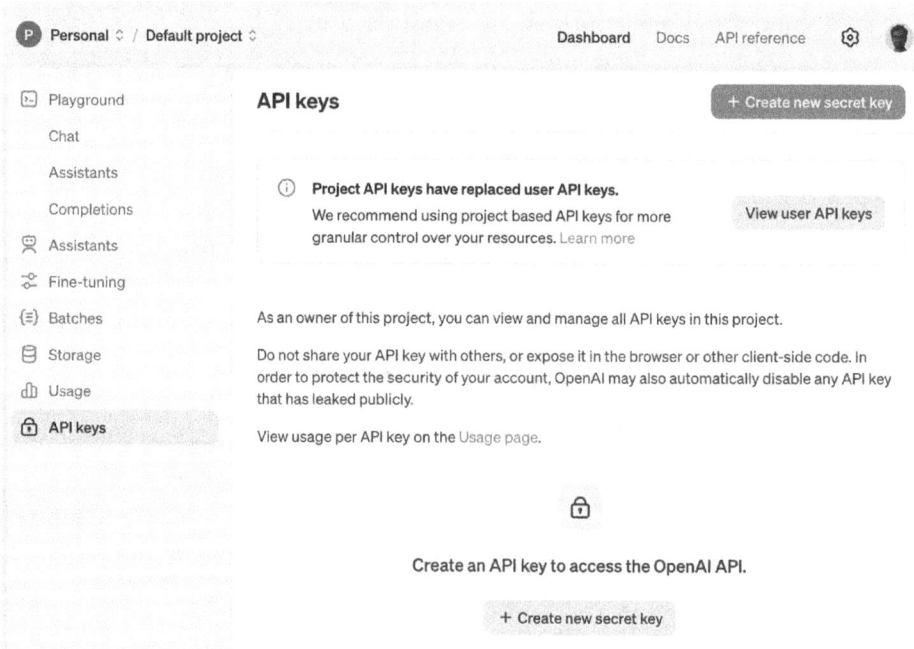

Figure A.1 API keys page in OpenAI

3   Click the Create a New Secret Key button. A modal will pop up prompting you for details (figure A.2).

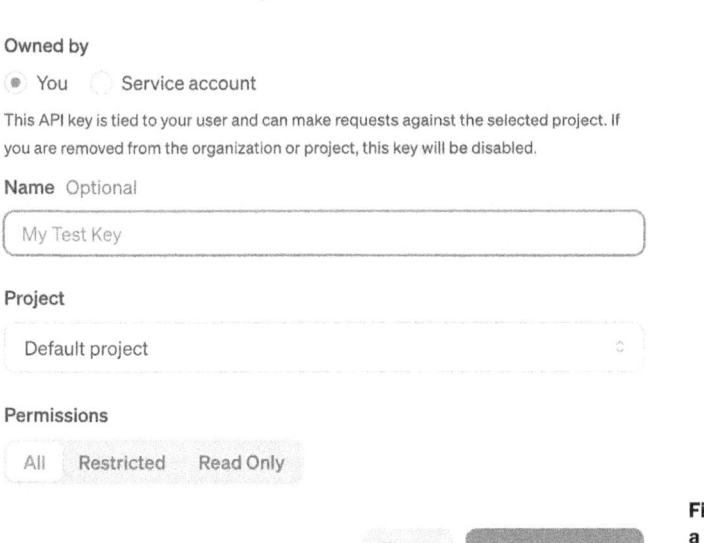

Figure A.2 Creating a new secret key in the OpenAI page

4   Fill in the form details in the model that appears. You have an option to configure individual API endpoint permissions.
5   Copy the generated secret key string and paste it into your clipboard. You won't be able to see it again otherwise, and you will have to create a new key to view it again.
6   Once you have your OpenAI API key, you need to add it to your project. In the root directory of the project you want to run, create a file named .env and add the secret key there:

```
OPENAI_API_KEY=your_secret_key_here
```

Now you should be able to access the AI model functionality.

NOTE   As of the end of 2025, OpenAI no longer provides free API credits or a free usage tier to new accounts by default. When creating a new account, you will be required to set up billing and prepurchase credits before you can use the API. The system will prompt you to start billing immediately, and API calls will not work without an active payment method and purchased credits. This applies regardless of using new phone numbers or email addresses.

> **NOTE** Always keep your API key confidential. Never commit it to version control or share it publicly.

By using this repository and following these instructions, you'll be able to run and experiment with all the examples from the book, enhancing your learning experience with hands-on practice. Most projects default to using Google's Gemini Flash model, which is free to use with a Google Cloud account—so you can complete all the examples at no cost if you use the default setup.

If you prefer to use OpenAI models instead, be aware that OpenAI requires a minimum of $5 in credits to activate API access. Running the examples with OpenAI models will generally cost no more than $1 to $2 total, as long as you avoid uploading large documents or books—particularly in the later chapters involving embeddings or fine-tuning.

A.3 Accessing Google AI APIs

If you are having trouble accessing the OpenAI API because of no available credits, then Google AI's Gemini API is a strong alternative. Unlike OpenAI, Gemini provides a free usable tier that allows you to experiment and test without immediate billing, making it more accessible for developers and learners.

Follow these steps to generate an API key for Google AI at the provided link:

1. Visit the Google AI Studio at https://aistudio.google.com/app/apikey. If you are not already signed in, click the Sign In button. Use your Google account credentials to log in. If you do not have a Google account, you will need to create one.
2. Access the API key section. Once signed in, navigate to the API key section of the Google AI Studio and click the Create API Key button (see figure A.3).

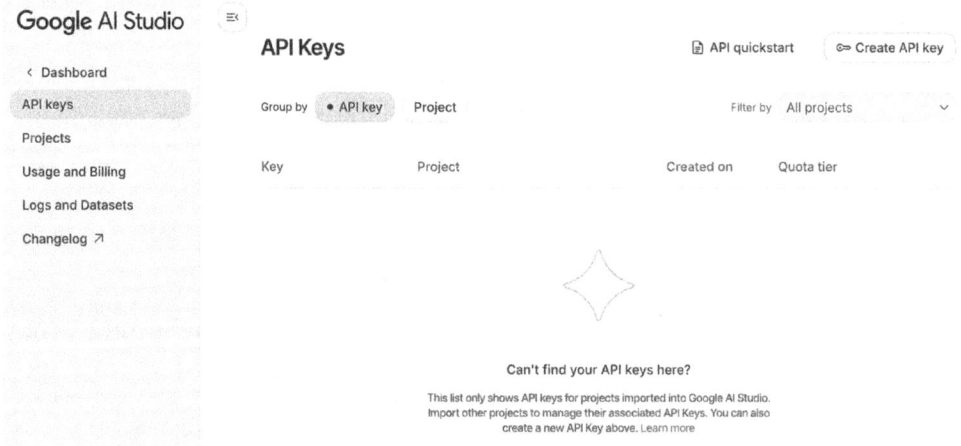

Figure A.3 Creating a new secret key in the Google AI studio page

3 Configure API key settings. You may be prompted to configure settings for your API key. This will include specifying the project that the key is assigned for (see figure A.4).

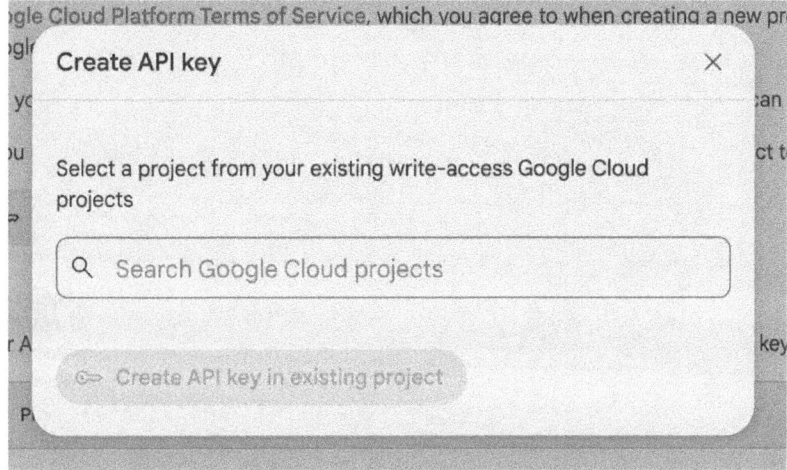

Figure A.4 Selecting a Google project to assign the API key

4 Generate the API key. After configuring the settings, click the Generate button. The system will create your API key. Once the API key is generated, it will be displayed on the screen. Make sure to copy this key and store it in a secure location, as you will need it to authenticate your requests to the Google AI services.

5 Once you have your Google API key, you need to add it to your project. In the root directory of the project you want to run, create a file named .env and add the secret key there:

GOOGLE_API_KEY=your_secret_key_here

Now you should be able to access the AI model functionality.

A.4 Accessing the Upstash Redis database

To integrate Upstash Redis into your full-stack AI web application, you need to create a Redis database and obtain the necessary connection details. Here's a step-by-step guide on how to do this:

1 Create an Upstash account. Go to https://upstash.com/ and create an account if you haven't already.

2 Once you have an account, log in to the Upstash console. You will see the page shown in figure A.5.

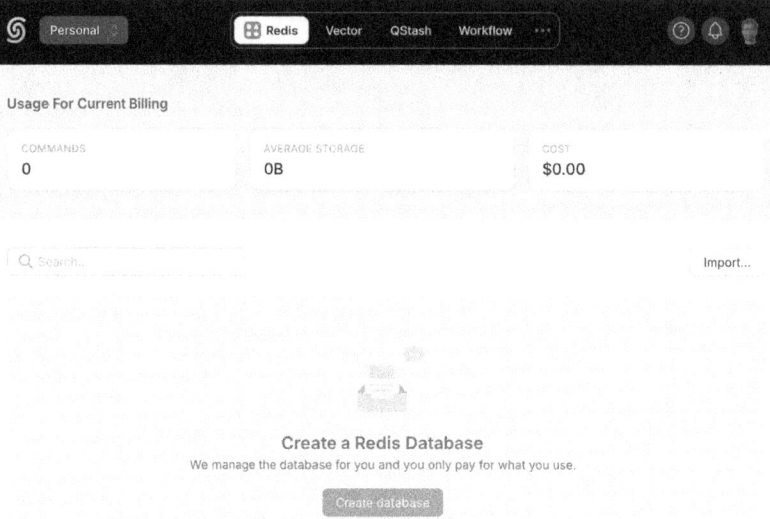

Figure A.5 Upstash main dashboard page

3 Create a new Redis database. In the Upstash console, click the plus sign in the middle to create a new database and fill in the details (see figure A.6).

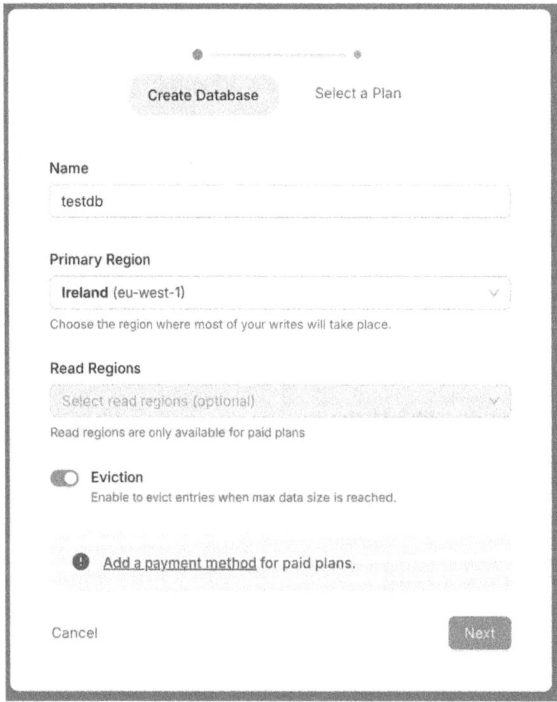

Figure A.6 Creating a new Redis database model

4   Obtain connection details. After creating the database, you will see a page with the connection details. Use the copy buttons to store the REDIS URL and Token in the clipboard (see figure A.7).

```
REST API
REST API enables you to access your Upstash database using REST
UPSTASH_REDIS_REST_URL    UPSTASH_REDIS_REST_TOKEN

  JavaScript   Python   cURL   .env                    Read-Only Token
1 UPSTASH_REDIS_REST_URL="https://nearby-sloth-44757.upstash.io"
2 UPSTASH_REDIS_REST_TOKEN="********"
```

Figure A.7   Obtaining Redis credentials

5   Set the following environment variables in your project:
   - UPSTASH_REDIS_REST_URL—The endpoint URL
   - UPSTASH_REDIS_REST_TOKEN—The API token to access the Upstash API

A.5 Integrating Clerk.js authentication

To integrate Clerk.js into your Next.js application for secure authentication, follow these steps:

1   Create a Clerk account. Go to https://clerk.com/ and create an account if you haven't already. Once you have an account, log in to the Clerk dashboard.
2   Create a new application. In the Clerk dashboard, click the Create Application button. Then, on the new page, select Email as the authentication method and unselect all other options. Then enter a name for your application (see figure A.8).
3   Get the API keys. Go to the Application Configure page and scroll down to find the API Keys section. Then use the Copy button to store the following environmental variables for the Next.js application:
   - NEXT_PUBLIC_CLERK_PUBLISHABLE_KEY—The public API key
   - CLERK_SECRET_KEY—The private API token
4   Configure restrictions. To restrict access during testing, you'll need to enable Restricted Sign-up mode in the Clerk dashboard. However, the Allowlist option must be configured *before* enabling Restricted mode.
5   While still in the default Public mode, navigate to the Restrictions page.

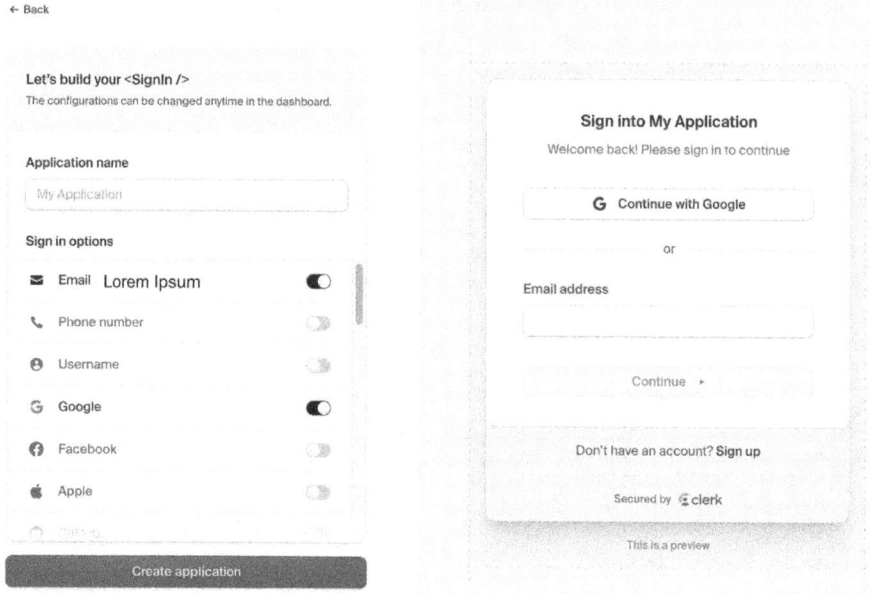

Figure A.8 Creating a new Clerk.js application

6. Enable the Allowlist toggle and add trusted email addresses you want to permit access.
7. Once your Allowlist is set, switch to Restricted Sign-up mode to ensure only those approved addresses can create or access accounts during testing (see figure A.9).

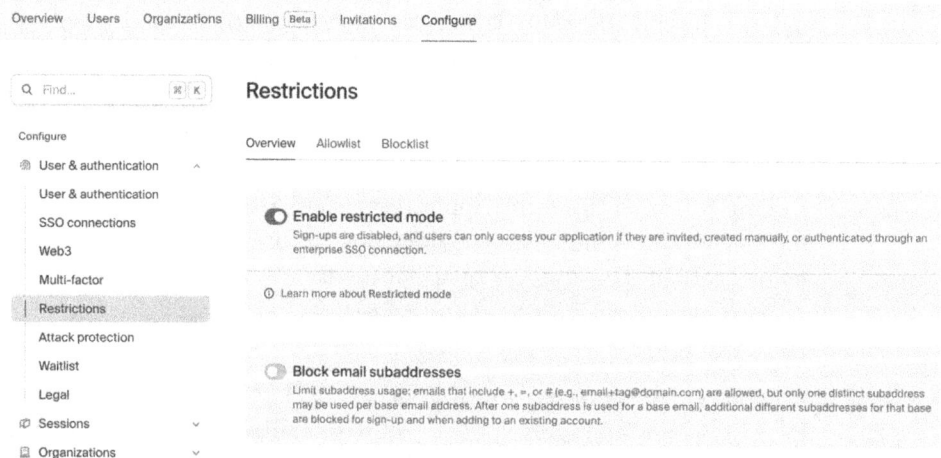

Figure A.9 Configuring signing restrictions when testing the application

index

Symbols

@ai-sdk/google   66
@ai-sdk package   60
/api/chat endpoint   269, 348
/chat endpoint   277
@google-cloud/dlp   289
@langchain/core/prompts package   171
@langchain/core/tools package   190
@next/ font module   52
@upstash/ratelimit library   281

A

abstract factories   75
    design pattern   73
abstraction layers   57
access control   139
adaptive interview difficulty   6
agents   188–194
    creating   190–192
    integration with Vercel AI SDK   192
    overview of   189
AI (artificial intelligence)
    connecting models with Vercel AI SDK, handling streaming responses with   61–72
    debugging techniques   232
    deployment, compliance and data protection   288–290
    future of web development   327
    generative vs. traditional AI   13–15
    generative AI web applications, generative AI lifecycle   26
    Google AI APIs   356
    integrating web apps with MCP   334–341
    state management   103–113
    workflows, building with LangChain.js   166
ai-fallback library   248
AI interview assistant   305
    additional considerations and improvements   315
    challenges during development   313–315
    overview of application   306–314
    choosing interview type   306
    interactive chat-based interview UI   308
    interview closing and summary   309
    interview parameters configuration   308
    past interview session review   310
    security measures implemented   313
    technical implementation   311
    technology stack overview   311–312
AI interviewer agents for simulated interviews   5
ai package   66, 69–71, 143
AIProvider   105

aiResponseStream 178
AI workflows, memory components 185–188
API configuration 42
API keys and secrets management 285–287
API rate limiting 326
APIs, OpenAI, accessing 354
app router 45
Astra AI 20, 76–79
    backend implementation 77–78
    frontend implementation 79
    integrating streaming into 69–72
    Vercel AI SDK with 58–61
augmentation, document augmentation 222
authentication 313
    with Clerk.js 306
autoscroll 29

B

backend 37–41
background processing 326
bias, handling 17

C

caching layers 7
callback handlers 253
CCPA (California Consumer Privacy Act) 16
chain execution errors 251–254
chain-of-thought prompting 130, 151–154
    example of 151
    general methodology for creating prompts 152
ChatBubble component 100
ChatList 32–37
    component 118
ChatMessageHistory format 185
ChatOpenAI model 170
ChatPage 32
chat routes 324
ChatThread component 311
ChuckNorrisFactCard component 348
chunked transfer encoding 63
citation-based grounding 225
Clerk.js
    authentication with 306, 318
    authentication with Next.js and 277–280
    integrating authentication 359
client-side processing 63

client validation 271
code generation, defined 4
completion, defined 63
compliance and data protection 288–290
components, defined 28
composition primitives 195
compound messages 138
computational cost 143
concrete factories 75
conditional auto-scrolling 31
configuration, Next.js 45–52
console logs 237
constrained validation 144
containerization, defined 7
content enhancement, defined 4
context length limitations 192
contextual grounding 225
contextual understanding 142
control tokens 136
conversational UIs (user interfaces)
    enhancing with multimedia content 79–86
    RSCs 90–103
conversation and state management, tool and function calling 121–125
ConversationChain component 187
conversations 88
    structured data generation 113–121
CORS (cross-origin resource sharing) 39, 42, 313
cosine similarity 144, 161, 163

D

data fetching and rendering
    advanced 51
data preprocessing 13
data sensitivity 271
debug chains 253
debugging, Next.js applications 233–241
    client-server problems 237–238
    memory profiling 240
    network monitoring 240
    performance monitoring 239–241
    rendering issues 233–237
    scroll behavior problems 235
    streaming responses problems 236
    state management 239
debugging techniques 232

decoupling, defined   75
deep learning, defined   13
deployment   268, 291–301
    alternative   299, 300
    authentication and authorization   275–285
    compliance and data protection   288–290
    example deployment to Vercel   294–299
    options for   291–292
    production checklist   292–294
    rate limiting   280–285
    secrets management   285
Docker   291
documents
    indexing   219–221
    ingestion   179
    preparing and storing for retrieval   179–185
    routes   324
    types   203
document summarization   198–216
    additional considerations for summarizing documents   212–216
    applying summarization chain and displaying to user   204
    architecture and workflow   198–202
    building   202–205
    caveats and limitations   205–208
    demonstration of app   208–211
    loading and preprocessing documents   203
    measuring cost of multiple LLM calls   207
    parsing and cleaning up documents   205
    project requirements   198
    splitting documents into manageable chunks   204
document summarization and RAG with LangChain.js, RAG web application   216–230
    adding grounding support   225–230
    key architectural components   217
    project requirements   216
    system components   219–223
    technical architecture overview   218
    web app demonstration   223
dotenv package   47
dynamic
    response generation for customer feedback   5
    updates   139

E

Elastic Stack (Elasticsearch, Logstash, Kibana)   250
embedding generation   179
embeddings   130
    IT support knowledge base   161–164
    machine language vs.   157
    restaurant menu analogy   154
    storing and retrieving with   160
    storing in database   158
    tied to particular model   157
    Vercel AI SDK   158–161
    visual representation of   156
encrypted storage   326
error boundary component   235
error handling   38, 41
Euclidean distance   161

F

factory method pattern   171
FakeLLM class   264, 266, 267
FakeRetriever class   264, 266, 267
FallbackModel class   249
feature extraction, defined   8
feedback page   312
fetch API   52
few-shot learning   146–151
    examples of   147–149
    general methodology for creating prompts   150
file-based routing   45
file uploader   84
fine-tuning   146
frontend, generative AI web applications   28
function calling   114

G

GANs (generative adversarial networks)   12
GDPR (General Data Protection Regulation)   16, 288
Gemini, vision queries   83–86
Gemini API key   44
generated content   332
generative AI   3
    AI tools and ecosystem   9
    capabilities of   4
    concerns and implications of   15–17
    generative vs. traditional AI   13–15

generative AI *(continued)*
  job loss and 16
  limitations of 15
  real-world uses of 5
  reliability of outputs 16–17
generative AI (artificial intelligence) web applications
  assessing first iteration 42
  building major components 28–42
  designing for better user experience 26
  example of 20
  generative AI lifecycle 26
  project goal and requirements 21–26
generative AI web application, Next.js 43
  configuration on 45–52
  routing and configuration on 45–52
  routing on 45–52
  running project 44
  setting up 44
generative chatbots for automated customer support 5
Google AI APIs 356
grounding, adding support 225–230
  types of grounding 225
  with log probabilities 227–230

H

hooks, defined 28
HTTP 429 (Too Many Requests) error 247
Hugging Face Spaces, alternative deployments 300
HumanMessage 188, 348
HyDE (hypothetical document embedding) 218

I

image
  component 52
  comprehension 80
  generation 4, 5
  processing 80
incremental delivery 63
incremental static regeneration 52
individual blog posts 48
information retrieval 180
input validation 269–275
  Next.js API handler 271
  overview 270–273
  server vs. client validation 271
  threat model 270
insufficient_quota error 26
integrating web apps with MCP
  architecture overview 335
  benefits of using MCP for web applications with LLMs 340
  building end-to-end integration with MCP in Next.js 336–340
  connecting Next.js and Vercel AI SDK with 334–341
integration testing, in React and Next.js 256–257
InterviewSidebar component 312
iterative refinement (reprompting) 115

J

JSX (JavaScript XML) 28

K

knowledge base grounding 225
knowledgebase routes 324
Kubernetes 291

L

LangChain agent 346
LangChain.js 269
  agents 188–194
  building AI workflows with 166–178, 194
  integrating MCP servers with 345–349
  memory components 185–188
  modules 194
  testing 264–267
  troubleshooting 250–256
LangGraph vs. LCEL 195
language model specification 74
LanguageModelV1 interface 249
layout components 48
lazy loading 52
LCEL (LangChain Expression Language) 168, 195
Live debuggers 237
LLMLingua 212
LLMs (large language models) 3, 7, 19, 130, 166, 268, 332
  techniques 164
log probabilities, grounding with 226–230
LTS (long-term support) 23

M

machine learning, defined   13
malware scanning   326
max tokens   39, 41, 134–136
maxWords   145
MCP (Model Context Protocol)   331
   architecture   333
   extending web applications   341–345
   future of   349–352
   importance of   332
   integrating web apps with
      architecture overview   335, 346
      benefits of using MCP for web applications with LLMs   340
      building end-to-end integration with LangChain.js   347–349
      building end-to-end integration with MCP in Next.js   336–340
      connecting Next.js and Vercel AI SDK with   334–341
      frontend   348
      integrating MCP servers with LangChain.js   345–349
   next steps with servers   352
mcpreg CLI tool   351
memory components   185–188
memory profiling   240
messages prompts   138
MFA (multifactor authentication)   277
middleware
   configuration   278
   layer   273–275
minWords   145
mocking LLM responses   143, 258
   challenges and concerns of   258
   exposing implementation details   259
   what to mock vs. what not to mock   259
MockLanguageModelV1   260
model fallbacks   246
model integration problems   254–255
models
   choosing   12–13
   performance considerations   13
   types of   12
model serving frameworks   7
MultiHop-RAG   218

multimedia content, enhancing conversational UIs with   79–86
   caveats of   82
   Gemini vision queries   83–86
   OpenAI vision capabilities   80–82
   overview of   80
multimedia generation   4
multimodal AI   81
MultiServerMCPClient   346

N

nested layout for blog section   48
Netlify, alternative deployments   299
network monitoring   240
next/cache module   237
next/dynamic module   52
Next.js
   authentication with Clerk.js and   277–280
   configuration on   45–52
   debugging   233–241
   environment variables   285–287
   generative AI web application   43–44
   input validation of API handler   271
   integrating web apps with MCP   334–341
   routing on   45–52
   separating AI and UI state in applications   103–104
   unit and integration testing in   256
nondeterministic outputs   142
npm dependencies   353
npm package   248

O

OAuth 2.0/social login   276
onFinish callback   185
onSubmit handler   84
OpenAI
   accessing APIs   354
   vision capabilities   80–82
OpenAIEmbeddings constructor   184
OpenAI/Google API   37
orchestration, defined   7
organizing prompts   139–145
   constrained validation   144
   mocking LLM responses   143
   semantic similarity scoring   144

organizing prompts *(continued)*
    testing   142
    versioning   141
output parsing   114

P

page and component terms   29
PageComponent   101
Performance.now() API   239, 241
personalized interview scenarios and feedback generation   6
PII (personally identifiable information)   16, 275
Pino logging library   238
post-processing   37, 115
preparing, documents for retrieval
    document retrieval   182
    full example   184
    text splitters   180
    vector stores   181
pretrained models   13
problem-solving, defined   4
prompt engineering   114, 129, 130, 131
    chain-of-thought prompting   151–154
    control tokens   136
    defined   132–137
    embeddings   154–164
    few-shot learning   146–151
    LLM techniques   164
    max tokens   134–136
    organizing prompts   139–145
    types of   137–139
prompts, defined   332
prompt templates
    integrating   173
    managing   171–173
propagation effects   192
props, defined   28
public
    endpoints   271
    environment variables   286

Q

quality control problems   15

R

RAG (retrieval-augmented generation)   4, 197–198
RAG agents   317
    challenges during development   325–327
    project walkthrough   318–325
        API routes   323
        application architecture   323
        authentication with Clerk   318
        chatting with knowledge base document   321
        creating new knowledge base   318
        DocumentUploader   323
        document uploading   319
        key features   318–322
        knowledgebase chat page   325
        knowledgebase upload page   323
        main dashboard page   318
        other functionalities   321
        technical implementation   322
        technology stack overview   322–325
RAG web application   216–230
    adding grounding support   225–230
    key architectural components   217
    project requirements   216
    system components   219–223
    technical architecture overview   218
    web app demonstration   223
rate limiting   246, 280–285
    message quota implementation   282–285
React
    separating AI and UI state in applications   103–104
    unit and integration testing in   256
    DevTools extension   237
    hooks   68
    library   28
ReAct (Synergizing Reasoning and Acting in Language Models)   199
RecursiveCharacterTextSplitter   180, 204
redact-pii library   289
redirects, unauthenticated   279
Redis database   357
refine type   204
regulatory compliance   16
requiredWords   145
resource intensiveness   15
Response
    generation   81
    transmission   38
    validation   41

restaurant menu analogy   154
Restricted Sign-up mode   359
retries, defined   41
retrieval
  document   221
  preparing and storing documents for   179–185
retrieval-augmented grounding   225
retrieverChain   184
root layout   48
route API handlers   50
route groups   47
route handler   59–61
routing, Next.js   45–52
RSCs (React server components)   89–103
  creating streamable UI components from LLM providers with streamUI   99–101
  generating and streaming UI components   98
  overview of   90–92
  streaming React components with createStreamableUI   101–103
  updating UI to use server actions   96–98
  using server actions for   93–96
Runnables interface   168–171

S

scalability, defined   139
scroll behavior problems   235
Scroll to Latest button   31
secrets management   285
  Next.js environment variables   285–287
security   16, 268
  and data protection pipeline   275
  authentication and authorization   275–285
  input validation   269–275
  measures   313
  middleware layer   273–275
  rate limiting   280–285
self-attention   15
self-hosted models   13
self-hosting   291–292
Self-Refine   164
semantic similarity scoring   144
Sentry   249
separation of concerns   56
server actions   93–96
  changes to   109, 118

updating UI to use   96–98
serverless functions, defined   7
server processing   63
server-side rendering   51
server validation   271
shadcn component library   311
sign-in page, creating   279
similarity search   163
simple messages   138
standaloneQuestionChain   184
state, defined   28
state management   54, 88, 239, 313
  UI state management   103–113
static site generation   51
StdioClientTransport   338
StdioServerTransport   336, 337
streamable React components   101
streaming
  handling responses with Vercel AI SDK   61–72
  overview of   62–64
  React components   101–103
  responses problems   236
  text   65–67
StreamingTextResponse   70
streaming UI components   98
  creating streamable UI components from LLM providers with streamUI   99–101
  streaming React components with createStreamableUI   101–103
StringOutputParser   168, 169
structured data generation   113–121
  integrating into web application   117–121
  overview of   113
  techniques for generating structured data from AI responses   114
  tools for implementing type-safe AI-generated content   115–117
stuffing method   201
stuff type   204
submitting image with prompt   84
system
  messages   135
  prompts   139

T

template-based generation   115
testing

generative AI web applications   41
prompts   142
strategies for AI applications   256–267
testing and debugging, Vercel AI SDK
 troubleshooting   241–250
 checking official Vercel AI SDK issue tracker   245
 common run-time errors   243
 handling error states in AI-generated content   242–246
 implementing robust error handling with user-facing fallbacks   243
 managing token limits and rate limiting   246–250
 model capability mismatches   243
 model fallbacks   248–250
 provider compatibility problems   242
 retrying failed requests   247
text
 generation   4–5
 prompts   137
 splitters   180
text-to-speech
 API route   312
 integration   314
threat model   270
tiktoken library   135
token count monitoring   247
tokenization   132
token limits   246
TokenTextSplitter   204
tool and function calling   121–125
 implementing custom tools and functions with Vercel AI SDK   123–125
 overview of   121
tool call messages   138
tools, defined   332
ToT (tree of thoughts)   164
trackVisibility prop   30
traffic-based requirements   292
transformer architectures   14
transformers, overview   14, 15
troubleshooting, LangChain.js   250–256
 adding debug chains for monitoring execution steps   253
 chain execution errors   251–254
 enabling verbose mode in models or tools   252
 missing integration problems   255
 troubleshooting model integration problems   254–256
 utilizing callback handlers   253
 vector dimensions mismatch   254
 wrapping execution with try/catch statements   251

U

UI design, defined   13
UI state management   103–113
 implementing patterns   108–113
 key components for   105–107
 separating AI and UI state in React/Next.js applications   103–104
UIs (user interfaces)   7–8
 generating and streaming components   98
 React hooks for   68
 updating to use server actions   96–98
unit testing, in React and Next.js   256
 integration testing   258
 overview of   257
upload route   324
Upstash Redis database   357
useActions hook   111, 112, 118
useAIState hook   111, 112
useChatFormSubmit hook   34, 35, 68–70
useChat hook   65, 68, 70, 78, 79, 340, 348
useCompletion hook   65, 68, 70
useContext hook   103
useEffect hook   34, 236
useInView hook   30
useIsAtBottom hook   30
useReducer hook   34
user input points   271
username/password   276
useState hook   34, 79, 103, 112
useUIState hook   111, 112
UX (user experience)   17, 26

V

validating AI-generated content   17
validation, server vs. client   271
variations in output   142
vector dimensions mismatch   254
vector stores   179, 181
 shared vs. dedicated user data in   325

vendor lock-in   54
verbose mode   252
Vercel
   dedicated providers   291
   example deployment to   294–299
Vercel AI SDK   55–61, 158–161, 122, 269
   agent integration with   192
   enhancing conversational UIs with multimedia content   79–86
   features and benefits of   55
   handling streaming responses with   61–72
   implementing custom tools and functions with   123–125
   integrating web apps with MCP   334–341
   integrating with LangChain.js   173–178
   practical integration with Astra AI   58–61
   storing and retrieving with embeddings   160
   strategic approach to integration   56–58
   structured data generation   113–121
   testing responses   260–264
   troubleshooting   241–250
   working with multiple AI providers   72–79
version control   139
versioning prompts   141
virtual DOM   28
VowelCount function   168–170

W

WeatherCard component   124
web applications
   document summarization   198–216
      additional considerations for   212–216
      applying summarization chain and displaying to user   204
      architecture and workflow   198–202
      building   202–205
      caveats and limitations   205–208
      demonstration of app   208–211
      loading and preprocessing documents   203
      measuring cost of multiple LLM calls   207
      parsing and cleaning up documents   205
      project requirements   198
      splitting documents into manageable chunks   204
   generative AI   4–9
   prompt engineering
      chain-of-thought prompting   151–154
      embeddings   154–164
      example of   151
      general methodology for creating prompts   152
web apps
   AI tools and ecosystem   9
   generative AI in, generative vs. traditional AI   13–15
   integrating with MCP
      architecture overview   335, 346
      benefits of using MCP for web applications with LLMs   340
      building end-to-end integration with LangChain.js   347–349
      building end-to-end integration with MCP in Next.js   336–340
      connecting Next.js and Vercel AI SDK with   334–341
      frontend   348
      integrating MCP servers with LangChain.js   345–349
workflows, AI
   building with LangChain.js   166–178, 194
   chaining calls   168–173
   integration with Vercel AI SDK   173–178
   LangChain Expression Language   195
   LangGraph   195
   preparing and storing documents for retrieval   179–185

Z

zero-shot learning   146
Zod schema validation   115

RELATED MANNING TITLES

Coding with AI
by Jeremy C. Morgan

ISBN 9781633437272
336 pages, $49.99
August 2025

Building Reliable AI Systems
by Rush Shahani

ISBN 9781633436732
325 pages (estimated), $59.99
Summer 2026 (estimated)

Generative AI in Action
by Amit Bahree
Foreword by Eric Boyd

ISBN 9781633436947
464 pages, $59.99
September 2024

AI for Everyday IT
by Chrissy LeMaire and Brandon Abshire
Foreword by Nitya Narasimhan

ISBN 9781633436428
376 pages, $49.99
May 2025

For ordering information, go to www.manning.com